School Effectiveness and Improvement Research, Policy and Practice

Challenging the orthodoxy?

Edited by
Christopher Chapman,
Paul Armstrong, Alma Harris,
Daniel Muijs, David Reynolds
and Pam Sammons

Routledge
Taylor & Francis Group

LONDON AND NEW YORK

First published 2012
by Routledge
2 Park Square, Milton Park, Abingdon, Oxon OX14 4RN

Simultaneously published in the USA and Canada
by Routledge
711 Third Avenue, New York, NY 10017

Routledge is an imprint of the Taylor & Francis Group, an informa business

British Library Cataloguing in Publication Data
A catalogue record for this book is available from the British Library

Library of Congress Cataloging in Publication Data
School effectiveness and improvement research, policy, and practice : challenging the
orthodoxy / [edited by] Christopher Chapman . . . [et al.].
    p. cm.
    1. School improvement programs. 2. Educational evaluation.
    I. Chapman, Chris, 1966–
    LB2822.8.S36 2012
    371.2'07—dc23
    2011030151

ISBN: 978-0-415-69894-8 (hbk)
ISBN: 978-0-415-69899-3 (pbk)
ISBN: 978-0-203-13655-3 (ebk)

Typeset in Galliard
by Swales & Willis Ltd, Exeter, Devon

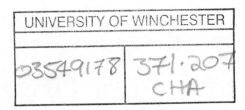

MIX
Paper from
responsible sources
FSC
www.fsc.org   FSC® C004839

Printed and bound in Great Britain by
CPI Antony Rowe, Chippenham, Wiltshire

School Effectiveness and Improvement Research, Policy and Practice

This book provides a contemporary overview of school effectiveness and improvement. It charts the development of theory and research in this area and looks at the contribution made to policy and practice. It also challenges some assumptions that have become ingrained into the theoretical and methodological traditions of the field. By challenging these orthodoxies, it provides a framework that sets a new agenda and repositions the field to meet the emerging challenges of the twenty-first century.

The book's contributors argue that traditional measures of school effectiveness are challenged as systems have attempted to adapt to a complex range of emerging agendas. New theoretical perspectives are required which consider 'education' and a 'broader set of outcomes'. This shift requires a rethink of how effectiveness and improvement have been understood by the field, and a reconstruction by policy makers and practitioners. Attention must be given to promoting equity as well as effectiveness so that one school or student's gain no longer means another's loss. The field must develop new methodologies based on a broader set of outcomes if inequities within education systems are to be challenged.

The two questions guiding this book are:

- How can educational effectiveness and improvement research and practice support the development of a more equitable education service?
- What are the key indicators of educational effectiveness and improvement and what are the new methodologies required to facilitate a shift from 'school' effectiveness and improvement to 'educational' effectiveness and improvement?

This book uses lenses of research, policy and practice to explore these key questions and articulate what such a repositioning may look like and how it may be achieved. It will prove invaluable for teachers, school leaders and anyone involved in policy and educational research.

Christopher Chapman is Professor of Education at the University of Manchester, UK.

Paul Armstrong is a researcher for the Effectiveness and Improvement Research Group at the University of Manchester, UK.

Alma Harris is Professor at the Institute of Education, University of London, UK.

Daniel Muijs is Professor of Education at the University of Southampton, UK.

David Reynolds is Professor of Educational Effectiveness at the University of Southampton, UK.

Pam Sammons is Professorial Senior Research Fellow at Jesus College, University of Oxford, UK.

Contents

Figures

Tables

Contributors

Paul Armstrong is a researcher for the Effectiveness and Improvement Research Group at the University of Manchester's School of Education. He is currently in the final year of doctoral research at the University of Manchester exploring the role of the school business manager in the changing organisational culture of schools in England. He has also completed an MSc in Educational Research. Whilst his background lies in Psychology, Paul has spent the last six years working as a researcher on a range of educational research projects, most recently evaluating the Teach First programme in England and investigating the effectiveness of a national strategy to develop school business management capacity. His primary interests are educational change, school culture and new forms of leadership and management.

Christopher Chapman is Professor of Education at the University of Manchester where he continues to develop his research interests and lead a series of externally funded research projects exploring the relationship between change, leadership, improvement, collaboration and organisational structure in urban and challenging contexts. He is editor of the international journal *School Leadership and Management* and has published widely on the themes of leadership, change and improvement. Chris's most recent books include *Radical Reforms* (edited with Helen Gunter) and *High Leverage Leadership* (with Denis Mongon).

Paul Clarke is Professor of Sustainable Education at St Marys University College in London and Director of Sustainable Leadership at Cambridge Education/Mott MacDonald. He is a Principal Consultant to His Royal Highness Prince of Wales charities and a founding Director of the influential Incredible Edible Programme, a community scheme now adopted in more than 30 towns in the UK. His interest in establishing the conditions for sustainable living are documented in education, urban planning and regeneration and across many community development initiatives in the UK and worldwide. His latest book *Education for Sustainability: Becoming Naturally Smart* is published in Autumn 2011.

David Egan is Emeritus Professor of Education at the University of Wales Institute Cardiff. He works as an educational adviser and consultant in the field of education research, policy and practice with particular reference to Wales. He is currently involved in the design and implementation of area-based strategies to address the link between poverty and low educational achievement.

Alma Harris is Professor and Pro-Director (Leadership) at the Institute of Education, London. Her research work focuses on organisational change, improvement and development. She is internationally known for her work on school improvement, focusing particularly on improving schools in challenging circumstances. She has been seconded to the Welsh Government since 2010 as a Senior Professional Adviser and is currently assisting with the process of system-wide reform. She is President Elect of the International Congress of School Effectiveness and School Improvement and will take up her Presidency at the 26th International Congress in Chile in 2013.

David Hopkins is Professor Emeritus at the Institute of Education, University of London, where until recently he held the inaugural HSBC iNet Chair in International Leadership. He is a Trustee of Outward Bound and is Executive Director of the new charity Adventure Learning Schools. He holds Visiting Professorships at the Catholic University of Santiago, the Chinese University of Hong Kong and the Universities of Edinburgh, Melbourne and Wales and consults internationally on school reform. Between 2002 and 2005 he served three Secretary of States as the Chief Adviser on School Standards at the Department for Education and Skills. Previously, he was Chair of the Leicester City Partnership Board and Dean of the Faculty of Education at the University of Nottingham. Before that again he was a Tutor at the University of Cambridge Institute of Education, a secondary school teacher and Outward Bound instructor. He is also an International Mountain Guide who still climbs regularly in the Alps and Himalayas. His recent books *Every School a Great School* and *System Leadership in Practice* are published by The Open University Press.

Anthony Kelly is Director of Research and acting Head of the School of Education, University of Southampton. He researches in the areas of policy, improvement/effectiveness theory, governance, and developing innovative quantitative approaches to educational research. He worked previously at the University of Cambridge and before that as a headteacher in Ireland. His headship coincided with some of the worst periods of political upheaval there and he was one of the leading figures in education in the border region where he developed new school governance structures. He is founding editor of the journal *Education, Knowledge and Economy*, and serves on the board of several other peer-reviewed journals and national steering groups. He is an elected Fellow of the Institute of Physics and the Institute of Mathematics, a Fellow of the Royal Statistical Society and the New York Academy of Sciences and a member of various national education research associations in Britain, the US and Australia.

Leonidas Kyriakides is Associate Professor in Educational Research and Evaluation at the University of Cyprus. His field of research and scholarship is the evaluation of educational effectiveness, whether of teachers, schools or educational systems. Currently his research agenda is concerned with the development of a dynamic model of educational effectiveness, and the application of effectiveness research to the improvement of educational practice. He has been involved in several international projects to increase the quality in education and was also responsible to develop the national reform policy on teacher and school evaluation in Cyprus. He is a member of the editorial board of various international journals with referee system and book review editor of the *School Effectiveness and School Improvement* journal. He is the author of more than 100 research papers, 7 books, and 80 chapters in books.

Ben Levin is Professor and Canada Research Chair in Education Leadership and Policy at the Ontario Institute for Studies in Education, University of Toronto. His career is about half as an academic and half as a senior civil servant. He is a native of the City of Winnipeg who holds a B.A. (Hons) from the University of Manitoba, an Ed. M. from Harvard University and a Ph.D. from OISE. He has worked with private research organisations, school districts, provincial governments, and national and international agencies, as well as building an academic and research career. As a civil servant, he served as Deputy Minister (chief civil servant) for Education for the Province of Ontario from 2004 to 2007 and again in 2008–2009. Earlier, from 1999 through 2002, he was Deputy Minister of Advanced Education and Deputy Minister of Education, Training and Youth for the Province of Manitoba. As an academic, he has published five books, most recently, *How to Change 5000 Schools*, and more than 200 other articles on education, conducted many research studies, and has spoken and consulted on education issues around the world. His current interests are in large-scale change, poverty and inequity, and finding better ways to connect research to policy and practice in education.

John MacBeath is Professor Emeritus at the University of Cambridge where he has held the Chair of Educational Leadership since 2000. Prior to that he was Director of the Quality in Education Centre at the University of Strathclyde in Glasgow. From 1997 to 2001 he was a member of the Tony Blair Government Task Force on Standards and from 1997 to 1999 a member of the Scottish Government Action Group on Standards. Other consultancies have included OECD, UNESCO and ILO (International Labour Organisation), the Bertelsmann Foundation and the European Commission on a school self-evaluation and member of an EU working party on European indicators. He has been working as a researcher and consultant to the Education Bureau in Hong Kong since 1997. He is currently Past President of the International Congress on School Effectiveness and Improvement, Director of Leadership for Learning: the Cambridge Network and Projects Director for the Commonwealth Centre for Education. He was awarded the OBE for services to education in 1997 and an honorary doctorate from the University of Edinburgh in 2009.

Daniel Muijs is Chair of Education at the University of Southampton. Previously he worked at the University of Manchester as Chair of Pedagogy and Teacher Development at the University of Manchester, School of Education, as Chair of School Leadership and Management at the University of Newcastle and as senior lecturer at Warwick Institute of Education. He is an acknowledged expert in the field of Educational and Teacher Effectiveness and Educational Leadership, and is co-editor of the journal *School Effectiveness and School Improvement*. He has published widely in the areas of educational effectiveness, leadership and research methods, and has conducted research for government agencies (DCSF, NCSL, QCA), Charitable Trusts (Gatsby) and Research Councils (ESRC).

Bernardita Munoz-Chereau is currently a PhD student working with Sally Thomas at the Graduate School of Education, University of Bristol. Her background in Psychology and Education lead her to work at the macro level (Ministry of Education) as well as at the micro level (schools) in Chile. Her empirical investigation aims to provide a useful contribution to the debate about the interpretation of secondary schools' examination results for accountability purposes in Chile by complementing raw league tables or a ranking approach with fairer and more accurate approaches – such as value-added – in order to provide a better picture of Chilean secondary school effectiveness. She is an active member of the AEA-Europe Doctoral Network.

Jim O'Brien is Professor Emeritus at the University of Edinburgh having recently retired from the Deanship of the Moray House School of Education. He continues to write and research and is an Associate Editor of Professional Development in Education. He has published numerous articles and papers and several books focusing on leadership and professional learning, his most recent book being *Coaching and Mentoring: Developing Teachers and Leaders* (Dunedin Academic Press).

Wen-Jung Peng is a researcher at the Graduate School of Education, University of Bristol. Her current research is related to quality in education in mainland China. In particular it looks at how Chinese stakeholders view about the quality of education from both quantitative and qualitative perspectives involving also teacher development in relation to professional learning community. In recent years, her work has included effectiveness, evaluation and improvement in the UK school context, and active citizenship via informal learning at school in the European context.

David Reynolds is currently Professor of Educational Effectiveness at the University of Southampton and has published widely on school effectiveness, school improvement and teacher effectiveness. He was responsible with others for the foundation of The International Congress for School Effectiveness and improvement and co-edited its journal *School Effectiveness and Improvement*. He has also had extensive links with the policy making and practice communities in England and more recently Wales, where he is currently Senior Policy

Adviser to the Education and Skills Department of Welsh government. His current research interests are cognitive neuroscience, comparative study and school effectiveness, particularly focusing upon within school variation and differential effectiveness.

Massoud M. Salim is a senior planning officer at the Ministry of Education and Vocational Training Zanzibar. His current work and research interests focus on evaluating education quality using school effectiveness approaches, in particular 'value-added' and school self-evaluation. He has extensive knowledge and experience of conducting large-scale projects on evaluating education quality in developing countries, including for the Southern and Eastern Africa Consortium for Monitoring Education Quality (SACMEQ). His other interests include policy development, management of education particularly strengthening Education Management Information System (EMIS) and education research methods both qualitative and quantitative including multilevel modelling techniques.

Pam Sammons is Professor of Education at the Department of Education, University of Oxford and a Senior Research Fellow at Jesus College, Oxford. Previously she was a Professor at the University of Nottingham (2004–2009). She spent 11 years at the Institute of Education, University of London (1993–2004) where she was a Professor of Education and Coordinating Director of its International School Effectiveness & Improvement Centre. She has been involved in educational research for the last 30 years with a special focus on school effectiveness and improvement, the early years and equity in education.

Sally M. Thomas is Professor of Education at the Graduate School of Education, University of Bristol. She has published widely on the topics of educational quality, effectiveness and improvement using a variety of research approaches – both qualitative and quantitative. In particular she has led extensive research studies funded by UKAID, ESRC and others using 'value-added measures of school effectiveness' and the application of these measures for different, or overlapping, purposes including: school improvement, evaluation and self-evaluation, assessing educational quality, international indicators and academic knowledge-base research. Her other research interests include, professional learning communities, pupil learning and citizenship and education in developing countries.

Tony Townsend is Chair of Public Service, Educational Leadership and Management at the University of Glasgow. He also has been Professor and Chair of the Department of Educational Leadership in the College of Education at Florida Atlantic University (2003–2009), and Associate Professor in the Faculty of Education at Monash University in Australia. He has given lectures, workshops, conference papers and presentations in more than 40 countries. His research interests include school effectiveness and improvement, school reform, leadership in schools and public sector organisations and strategic planning. He has published extensively in the areas of school effectiveness, school improvement and teacher education in Australia, Europe and North America.

Mel West is Professor of Educational Leadership and Head of the School of Education at the University of Manchester. His work has principally been in the fields of school management and school improvement. In the mid-1980s, he was one of the architects of the influential Improving the Quality of Education for All (IQEA) programme. This programme, which is still going strong in several parts of the world, has been used by some hundreds of schools, and has become one of the most widespread approaches to school development. He has contributed to school improvement and management development programmes in Iceland, Laos, Chile, Hong Kong, China, Puerto Rico and Malawi, working with a number of international agencies including the British Council, DfID, OECD, UNESCO and Save the Children. Current projects include school improvement programmes in Beijing (DfID funded) and Hong Kong (Hong Kong Education Ministry) and a headteacher development programme in the West of China (APEC).

Introduction

Paul Armstrong, Christopher Chapman,
Alma Harris, Daniel Muijs,
David Reynolds and Pam Sammons

Over the past three decades school effectiveness and school improvement (SESI) research and practice have become an influential driver of educational policy and practice across many educational systems (Teddlie and Reynolds, 2000). A plethora of effectiveness studies have identified factors associated with more and less effective systems (Levin and Lockheed, 1993), schools (Sammons *et al.*, 1995; Stoll and Myers, 1998) and classrooms (Creemers, 1994; Muijs and Reynolds, 2001) whilst school improvement research and practice have identified a number of processes associated with improvement in a range of different contexts (Hopkins *et al.*, 1994; Harris *et al.*, 2006; MacBeath *et al.*, 2007). Despite a series of critiques (Slee *et al.*, 1998; Thrupp, 1999; Coe, 2009; Gorard, 2010) SESI has continued to play an important role in shaping educational systems, acting as an important source for educational change whilst retaining close relationships with policy makers and practitioners in the field.

SESI's contribution to raising educational standards has been well documented (Fielding, 2001; Barber 2007). However, some recent evidence suggests variable impact in different settings (Sammons *et al.*, 2007; DfES, 2007) and diminished effect over time (Earl *et al.*, 2003). In addition, the field has struggled to cope with a number of emerging challenges. It has become apparent there are high levels of variation within many systems; with different groups of learners performing at different levels and progressing at different rates. SESI research has also continued to focus on ways of improving test scores at the expense of other areas. Put simply, SESI research and practice has failed to address issues of equity and promoted a narrow view of what constitutes educational achievement (Chapman and Gunter, 2009).

It would seem the field requires a fundamental rethinking of its position from one where school effectiveness and school improvement is reconceptualised as educational effectiveness and improvement (EEI). We also suggest there is much to be learned about achieving this shift from within the United Kingdom where the subtle but important differences between the English, Welsh, Scottish and Northern Irish systems provide the opportunity to explore such a reconceptualisation in detail from a range of national perspectives. The launch of the British Educational Research Association Educational Effectiveness and Improvement SIG (BERA SIG) in December 1997 initiated debate, providing a forum for academic, policy maker and practitioner communities to discuss their perspectives on the current position and future direction of the field. Initial discussions suggested the core issues related to equity and focus. With these two key themes in mind, a series of seminars aimed at challenging the orthodoxy of SESI was developed. At its outset the series was underpinned by the following research questions:

- How can educational effectiveness and improvement research and practice support the development of a more equitable education service?
- What are the key indicators of educational effectiveness and improvement and what methodologies are required to assess educational effectiveness and associated improvement processes?

The seminar series was funded by the Economic, Social and Research Council (ESRC) and it was designed to bring together educational practitioners, policy makers and academics to explore the key issues in hand. Using keynote papers as stimuli for discussion the intention was to generate new theoretical, intellectual and practical insights designed to meet the challenge of developing a more equitable educational system measured on a broader range of outcomes. As the series evolved these two important areas generated much discussion and, as illustrated by the contributions in this book, were complemented, enriched and at times superseded by many other important contemporary issues and themes.

This book documents the outcomes from the seminar series. Each chapter in the book is based on a paper or key theme from one of the three meetings held in Manchester, Cardiff and Glasgow between November 2009 and June 2010. In this sense the chapters serve as standalone reflections on SESI and EEIR but also offer a commentary documenting the key debates to provide a structured narrative of the series. The book is organised in three parts. Part I reflects on the foundations of the field. Part II focuses on cases of current practice to highlight issues, tensions and dilemmas associated with SESI research, policy and practice. Here we draw on the individual education systems within the United Kingdom and supplement this with examples of SESI in emerging contexts. The third concluding part focuses on recent developments and future perspectives in SESI.

In the first chapter Pam Sammons focuses on educational effectiveness research (EER), examining a number of key issues relating to methodology and measurement. Sammons also argues for a greater emphasis on theory development in EER and makes the case for considering new approaches to model development. In conclusion Sammons reflects on the potential value of adopting a pragmatic philosophical approach with mixed methods designs in EER and examines possible directions for future research.

In Chapter 2 Christopher Chapman reflects on the development of school improvement research and practice considering where the key contributions and advancements have occurred and where future developments may take the field. Chapman argues the phases and waves of improvement research, policy and practice have been useful but we now need to develop new sets of frameworks and ways of thinking if we are to further improve student experience, schools and whole systems.

In Chapter 3 Leonidas Kyriakides offers a critical analysis of current approaches to modelling school effectiveness. He argues the dynamic model of educational effectiveness, recently developed to address the weaknesses of the integrated models, could contribute in establishing a theory-driven and evidence-based approach to school improvement. The central characteristics of the model are then presented with findings from research studies to support its validity.

In the final chapter of Part I Daniel Muijs suggests the growing sophistication of research designs in SESI research since the 1970s has led to a crystallisation of methods, to the extent that it is now possible to talk of a methodological and analytical orthodoxy. He puts this hypothesis to the test via analysis of empirical research articles published in the academic journal *School Effectiveness and School Improvement* before discussing the implications of the findings in light of the direction and make-up of future research in the field.

In the first chapter of Part II (Chapter 5) Mel West begins by considering the English context via four basic types of school improvement policy intervention before taking a closer look at the assumptions underpinning these intervention strategies and the role played by schools in reducing educational disadvantage. He then reviews the evidence regarding the impact of these interventions to ask what lessons have been learned with regard to implications for policy, practice and research.

In Chapter 6 Anthony Kelly discusses educational effectiveness and school improvement in Northern Ireland, first focusing on the educationally divisive areas of religion and selection before considering the ways in which the requirement for school improvement has united the system. He then highlights the challenges and opportunities for EER in Northern Ireland before discussing some of the ironies, issues and implications in relation to education and schooling in the country.

Chapter 7 moves on to focus on the Scottish context. John MacBeath begins by outlining some of the key distinctions between the education systems in Scotland and England, considering the unique roles played by the local authority and the teacher unions in Scotland. He also discusses the Scottish tradition of school effectiveness and how this might be improved whilst highlighting recent educational initiatives in Scotland. Finally, he deliberates how the purpose of the school might be defined as we look to the future.

In Chapter 8 David Egan examines the Welsh education system, discussing the extent to which improvements have been achieved in Welsh schools over the last twenty years and whether a body of Wales-specific knowledge on SESI has emerged during this period. Egan also reports on the implementation of a national programme aimed at developing a system-wide approach to school effectiveness and considers the challenges facing the Welsh educational system in introducing this programme.

In the final chapter of Part II, Sally Thomas and colleagues turn our attention to contexts where educational effectiveness is an emerging concern. Drawing on their work in China, South America and Africa the authors discuss educational quality effectiveness and evaluation in these diverse settings.

Part III of this book begins with Jim O'Brien's assessment of some of the key components of the SESI movement. O'Brien explores continuing professional development (CPD), teacher quality (standards and CPD), the emergence of teacher standards in the UK, and the success and impact of the Scottish standards. He then highlights the need for further research into the link between CPD for teachers, enhanced teacher quality and the attainment and achievement of students.

In Chapter 11 David Hopkins highlights recent efforts at system improvement and attempts to understand the dynamics of system change before introducing the concepts of system leadership and segmentation as the basis of system transformation. This then leads into a discussion of the idea of an operating system or innovation clusters as a means of achieving system improvement at various stages of development.

In Chapter 12 Tony Townsend claims that education has moved through four major phases of thinking and action. Townsend suggests the evidence does not support claims these changes have generated significant improvement in student achievement and, therefore, a new approach involving thinking and action at the both local and global level is necessary.

Paul Clarke and Anthony Kelly use Chapter 13 to explore the applicability of the linear neo-liberal model in the current climate. They argue it is no longer relevant, suggesting that the way we relate to our world is outdated, destructive and unsustainable. What happens next, they suggest, largely depends upon how and if we can we learn to live more sustainably in our built landscapes and communities around the planet, which is ultimately an educational challenge, a challenge of how to respond to a crisis with practical sustainable solutions.

In Chapter 14 David Reynolds considers the future progress of SESI depends on a closer association between the field and the practical needs of educational policy, which therefore involves seeking out a closer relationship between the discipline, educational policy makers and politicians, and additionally better relating to their concerns.

In the following chapter Ben Levin suggests that we should be cautious about embracing transformation and innovation as the requirements for schooling. Instead he takes the view that the real benefits are to be gained from deeper and wider use of existing knowledge about good teaching and learning and the supports needed for them – such as leadership and professional development.

The final chapter draws together the key themes from the book to reflect on effectiveness and improvement research in education. This chapter highlights the relative strengths and weakness associated with effectiveness and improvement theory, research, policy and practice and outlines five key issues for the development of the field.

The collection of chapters in this volume illustrates the significant contribution the field has made in a remarkably short time. The chapters also highlight the diverse range of perspectives held by those involved in effectiveness and improvement research. With this in mind we have attempted to ensure each contributor's voice comes through in their writing. One consequence of this approach is the variation in terminology throughout the volume. Most notably authors slide between 'school' and 'educational' effectiveness and improvement. We have not edited this for consistency. Rather, we use these inconsistencies to highlight variations in perspectives and understanding.

We hope this book and the forthcoming *International Handbook of Educational Effectiveness Research* to be published by Routledge will begin to question some of the orthodoxies that have emerged within the field and provide a platform the next phase of development.

Christopher Chapman, Paul Armstrong, Alma Harris, Daniel Muijs,
David Reynolds and Pam Sammons
Manchester, London, Southampton and Oxford
November 2011

Part I
Foundations of the field

1 Methodological issues and new trends in educational effectiveness research

Pam Sammons

Introduction

Over the last thirty years or more school effectiveness research (SER) has emerged as a fast growing and dynamic field of study with a growing international profile (Scheerens and Bosker, 1997; Mortimore, 1998; Teddlie and Reynolds, 2000; Muijs, 2006; Sammons, 2006a and 2006b, 2007; Van Damme *et al.*, 2006; Townsend, 2007; Creemers and Kyriakides, 2008; Creemers *et al.*, 2010) that explicitly focuses on studying the variation between schools, departments and teachers in their effects on students' outcomes and the school and classroom processes that seem to support better outcomes. In addition to the study of school and, more recently, of teacher or class level effects and attempts to delineate the characteristics of effective schools and effective teaching (Muijs and Reynolds, 2010; Ko and Sammons, 2011), the field is now paying greater attention to contextual influences including the role of local authorities and school districts, for example (Tymms *et al.*, 2008; Reynolds *et al.*, 2011) and the role of comparative studies in different international contexts (Reynolds *et al.*, 2002; Teddlie *et al.* 2006; Van de Grift *et al.*, 2007). Moreover, SER-type studies of institutional effects are also addressing other areas of education including pre-school settings and nurseries (Sammons *et al.*, 2008; Melhuish *et al.*, 2008; Sylva *et al.*, 2010), and colleges and higher education settings that serve students who are beyond the compulsory school leaving age. Given these developments the term *educational effectiveness research* (EER) is becoming increasingly used (Muijs, 2006; Creemers *et al.*, 2010; Reynolds, 2010; Teddlie, 2010). This is a more appropriate description because it recognizes the broader remit of recent research (Creemers and Kyriakides, 2008) and a wider focus of enquiry than just the study of the effects of individual schools. For example, there is an increasing interest in the way EER can promote school improvement (Stringfield *et al.*, 2008a) using the evidence base from High Reliability Schools research and can be used to evaluate educational initiatives, for example in England the introduction of Federations (Lindsay *et al.*, 2007).

More than a decade ago I posed the question 'Has school effectiveness come of age?', noting the turbulent debates both methodological and philosophical that had accompanied this growth and the high policy profile accorded SER in some countries (Sammons, 1999). In 1999 I suggested that, at the turn of the millennium, SER could be seen as still in its adolescent phase, affected by heated controversy over its political and philosophical underpinnings, given the policy emphasis on raising standards and increasing accountability adopted by many education systems, as well as in relation to the role of local and national context in shaping school and teacher performance.

A few years later a special issue of the journal *School Effectiveness and School Improvement* was devoted to the topic 'Critique and Response to twenty years of SER' edited by Townsend (2001). Interestingly, at this time the focus of criticism remained largely on political and philosophical grounds rather than on methodological issues although there was evidence of a strong anti-quantitative stance. Yet the methodology of EER remains crucially important in efforts to enhance the knowledge base and the practical application of findings (Luyten and Sammons, 2009). After a lull, critiques of the field and its methodology have resurfaced recently (Gorard, 2010). Such arguments have been addressed by Muijs *et al.* (2011), who have comprehensively demonstrated flaws in the statistical critiques and knowledge of the field of EER.

More than a decade on from my comments on SER as still in its adolescent phase, the EER field can be seen to have matured and evolved as the various contributions to this volume demonstrate. This chapter seeks to provide a brief review of the current state of EER, its achievements and limitations, and to suggest some fruitful directions for future research. First, the chapter examines methodological and measurement issues before discussing the need for a greater emphasis on theory development in EER and the role of new approaches to model development. The third section explores the potential value of adopting a pragmatic philosophical approach and the role of mixed methods designs in EER that combine and integrate qualitative and quantitative approaches. The concluding section examines possible directions for future studies.

1. Methodological and measurement issues

Methodological debates were particularly evident in the early development of the SER field. For example, the seminal *15000 Hours* (Rutter *et al.*, 1979) study of London secondary schools was criticized severely by statisticians, amongst others, due to certain features of the methodology, including the small sample size of schools and inability to take account of the clustering of the student sample. Such criticisms stimulated significant advances in subsequent SER designs and approaches to analysis. Most notably, the development of hierarchical regression approaches using multilevel modelling that recognizes the impact of clustering in educational datasets and the need for longitudinal samples with individual student level data to compare school performance were led by authors such as Goldstein (1995) and Bryk and Raudenbush (1992). Improvements in the size, scale and statistical approaches used in EER during the late 1980s and 1990s (e.g. work by Hill and Rowe, 1998, that demonstrated not only that teacher effects tend to be larger than school effects, but also that in combination they could account for a substantial proportion of the variance in student outcomes). More recent methodological advances have been discussed by Creemers *et al.* (2010).

However, despite the methodological limitations of pioneering earlier studies such as *15000 Hours* many of the key findings have been supported by later, more sophisticated multilevel research. For example, another study of secondary school effectiveness also conducted in inner London but almost two decades later (*Forging Links: Effective Schools and Effective Departments*, Sammons *et al.*, 1997) supported and extended the original conclusions of *15000 Hours* using a much larger sample of schools and multilevel approaches with longitudinal data for three successive student cohorts. In addition, a replication and extension of the Forging Links research conducted in Ireland (Smyth, 1999) also supported and extended the findings of the Forging Links research. As well as examining the size of school effects on students' academic outcomes, both these studies addressed three important features of theoretical and practical importance – namely the size, stability and consistency of school effects and drew attention to the importance of departmental differences in academic effectiveness. Sammons *et al.*, (1997) concluded that there is considerable internal variation in school effectiveness and that school effectiveness is best seen as a *relative, retrospective concept* dependent both on the choice of appropriate outcome measures and the timescale and methods of analysis used, including the adequacy of the intake predictors available for inclusion in appropriate multilevel models. The topic of within school variation (WSV) remains relatively unexplored however and is identified as an important focus of future enquiries (Reynolds, 2008).

The creation of the International Congress for School Effectiveness and Improvement (ICSEI) in 1990 helped to promote international collaborations and the development and wider dissemination of SER approaches. The first *International Handbook of School Effectiveness Research* (Teddlie and Reynolds, 2000) examined the methodology and scientific properties of SER, and summarized the research knowledge base, achievements and limitations and some important issues for future development. The next (Townsend, 2007) sought to link the school effectiveness and improvement fields more closely, gave greater attention to context issues, the classroom and international comparative perspectives, but paid little attention to methodological issues. However, despite wider recognition of the need for appropriate research designs and statistical techniques by those engaged in SER, it was only in 2005 that the MORE (Methodology of Research in Educational Effectiveness) group was established as part of ICSEI to stimulate further methodological advances in the EER field. Similarly, although the Educational Effectiveness SIG (Special Interest Group) at EARLI has only been in existence for a couple of years it too has sought to encourage more rigorous and innovative approaches and promote further international collaborative work, including the development of relevant instruments to measure school and classroom processes of theoretical and practical interest that could be used in a range of contexts (Teddlie *et al.*, 2006). It is recommended that closer links be promoted between such groups to further encourage and enhance future EER studies. The increased emphasis on methodological issues evident during the last decade is illustrated by the production of a new volume on Methodological Advances in Educational Effectiveness Research (Creemers *et al.*, 2010) that seeks to document: the current state of the art in EER and the challenges it faces; the contribution of different methodological orientations to the development of EE research, and to provide a conceptual map for further methodological advancement in EER studies.

There have been a number of important methodological achievements in EER, particularly related to the use of multilevel models and large-scale longitudinal research that recognizes the complexity and hierarchical structure of most educational systems. Gorard (2010) has recently criticized EER methodology based on the use of contextualised value-added indicators, arguing that simplicity is important in educational research. Yet education is a feature of complex social systems that demonstrate a hierarchical structure in many aspects of life (because of clustering effects linked to neighbourhoods, schools or classes) and complexity cannot be avoided as Goldstein (1998: 2) argued: 'in order to describe the complex reality that constitutes educational systems we require modelling tools that involve a comparable level of complexity'. Goldstein and Noden (2004) and Plewis and Fielding (2003) have drawn attention to the value of multilevel statistical modelling in a range of fields because of its ability to answer questions at a much greater level of detail and complexity. Muijs *et al.* (2011) similarly argue the case for the use of appropriate multilevel models and other appropriate statistical techniques in order to investigate institutional influences.

Many in the EER field have warned against the use of single measures of school performance for accountability or research purposes (e.g. Mortimore *et al.*, 1988, 1989; Nuttall *et al.*, 1989; Sammons *et al.*, 1993, 1995; Goldstein, 1995, 1998; Teddlie and Reynolds, 2000). In standard SER designs, the residual estimate of an individual school's effectiveness is always based on its relative position in comparison with other schools, taking into account differences in student intake this is often known as a contextual value-added (CVA) indicator. There is a need to consider the confidence limits (CL) associated with individual school, departmental or class level residuals derived from multilevel value-added analyses. This prevents fine (rank ordered) distinctions being made between most schools, and thus the production of ranked 'league tables' is regarded as statistically invalid (Goldstein, 1997). A consequence of using multilevel value-added approaches is that the extent a school is identified as more or less effective is thus largely determined by the performance of the other schools to which it is compared and the adequacy of intake controls to ensure more appropriate 'like with like' comparisons of relative performance levels. Of course a similar argument about the adequacy of model fit can be made with respect to the interpretation of estimates and effect sizes for individual predictors included in any multivariate analyses, but an advantage of multilevel analysis over traditional regression approaches is that this allows more precise estimates to be obtained because of the control for variance attributable to higher levels such as the school or teacher level (Goldstein, 1995; Elliot and Sammons, 2004). The use of CLs for school residual estimates means that it is most appropriate to identify groups of schools whose performance is either significantly better or poorer than other schools in a given sample for a given outcome (Sammons, 1996). This has important implications for educational policy makers and practitioners in education systems that seek to promote greater educational accountability by publishing school performance data.

In England, CVA indicators have been made available and welcomed by most schools as fairer than raw results for evaluating their performance. However, it is unfortunate that raw results are still used as the main means of judging school performance and continues to penalize schools serving disadvantaged communities (Sammons, 2008). Moreover, any one measure is both outcome and time specific and to evaluate schools appropriately more attention needs to be paid to WSV (Sammons *et al.*, 1997; Reynolds, 2008; Muijs *et al.*, 2011).

Luyten and Sammons (2010) provide a brief summary of multilevel approaches and their application to datasets that are hierarchically structured. In those cases two or more levels can be distinguished with the units at the lower levels nested within the higher level units, typically this can be a dataset of students nested within classrooms and schools. The hierarchical structure may be extended further, if one takes into account the nesting of schools within geographical units (such as local communities, regions or nations). They argue that the advantages of multilevel analysis include its flexibility and capability to deal with unbalanced data and data with incomplete records on the outcome measures. In addition to the analysis of longitudinal data the multilevel approach may also be useful for analysis of data with two or more distinct outcome measures per individual (multivariate multilevel modelling).

The ability to take account of the role of clustering in educational data and identify variance at different levels in hierarchical structures also has the advantage that it provides more efficient and accurate estimates of the effects of predictor variables and their associated standard errors. It also allows the estimation of overall size of effects at higher levels (e.g. school or classroom/teacher) in terms of the proportion of unexplained variance attributable to each level using the intra-class correlation. Comparison of the null model (partitioning the variance at different levels in an empty model with no predictors) with various more complex models allows the researcher to show the percentage of total variance and the percentage of student or of teacher or school level variance explained (accounted for) by different sets of predictors.

Of course, good control for student prior attainment and background characteristics remains essential for value-added analyses of possible school or teacher effects, because poorly specified models may lead to over-estimates of institutional differences in student outcomes through failure to control sufficiently for pre-existing student intake differences (Elliot and Sammons, 2004; Van de Grift, 2009). In addition, there is a need to explore more complex models that test random variation at higher levels to study differential effects and possible cross-level interactions. Work by Opdenakker and Van Damme (2006, 2007) illustrates the use of more complex models to study the relationships between measures of school type, school context, group composition, school practices and school effects on student outcomes including multilevel growth curve modelling.

Multilevel meta-analysis

Further refinements in multilevel approaches include multilevel meta-analysis that has the potential to provide better estimates of the size and variation in educational effectiveness for a range of outcomes, phases of education and contexts (Hox and De Leeuw, 2003). Meta-analysis uses statistical results from a range of studies that address a similar research question and often seeks to establish an average effect size and estimate of the statistical significance of a relationship. In EER this might be the effects attributable to a particular approach to teaching, or of a school reform programme. However, one might also be interested in the variation in effect sizes *across* studies of interest as in a random effects analysis which seeks to distinguish variance that is the result of sampling variance and that is attributable to real differences between studies. Thus meta-analysis can be viewed as a special case of multilevel analysis. In meta-analysis typically there is limited access to original data, usually results are published in the form of selected statistics such as effect sizes, means, standard deviations or correlation coefficients. The advantage of multilevel approaches to meta-analysis is its flexibility to include a range of potential explanatory variables and multiple outcomes. This has been illustrated using data on various interventions intended to enhance students' self-concept (Marsh, 1993; Marsh and Craven, 1997).

A study of self-concept research in school settings using a multivariate multilevel model meta-analysis by O'Mara *et al.* (2005) provides an example of new developments in multivariate multilevel models. Multivariate analyses allow the researcher to incorporate a range of different outcomes of interest. An advantage of such a multilevel multivariate approach is that it also addresses the issue of independence that has affected traditional meta-analysis approaches and provides better estimates of the effect sizes of interventions and their statistical significance.

O'Mara *et al.* (2005) note evidence of a reciprocal relation between self-concept and skill building, such that direct self-concept interventions can enhance both students' self-concept and related performance outcomes. The findings revealed that self-concept was enhanced through various intervention treatments. The estimate for mean effect size of 0.31 identified in the fixed effects model increased to 0.47 in the multilevel analysis, indicating that traditional analysis may underestimate the average effect of interventions. Significant heterogeneity was also found in the effect sizes between different studies and a number of predictor variables were tested that improved the model fit. The results confirm that the fixed effects model was less accurate in identifying statistically significant relationships and the findings from the multilevel models supported the construct validity approach, it provided greater confidence in the accuracy of the results and allowed the results to be generalized to the greater population of studies.

Cross-classified models for the study of complex hierarchical and non-hierarchical structures

The principles underlying cross-classified models and their analysis have been described by Rasbash and Goldstein (1994) and Goldstein (1995, 2003). Such an approach allows the researcher to study two sources of higher level influence simultaneously. In EER this is of particular interest because students may be clustered (i.e. be members of) different institutions or other higher level units at the same time point or at different time points. For example, a student may live in one neighbourhood and attend one school at the same time for a period of years. Both are forms of clustering that are of interest to those studying the sources of variation in individual students' educational outcomes over time. We can hypothesise (as social geographers do) that the neighbourhood a student lives in may shape students' outcomes, perhaps through peer influences or other opportunities that vary on a spatial scale. In addition, the school a student attends is also likely to have an influence on their outcomes. Although there may be a strong relationship between the neighbourhood and school attended, in most systems young people in some neighbourhoods will attend a range of schools, while in any one school students may come from homes in a number of different neighbourhoods. This is especially likely to occur in education systems that encourage choice and diversity of provision or that involve selection of some kind, as in England.

Cross-classified models that follow up student progress across phases (e.g. primary to secondary), allowing for the impact of multiple school membership and where data is available, can also be used to test for interactions with neighbourhood effects, recognizing the complexity of real world nested structures in educational research (Leckie, 2009). Multiple membership models allow for pupil mobility and Leckie (2009) built on the work of Goldstein *et al.* (2007) to present a more detailed study of pupil mobility between schools and between neighbourhoods to allow the relative importance of secondary schools, neighbourhoods and primary schools on both achievement and progress to be investigated using a very large data set. Leckie (2009: 4) argues that

> research into pupil mobility has been held back by both a lack of data on pupil movements and also by the absence of appropriate multilevel methodology. However, the recently established national pupil database in England and the development of cross-classified and multiple-membership multilevel models now make it possible to analyse a wide range of complex non-hierarchical data structures in models of educational achievement (Fielding and Goldstein, 2006; Rasbash and Browne, 2001).

Leckie's (2009) work illustrates how the contribution of secondary schools to the variance in outcomes for a given student varies as a function of the number of schools that the student attends and the time they spent in each school. Models that ignore the multiple membership structure lead to biased estimates of school effects and that the bias increases with the degree of student mobility.

Alternative methods for assessing school effects and schooling effects

In a special issue of the journal *School Effectiveness and School Improvement* focusing on 'Alternative Methods for Assessing School Effects and Schooling Effects', Sammons and Luyten (2009) drew together a number of articles to provide examples of recent innovative EER studies. While these typically all use multilevel analysis they move beyond the most common form of studies where effects are studied using a clustered student sample and a focus on progress over only two time points. Three different approaches were illustrated in this special issue: regression-discontinuity, growth curve analysis and seasonality of learning. Growth curve modelling is becoming more widely applied and represents a further refinement on more traditional multilevel analysis by modelling student growth in academic or in attitudinal or social behavioural outcomes across more than two time points. Guldemold and Bosker (2009) illustrate the curvilinear nature of growth curves for children's academic outcomes from kindergarten through to grade 6 and show how growth rates differ for low SES students compared with others. Van de gaer *et al.* (2009) by contrast examine non-cognitive outcomes and secondary age students using multivariate latent growth curve approaches to the study of developments in student motivation and academic self-concept. This revealed variation between student groups (boys/girls) in the rate of decline in motivation and academic self-concepts and some evidence of variation in school effects on this.

Seasonality of learning research can be seen as a special case of growth curve analysis. Examples were illustrated by Verachtert *et al.* (2009) and von Hippel (2009). In these studies student progress or learning rates during the school year and the summer vacation were compared. The basic assumption is that during the school year learning gains would be affected both by in- and out-of-school influences, whereas during the summer vacation it is assumed that only out-of-school factors operate. These authors' work indicates that learning rates in summertime vary for different student groups and thus provides potentially a more valid measure of overall variation in school effects and the extent to which some schools are more successful in promoting term-time learning for specific student groups. While providing possibly more valid and precise estimates of the size of school effects and illustrating the way summer learning rates may differ for students from different groups (advantaged/disadvantaged), von Hippel also acknowledges that such models may prove less reliable, although he suggests that enhanced validity may be preferable even at the cost of somewhat lower reliability in estimating school effects. A potential practical disadvantage of a focus on seasonality of learning models to study school effects is the need for additional points of assessment at the start and end of the school year to allow vacation learning (or fall back) to be examined as this is likely to increase the resource requirements, in contrast to the case of regression-discontinuity that can use cross-sectional data.

Regression-discontinuity is based on a comparison of students' outcomes in adjacent grades and uses cross-sectional data. This approach capitalizes on the fact that students' date of birth is the primary criterion for assignment to grades in most countries. The difference in achievement between students from adjacent grades minus the effect of age is therefore assumed to be a valid measure of the overall effect of extra time (an additional year) in schooling. This implies that the effect of education is equal to zero if the difference in achievement can be accounted for solely by the effect of students' ages in the statistical model. An important practical advantage of the approach is that it does not require longitudinal data (a major inhibitor of EER in many countries). Although longitudinal student level data are indispensable for some specific research questions (e.g. on the reciprocal relation between attitudes and achievement, or mapping changes in students' progress or growth trajectories), they also require more time and resources to collect. Kyriakides and Luyten (2009) and Luyten *et al.* (2009) provide illustrations of the application of regression-discontinuity to the study of the absolute effects of time in school. Their results point to the potential value of the regression-discontinuity approach in allowing analyses of the absolute effects of schooling as well as estimates of variation between individual schools (relative school effects) in the grade effect in the same analysis. In interpreting such estimates it is also important to use the CI associated with estimates for individual school residuals.

As yet, the number of regression-discontinuity and seasonality EER studies is very small but it is suggested they may provide a fruitful avenue for further enquiry in a range of contexts and an important addition to the EER toolkit, although they are mainly suited to systems where there is very little grade retention or promotion, with clear policies on age at entry to school so that whole age cohorts move through school grades together.

Better reporting of multilevel results in EER

Dedrick *et al.* (2009: 96) provide a review of methodological issues and applications in multilevel modelling. It is argued that:

> The complexity and relative newness of multilevel models requires researchers to take greater care in their descriptions of their methods and results . . . Primary researchers should thoroughly describe their methods and results. In addition manuscript reviewers and journal editors should require sufficient detail in submissions to allow appropriate evaluation of research quality.

They provide a seven-point set of guidelines on reporting multilevel results. While the article is welcome and the guidelines suggested are generally sound it is disappointing that these authors did not include the international *School Effectiveness and School Improvement* journal in their review and thus did not cover many important EER studies that have used multilevel modelling and provide good examples of informative reporting of results. This seems to reflect a lack of awareness of the important contribution of European and other researchers in non-American contexts and of the widespread use of multilevel modelling in EER in particular. It is suggested that the development of further guidance on appropriate reporting of multilevel results in EER studies and the highlighting of examples of articles that illustrate good practice should be a strong priority for the EER field to refine and extend the advice provided by Dedrick *et al.* (2009) and to draw attention to the achievements of EER over the last decade or so.

2. The potential of mixed methods studies in EER

Teddlie and Sammons (2010) argue that the flexibility of mixed methods (MM) research in simultaneously addressing multiple and diverse research questions through integrated qualitative (QUAL) and quantitative (QUAN) techniques is one of its attractions. They note the growing use of MM designs as a third paradigm to rival the dominant post-positivist and constructivist traditions of social research and that it offers the potential to enhance theory development as well as providing new knowledge or relevance to practitioners. The combination of general statistical findings and thick descriptions of specific cases exemplifying those findings has the potential to generate a synergy that neither can alone (for examples of such mixed methods EER studies see Teddlie and Stringfield, 1993; Sammons *et al.*, 1997; Sammons *et al.*, 2005; Siraj-Blatchford *et al.*, 2006; Day *et al.*, 2008; Jang *et al.*, 2008). By the generation of new knowledge that goes beyond the sum of the individual QUAL and QUAN components, MM research adds 'extra value' to EER research that seeks to better describe, predict and understand the variation in, and contributors to, differences in educational effectiveness. The integration and synthesis of QUAL and QUAN evidence can foster mutual illumination and so has the potential to enable the development of new synergistic understandings. It is argued that MM research is particularly valuable in the testing and development of EER theories and is also necessary to inform and support closer links with applied research and evaluations that can promote effective school improvement initiatives and teacher development programmes.

Much SER and school improvement activity has suffered from the rather unhelpful dichotomy and antagonism that has arisen between QUAL and QUAN approaches, which reflects the legacy of the 'paradigm wars' in social research evident during the last thirty years (Sammons, 2010; Teddlie and Sammons, 2010). This is reflected in the QUAN paradigm becoming primarily associated with larger-scale EER investigations that seek to identify and measure differences in school or teacher effectiveness in promoting students' educational outcomes, and with the statistical prediction and explanation of variance in student outcomes. This also led to a focus on the development and largely QUANT focus of testing of theoretical models that seek to account for such variations in educational effectiveness, as discussed previously in relation to Creemers' (1994) Comprehensive model of educational effectiveness. By contrast, the QUAL paradigm has mostly been used in school improvement and teacher development studies and is associated with action research and interpretivist approaches to enquiry in SER. Here the focus has largely been on generating 'thick' descriptions, to aid understanding school and classroom processes and participants' perspectives, usually with only limited attention given to investigating the impact of processes on student outcomes.

Much work in the school improvement and development traditions has involved mainly QUAL case studies of particular institutions, such as improving or 'turnaround schools', and others that can be viewed as more effective despite disadvantaged contexts. Such research has sought to stimulate and study the processes of change, and explore the perceptions and experiences of participants, and has generally paid less attention to the study of student outcomes than EER. A number of different approaches to promoting school improvement have been identified as relevant for schools depending on their organizational history and current performance level (Harris, 2003) and much attention has been given to studying the improvement of schools in disadvantaged contexts (Chapman and Harris, 2004; Harris *et al.*, 2006). Two examples of voluntary school improvement programmes that have incorporated EER evidence and give a strong emphasis to student outcomes are the Improving the Quality of Education for All (IQEA) project (Hopkins, 2001, 2002) and the High Reliability Schools project (Stringfield *et al.*, 2008). Nonetheless, there have been a growing number of evaluations of the impact of various school reform or improvement programmes in the US that have examined the effects on student outcomes (Boreman *et al.*, 2003), but these have largely been conducted using QUAN rather than QUAL perspectives and often involve the use of quasi experimental approaches including randomized controlled trials. These have identified sustained impacts for the most successful intervention programmes such as 'Success for All'.

Although there are therefore distinctive QUAL and QUAN traditions in both teacher and SER studies, there have been relatively few that utilize MM techniques intentionally to conduct large-scale studies with complex research questions (e.g. Brookover *et al.*, 1979; Mortimore *et al.*, 1988; Teddlie and Stringfield, 1993; Sammons *et al.*, 1997; MacBeath and Mortimore, 2001; Jang *et al.*, 2008; Sylva *et al.*, 2010).

In order to achieve mutual illumination such MM studies must be designed to ensure that different phases of QUAN and QUAL data collection and analysis can feed into each other in a productive way that enhances both and integrates findings and interpretations to enable meta-inferences that go beyond and enrich the QUAN and QUAL results considered in isolation. In this way, emerging findings from QUAL interviews, for example, may be used to help shape the topics covered in a larger-scale QUAN survey. Following analysis, the survey results may then feed into a second round of follow-up interviews in an iterative cycle. The identification of outlier schools or teachers that are classified as more effective, or by contrast, less effective, and those that are broadly typical in their effectiveness based on QUAN multilevel analyses of student outcomes, may be used to help identify a purposive case study sample of schools or teachers for in-depth investigation using largely QUAL approaches. These case studies, in turn, may suggest additional questions or hypotheses that can be further tested in subsequent analyses using the larger QUAN datasets.

This 'to and fro' process of MM research (using inductive and deductive reasoning for ongoing theory generation and testing) represents a cyclical rather than linear approach to enquiry. It suggests that MM researchers are endeavouring to create deeper understandings of a topic rather than only seeking to formulate static, constant, linear 'truths' or 'laws' about a phenomenon and this is deemed more appropriate for the study of educational institutions and processes that are continuously subject to change internally and externally and so are inherently dynamic in nature (as discussed previously in relation to the dynamic model). Teddlie and Sammons (forthcoming) suggest that, in general, EER has given too much emphasis to purely large-scale, QUAN methodologies, particularly those involving multilevel modelling approaches to study variations between schools, departments or classes in the 'value added' to student outcomes. While this has been necessary to enable the development of a sound evidence base on the appropriate measurement of variations in student outcomes and of differences in effectiveness, and to answer important questions concerning the size of school and teacher effects (Teddlie and Reynolds, 2000; Creemers and Kyriakides, 2008; Luyten and Sammons, 2009), it has led to a stronger focus on producing generalizations, rather than fostering illumination and understanding of educational effectiveness topics that are of value to practitioners. It is argued that MM research is a third paradigm (Tashakkori and Teddlie, 2003, 2010) that is likely to become increasingly important in EER in the twenty-first century as it offers approaches that help to bridge the unhelpful QUAL versus QUAN paradigm divide that has tended to separate the EER and school improvement research communities.

Although much EER is situated within the post-positivist QUAN-oriented tradition, there are examples of both QUAL and QUAN research in TER and SER, with a relatively small but growing number of studies that use MM research techniques (for example, Mortimore *et al.*, 1988; Teddlie and Stringfield, 1993; Sammons *et al.*, 1997; MacBeath and Mortimore, 2001; James *et al.*, 2006; Day *et al.*, 2007, 2011; Sylva *et al.*, 2008, 2010). Teddlie and Sammons (2010) argue that it is valuable to consider some of the differences between post-positivism and pragmatism as research paradigms, and how pragmatic MM research can enhance post-positivistic EER. They make comparisons of these approaches in terms of three dimensions that are seen to be especially relevant to the design of better EER and SI research and evaluations: these are concerned with *methods, logic* and the possibility of *generalizations.*

Rather than maintaining the artificial QUAN versus QUAL opposition evident in the 'paradigm wars', between post-positivist and constructivist/post-modernist approaches, they claim that the pragmatic philosophical position underpinning most MM designs focuses on the value and fruitfulness of using evidence from both paradigms to address a broader range of research questions and produce more robust and interesting findings, than either approach could do in isolation and so has the potential to prove of value to both practitioners and policy makers.

A range of typologies of MM designs can be identified (Tashakkori and Teddlie, 2003, 2010). Of particular interest to EER and school improvement studies and evaluations are *multilevel mixed designs* that can be used to examine organizations that have a hierarchical structure such as schools and classrooms (Tashakkori and Teddlie, 1998). This fits well with the emphasis on multilevel modeling evident in much existing EER (where the QUAN methods linked with a post-positivist paradigm view have traditionally dominated as noted above), as it focuses on the clustering in data typical in educational settings, and also allows the possible impacts of school and neighbourhood context measures to be explored, because students may be nested within neighbourhoods as well as within schools. However, multilevel mixed designs extend the kinds of research questions that can be addressed via reliance only on the dominant QUAN tradition, particularly in relation to the influence of context. Tashakkori and Teddlie (2003) and Teddlie and Sammons (2010) suggest that 'Fully integrated mixed designs' are probably the most complete manifestation of MM research designs in which the mixing of the QUAL and QUAN approaches occurs in an interactive manner across all stages of a study.

The further development of fruitful linkages between EER and school improvement research is likely to require greater use of such multilevel and fully integrated designs in order to produce findings of greater relevance to both policy and the improvement of practice (Tashakkori and Teddile, 2010).

3. Theoretical models and EER

A number of EER researchers have highlighted the need to strengthen the theoretical underpinnings of EER to better understand the mechanisms that link school and classroom processes and student outcomes through the development of better theoretical models. There are strong links between the methodological and measurement developments in EER discussed previously and theoretical advance.

There have been interesting developments moving on from Creemers' (1994) Generic Educational Effectiveness Model to the recent notion of a *Dynamic Model of Educational Effectiveness* (Creemers and Kyriakides, 2008) that places *change* at the centre of the model and thus offers the prospect of better correspondence with the study of improvement processes. Similarly, work by Stringfield *et al.* (2008a and b; Reynolds, 2010) has developed the concept of schools as High Reliability Organizations (HRO). This seeks to integrate robust EER evidence and a theoretical model of a HRO to foster school improvement. Further study of the application of such models offers a way to promote stronger links between the improvement and effectiveness fields.

Despite attempts to promote greater synergy, the paradigms of school effectiveness and school improvement remain fairly distinct, particularly in terms of theory and methodology (a point discussed further later in this chapter). Creemers and Kyriakides (2008) provide a comprehensive integrated framework for effective school improvement through developing the concept of a *Dynamic Model* of EER that they claim can guide the study of educational change and improvement processes. It also offers a valuable basis to guide future research and the development of new programmes for school improvement that are grounded in the existing EER evidence base and enable the testing of key theoretical concepts.

The authors argue that this offers a better basis for policy makers and practitioners to improve practice through the combination of a *theory driven* and *evidence based approach*. This includes explicit recognition of the multilevel nature of schools and education systems, better articulation and measurement of relevant constructs and advocates further exploration of the relationships between different factors that operate at a number of levels (student, teacher/classroom, and school and context levels).

In addition to identifying the correlates or characteristics of effective schools and teachers, the need to establish and test theories that seek to explain why and how some schools and teachers are more effective in promoting better student outcomes than others has formed an important focus in earlier SER and TER with significant contributions by researchers such as Bosker, Creemers, Scheerens, Stringfield and Teddlie in particular. Major reviews of EE models have been provided by Scheerens and Bosker (1997) and Teddlie and Reynolds (2000). However, until recently, models of EE can be regarded as essentially static in nature. The Creemers and Kyriakides (2008) model represents a major shift in thinking because it seeks to place the study of *change* (in contexts, processes and student outcomes) at the heart of the model. Given this, it does not consider effectiveness necessarily as a relatively stable feature of schools but rather as one that, by definition, must *evolve* over time. This approach is thus better suited to those concerned with a longitudinal perspective who seek to examine the issue of school improvement and the way different factors may influence changes in effectiveness over time.

The model views both school and teacher effects (and their relationships) as dynamic concepts that occur within multilevel, hierarchical and dynamic structures. In other words, they recognize that not only do students' achievement and other outcome trajectories change over time, so too may the organizations, individuals (schools and teachers) and other contextual features (educational policy contexts, neighbourhood and societal contexts) that help to shape them.

The lack of appropriate models that focus on change has probably hindered the uptake of both SER and school improvement results and insights by practitioners in schools. A well-grounded model that draws on existing work has the potential to aid understanding of EER findings and may also help to identify and map areas for future research (both confirmatory and exploratory) and can thus strengthen, refine and extend existing EER knowledge. Creemers and Kyriakides (2008) argue that longitudinal data can enhance the validity of making tentative causal claims in non-experimental research (see also Chapter 3 by Kyriakides in this volume).

Of particular relevance to those interested in school improvement, the dynamic model assumes that the impact of both school and context level factors must be measured over time and in relation to diagnoses of weaknesses in the school, particularly features related to policy on teaching and actions to improve teaching, but also in terms of culture. Van der Werf *et al.* (2008) provide an analysis that tests the application of the dynamic model.

School improvement researchers increasingly recognize that the impact of school and context factors will depend on the current situation in a school. This is an important new theoretical feature of the dynamic model, in comparison with earlier EER models. It fits with findings from studies of schools in disadvantaged contexts (Muijs *et al.*, 2004; Harris *et al.*, 2006; Reynolds *et al.*, 2006). Similarly, a study of school leadership and pupil outcomes in England has compared improvement processes and strategies reported by head teachers and staff in different groups of improving effective and schools divided according to their attainment starting point, Low start, Moderate start and High start (Gu and Sammons, 2008), and identified significant differences for the Low start group in intensity of actions taken to promote improvement.

Summary and conclusions

This chapter argues that we need to pay more attention to identifying the best ways to promote greater understanding of the use and limitations of EER, given the growing interest internationally in raising educational standards and promoting school improvement and the quality of teaching. There have many criticisms of EER and the school improvement fields that have stimulated reflection and further research, though it should be acknowledged that not all such criticisms are well founded. The application and testing of EER models and the use of MM designs can provide an appropriate basis for the development of better improvement strategies and for the evaluation of improvement initiatives at system and at school level. There is growing evidence on the size and significance of school and teacher effects and recent research points to the importance of pre-school effects (Sylva *et al.*, 2010). The academic effectiveness of the primary school attended and the quality of the pre-school experience can both shape children's attainment and progress, and in combination they can be substantial (Sammons *et al.*, 2008; Anders *et al.*, 2010). Existing evidence suggest school effects vary and are more important for disadvantaged groups (Scheerens and Bosker, 1997) but further studies are needed to establish whether particular approaches to teaching and methods of organization promote better outcomes for disadvantaged students and the sustainability of school effects. For example, the role of direct instruction versus constructivist approaches has been analysed by Rowe (2006). This showed that direct instruction offered significant benefits in teaching early literacy and that this was especially important for low attaining and disadvantaged children.

Differential effectiveness and stability and consistency of effects also require further investigation. Student and family background factors that predict educational outcomes and the size of the equity gap in achievement remain foci of continued interest, particularly how they may interact with school and classroom process measures (Sammons, 2010; Kelly and Downey, 2010). High quality longitudinal data with appropriate controls are required to conduct rigorous EER in a variety of contexts. There is also a need for further study of contextual effects on both student outcomes and processes in a range of contexts and across sectors.

EER studies should investigate a wider range of student outcomes, including goals of citizenship, social cognition and well-being, as well as in terms of academic outcomes (Van de Wal and Waslander, 2007). There is no discrepancy between schools achieving objectives in the cognitive domain and in the area of well-being and relationships can often be reciprocal, with academic achievement promoting motivation and feelings of well-being that in turn promote further cognitive gains.

Research into the relationships between academic and behavioural self-concept and attainment has demonstrated such reciprocal links (Marsh *et al.*, 2005).

The development of new methods to study educational effects such as regression-discontinuity, growth curve modelling and 'seasonality' studies of student progress while schools are in session compared with progress during holiday periods offer potentially powerful additional resources for EER.

There is also a need for greater conceptual clarification and the development of better instruments to measure key constructs and processes. The lack of standardized and validated instruments is a barrier to the development of future EER studies. Recent attempts to develop an international classroom observation and teacher feedback instrument (ISTOF) by Teddlie *et al.* (2006) and of classroom and school climate (Van Damme and Dhaenens, 2007) offer the prospect of potentially fruitful comparisons within and between sectors and countries of the features of effective classroom practice. This should shed further light on the extent to which overall teacher effectiveness is best viewed as a more global, generic, stable characteristic of teachers or a differentiated, context and time dependent characteristic (varying between lessons, over time and in relation to different student groups). A study of Effective Classroom practice in England has used the ISTOF instrument to explore variations in teacher practice and provides evidence to support both the generic and the differentiated views of effective teaching (Ko and Sammons, 2008; Day *et al.*, 2008). In addition, the use of international instruments such as the Early Childhood Environment Rating Scale (ECERS-R, Harms *et al.*, 1998; and ECERS-E, Sylva *et al.*, 2003) offer further potential for the development of EER in the early pre-school phases of education (Sylva *et al.*, 2006, 2010).

The value of mixed methods approaches to the study of educational effectiveness is also becoming increasingly recognized, as is the important role of multilevel meta-analyses of EER results to provide a better guide to the robustness of empirical findings.

In examining the EER legacy a number of conclusions can be drawn:

- Individual schools and teachers can make a significant difference to the development, progress and achievement of students.
- There is evidence for variation in absolute schooling effects as well as in differences in relative effects.
- Effectiveness is best seen as a dynamic, retrospective and relative concept that is time and outcome dependent and influenced by the sample and predictors and the adequacy of statistical models.
- There can be significant internal variation in school effects and fine (rank ordered) distinctions of school performance are inappropriate.
- Effectiveness research should focus on a broader range of learning outcomes; including academic, affective, behavioural, practical, creative and social.
- Teacher/classroom effects are generally larger than those attributable to schools and thus the improvement of teaching quality and classroom climate should remain a strong focus for improvement initiatives.

- Schools improve most by focusing on the quality of learning and teaching, while also addressing their culture and internal conditions.
- Intervention work for school or system improvement needs to be based on appropriate research findings and theoretical models.

Future directions for EER

The traditional focus of SER on the school as an institution needs to be broadened if it is to remain relevant to the many changes affecting education systems in the twenty-first century.

> Moves towards more flexible school organization such as networks of schools, a broader role for schools reconceptualized as community centers, the emergence of new providers outwith the public sector, the increasingly internationalised nature of research and moves towards greater use of distance learning and home schooling all mean that this focus may rapidly become outdated.
>
> (Muijs, 2006: 141)

Muijs (2006) endorses a renewed focus on a broader field of EER studies conducted in an open minded and empirical way. Creemers *et al.* (2010) have also outlined a number of areas for future research in the field addressed in terms of a 'road map'.

As I hope this chapter illustrates, the topic of educational effectiveness remains a dynamic field of enquiry and if no longer in its adolescence is certainly still in an early stage of maturity. EER remains an exciting area with many possibilities to influence policy and practice. There remains a need to study the processes of improvement and the role of external interventions (Borman *et al.*, 2003; Slavin, 2010; Bosker, 2011), new approaches to school leadership (see Chapman 2006; Chapman *et al.*, 2010; Day *et al.*, 2011) and forms of school and educational organization. There are numerous opportunities to consolidate, refine and extend the existing knowledge bases of school and teacher effectiveness and to investigate wider phases of early or later education, or the role of the shadow education system that is very active in some contexts. There is significant scope for methodological advance and the further development and testing of EER theories. The need for better links with, and contribution to, thoughtful school improvement and evaluation studies remains urgent. The EER and SI fields can play an important part in the evaluation and critique of education policy reforms in many contexts (Sammons, 2008; Chapman and Gunter, 2009). Some possible foci for future directions are suggested below but the list is by no means comprehensive:

- exploring student progress over the longer term across different phases of education to establish the extent, nature and cumulative impact of educational influences (pre-schools, primary and secondary schools and colleges);
- exploring whether and how different classroom and school processes

vary in their impact on different groups of students and their educational trajectories;

- using EER approaches to inform and evaluate the impact of school improvement initiatives and educational policy reforms to enhance understanding of the processes of educational and institutional change;
- using new methodological approaches (such as seasonality or regression-discontinuity analysis, multilevel meta-analysis and multilevel structural equation models) to enhance and broaden the scope of existing studies of variations in educational effectiveness;
- more explorations of equity in EER investigating the way educational influences can reduce or increase inequalities in outcomes for disadvantaged groups (relevant to the narrowing the gaps equity in education aims of policy makers in many systems);
- studying a broader range of student outcomes covering new goals of education and approaches to learning and developing new instruments to foster this;
- investigating the role of 'within school variation' further and its implications for learning from best practice, and examining the differential effectiveness of schools and teaching approaches for specific sub-groups of students;
- greater international collaborations and comparative studies, for example, using international comparative datasets such as PISA, TIMSS, PIRLS, etc., and the development of common instruments to measure key features of institutions and teaching;
- providing reviews and syntheses of evidence on effective teaching and educational reforms to inform school improvement studies;
- greater use of quasi-experimental approaches and randomized controlled trial (RCT) in EER to examine promising interventions;
- developing improvement initiatives based on the EER knowledge base and theoretical models to test their value and further inform theory development.

In summary, further advances of EER are likely to emerge through the combination of better use of existing methods and the development of new approaches, more rigorous use of theory and the application of causal models and experimental designs. A stronger focus on within school variation and the role of context, coupled with the use of theory and evidence to develop better focused improvement approaches and interventions, offers the prospect of forging better links between the SI and EER traditions with mutual benefits to both.

2 School improvement research and practice

A case of back to the future?

Christopher Chapman

Introduction

The emergence of the concept of school effectiveness has popularised the argument that schools can, and do, make a difference to academic outcomes and ultimately to the life chances of children (Teddlie and Reynolds, 2000; Sammons, 2008). Recognition that schools can have positive (and therefore also negative) impacts on student outcomes has also supported the rise of school improvement research and practice. These two related fields have made a considerable contribution to our understanding of the factors associated with effective schooling and the processes linked to enhancing them.

Policy makers world-wide have drawn on this research to develop interventions designed to raise educational standards in schools and recent policies across several systems have reflected a zero tolerance approach (Sammons, 2008a). These include No Child Left Behind and Race to the Top in the USA and The National and City Challenge Programmes in England. Policy makers have also listened to the arguments of academics and researchers calling for improvements to be made from within schools (Barth, 1990; Hopkins *et al.*, 1994; Stoll and Fink, 1996). Policies designed to support internally generated improvement can often be traced back to the ideas associated with Kurt Lewin (1946) on action research, the development of professional practice, and school self-evaluation for school improvement.

This chapter explores the development of this field and reflects on conceptualisations of school improvement. This reflection leads us to consider a number of challenges for the development of school improvement research and practice. I argue that school improvement researchers and activists have shifted the focus of their attention from improving the work of teachers in classrooms and schools to influencing policy makers in the hope of delivering systemic improvement. In conclusion, I argue that, while this shift has delivered some returns, the field has become disconnected from the work of schools and teachers and therefore requires a reconfiguration of relationships and priorities if research and practice are to penetrate classrooms in meaningful ways.

The development of school improvement research and practice

School improvement (SI) research and practice has taken a related but different evolutionary pathway to school effectiveness (SE) research. SE researchers have tended to focus on exploring differences between more or less effective schools from a positivist perspective. As is evident from other chapters in this book, research methodology in SE often involves quantitative measurement of a range of parameters associated with educational performance in attempts to assess the scale of impact (Gray, 1981; Rutter, *et al.*, 1979; Tymms, 1992). A second common feature of effectiveness studies has been to identify the characteristics of more effective schools (Purkey and Smith, 1983; Rutter *et al.*, 1979; Sammons *et al.*, 1995). As the knowledge base at school level has grown, researchers have turned their attention to various aspects of effectiveness, including the quantification of school effects for different groups of pupils and their stability over time (Smith and Tomlinson, 1989; Nuttall *et al.*, 1989). More recently, researchers have investigated the differential effectiveness of departments (Harris *et al.*, 1995; Sammons *et al.*, 1997) and contemporary research in this field takes the classroom level as the unit of analysis, focusing on teacher effectiveness (Muijs and Reynolds, 2002). Most recently, SE researchers have become preoccupied with studying variations in effectiveness at different levels within the system, particularly within school variation.

In parallel to the development of SE research a second, related approach to school performance has emerged. SI research and practice has evolved and, until recently, there has been little communication between proponents of the different educational theories. Although intrinsically related, these two approaches clearly have their own histories and traditions.

In contrast to SE research the SI movement has tended to consider schools as social organisations while inquiring into the processes associated with improvement. The successful implementation of change has underpinned much of the work in this area and, in contrast to SE research, this has usually involved a bottom up rather than top down approach to change, locating power and control with those actually tasked with securing improvements. The methodologies relied upon to research and record these aims have been largely qualitative, often using case studies to illustrate initiatives that have worked at a particular level within a specific school rather than generating large datasets. Table 2.1 summarises the separate traditions of school effectiveness and school improvement research and practice.

What is school improvement research and practice?

SI research and practice is concerned with making schools 'better' places for students, teachers and the wider community (Reynolds *et al.*, 1996). Practice has tended to rely on the engagement of teachers through continuing professional development (CPD). This approach has drawn on principles of inquiry, reflection and self-review as a spur to improvement (Hopkins *et al.*, 1994).

The term school improvement is commonly used in two ways. As noted above it can be a common-sense term to describe efforts to make schools better places for students. Alternatively, it can be used in a more technical sense to describe the processes that contribute to raising student achievement (Hopkins *et al.*, 1994). Definitions relating to school improvement have evolved to reflect an increased focus on student achievement and capacity building. For example, an early definition from the International School Improvement Project (ISIP) defined school improvement as

> a systemic, sustained effort aimed at change in learning conditions, and other related internal conditions, in one or more schools, with the ultimate aim of accomplishing educational goals more effectively.
>
> (van Velzen et al., 1985: 48)

By the mid-1990s researchers had drawn on their experiences of researching on and working with schools to develop a tighter a definition focusing on capacity to manage change and enhance student outcomes:

> In this sense school improvement is about raising student achievement through focusing on the teaching and learning processes and the conditions that support it. It is about strategies for improving the school's capacity for providing quality education in times of change, rather than blindly accepting the edicts of centralized policies and striving to implement these directives uncritically.
>
> (Hopkins et al., 1994: 3)

The principles of improving student outcomes by attempting to develop organisational culture and capacity have become central to contemporary school improvement research and practice (Barth, 1990; MacBeath, 1996, 1999; Brighouse, 2000; Harris, 2002; Chapman and Hadfield, 2010). Increased emphasis on student

Table 2.1 The separate traditions of school effectiveness and school improvement

School effectiveness	*School improvement*
1 Focus on schools	Focus on teachers
2 Focus on organisation	Focus on school processes
3 Data-driven, emphasis on outcomes	Empirical evaluation of changes' effects
4 Quantitative in orientation	Qualitative in orientation
5 Lack of knowledge about how to implement change strategies	Exclusively concerned with change in schools
6 More concerned with change in pupil outcomes	More concerned with journey of school improvement than its destination
7 More concerned with schools at one point in time	More concerned with schools as changing entities
8 Based on research knowledge	Focused on practitioner knowledge

(Adapted from Reynolds et al., 1996)

outcomes and capacity building have ensured continued commitment to these principles decades after their introduction in the literature.

In addition (and in many cases in contrast to school effectiveness), the school improvement movement has argued that improvement and the capacity to improve come from within, rather than beyond organisations. Therefore, proponents of school improvement have tended to view it as a bottom up rather than top down approach to change, thereby putting students and teachers at the core of improvement efforts. Essentially, teachers and school leaders are the key agents of change (Fullan, 1991; Hopkins, *et al.*, 1994; MacBeath, 1999, 2009). This said, as shown in David Hopkins' valuable contribution in Chapter 11, over the past decade or two there has been a shift in focus from school to system improvement. The next section of this chapter offers a range of perspectives that highlights this development.

Perspectives on school improvement research and practice

School improvement research and practice is a relatively young field of inquiry yet it has made significant progress and influenced many educational systems in a short period. Since its inception in the 1970s commentators have argued that it developed in a series of waves or phases (Hopkins *et al.*, 1994; Hopkins and Reynolds, 2001). Most recently, the field has been described in terms of five phases, summarised as follows:

- *Phase 1* – specific intervention and the highlighting of the importance of culture in any change process.
- *Phase 2* – focus on teacher action research and school self-review.
- *Phase 3* – builds on the emerging school effectiveness knowledge base. It sees the school as the unit of change. Approaches address both organisational and classroom improvement and increasing emphasis on the importance of school leadership.
- *Phase 4* – scaling up reforms. Development of large-scale professional learning communities offers one way to reinvigorate and recommit individual schools and educators to the process of improvement.
- *Phase 5* – the spread of the knowledge base globally alongside learning more about achieving school improvement at scale – systemic reform.

(Hopkins *et al.*, 2011)

These phases provide us with a helpful framework for reflecting on the evolution of school improvement. They provide a historical overview of the development of the field rather than a diagnostic tool or map on which education systems can be located with associated recipes for policy makers and practitioners to wade through, in attempts to move their system, schools and classrooms from one phase to another.

Furthermore, it does not necessarily follow that phase five systems are of higher capacity and more effective than those focusing on phase one or two. This is not a case of moving from poor to fair to good and ultimately to great (McKinsey, 2011). We might reflect that education systems, like schools, exhibit significant internal variation. This suggests that there are elements in all systems that can be described as 'great' or 'leading edge' and elements that are 'poor' or 'trailing edge'. Therefore, much can be learned from within, drawing on the capacity of the leading edge to support the development of the trailing edge. Systems should not be treated as linear or hierarchical but seen as operating in broad and overlapping phases, with the expectation that most have layered activity from all phases in action in the field.

With these thoughts in mind it is no surprise that some strands of activity from earlier phases continue to be powerful drivers for change in the most advanced educational systems world-wide. For example, Ben Levin (2008) refers to the importance of cultural change and inquiry in transforming 5,000 schools in Ontario, Canada. Other systems, including in Australia and Japan, have engaged in various forms of action research, lesson study and school self-review to support the school improvement process. In some of the strongest systems, such as Canada, phase one and two activities have not been superseded by phase three, four or five activity. Rather they became recognised as powerful levers for change and have become part of the infrastructure for self-renewal and sustained improvement, indicating a layered approach to change and improvement.

MacGilchrist (2000) offers a second conceptualisation, arguing that self-improvement is multi-dimensional in nature. She claims self-improvement is underpinned by three types of self-evaluation:

1   *Macro self-evaluation* – focusing on the school as a whole; in other words, the 'big picture'. It is concerned with the extent to which the school uses an intelligent approach to maximising overall effectiveness as a learning community.
2   *Means-ends self-evaluation* – focusing on the extent to which school-wide plans for improvement are not only strengthening management arrangements but also having a direct impact on classrooms and, more importantly, on pupils' progress and achievement.
3   *Micro self-evaluation* – focusing not on learning outcomes but on the quality of learning that takes place in classrooms.

This multi-dimensional approach to self-evaluation provides a means whereby a school can systematically keep under review a number of elements, including:

• its effectiveness as a learning community;
• the effectiveness of its school improvement processes, particularly regarding school culture and impact on pupils' progress and achievement;
• the effectiveness of the learning actually taking place in classrooms.

This three-pronged approach to self-evaluation for self-improvement also highlights the need to work at, and keep under regular review, not only relationships between leadership and management across the school as a whole with the culture of departments and classrooms but also the interface between the school and its local and national communities.

School improvement's focus on self-review, culture and inquiry are key components of phase 1 and 2 school improvement and remain central to contemporary efforts concerned with organisational or within-school improvement.

Focus on the organisation as the key unit of analysis leads us to a third conceptualisation of improvement. Rather than considering improvement in terms of evolutionary phases it is helpful to think in terms of foci and units of analyses. This leads us to reflect on three key levels of improvement effort:

1   Improvement *within schools* – focusing on improving structures and processes to support the development of teaching, learning and capacity for change within the organisation.
2   Improvement *between schools* – focusing on developing structures and process to support the development of teaching, learning and capacity for change laterally across organisational boundaries.
3   Improvement *beyond schools* – focusing on developing structures and processes that support young people's capacity to engage in meaningful learning experiences outside formal schooling. This third perspective may offer an alternative way of thinking about developing coherent approaches to systemic improvement.

The evidence base concerning within school improvement is the most secure. It suggests that efforts should focus on the following key areas:

•   developing teaching and learning and leadership;
•   development of high expectations and strong cultural norms;
•   application of appropriate accountability mechanisms;
•   relentless use of data to identify organisational strengths and weaknesses and inform decision-making;
•   combining short-term tactical responses to change the 'here and now' with longer-term strategic responses that attend to medium- and longer-term capacity building, all matched to context;
•   attention to detail to achieve consistent application of school policies;
•   unrelenting investment in individuals' personal and professional development;
•   protection from inappropriate local and national policy initiatives by filtration and adaptation or rejection of external interventions.

The evidence base pertaining to between school improvement is less secure. There has been considerable attention paid to networking and collaboration activity but, in spite of this, we have less understanding about what works and why. However, the emerging knowledge base suggests between school improvement:

- can achieve economies of scale;
- involves surrendering some autonomy to an overarching super-structure;
- supports succession planning and career management across schools and localities;
- promotes the movement of key staff around groups of schools to identify issues and support capacity building;
- can support the development of shared governance arrangements between high and low performing schools;
- promotes centralised functions to support quality assurance and coordinate action between schools (e.g. Charter Management Organisations for Charter Schools);
- promotes two-tier governance structures – strategic (central) and operational (local);
- provides opportunities for sharing expertise across organisational boundaries in a systematic and meaningful way;
- enhances opportunities for CPD;
- provides commitment to promoting the 'brand' of the group (e.g. KIP charter schools, United Learning Trust Academies).

The knowledge base for improvement beyond schools is even less robust. However, it tends to be concerned with:

- achieving the right blend of school improvement and community development approaches across localities to support appropriate levels of consistency and fidelity of implementation without stifling innovation – *Designing approaches tailored to the needs of specific communities.*
- inter-dependence for capacity building across groups of schools and the wider system – *Creating a workforce and generation of leaders who think beyond their own brand and understand the interplay between education and other public services.*
- the development of coherent and connected policies to promote joined-up practice across public services – *Promoting inter-professional arrangements which generate shared understanding of different professional contexts and the relationship between educational and social improvement.*
- creating a system that assumes joint responsibility for all children in a locality, not just those on roll in one school or one federation of schools – *Developing accountability mechanisms that promote shared responsibility for all children across a locality and, ultimately, the system.*

Systems where within school improvement dominates the discourse tend to be underpinned by *individualistic improvement*. Schools and their leaders are in constant competition for resources and focus their energy on preserving the status quo by protecting their organisational interests. These systems can never generate high leverage improvement.

Systems where between school improvement dominates lead to *federal improvement.* In these systems, groups of schools join forces to form improvement alliances as federations, chains and other types of collaboratives. Schools and their leaders work collaboratively within their 'club' but are wary of being 'taken over' or 'beaten' by other improvement alliances. Ultimately, competition within the system is pervasive and federal improvement suffers a similar fate to its individualised counterpart, limiting potential for systemic improvement. Both individualised and federal approaches tend to be favoured in systems underpinned by neo-liberal agendas. Table 2.2 highlights the key features of individualised and federal improvement.

Systems where beyond school improvement dominates, lead to improvement becoming systemic. The features of these systems create the conditions whereby school improvement is viewed in a much broader context in terms of processes and outcomes. This involves developing a coherent approach to school and societal improvement whereby strong connections between different agencies and government departments facilitate a shared language about public policy values and outcomes.

The various perspectives outlined above offer a number of insights into how we have thought about and pursued the improvement agenda over the past few decades. In the following section I move on to reflect on some of the challenges presented by our current view of improvement.

Table 2.2 Key features of individualised and federal improvement

Type 1: Individualised Improvement	Type 2: Federal Improvement
High levels of both autonomy and accountability at school level. Principal has control over most decisions.	Some loss of autonomy at school level but accountability remains high. Most key decisions made at federal level.
Deep understanding of individual school context. Opportunities tailored to individual needs and matched to school context and capacity for change.	Standardised approaches across the federation considered a key benchmark leading to tensions between school and federation perspectives.
Success considered fragile (even when sustained) – reliant on personnel in key leadership positions and other internal factors e.g. teacher retention.	Successes less fragile than for Type 1 improvement but could be catastrophic if whole federation is viewed as failing.
Individual school vulnerable to changes in external environment – e.g. political decisions, demographics.	Federation is less vulnerable to changes in external environment and more easily draws in external resources.
Individual school gains have limited or even negative effect on other schools in the area.	Commitment to the federal brand limits potential for genuine collaboration with other local schools.
No commitment to children attending other schools in the locality.	Still no commitment to children attending other local schools.
Potential for systemic improvement is LIMITED.	Potential for systemic improvement remains LIMITED.

School improvement research and practice: the seduction of systemic improvement

The phases of improvement and the focus on work within, between and beyond schools indicate a shift in interest from improving classrooms to improving systems. Governments have sought the advice, guidance and opinions of successful practitioners while academics have moved between policy and university roles. There is a belief within the system that if those in the field can influence policy then classrooms will change for the better. This situation is problematic for a number of reasons.

First, there is an issue of *political interference*. Findings from the field have been used selectively and sometimes distorted to serve political needs. While government has invested in programmes of research and evaluation, the extent to which their findings are disseminated and fed into policy decisions appears to depend upon political expediency. Policies tend to be driven by expediency, not empirical evidence, and this has produced a distorted view of the evidence base and marginalised the voices of those in the field.

Second, the nature of the *policy–practice divide* is problematic. The relationship between policy makers and practitioners limits the potential for policymaking mechanisms to have significant impact on classrooms, except for those identified as in crisis which are subject to high levels of intervention and monitoring. For the majority of schools in many systems, by the time government policy gets into classrooms it has been so extensively diluted or deconstructed that it barely resembles its initial formulation. Put simply, we do not have appropriate mechanisms or, perhaps more importantly, relationships that enable transfer of central government policy into schools and classrooms.

Third, obtaining a consensus about the nature of policy design and content is problematic. For example, to what extent is the application of policy prescribed and regulated and to what extent do schools have flexibility to adapt a policy to suit context? How does this sit with the concept of earned autonomy, which underpins many systems? It may be precisely those schools without earned autonomy that most need the flexibility to do something radical to bring about change. Developing context-specific policies seems problematic without a close relationship between schools and those involved with policy development. Furthermore, how can context-specific policies be developed if policy makers have little understanding of context? Some systems would claim that this relationship does exist, either directly between school leaders and policy makers or indirectly through a mediating critical friend in the middle tier, linking schools to policy. A key issue here is whether these relationships facilitate honest communication whereby the realities of contexts are communicated and understood. Similarly, all too often a limited number of high profile school leaders feeds the process, again providing limited and potentially biased insights. If we are to tap into the wealth of knowledge and expertise that exists within the system we need trusting relationships whereby narratives can be developed without fear of reprisal or compromise.

Fourth and related to the previous issues, our preoccupation with scaling up to achieve systemic change appears misguided. Policy makers are constantly looking for solutions that can go to scale. The tension here is clear. How does one move to scale while attending to individual context? Such models tend to be prohibitively expensive because of the need for people to be immersed in specific contexts. They rely heavily on leadership capacity at the local level, generating mixed results, based on the extent to which leadership capacity can connect people to bring about change (Chapman, 2006).

The four issues outlined above all highlight the importance of relationships in the improvement process. Relationships between policy makers, researchers and practitioners need to be reconfigured in order to achieve systemic improvements. The final section of this chapter sets out an argument for redefining these relationships and offers practical examples of how this might be done.

Redefining relationships: a case of back to the future?

As the field has evolved and the school improvement knowledge base developed there has been a tendency to assume that the best way to improve schools and children's educational experiences is to operate at system level. This discourse has been further reinforced by the globalisation of school improvement, led by consultants and private companies generating influential reports comparing more and less successful systems and offering technical–rational solutions with little regard for stark differences in contexts, cultures or values.

What if the greatest leverage is not at system level? Despite the investment of significant resources, the limited and patchy impact of school improvement efforts and the nature of relationships between politicians, policy makers and those in the field indicate misplaced optimism. Here is an interesting parallel with schools. I once heard a primary school teacher justify a push for promotion on the grounds of wanting to influence the lives of more children – to make a bigger difference. The argument was that, each year, a teacher could only have an impact on the lives of the 25 children in one class but a headteacher would have an impact on all 200 or so children in a school. In terms of impact, we know from school effectiveness research that what happens at classroom level is around four times more important than what happens at whole school level. Perhaps we need to consider the nature of the impact we can make and the relationships that are needed to achieve it. Ultimately, it is what happens in classrooms that makes the real difference – have school improvement researchers and activists lost sight of this?

Perhaps school improvers should think about refocusing attention by redefining relationships with practice. Conversations within the school improvement community – at conferences such as ICSEI – and experiences in the field over the past decade indicate that SI research has become much more policy orientated and is in danger of losing its core constituency, namely teachers and school leaders.

For those of us located in universities the current economic and social climate provides an opportunity to move 'back to the future'. The time is right to reconnect with schools and teachers, rediscovering our voice and passion as activists researching and working on the front line and directly making a difference to teachers' values, beliefs and behaviours – ultimately to the educational experiences and outcomes of young people.

Reconnecting school improvement research and practice

In an attempt to reconnect school improvement research and practice, a group of researchers at the University of Manchester has refocused to work directly with schools. This is not to say that they disregard their policy interests or commitments or ditch their national and international projects. They have reaffirmed their commitment to build on the body of school improvement work developed over recent decades by returning to the core business – spending more time working with schools and teachers.

This shift in emphasis is driven by two factors. First, as I have already argued, recent relationships between researchers and policy makers have not delivered the results we hoped for. Therefore, it would seem sensible to reconnect and redefine relationships with schools in an attempt to maximise impact where we know a difference can be made. Second, in England, changes in the national context mean there is space within the system to attempt such a repositioning. As the traditional system is being dismantled, universities and schools have to reflect on a number of important changes including: how initial teacher training will be organised in the future; changing measures of impact; the demise of local authorities, the entrenchment of the private sector within education and reduced funding arrangements.

Given the nature of these challenges and mutual interests it seems sensible to build coalitions between schools and universities, tackling them in partnership. For our team of school improvement researchers this has meant engaging in a range of activities, including:

- developing a coalition of schools committed to using research to drive improvement efforts;
- working with individual schools to support the development of teaching and learning;
- developing 'embedded' doctoral researchers in schools.

We do not claim that these approaches are unique or even 'leading edge'. Rather, given our combined interests, experience and context we view this as an appropriate direction of travel for our team.

1 Working with a group of schools: the Coalition of Research Schools

The Coalition of Research Schools is a joint project for the university team and a group of eight schools in Greater Manchester. Seven of the schools have been recognised as 'outstanding' in their most recent Ofsted inspections. The group includes primary, secondary and special schools, faith schools and an academy.

They are interested in gaining 'Teaching School' status and will identify and co-ordinate expertise in partner schools, using the best leaders and teachers to:

- work with other strategic partners, including universities, to train new entrants to the profession;
- lead peer-to-peer learning;
- spot and nurture leadership potential;
- provide support for other schools when needed.

(NCSL, 2011)

This diverse and excellent group is bonded together by a strong commitment to research and inquiry. One of the head teachers has just completed a Master's in Educational Leadership and Improvement and plans to enrol on a PhD. An Assistant Head at another school is part way through an Ed.D programme and staff in all schools are enrolled on MA and CPD programmes. In addition to the individual commitment of staff, a culture of learning is pervasive. School leaders understand that while they have very successful schools, they still fail some students. Staff commitment to research and inquiry is driven by the desire to gain a deeper understanding of context and develop context specific solutions to the challenges they face in improving outcomes.

In addition to improving their own schools they are keen to develop approaches that can be used to promote learning in others. One secondary head commented:

> It is not enough to make your own school better if you have the capacity to make the system better.

The coalition is in its early stages of development but the signs are encouraging. Relationships between university staff and schools are strong; motivation to work in an inquiry-based mode is high; there is interest in using the SE/SI knowledge base to develop evidence-based approaches rather than reinventing the wheel in isolation and, perhaps most importantly, the coalition is committed to developing new approaches to tackle the underachievement of specific groups of children and to developing models and ways of working that can support improvements across institutional boundaries.

The exact nature of schools' partnership with the university varies. However, the generic model involves a university team of two professors (one as designated lead) and a senior researcher, supported by a doctoral student with teaching experience ranging from classroom teacher to Assistant Head Teacher, working with a group of staff from the school. Usually, this group of school staff numbers between five and seven and includes the head teacher, but it can be as large as 15.

Initial visits focus on the university team getting a feel for the school through discussions with staff and students, sweeps, walk-throughs and tours with students. Impressions from initial contact are used to produce a school portrait and highlight emerging issues, tensions and dilemmas. These are presented to the staff group to stimulate discussion that identifies an area of focus for research and research questions. A series of workshops provides the staff group with the necessary expertise to operationalise their research. University staff provide bespoke support to guide and facilitate the research process. When appropriate, schools are brought together for joint seminars and activities. However, school-to-school networking across the coalition is not a priority. These schools are already very well networked and belong to many 'clubs'. The coalition's two priorities are to support each school to develop its own capacity for research and develop a model that each school can use to support improvement in other schools across its various networks.

2 Working with an individual school: a case of lesson study

Members of the university team have worked with the English department of an academy in the north-west of England to develop a lesson study approach to CPD. This has supported the development of shared expectations and language about teaching and learning. The initiative commenced with a workshop led by university staff to negotiate a protocol for setting up lesson study groups. Then, over four weeks, the departmental team adopted the following process:

1 Staff formed trios comprised of colleagues with varied levels of experience. Trios worked together to trial and evaluate lesson study as a means of strengthening learning and teaching.

2 Each trio chose and planned a lesson that they taught. Their aim was to put together the best available expertise on how to engage participation of all members of the class – this included an emphasis on reading for learning techniques and, where relevant, the use of technology.

3 As each of the trio taught the lesson, their colleagues observed, focusing specifically on students' responses. The lesson was videoed and a group of students was interviewed to determine their reactions and the extent of their learning.

4 After each lesson the trio reflected on what had happened, using their notes, the views of students and the video to analyse processes and outcomes. They adjusted the lesson plan before it was taught by the next member of the trio.

5 Once the lesson had been taught by each, a short report was prepared, summarising findings and making recommendations for future practice.

At the end of the lesson study period each trio presented their findings and conclusions at a departmental meeting. The school followed this with a seminar to consider wider implications for policy and practice across departments. Lesson study has been adopted across several departments and further cycles have involved the wider group revising and testing lessons. Analysis of the evidence leads the group to consider ways of continuing to improve lessons and further involving students in the process.

The framework for lesson study has been a powerful method for challenging assumptions and developing new and innovative approaches to teaching that promote higher levels of student engagement and achievement. This approach was expanded across the whole school and has become an integral part of its CPD programme. Most recently the approach has been developed further and is now used across the whole chain of academies.

3 Using Embedded Researchers to reconnect school improvement research and practice

During the past three to four years a team of researchers at the University of Manchester has developed the concept of 'Embedded Researchers'. The nature of the relationship between the researcher and host institution varies according to context. However, arrangements are underpinned by a set of core principles:

- The host organisation provides unlimited access for research purposes.
- Researchers focus on a programme of work of mutual benefit to them and to the host organisation and university.
- The researcher generates outputs of relevance to the host organisation.
- The researcher successfully completes a PhD.
- There is joint agreement concerning operational and strategic arrangements.
- The host organisation provides some form of sponsorship for the student.
- The university link provides supervision for the student and critical friendship to the organisation.

Embedded researchers from the university's School of Education have been located in individual schools, chains of schools and local authorities. Their work is varied and covers a diverse range of topics that compliments the SI research interests of their supervisors.

Undertaking an embedded research project provides researchers with a range of opportunities and experiences beyond what is normally available to PhD students on 'traditional' programmes of study. First, they have unparalleled access to a research setting. This allows the possibility of developing an in-depth ethnographic study. Researchers are commonly regarded as part of the organisation and quickly treated as just another member of staff. Second, the relationship between the host organisation, researcher and supervisor is often very complex. This provides opportunities for the researcher to see senior academics at work in ways a 'traditional' PhD student does not, for example, in the steering group and board meetings of a school trust. That does not mean that the nature of Embedded Researchers is unproblematic. The relationships themselves often create issues, tensions and dilemmas that would not exist on a more traditional route. There are also a number of research issues relating to the role and purpose of an Embedded Researcher. Who owns the data? How does one deal with the insider/outsider dilemma? How can you maintain rigour and independence when one is (at least) partly funded by the research subject? These are all serious questions that professional researchers have to grapple with and it does no harm for PhD students to consider the realities of real world research.

The relationship between host and supervisor is critical. While the researcher's work is important, the host and supervisor are key to reconnecting school improvement research and practice. Critical friendship between the university and host can lead to other unintended mutual benefits. For example, the site gains access to the knowledge base and, if it wants to, can become a hub for research activity. Joint D & R projects can be developed and mutual benefit gained through access to each other's networks. The possibilities are endless. The development of Embedded Researchers can play a key role in reconnecting SI research to practice.

Three examples and a common framework for linking research and practice

A common framework of inquiry underpins the approach to working with schools on the types of projects outlined above. This framework draws on research evidence and on our experiences of working with schools and school-based networks to promote effective learning for all. Both the research base and our own experience lead us to conclude that:

- *Schools know more than they use.* A major thrust for developing improved learning experiences for all pupils can be created through making better use of existing expertise and creativity – within and across schools.
- *The professional expertise of teachers and educational leaders is largely unarticulated.* Therefore, in order to access the reservoir of unused expertise, it is necessary to create a common language of practice that facilitates mutual reflection and the sharing of ideas.
- *Evidence is the engine for change.* Specifically, it can help to create space for re-appraisal and re-thinking by interrupting existing discourses and focusing attention on previously overlooked possibilities for moving practice forward.
- *Collaborative learning is a socially complex activity.* Successful collaborative learning requires new thinking and new relationships at system level that foster active connections amongst stakeholders.
- *'Leadership for Learning' must foster inter-dependence.* Specifically, there is a need for forms of leadership that encourage the trust, mutual understandings and shared values and behaviours that bind individuals together and make cooperative action possible.

Together, these conclusions lead us to suggest a *Framework for Collaborative Learning* (see Figure 2.1). This is designed to provide a structure for adult learning within an organisation. For example, a group of staff may identify an issue or come together around a common concern (such as under-achievement in white working-class students). The framework provides a structure for systematic inquiry into the issue. Each of its four, interlinked elements has its own questions to address; these provide 'interruptions' which can facilitate reflection on

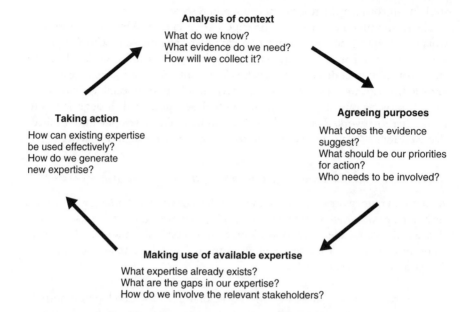

Analysis of context

What do we know?
What evidence do we need?
How will we collect it?

Taking action

How can existing expertise
be used effectively?
How do we generate
new expertise?

Agreeing purposes

What does the evidence
suggest?
What should be our priorities
for action?
Who needs to be involved?

Making use of available expertise

What expertise already exists?
What are the gaps in our expertise?
How do we involve the relevant stakeholders?

Figure 2.1 A framework for collaborative learning (adapted from Chapman, 2008)

taken-for-granted methods and analyses and encourage collaborative learning, while fostering the development of relationships and opportunities for learning as a social activity. We use the questions to provide a series of prompts at the various stages of the collaborative learning cycle highlighted in the framework. While this framework has been designed with adult learning in mind, it can also be used with school age pupils.

Experiences of working with schools through this framework suggest that as teachers engage in the analytical process and begin to scrutinise existing methods, the sorts of practices outlined in the first part of this chapter are commonly developed as practical, local strategies. Thus, scrutiny of and reflection on practice often lead to solutions, which are supported by research findings.

Conclusion

This chapter set out to offer a commentary on the development of school improvement research and practice and reflect on its progress to date. It highlights the significant contribution the field has made in a relatively short time and raises issues about the nature of the field's relationship with politicians and policy makers. This leads us to question at what level the field should focus its attention. The practical examples highlighted above chart one team's attempts to redefine relationships and reconnect school improvement research and practice.

Working with politicians and policy makers to influence systemic change and working with schools and teachers are not mutually exclusive activities. It has long been recognised that a complex mix of top-down and bottom-up activity, tailored to specific contexts, is required to optimise improvement efforts. I have highlighted here the importance of developing a layered approach to these efforts.

There are also questions about the current blend of activities. It seems that the balance has become distorted. Our attention has come to be focused on influencing politicians and policy makers. With a few notable exceptions, we tend to neglect what was a major strength of the field – working directly with schools and teachers. Historically, school improvement activists had a strong influence on teachers' values, beliefs and ultimately behaviours – this was *the* key lever for improvement.

This would be fine if our new endeavours had brought significant rewards, revitalised systems and built capacity for improvement. But where are the significant returns for the considerable energy we have expended? National policies appear to be watered down as they travel through systems. In England, the National Strategies have been scrapped and, except for those in severe difficulty, schools seem to carry on regardless. Policy just does not penetrate where it counts most – in the classroom.

Perhaps, the current volatile environment with its acute economic and social concerns, is the time to reflect on progress and consider how best to target future efforts and engage the system. Put simply, we need a recalibration of relationships, maintaining relationships with politicians and policy makers and re-engaging schools and school networks. We need to work in partnership to undertake high quality improvement research linked to support for sustainable improvement practice. This is where we will get the greatest return for our effort.

3 Advances in school effectiveness theory

Leonidas Kyriakides

Introduction

School Effectiveness Research (SER) has expanded rapidly during the last three decades. Methodological advances have enabled more efficient estimates of teacher and school differences in student achievement to be obtained (Goldstein, 2003). In regard to the theoretical component of the field, progress was made by a more precise definition of the concepts used and the relations between the concepts (e.g. Levine and Lezotte, 1990; Scheerens and Bosker, 1997). However, there is a shortage of rational models from which researchers can build theory. The problem is aggravated by infrequent use of whatever models exist (Kyriakides, 2005). As a consequence, most of school effectiveness studies are concerned with the establishment of statistical relationships between variables rather than with the generation and testing of theories that could explain those relationships.

There are several reasons to argue that there is a need to develop and test models of school effectiveness. First, a model serves to explain previous empirical research parsimoniously. Second, the establishment and testing of models help us generate a guide to the field to prevent the new entrants from re-inventing the wheel by conducting already existing research. It also maps a series of avenues for future research. Finally, a model may provide a useful road map for practitioners, and indeed there are hints that it has been partially an absence of school effectiveness theory that has hindered the take up of effectiveness knowledge by practitioners in schools (Creemers and Kyriakides, 2006).

In this chapter, a critical analysis of current approaches to modelling school effectiveness is provided and the importance of considering the dynamic nature of educational effectiveness is stressed. It is argued that the dynamic model of educational effectiveness (Creemers and Kyriakides, 2008), which has recently been developed in order to address the weaknesses of the integrated models, could contribute in establishing a theory-driven and evidence-based approach to school improvement. Thus, the essential characteristics of the dynamic model are presented and the main findings of studies testing the validity of the model are outlined. Finally, suggestions for research on modelling school effectiveness are drawn.

A critical analysis of the models of SER

In the literature of school effectiveness modelling, three basic approaches have been used. First, the economic approach is focused on estimating the relationship between the 'supply of selected purchased schooling inputs and educational outcomes controlling for the influence of various background features' (Monk, 1992: 308). Resource input variables such as student/teacher ratio, teacher salary and overall measures of per student expenditure were of primary interest in the earlier studies. The emerging 'education production' models (e.g. Brown and Saks, 1986; Coates, 2003; Elberts and Stone, 1988) are based on the assumption that increased inputs will lead to increments in outcomes and their main characteristics are concerned with: a) the selection of resource inputs as the major type of selection of antecedent condition; b) the measurement of direct effects; and c) the use of data at only one level of aggregation (i.e. either at micro (e.g. student) level or aggregated (e.g. school) level). However, the research done using these models revealed that the relation between input and outcomes is more complex than was assumed. For example, studies from Hanushek and Hedges (e.g. Hanushek, 1986, 1989; Hedges *et al.*, 1994) show that reducing student/teacher ratio and/or increasing the amount of funding education per student does not necessarily result in higher student outcomes.

The second approach to effectiveness modelling is similar to the economic approach but is focused on a different choice of antecedent conditions since it is mainly focused on variables at student level, which are assumed to predict student outcomes. Some attention is also paid on processes from two different perspectives concerning learning and school as organisations. Within this approach, educational psychologists focused on student background factors such as 'learning aptitudes', 'personality' and 'motivation', and on variables measuring the learning processes which take place in classrooms. Carroll's model (Carroll, 1963) is considered as the starting point of this approach to modelling effectiveness. It consists of five classes of variables that are expected to explain variation in student achievement: aptitude; opportunity to learn; perseverance; quality of instruction; and ability to understand instruction. All classes of variables (factors) are related to the time required to achieve a particular learning task. In a more recent attempt to formulate an encompassing model of educational productivity, Walberg (1984) made use of the basic factors of Carroll's model and added a new category of variables concerned with the learning environment. Numerous research studies and meta-analyses have confirmed the validity of Carroll's model (e.g. Doyle, 1986; Scheerens and Bosker, 1997; Stallings, 1985), but as Carroll (1989) pointed out, 25 years after the construction of his model, the one factor in his model that needed further elaboration was 'quality of instruction'.

On the other hand, the sociological perspective is focused on factors that define the educational background of students such as SES, gender, social-capital and peer group. This perspective does not only examine student outcomes but also the extent to which schools manage to reduce the variance in student outcomes compared to prior achievement. Through their emphasis on the importance of reducing the variance in student outcomes compared to their prior achievement educational gap, two dimensions of measuring educational effectiveness concerning both quality and equity emerged. In this respect, studies on the effects of contextual factors (Opdenakker and Van Damme, 2006) and on the extent to which teachers and schools are equally effective with different groups of students (i.e. differential school effectiveness) have been conducted (e.g. Campbell *et al.*, 2004; Strand, 2010). Moreover, the sociological perspective raises attention for process variables that emerged from organisational theories, which were treated as school-level factors associated with student achievement.

Organisational theories often adhere to the thesis that the effectiveness of organisations cannot be described in a straightforward manner. Instead, a pluralistic attitude is taken with respect to the interpretation of the concept in question. Thus, organisational approaches to effectiveness indicated a range of models, each emphasising a different type of criteria to judge effectiveness. The major categories are as follows: productivity; adaptability; involvement; continuity; and responsiveness to external stakeholders (Scheerens *et al.*, 2003). However, most empirical school effectiveness studies are concerned with the productivity criterion. Scheerens (1992) argues that this position can be legitimised from the point of view of a means to an end ordering of the criteria, with productivity taken as the ultimate criterion. Other authors see the criteria as 'competing values' (Fairman and Quinn, 1985) or claim that the predominance of any single criterion should depend on the organisation's stage of development (Cheng, 1993).

Since school effectiveness is a causal concept, not only the type of effects but also the dimension of the causes or means should be considered. In doing so, the question that is dealt with, from this perspective of SER, concerns the distinction of all the possible features of the functioning of schools that are malleable in order to reach the effects that are aimed for. Thus, the following six categories are used as a core framework to further distinguish elements and aspects of school functioning: goals; structure of authority positions or subunits; structure of procedures; culture; organisation's environment; and organisation's primary process. Each of these main categories was treated by researchers in the field as an area that can be influenced by the school or external change agents. However, the structure of procedures (particularly school management) and the culture have received the most emphasis in the practice of empirical effectiveness research, but the empirical basis for the importance of these factors still needs to be strengthened (Freiberg, 1999; Maslowski, 2003).

Finally, the models of the third approach emerged by researchers attempt to integrate the findings of school effectiveness research, teacher effectiveness research and the early input-output studies. Thus, the models of this approach (e.g. Creemers, 1994; Scheerens, 1992; Stringfield and Slavin, 1992) have a multilevel structure, where schools are nested in contexts, classrooms are nested in schools, and students are nested in classrooms or teachers. Although these models make use of both organisational theories and theories of learning and refer to multiple factors at different levels, each of them is either focused on the classroom or the school level. Depending on this, more emphasis is given either to theories of learning (e.g. Creemers, 1994) or to organisational theories (e.g. Scheerens, 1992).

A first example of this approach is Scheerens' integrated model of school effectiveness (Scheerens, 1990). The model is based upon a review of the instructional and school effectiveness research literature. The general assumption is that higher-level conditions somehow facilitate lower-level conditions. A second example is the QAIT/MACRO model (Stringfield and Slavin, 1992). QAIT stands for: Quality, Appropriateness, Incentive, and Time of instruction. MACRO is the acronym for: Meaningful goals, Attention to academic focus, Coordination, Recruitment and training, and Organisation. This model has four levels: a) individual student and learner; b) (para-) professionals who are in direct interaction with students; c) schools, with head teachers, other school level personnel, and programs; and d) the 'above schools' level, comprising the community, the school district, state and federal sources of programming, funding and assessment.

The third example is the comprehensive model of educational effectiveness (Creemers, 1994), which is considered as one of the most influential models in the field (Teddlie and Reynolds, 2000). Creemers (1994) developed Carroll's model of learning by adding to the general concept of opportunity, the more specific opportunity to learn. In Creemers' model, time and opportunity are discerned both at the classroom level and at the school level. In this way, Creemers made a distinction between available, and actually used, time and opportunity. Creemers' model was also based on four assumptions. First, time-on-task and opportunity used at the student level are directly related to student achievement. Second, quality of teaching, the curriculum, and the grouping procedures influence the time on task and opportunity to learn. For example, some teachers spend more time actually teaching than others who spend more time on classroom management and keeping order. Teachers are, therefore, the central component in instruction at the classroom level. Third, teaching quality, time, and opportunity at the classroom level are influenced by factors at the school level that may or may not promote these classroom factors. It is, finally, acknowledged that although teachers are able to influence time for learning and opportunity to learn in their classrooms through the quality of their instruction, it is students who decide how much time they will spend on their school tasks and how many tasks they will complete. Thus, achievement is also determined by student factors such as aptitude, social background and motivation.

Creemers (1994) claims that there are four principles operating in generating educational effectiveness. First, the variables at the different levels should support each other in order to improve students' achievement. This is called the *consistency* principle. It is argued that there should be consistency of effective characteristics within and between levels. A second formal criterion is *cohesion*, which implies that all members of the school team must show characteristics of effective teaching. Moreover, Creemers (1994) argues that there should be *constancy*, meaning that effective instruction is provided throughout the school career of the student. Finally, the model states that there should be *control*, meaning that goal attainment and the school climate should be evaluated. Consistency, cohesion, constancy and control are formal principles, which are difficult to observe directly, but we can argue that they exist when the same factors operate across instructional components, subjects, classes and grades.

Six studies examined the validity of Creemers' model (de Jong *et al.*, 2004; Driessen and Sleegers, 2000; Kyriakides, 2005; Kyriakides *et al.*, 2000; Kyriakides and Tsangaridou, 2008; Reezigt *et al.*, 1999) and provided some empirical support. These studies revealed that the influences on student achievement are multilevel. This finding is in line with the findings of most studies on school effectiveness conducted in various countries (Teddlie and Reynolds, 2000) and provides support to the argument that the theoretical models of SER should be multilevel in nature. However, these studies also revealed that next to the multilevel nature of effectiveness the relationship between factors at different levels might be more complex than assumed in the integrated models (Kyriakides, 2008). This is especially true for interaction effects among factors operating at classroom and student level, which reveal the importance of investigating differential effectiveness (Campbell *et al.*, 2004). A synthesis of these studies has also revealed suggestions for further development of the model, especially by taking into account the dynamic nature of educational effectiveness (Kyriakides, 2008). Studies testing the validity of the comprehensive model and studies investigating the stability of school effects (e.g. Gray *et al.*, 1996; Gray *et al.*, 2001; Thomas, 2001; Thomas *et al.*, 2007) revealed concerns about the attempt of integrated models to study school effectiveness as a rather stable phenomenon. Teaching and learning are dynamic processes that are constantly adapting to changing needs and opportunities. Effective schooling should, therefore, be treated as a dynamic, ongoing process. This idea is also consistent with the contingency theory (Donaldson, 2001; Mintzberg, 1979). In this context, Creemers and Kyriakides (2008) have developed a dynamic model of educational effectiveness, which attempts to define the dynamic relations between the multiple factors found to be associated with student achievement.

The dynamic model of educational effectiveness: an overview

The dynamic model is based on the following three main assumptions. First, the fact that most of the effectiveness studies are exclusively focused on language or mathematics rather than on the whole school curriculum aims (cognitive, metacognitive and affective) reveals that the models of SER should take into account the new goals of education and, related to this, their implications for teaching and learning. This means that the outcome measures should be defined in a more broad way rather than restricting to the achievement of basic skills. It also implies that new theories of teaching and learning are used in order to specify variables associated with the quality of teaching. Second, an important constraint of the existing approaches of modelling school effectiveness is the fact that the whole process does not contribute significantly to the improvement of school effectiveness. Thus, the dynamic model is established in a way that helps policy makers and practitioners to improve educational practice by taking rational decisions concerning the optimal fit of the factors within the model and the present situation in the schools or educational systems (Creemers and Kyriakides, 2006). Finally, the dynamic model should not only be parsimonious but should also be able to describe the complex nature of educational effectiveness. This implies that the model could be based on specific theory but at the same time some of the factors included in the major constructs of the model are expected to be interrelated within and/or between levels.

The main characteristics of the dynamic model are as follows. First, the dynamic model takes into account the fact that effectiveness studies conducted in several countries reveal that the influences on student achievement are multilevel (Teddlie and Reynolds, 2000). Therefore, the model is multilevel in nature and refers to factors operating at the four levels shown in Figure 3.1. The teaching and

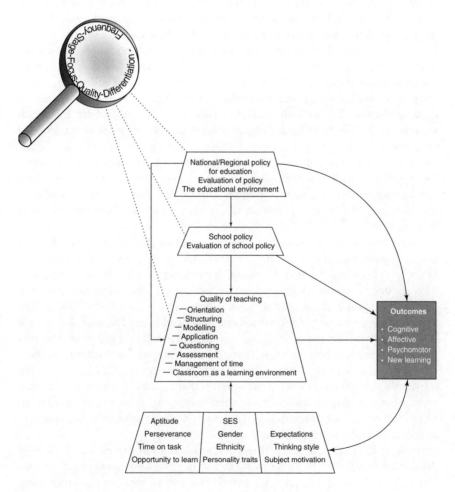

Figure 3.1 The dynamic model of educational effectiveness

learning situation is emphasised and the roles of the two main actors (i.e. teacher and student) are analysed. Above these two levels, the dynamic model refers to school-level factors, which are expected to influence the teaching–learning situation by developing and evaluating the school policy on teaching and the policy on creating the School Learning Environment (SLE). The system level refers to the influence of the educational system through a more formal way, especially through developing and evaluating the educational policy at the national/regional level. The teaching and learning situation is also influenced by the wider educational context in which students, teachers, and schools operate. Factors such as the values of the society for learning and the importance attached to education play an important role both in shaping teacher and student expectations as well as in the development of the perceptions of various stakeholders about effective teaching practice.

Second, the model supports that factors at the school and system level have both direct and indirect effects on student achievement since they are able to influence not only student achievement but also the teaching and learning situations.

Third, the dynamic model assumes that the impact of the school- and system-level factors has to be defined and measured in a different way than the impact of classroom-level factors. Policy on teaching and actions taken to improve teaching practice must be measured over time and in relation to the weaknesses that occur in a school. The assumption is that schools and educational systems, which are able to identify their weaknesses and develop a policy on aspects associated with teaching and their SLE, are also able to improve the functioning of classroom-level factors and their effectiveness status. Only changes in those factors for which schools face significant problems are expected to be associated with the improvement of school effectiveness. This implies that the impact of school- and system-level factors depends on the current situation of the objects under investigation.

Fourth, the model assumes that there is a need to carefully examine the relationships between the various effectiveness factors that operate at the same level. Walberg's (1984) model, which is one of the most significant educational productivity models, attempts to illustrate such relationships. Aptitude, instruction and the psychological environment are seen as major direct causes of learning. They also influence one another and are in turn influenced by feedback on the amount of learning that takes place. Walberg's model was tested as a structural equation model on science achievement, indicating more complex, indirect relationships (Reynolds and Walberg, 1990). This implies that there is a need to refer to the relationships between the effectiveness factors that operate at the same level. Such approach to modelling school effectiveness may reveal grouping of factors that make teachers and schools effective. Therefore, strategies for improving effectiveness that are comprehensive in nature may emerge.

Finally, the dynamic model is based on the assumption that each factor can be defined and measured by using five dimensions: *frequency, focus, stage, quality,* and *differentiation*. Frequency is a quantitative way to measure the functioning of each effectiveness factor whereas the other four dimensions examine qualitative characteristics of the functioning of each factor at the system/school/classroom level. A brief description of the four dimensions concerned with the qualitative characteristics of effectiveness factors is given below.

Two aspects of the *focus* dimension are taken into account. The first one refers to the specificity of the activities associated with the functioning of the factor whereas the second one refers to the number of purposes for which an activity takes place. The measurement of the focus of an activity, either in terms of its specificity or in terms of the number of purposes that it is expected to achieve, may be related in a non-linear way with student achievement. For example, guidelines on parental involvement which are very general may not be helpful at all in establishing good relations between parents and teachers, which, when good, can result in supporting student learning. On the other hand, a school policy which is very specific in defining activities may restrict teachers and parents from being productively involved and creating their own ways for implementing the school policy.

The *stage* at which tasks associated with a factor take place is also examined. It is expected that the factors need to take place over a long period of time to ensure that they have a continuous direct or indirect effect on student learning. The *quality* refers to the properties of the specific factor itself, as these are discussed in the literature. Finally, *differentiation* refers to the extent to which activities associated with a factor are implemented in the same way for all the subjects involved with it (e.g. all the students, teachers, schools). It is expected that adaptation to specific needs of each subject or group of subjects will increase the successful implementation of a factor and will ultimately maximise its effect on student learning outcomes. The use of different measurement dimensions reveals that looking at just the frequency dimension of an effectiveness factor does not help us identify those aspects of the functioning of a factor that are associated to student achievement. Considering effectiveness factors as multidimensional constructs not only provides a better picture of what makes teachers and schools effective but may also help us develop specific strategies for improving educational practice.

Based on the main findings of teacher effectiveness research (e.g. Brophy and Good, 1986; Muijs and Reynolds, 2001; Rosenshine and Stevens, 1986), the dynamic model refers to factors that describe teachers' instructional role and are associated with student outcomes. These factors refer to observable instructional behaviour of teachers in the classroom rather than on factors that may explain such behaviour (e.g. teacher beliefs and knowledge and interpersonal competences). The eight factors included in the model are as follows: *orientation, structuring, questioning, teaching-modelling, application, management of time, teacher role in making classroom a learning environment,* and *classroom assessment.* These eight factors do not refer only to one approach of teaching such as structured or direct teaching (Joyce *et al.*, 2000) or to approaches associated with constructivism (Schoenfeld, 1998). The eight teacher factors are presented in Table 3.1. It is shown that an integrated approach in defining quality of teaching is adopted. Specifically, the dynamic model does not refer only to skills associated with direct teaching and mastery learning such as structuring and questioning but also to orientation and teaching modelling, which are in line with theories of teaching

Table 3.1 The main elements of each teacher factor included in the dynamic model

Factors	Main elements
1 Orientation	a) Providing the objectives for which a specific task/lesson/series of lessons take(s) place; and b) challenging students to identify the reason for which an activity takes place in the lesson.
2 Structuring	a) Beginning with overviews and/or review of objectives; b) outlining the content to be covered and signalling transitions between lesson parts; and c) calling attention and reviewing main ideas.
3 Questioning	a) Raising different types of questions (i.e., process and product) at appropriate difficulty level; b) giving time to students to respond; and c) dealing with student responses.
4 Teaching modelling	a) Encouraging students to use problem-solving strategies presented by the teacher or other classmates; b) inviting students to develop strategies; and c) promoting the idea of modelling.
5 Application	a) Using seatwork or small group tasks in order to provide needed practice and application opportunities; and b) using application tasks as starting points for the next step of teaching and learning.
6 The classroom as a learning environment	a) Establishing on task behaviour through the interactions they promote (i.e. teacher-student and student-student interactions); and b) dealing with classroom disorder and student competition through establishing rules, persuading students to respect them and using the rules.
7 Management of time	a) Organising the classroom environment; and b) maximising engagement rates.
8 Assessment	a) Using appropriate techniques to collect data on student knowledge and skills; b) analysing data in order to identify student needs and report the results to students and parents; and c) evaluating their own practices.

associated with constructivism. Moreover, the collaboration technique is included under the overarching factor contribution of the teacher to the establishment of the classroom learning environment.

In regard to the school factors, the dynamic model gives emphasis to the following two main aspects of the school policy which affect learning at both the level of students and teachers: a) school policy for teaching; and b) school policy for creating a learning environment at school. Guidelines are seen as one of the main indications of school policy and this is reflected in the way each school level factor is defined. However, in using the term 'guidelines' we refer to a range of documents, such as staff meeting minutes, announcements, and action plans, which make the policy of the school more concrete to the teachers and other stakeholders. These two factors do not imply that each school should simply develop formal documents to install its policy. The factors concerned with the school policy mainly refer to the actions taken by the school to help teachers and other stakeholders have a clear understanding of what is expected from them. Support offered to teachers and other stakeholders to implement the school policy is also an aspect of these two school factors.

Based on the assumption that the essence of a successful organisation in the modern world is the search for improvement, the dynamic model is also concerned with the processes and the activities that take place in the school in order to improve the teaching practice and its learning environment. For this reason, the processes that are used to evaluate the school policy for teaching and the SLE are investigated. Thus, the following four overarching factors at the school level are included in the model:

1 school policy for teaching and actions taken for improving teaching practice;
2 evaluation of school policy for teaching and of actions taken to improve teaching;
3 policy for creating a SLE and actions taken for improving the SLE; and
4 evaluation of the SLE.

In regard to the school factor concerned with teaching, the dynamic model is concerned with aspects of school policy for teaching associated with: a) quantity of teaching; b) provision of sufficient learning opportunities; and c) quality of teaching. Actions taken for improving the above three aspects of teaching practice, such as the provision of support to teachers for improving their teaching skills, are also taken into account. Specifically, the following aspects of school policy on quantity of teaching are taken into account: a) school policy on the management of teaching time (e.g. lessons start on time and finish on time; there are no interruptions of lessons for staff meetings and/or for preparation of school festivals and other events); b) policy on student and teacher absenteeism; c) policy on homework; and d) policy on lesson schedule and timetable. School policy on provision of learning opportunities is measured by looking at the extent to which the school has a mission concerning the provision of learning opportunities and this mission is reflected in its policy on curriculum. We also examine school policy on long-term and short-term planning and school policy on providing support to students with special needs. Furthermore, the extent to which the school attempts to make an effective use of school trips and other extra-curricular activities for teaching/learning purposes is investigated. Finally, school policy on the quality of teaching is seen as closely related to the classroom-level factors of the dynamic model, which refer to the instructional role of teachers. Therefore, the way school policy for teaching is examined reveals that effective schools are expected to make decisions on maximising the use of teaching time and the learning opportunities offered to their students. In addition, effective schools support their teachers in their attempt to help students learn by using effective teaching practices.

In regard to the factor concerned with the school learning environment, the dynamic model investigates school policy on the following five aspects which define the environment of the school:

1   student behaviour outside the classroom;
2   collaboration and interaction between teachers;
3   partnership policy (i.e. the relations of school with the community, the parents, and the advisors);
4   provision of sufficient learning resources to students and teachers; and
5   values in favour of learning.

The first three aspects refer to the rules that the school has developed for establishing a learning environment inside and outside the classrooms. Here, the term 'learning' does not refer exclusively to the student learning. For example, collaboration and interaction between teachers may contribute in their professional development (i.e. learning of teachers) but may also have an effect on teaching practice and thereby this factor is able to improve student learning. The fourth aspect refers to the policy on providing resources for learning. The availability of learning resources in schools may not have only an effect on student learning but may also encourage the learning of teachers. The last aspect of this overarching factor is concerned with the strategies that the school has developed in order to encourage teachers and students to develop positive attitudes towards learning.

Testing the validity of the dynamic model

Some supportive material for the validity of the dynamic model has been provided. Specifically, a longitudinal study measuring teacher and school effectiveness in three different subjects (i.e. mathematics, language and religious education) was conducted in order to test the main assumptions of the model. Using Structural Equation Modelling (SEM) techniques, it was possible to demonstrate that classroom and school factors can be defined by reference to the five dimensions of the dynamic model (see Kyriakides and Creemers, 2008; Creemers and Kyriakides, 2010a). The added value of using these five dimensions of the classroom- and school-level factors to explain variation on student achievement in both cognitive and affective outcomes of schooling was also demonstrated. Finally, it was possible to generate evidence supporting the assumption that the impact of school factors depends on the current situation of the school and on the type of problems/difficulties that the school is facing. Specifically, school factors were found to have situational effects. The development of a school policy for teaching and the evaluation of school policy for teaching were found to have stronger effects in schools where the quality of teaching at classroom level was low (Creemers and Kyriakides, 2009).

Second, a study investigating the impact of teacher factors on achievement of Cypriot students at the end of pre-primary school was conducted (Kyriakides and Creemers, 2009). By comparing the results of this study with the findings of the first study testing the validity of the model, it was shown that almost all teacher factors were associated with achievement in language and mathematics at both phases of schooling (see Kyriakides and Creemers, 2009). Some factors were also found to be more important for one age of schooling, indicating the possibility of having differential effects. For the purpose of testing the generic nature of the model, this difference does not question the importance of teacher factors within the model. These differences in effect sizes might be attributed to differences in the developmental stages of the two groups of students and, related to that, to the functioning and the curriculum of each phase of schooling. Therefore, the assumption that the factors included in the dynamic model are generic was supported.

Third, the validity of the dynamic model at the school level was supported by the results of a quantitative synthesis of 67 studies exploring the impact of school factors on student achievement (Kyriakides *et al.*, 2010). This meta-analysis revealed that effective schools are able to develop policies and take actions in order to improve their teaching practice and their learning environment. Factors excluded from the dynamic model were found to be weakly associated with student achievement.

Finally, a follow-up study testing the validity of the dynamic model was conducted during the school year 2008–09 (Creemers and Kyriakides, 2010b). The methods used were identical to those followed by the original study testing the validity of the model. This study provided support to the generalisability of the original study. Very similar results on the impact of teacher and school factors upon student achievement emerged from both the original and the follow-up study. Since the follow-up study took place in the same schools where the original study took place, changes in the effectiveness status of schools and in the functioning of effectiveness factors were also identified. Discriminant function analysis reveals that changes not only in the functioning of some school factors but also of the quality of teaching practice can help us classify the schools into those which improved their effectiveness status or remained equally effective or even reduced their effectiveness status (see Creemers and Kyriakides, 2010b). Thus, this study was able to test one of the essential differences of the dynamic model, which has to do with its attempt to relate changes in the effectiveness status of schools to the changes in the functioning of school factors.

Although the studies mentioned above provided support to the main characteristics and assumptions of the dynamic model, we need further research to test the generalisability of the findings of these studies. Moreover, comparative studies should be conducted in order to find out whether the factors of the model are associated with student achievement in different countries. In this context, a comparative study is currently being undertaken in eight European countries in order to find out whether teacher and school factors of the dynamic model are associated with student achievement gains in mathematics and science. It also attempts to provide evidence about the effects of the system-level factors, but further international studies are needed in order to help us understand better the characteristics of effective educational systems. By investigating the impact of the overarching system factors of the dynamic model, researchers may explore relations of these factors with student outcomes in different countries and may also search for their impact on the functioning of teacher- and school-level factors. Such comparative studies may also be used to develop the dynamic model at system level further and formulate research questions on the impact of specific national policies on outcomes in different socio-cultural contexts. Such studies may eventually contribute in the establishment of the international dimension of SER (Reynolds, 2006).

Conclusions and suggestions for further research

In this chapter, it is demonstrated that useful contributions were already being made in the area of theory in the 1990s but there is a need to take them further. Studies testing the validity of the comprehensive model revealed that the variation in 'what worked', if it could be explained and theoretically modelled, would force the field towards the development of more complex and multifaceted accounts than the 'one size fits all' mentality that had hitherto existed in the field during the 1990s. In this context, the dynamic model of educational effectiveness has recently been developed. This model attempts to illustrate the complex and dynamic nature of educational effectiveness and takes into account the findings of research on differential effectiveness. In this chapter, the dynamic model is outlined and studies supporting the validity of the model are briefly presented. Since the dynamic model was designed in order to establish stronger links between SER and improvement of practice, experimental studies and/or case studies should also be conducted to identify the extent to which schools can make use of the dynamic model for improvement purposes. These studies may help us identify when and under what conditions schools can make use of the dynamic model and establish a theory-driven and evidence-based approach to school improvement. Moreover, research is needed in order to identify the *obstacles that schools face in introducing an improvement strategy*. Mixed method approaches might be employed to find out how teachers and schools could move from being resistant to change to becoming committed to school improvement strategies. A topic that looks at the other end of the continuum is concerned with the efforts that the most effective schools take in order to remain effective. Currently, there are almost no studies looking at the improvement strategies that effective schools take in order to remain effective or why others decline (Gray *et al.*, 1996; Thomas *et al.*, 2007). However, a study following 50 schools for a period of five years has shown that schools which were among the most effective had to improve the functioning of the school factors in order to remain among the *most* effective, otherwise they dropped to a typical level (Creemers and Kyriakides, 2010b). Moreover, a mixed method study by Day *et al.* (2009) investigated schools that remained academically effective over at least three years and pointed to the importance of adopting a range of strategies to improve. Further studies testing the generalisability of these findings are needed in order to help us better understand the dynamic nature of school effectiveness and expand the theoretical framework of SER by establishing models that are not only concerned with factors associated with student achievement but also refer to factors which are able to explain changes in the effectiveness status of schools. Such models can help us understand the process of school improvement and establish effective strategies and actions aiming to improve the quality of education.

4 Methodological change in educational effectiveness research

Daniel Muijs

Introduction

School effectiveness and school improvement have now been part of the academic landscape for more than three decades. During that period the field has played an important part in developing and refining methods in educational research. Two areas in particular have benefited from the work of researchers in educational effectiveness and improvement.

On the quantitative side, the development of multilevel modelling techniques has been driven to a significant extent by educational effectiveness researchers, concerned as they are with the consequences of hierarchical sampling methods on traditional statistical tests, and through their natural interest in the impact of school- and classroom-level factors on individual pupil outcomes (see e.g. Snijders and Bosker, 1999; Goldstein, 1987; D'Haenens *et al.*, 2010). Multilevel models deal with the analysis of data where observations are nested within groups, and it is therefore not surprising that they received a major impulse from researchers working in our field, where a substantive interest in school-level effects on pupil outcomes makes the use of such a hierarchical sampling framework imperative. Traditionally, fixed parameter linear regression models were used for the analysis of such data. However, as Aitkin and Longford (1986) demonstrated, the aggregation over individual observations may lead to misleading results. Aggregation of, for example, pupil characteristics over schools allow a school-level analysis to take place, but in the process all individual information is lost. As within-group variation frequently accounts for most of the total variation in the outcome, this loss of information can have an adverse effect on the analysis and lead to distortion of relationships between variables. The alternative, disaggregation, implies the assignation of all class, school, and higher-level characteristics to the individual students. In the process, the assumption of independent observations, a key assumption in linear regression, no longer holds. Both the aggregation of individual variables to a higher level of observation and the disaggregation of higher order variables to an individual level have therefore been somewhat discredited (Bryk and Raudenbush, 1992). Multilevel models, which allow variance to be partialled out between levels, was developed for use with educational data and was quickly taken up by the SER community (see for early examples, Gray and

Jesson, 1990; Aitkin and Longford, 1986; Nuttall *et al.*, 1989). Recently, due to its applicability to any situation in which data are hierarchically nested, multilevel modelling has seen a great deal of growth, and is now widely used in biology (e.g. Baxter-Jones *et al.*, 2003), health research (e.g. Diez-Roux, 2000), psychology (e.g. Jayasinghe *et al.*, 2003), demography (e.g. Sacco *et al.*, 2009), medicine (Goldstein *et al.*, 2002), geography (e.g. Jones and Duncan, 1996) and others. However, educational effectiveness researchers are still at the forefront of research and development in this area, with developments such as multilevel modelling for meta-analysis (Goldstein *et al.*, 2000); cross-classified multilevel modelling, that takes account of the fact that pupils often attend more than one school over their school years (Heck, 2009); multilevel approaches to confirmatory factor analysis (D'Haenens *et al.*, 2010); and multilevel design efficiency, determining the power and accuracy of models and the sample sizes necessary to achieve them (Cools *et al.*, 2009). These have all seen significant development, originating at least in part in the field of educational effectiveness research (EER). It is fair to say that this represents a rare example of an educational discipline being at the forefront of methodological developments.

Researchers in educational improvement have, meanwhile, made an important contribution to the development of mixed methods research approaches in education (e.g. Tashakkori and Teddlie, 2003). Mixed methods research has a long history, starting with two-method quantitative-qualitative or qualitative-quantitative designs in the 1960s, but has evolved very significantly since then (Tashakkori and Teddlie, 2003). While contested in some fields, mixed methods were enthusiastically taken up by researchers in school effectiveness and school improvement. Working within a pragmatic paradigm that essentially rejects paradigmatic fundamentalism, and interested in both quantifiable impacts and the complex processes related to them, mixed methods were seen as providing a route towards integrating these two interests. Early school effects studies frequently used a mixed quantitative-qualitative design, where effective schools were identified through quantitative means, while case studies were used to study the factors that made them so (e.g. Edmonds, 1977). Improvement researchers also frequently employed similar mixed methods designs, where, again, schools were selected on the basis of performance trajectories (have they improved significantly), which is then followed by case study work to ascertain what factors were related to this improvement trajectory. Harris *et al.* (2006) is a recent example of this type of design in school improvement research. Improvement researchers have also developed more complex designs, frequently integrating quantitative and qualitative methods, such as surveys, interviews and documentary analysis within a case-study design (e.g. Stoll and Fink, 1994). In many cases, however, the integration of qualitative and quantitative data in these studies has been limited, and it is here that significant work is progressing in the field of educational effectiveness and improvement. Teddlie and Tashakkori (2009) have developed a typology of ways of integrating data, while Day *et al.* (2006) employed an integrated synergistic research design that combined quantitative and quantitative data in innovative ways. For example, the results from multilevel analyses of effectiveness were incorporated into teacher profiles and were then used as one of several important attributes included in subsequent qualitative analyses of teacher identity, professional life phase and variations in effectiveness.

It is therefore clear that the field has been at the forefront of some important methodological developments, and, more generally, the sophistication of the research methods employed has grown strongly over time. However, whenever a field strengthens and consolidates as an area of research with defined parameters, methods, and indeed practitioners, there is a danger that methods become overly crystallised and fixed. From my work as an editor and reviewer in the field I have gained the impression that this may indeed be occurring, to the extent that it is now possible to talk of a methodological orthodoxy in both effectiveness and improvement research, consisting of case studies, mixed methods studies and surveys, with use of mainly thematic analysis and multilevel statistical models to analyse the data.

Methods in EER

To test this hypothesis, I looked at articles published in *School Effectiveness and School Improvement* between issue 1 of 2005 and issue 2 of 2010. *School Effectiveness and School Improvement* was selected as it is the only journal specific to our field to be ranked in the Social Sciences Citation Index, and is thus likely to be representative of the best research in the field. Articles were selected that reported on empirical research studies. We did not select theoretical papers, methodological explorations or editorials. A total of 83 articles fit these criteria. We then determined:

1   What the principle data collection method used in the study was; and
2   What the principle data analysis method used was. This was determined as the main or most sophisticated method used.

All papers were read and coded using a thematic analysis framework. A coding framework was used that classified a range of data collection and research methods according to key delineations found in the Research Methods literature (e.g. Cohen *et al.*, 2007). Main themes and methods were identified. Where more than one method emerged, the extent to which the methods informed the conclusions was used as the key indicator (e.g. some quantitative papers contain descriptive statistics, but the main conclusions follow from subsequent regression analyses).

With regards our research hypothesis, a first significant finding is that very few published papers used a mixed methods approach – 68.7 per cent of empirical papers reported on quantitative studies, 26.5 per cent on qualitative studies, and 4.8 per cent on mixed methods studies.

We then looked at what data collection methods were used within quantitative and qualitative studies.

As can be seen in Tables 4.1 and 4.2, both quantitative and qualitative studies are dominated by a limited range of data collection methods. Over 80 per cent of

Table 4.1 Research methodologies in recently published quantitative papers

Research method	Percentage of articles
Survey research	59.7
Secondary data	22.9
Quasi-experimental	15.7
Other	1.7

Table 4.2 Research methodologies in recently published qualitative papers

Research method	Percentage of articles
Case studies	81.8
Interviews	18.2

qualitative studies reported on are case studies, with the remainder being other interview methods. Of quantitative studies, almost 60 per cent are survey studies, and just under 23 per cent use secondary data, such as international studies (e.g. PISA) and national or local accountability data sets (such as the National Pupil Database in England). Almost 16 per cent of studies used quasi-experimental designs. Main data analysis methods are depicted in Tables 4.3 and 4.4.

In quantitative studies, almost 50 per cent of papers used multilevel methods (MLM), while a further 35 per cent used what I have termed 'traditional' statistics, such as regression and parametric or non-parametric tests. In all cases the methods used were appropriate for the data collected. A smaller number of papers used econometric, SEM or IRT models. In qualitative papers the vast majority of studies used some form of thematic analysis.

In terms of our hypothesis we can therefore see quite a limited range of data collection and analysis methods, and it can be said that the typical quantitative

Table 4.3 Data analysis methods in recently published quantitative papers

Research method	Percentage of articles
Multilevel modelling	46.7
Traditional statistics	35.0
Econometric techniques	6.7
Structural equation and latent growth curve modelling	6.6
Item response theory	5.0

Table 4.4 Data analysis methods in recently published qualitative papers

Research method	Percentage of articles
Thematic analysis and equivalents	81.8
Other	18.2

study is a survey study using either MLM or traditional statistics, with some use of secondary data analysis, while the typical qualitative study in our field is a case study. There were surprisingly few mixed methods studies.

Of course, in some ways we can say that this is a logical development. The complexity of educational organisations probably lends itself more easily to survey research than to other methods of quantitative data collection such as experimental designs, and the hierarchical nature of most datasets used lends itself to multilevel modelling. Similarly, if one wants to study processes of, for example, leadership or school improvement, case studies provide a valid and robust way of doing so. However, where methodologies become too standardised, the further growth of the field may be limited, as the methods we use constrain our thinking and in part determine our findings and designs.

Issues with quantitative designs and methods

As we have seen above a large proportion of quantitative studies employ multilevel modelling as their basic method. Of course, multilevel modelling is a key approach in EER. Data typically have a hierarchical structure in our field, with pupils nested in classrooms, and classrooms nested in schools. This is not just, as in some other fields of research, a pragmatic decision due to the greater ease of reaching pupils through schools rather than individually, but is fundamental to the interest of the field in school- and classroom-level factors as they relate to pupil level outcomes. As is well known, multilevel modelling both alleviates the problem of attenuated standard errors in hierarchical samples, and allows more accurate modelling of school and pupil level impacts to be done (Muijs, 2004). Of course, the use of multilevel modelling has itself become more sophisticated over time. A better understanding of the need to include all relevant levels in the model (Opdenakker and Van Damme, 2000), greater use of cross-classified models to account for changes between schools (Meyers and Beretvas, 2006), and the development of multilevel growth curve models (van der Werf *et al.*, 2008) have all, for example, led to greater accuracy and enhanced the validity of the models used.

However, the reliance on multilevel models does have a number of less positive consequences. One issue is to do with the way the methods we use can shape our conceptual thinking. A key part of multilevel modelling is of course the partialling out of variance between the different levels, typically schools, classrooms and pupils. This is accompanied by a division of variables as belonging to these different levels, so we can distinguish school, classroom and pupil level variables. While useful, this can lead to us to overstate these distinctions, and understate the extent to which variables at the different levels interact and inform one another. For example, pupil background and ability may interact in complex ways with teacher behaviours and school policies, which makes the distinction between different levels problematic (e.g. Cummings *et al.*, 2008).

Another issue is the fact that multilevel modelling is a subset of the general linear model that is typically configured as a direct effects multiple regression model. This means that independent variables in the equation are usually modelled as directly affecting dependent variables. However, in educational effectiveness many processes operate indirectly. Factors such as school leadership do not impact directly on pupil outcomes, but rather create the conditions under which teaching and learning can take place. Not only are these types of effects indirect, but they are also frequently reciprocal. Leadership, for example, influences organisational processes and culture, but organisational culture and processes themselves influence leadership (Hallinger and Heck, 2010). Multilevel models may thus in many cases oversimplify the processes of educational effectiveness.

As well as a strong reliance on multilevel modelling, our field appears to rely on a limited range of data collection methods, in particular surveys and secondary datasets. One problem with these is that each survey or international study tends to develop its own definitions and data collection instruments, rather than relying on existing constructs. Key elements of educational effectiveness like school climate and leadership are therefore defined and measured differently from study to study. This leads to a lack of comparability between studies, which have proven problematic in, for example, the development of meta-analytic summaries, and leads to divergent findings that don't help us to develop authoritative conclusions on the strength of effects in our area. This constant reinvention of the wheel, most strongly present in leadership research, means that the field can tend towards a rather circular development mode, where findings are revisited under slightly different definitions and names, rather than moving forward in a more linear manner. There is also a lot of variance in the types of instruments used, and in the way they are constructed, and at times lack of interest in measurement as a science in educational effectiveness, notwithstanding the importance of measurement as a practical activity to the field.

Issues with qualitative designs and methods

The range of qualitative designs in the field seems even more limited than the range of quantitative designs, being largely premised on case studies. That said, case study is a flexible and varied set of methodologies, which can, in epistemological terms, range from Yin's (1994) positivistic pattern-matching methods to the constructivist orientation that Wells (1995), for example, espouses. Similarly, within case studies various data collection mechanisms are possible, from interviews and questionnaires to observational and ethnographic methods, and the analysis of documentary evidence. The number and types of cases are also varied. However, when we look at the work in our field, it is clear that the methods used are somewhat more limited than the above suggests. Nearly all case studies reviewed rely primarily on interview data (while the few non-case study examples of qualitative research likewise were based on interviews). Lip-service is sometimes paid to the collection of documentary evidence, but rarely is any analysis of this data presented.

This reliance on interview data is problematic in a number of ways. First, there is a significant risk of attributional bias, the natural human tendency to attribute success to internal factors and failures to environmental ones. Therefore, we tend to see that improvements in schools are presented as the work of our interviewees, while setbacks are frequently down to others in the organisation, or policy and environmental factors. It is clear that the reliability of some of these findings needs to be questioned. Of course, this is not merely an issue for qualitative interview methods, but applies equally to many of the survey methods used in quantitative studies. Our own research in colleges of further education, for example, uncovered the interesting finding that most survey respondents were transformational leaders, while their line managers were almost invariably described as employing transactional forms of leadership (Muijs *et al.*, 2006). Related to this is the fact that many case study research designs, particularly in the area of school improvement, use retrospective methods, where interviewees are asked to comment on a process of change that may have started three or more years ago. This means that the processes of attributional bias are linked to bias resulting from hindsight, leading to further validity issues.

An additional issue here is the interviewer expectancy effect. This is the phenomenon whereby interviewees will tend to want to give an 'acceptable' response to the interviewer, for reasons of self-presentation or conviviality (Singer and Kohnke-Aguirre, 1979). This effect, which also exists in survey research, is particularly prevalent in interview situations as a result of the face-to-face interaction between interviewer and interviewee. The effect may be influenced by interviewer characteristics such as age, gender, appearance and institutional affiliation, or by interviewee characteristics such as training in particular areas. In EER the latter is often an issue, as many interviewees have partaken in training programmes, for example the National Professional Qualification for Headteachers in England, which inculcate certain expectations of 'good' behaviours and values, that in turn are easily reproduced in interview situations regardless of actual behaviours or beliefs. It has also become increasingly easy for interviewees to discover the actual views and beliefs of interviewers through use of the internet, making reliance on visible characteristics lower, and the probability of being able to provide the 'right' response greater.

Finally, there is the issue of what case study research actually means in this context. Typically, the stated aims of case studies are to develop an in-depth understanding of the context and characteristics of the case, leading to a richer contextual understanding than is possible using quantitative methods. However, where one is not an insider-researcher, gaining a genuine in-depth understanding of an educational organisation (which, as we are so frequently reminded by qualitative researchers, will be complex) will surely take some time and immersion in the case. It is therefore somewhat unfortunate to find that most case studies reported appear to consist of a limited set of interviews, conducted in during limited time period of typically a few days.

So where do we go from here?

Obviously the above by no means implies that we should give up on our present research and analysis methods. Survey and case study research, multilevel modelling and thematic analysis are important and should remain a central part of our methodological arsenal. However, it would be beneficial to the field if we extended our array of methods somewhat. The first area for expansion is clearly the use of mixed methods. It was somewhat surprising and disappointing to discover the dearth of mixed methods studies in extant educational effectiveness research. In view of the much-documented advantages thereof (see Tashakkori and Teddlie, 2003) more use should be made of mixed methods designs, especially where methods can truly lead to greater levels of information from and integration of data.

More promising was that the use of quasi-experimental methods accounted for over 15 per cent of papers in SESI. The enhanced ability to test causal models using these methods make them potentially particularly powerful in EER, and we would support further development and expansion of these methods. This is of course not to say, as some have done, that only (quasi-)experimental research can truly be termed scientific, and to consider this form of research as somehow on a higher plane than other types (Schneider and Keesler, 2007). However, in view of the issues of response bias in surveys and interviews mentioned above, this method does deserve greater emphasis in future. In particular, the use of randomised controlled trials can lead to more robust findings on factors such as effective teaching methods.

Quantitative studies also need to employ a greater range of analysis methods. Causal mechanisms are often better studied using Structural Equation Modelling methods, while econometric models are particularly strong in accounting for the possible impact of endogenous variables. Both deserve greater use in our field.

In terms of qualitative designs, there is a clear need for more inventiveness in the way we study effectiveness and improvement. Two main issues need expanding here; methods that are less prone to attributional bias, and methods that are more truly in depth. Both issues really lead one in the same direction: the need for more longitudinal research, where the researchers spend more time in the schools they are researching, either through longitudinal case studies or more ethnographic methods. In particular, it would be useful to design studies where researchers follow a process of change in one or more schools over time, from the onset of the change (for example, a new school improvement initiative) to a time point sufficiently long removed from the starting point that change may have happened and be demonstrated (or not, as the case may be). This more longitudinal perspective needs to be coupled with a greater variety of data collection methods, and in particular with greater use of observational methods that can alleviate the over-reliance on self-report data.

However, probably the most important element in moving the field forward in methodological terms is to come to greater agreement over definitions, constructs and concepts. The tendency to constantly re-invent the wheel in terms of defining key concepts is unhelpful, though common in educational research in general, and hinders the development of a robust and consistent knowledge base. This is particularly apparent when we compare the robustness and development of knowledge in educational research to developments in psychology, where far greater care is taken to standardise definitions and measurement. The field of self-concept research is a good example. Following the convergence on agreed models of self-concept in the late 1970s and early 1980s, and the development of a number of standard research instruments, the field has been able to test a range of theories and hypotheses, retest these in a range of contexts and so come to develop a robust set of findings and relationships (Shavelson *et al.*, 1976; Marsh, 1984; Moller *et al.*, 2008). We urgently need to engage in the task of agreeing on what our key concepts are and mean, and stop the unhelpful practice of constantly inventing new labels, often for old wine (leadership being a particular culprit here). This will require a sustained intellectual endeavour on the part of the field, and one in which our organisational structures such as ICSEI, and the BERA, AERA and EARLI Special Interest Groups could play a key role.

In quantitative research in particular, this also requires greater attention to measurement science. Item Response Theory (IRT) represents a great leap forward in terms of developing valid research instruments and measures, and needs to be more strongly integrated into EER. At present, one of the factors holding back the development of social scientific research in general is the high level of measurement error in our instruments. Fox (2004) demonstrated that integrating IRT models into multilevel designs significantly improved the reliability of findings and, incidentally, significantly increased the percentage of school-level variance in pupil outcomes, suggesting that weak measurement may be constraining our ability to pick up on the full extent of the school effect in educational outcomes.

While all this is an ambitious endeavour, especially in a period in which funding for educational research is rather more likely to decrease than to increase, it is in my view worth considering ways in which we as a community can attempt to collaborate to increase the quality, rather than the quantity of our research, and maintain educational effectiveness and improvement's leading role in producing valid, reliable and useful research in education.

Part II
Educational effectiveness and improvement in practice

5 Closing the gap?

A critical reflection on the impact of school improvement policies in England

Mel West

Introduction

The picture of United Kingdom education systems that emerged from the OECD study of social disadvantage and educational outcomes (OECD, 2006) was a bleak one. The study reported that in the United Kingdom socio-economic circumstances had a greater influence on educational attainment than almost anywhere in the world, with both England and Scotland ranking in the bottom five of the 52 countries surveyed. This despite the fact that the last 20 years have seen successive governments impose policy upon policy, in deliberate and focused attempts to bring about improvements in the quality and performance of individual schools in England, particularly those serving disadvantaged communities. It would seem that the efforts to create a more equitable educational system in which educational policies offset key aspects of socio-economic disadvantage that hold back educational attainment have had little impact. England remains a place where social differences are likely to be magnified rather than eliminated through schooling, a place where privileged home circumstances seem more important than schooling in determining the life chances available to young people.

However, the same OECD report is clear that it is possible to design educational policies that offset some of the factors that accompany social disadvantage. What is more, it argues that such policies will not necessarily reduce the performance of more 'advantaged' students. Some such policies relate to the regulation of school admissions or 'sorting systems', others focus on the development of schooling experiences that build those cognitive and social skills that children from disadvantaged backgrounds need in order to thrive within schools. Sadly, despite unprecedented levels of policy, prescription and monitoring, English governments have achieved neither. Indeed, if the same narrow principles used to gauge school effectiveness by successive administrations is applied to assessing their own performance, there is little doubt that we would have seen a government in 'special measures' before now. This chapter looks back over some of the main government initiatives in recent years, and asks what we can learn from these that might lead to more effective and more equitable schooling in the future.

Intervention, intervention, intervention . . .

Few were surprised when Tony Blair famously described New Labour's key priorities as 'Education, education, education' in the run-up to the 1997 election. After almost ten years of sweeping reforms from a Conservative government that had dramatically altered the balance of powers within the education system away from local control towards centrally dictated policies, many assumed this signalled that local influence would be restored. They were to be quickly disabused of this notion however, as the new government embarked on a series of policy initiatives that were even more prescriptive and set in place mechanisms for micro-management of every aspect of schooling. The scope and pace of interventions to 'improve' schools accelerated rapidly, sometimes moving further in directions already signalled by the previous government, sometimes finding new aspects of schooling in need of central direction and control. There are a number of ways these interventions might be grouped. We have previously suggested that they can be considered to be of four basic types: targeted interventions, general interventions, within-school interventions and structural interventions (see Kerr and West, 2011).

Targeted interventions

These initiatives have been aimed directly at improving the performance of schools in socio-economically disadvantaged areas. The underlying premise is that in such areas ineffective schools 'fail' pupils who already have the odds stacked against them, and so merely perpetuate existing inequities. As a first consequence, such schools are often placed in an Ofsted category and become subject to direct interventions and regular monitoring, coordinated by the local authority but dictated by central government. But in some areas groups of schools have been targeted simultaneously in more sweeping interventions. This process began with the identification of Education Action Zones (EAZs) by the Conservative administration during the early 1990s. It was been continued into the Excellence in Cities (EiC) programme, which required groups of secondary schools in deprived inner-city areas to collaborate for the benefit of the students in all of their schools. Such collaborative arrangements continued to be developed through Excellence Clusters, and through the Leadership Incentive Grant. As they have developed, interventions have targeted collaboration beyond schools, for example between schools, parents and community groups. Arguably the most significant example of this approach is the London Challenge, which, over the last seven years or so, has been focused on raising the attainment levels of disadvantaged learners in Greater London, whilst at the same time improving the overall performance of all schools and pupils. The perceived success of this intervention led to its extension to the City Challenges established in the Black Country and in Greater Manchester. It also influenced the approach used more recently in a particularly controversial initiative, the National Challenge. This targeted over 600 'low performing' secondary schools, which are predominantly located in areas of socio-economic disadvantage.

General interventions

These aim to improve the overall quality and effectiveness of all schools, particularly in relation to the strengthening of leadership and teaching quality. Again, the underlying assumption is that (at least part of) the reason for differences in educational attainment levels lies in the limited effectiveness of some schools. Improving schools generally can therefore be seen as a way of improving the outcomes of those serving disadvantaged pupils, leading in turn to an improvement in their life chances. This type of intervention was particularly popular during the early period of the New Labour government in the late 1990s, initially in the form of the National Literacy and Numeracy strategies, and later the Key Stage 3 strategy. Subsequently these were incorporated into the National Strategies, a set of system-wide improvement approaches commissioned by government from a private sector education service provider and supported by teams of consultants employed nationally, regionally and within each local authority. More recently, as the really quite modest improvements in test and examination scores occurring in those years have tended to level off, these 'one-size-fits all' approaches have been phased out. Officially, they have done their job and so are no longer needed, though many would say that they were expensive but relatively ineffective strategies and that funding such interventions could no longer be justified.

Within-school interventions

While the first two types of intervention focus on improvement at the whole-school level, this third type is aimed at improving outcomes for underachieving groups within schools. These approaches are therefore rooted in the view that pupil outcomes show significant within-school variation. This differential attainment for different student groups implies that many (most?) schools do not work equally well for all of their pupils. In national policy documents – such as those associated with the recent 'Extra Mile' initiative – these approaches are usually referred to as being about 'narrowing (or closing) the gap' between high and low performing groups. So, for example, there have been interventions that have specifically focused on the underachievement of boys, particularly those from white working-class backgrounds; learners from certain minority ethnic backgrounds; bilingual learners; children in local authority care; travellers; gifted and talented children; and children with special educational needs. Specific attention has also been given to improving access to university education amongst students from disadvantaged backgrounds through the Aim Higher initiative. This involves universities working closely with local schools to help raise awareness and aspirations and to open up pathways for young people from those communities that have no established tradition of university education.

Structural interventions

Recent years have seen the introduction of a number of new categories of schools. The creation of these schools has typically involved changes in school governance arrangements – Academies, Federations, Trusts, All-through Schools and, now, Free Schools too – so that increased freedom from the already severely diminished influence of the local authority is a key feature of such schools. Sometimes, such schools have been established as a result of local ambitions, sometimes as a result of central government's dissatisfaction with existing local arrangements. These interventions seem to operate from the assumption that a partnership of strong schools and strong government is all that is needed to improve schooling outcomes. Curiously, a feature of the 'new' schools created by these policies is the relative freedom granted to these schools in relation to the curriculum. While government has never conceded officially that one factor generally holding back attainment among disadvantaged groups may be an inappropriate National Curriculum, which meets neither the needs nor the interests of many pupils, it is interesting that greater freedom to abandon National Curriculum prescriptions is typically available within the new categories of schools.

A closer look at the assumptions underpinning intervention strategies and the role played by schools in reducing educational disadvantage

As noted above, all of these interventions see the school as the primary focus for national improvement efforts. In this way they also imply a central role for the school in improving equity within education systems. This has led to a strong emphasis on accountability of individual schools for the performance of their students, leading to what some have seen as unreasonable pressure on schools to solve the problem of disadvantage (Muijs and Chapman, 2009).

Emphasis is also placed on support for schools through the involvement of expert advisers and consultants, professional development opportunities, targeted financial support and support in terms of human resources. Different interventions vary with respect to how much they emphasise support as opposed to accountability, and can be placed along a continuum, from those that are mainly supportive (e.g. improving schools programmes), to others that are mainly punitive (e.g. various forms of school reconstitution and closure).

Interventions also differ in terms of their prescriptiveness. Some, such as those provided through the National Strategies, come with very detailed guidelines and training on how they are to be implemented. Others allow rather more local discretion and encourage schools to innovate, resulting in strategies like 'lending' one another teachers, as emerged through the Leadership Incentive Grant initiative (see West, 2010). An important strand within national school improvement efforts has been an emphasis on such forms of school-to-school collaboration. On the surface this may seen strange within a policy context in which competition between schools remains the key strategy for 'driving up standards'. On the other hand, there is increasing evidence that collaboration between schools has enormous potential for fostering system-wide improvement, particularly in challenging contexts (e.g. Ainscow and West, 2007). It does this by both transferring existing knowledge and, more importantly, generating context-specific new knowledge.

The interventions listed above seem to be driven by two underlying assumptions. First, that the traditional governance arrangements do not produce schools able to overcome the disadvantages that children in areas of economic and social deprivation bring into school with them – that is, these arrangements are failing the children they should serve. Second, that boosting academic attainment levels among these children will increase their life chances, and thus help reduce inequities within society. Of course, while these assumptions may well have some substance, there is also room for doubt.

The notion that increased attainment is itself life-changing is perhaps overly simplistic. In reality, exam success is at best a proxy for educational quality, and there is ample evidence that improving 16-plus qualifications by a few percentage points does little to influence either post-school choices or opportunities. Equally, it can be argued that the attainment gains themselves are not attributable to the new forms of governance, but rather to the substantial additional resources that have tended to come along with such interventions. Had the schools that have been closed down and replaced enjoyed the facilities and resources available to Academies, who can say they would not have achieved as much, if not more? However, few can question that additional resources are justified – these schools tend to be located in areas of high deprivation, with a much greater proportion of pupils qualifying for free school meals, having special needs, or with English as a second language.

However, as we have noted above, the notion that at least part of the reason for the differential achievement of different student groups lies in the quality of the school provision they experience is a general assumption driving the educational reform process. Whilst there is some evidence to support this, there is also evidence that points to its limitations. There is strong evidence that the school effect on attainment is significant, and similar in effect size to that of pupil social background (Muijs, 2008). However, this school effect must not be overstated, as it has sometimes been by national policy makers. According to studies in the UK, typically between 10–25 per cent of the variance in attainment outcomes between students can be explained at the school level, though this does not mean all of that variance is down to school factors (see, for example, Sammons, 2007; Muijs, 2006; Teddlie and Reynolds, 2000). However, it is mistaken to assume that the remaining variance – at the student level – is all associated with social background. In fact, whenever researchers use actual measures of social background – such as mothers' education level (the measure that best predicts outcomes among measures of social background), parental income, or job classification – the variance explained is typically below 10 per cent. Rather, the research suggests that the largest factors associated with learner outcomes relate to measures of general ability and prior learning.

There is some research evidence that suggests the impact the school has on students from disadvantaged backgrounds is larger than on all students generally, the 'school effect' being up to three times greater on the attainment levels of those students (Muijs and Reynolds, 2003). This implies that interventions to improve school effectiveness will bring greater proportional benefits to these students, thereby improving educational equity too. However, there is also some evidence that schools in areas of socio-economic disadvantage face greater operational problems, for example in recruiting and retaining high-quality teachers (Maguire *et al.*, 2006), which may further disadvantage students in these schools. This is one of the reasons put forward to explain why various national school improvement interventions have used relatively prescriptive approaches, in an attempt to develop teacher competence and to ensure there are tight management arrangements for consistent implementation and monitoring.

Some researchers draw attention to the in-built limitations of improvement efforts that focus solely on within-school factors. Some argue that schools reflect the massive inequalities that exist within British society, an analysis that offers little encouragement to school improvement as a means of breaking the link between home background, educational outcomes and life chances. Others take a more optimistic line, suggesting that efforts to improve individual schools are needed but that these must be linked to wider actions to break down the additional barriers faced by disadvantaged groups.

What evidence is there regarding the impact of these interventions?

There is considerable debate about the impact of these efforts, both in improving schooling generally and in enhancing life chances for learners from disadvantaged backgrounds specifically. Predictably, government statements point to improvements in test and examination scores, arguing that the impact has been significant. Within the research community, however, there are a variety of views, including some that argue that there has been very little real impact, particularly on learners from disadvantaged backgrounds, and that even the apparent improvements in measured performance are not always supported by a detailed analysis of national data (Gorard, 2006). Concern has also been expressed that such improvements that have been achieved in test and examination scores may have been achieved by the use of dubious tactics – such as orchestrated changes in school populations, the exclusion of some students, the careful selection of which courses students follow and the growth in so-called equivalent qualifications that may inflate reported attainment levels. Another problem is that where strategies do work, they may well work just as well for advantaged students, so that overall improvements may even widen the 'gap'.

This underlines that the evidence for impact of these interventions is, at best, mixed, not least because of the limited extent to which reliable evidence has been systematically collected and analysed. Where systematic larger-scale evaluations have been carried out, what is often found is that impact is patchy, with evidence of progress in some schools, but little overall improvement in learner outcomes, particularly learners from disadvantaged groups, has been sustained (Tikley *et al.*, 2006). At the same time, there is an accumulating volume of accounts from both individual, and networks of schools in socially disadvantaged areas that report significant progress in improving student performance.

These positive examples reinforce the importance of factors that are now well established within the school effectiveness research base, such as the need to raise expectations, the strengthening of teaching practices, the systematic use of data to guide classroom-level strategies and the way change is managed at school level. They also suggest the need to develop strategies that relate to the immediate contexts, both inside and outside the school. In the case of schools that are relatively low performing, for example, initial emphases on strengthening systems and procedures through the tightening of management arrangements and the standardising of classroom practices seem most effective. Here the partnering of schools – where a relatively stronger school provides support to a weaker school – has been found be a useful approach. But for schools that are performing more effectively, further standardisation seems less helpful; engagement with specific data about aspects of school performance, looking at within-school performance variation or listening more closely to pupil voice for example, and encouraging experimentation in the classroom seem to be more successful approaches.

Turning to specific initiatives, there has been little in the way of systematic, rigorous evaluation of the impact of targeted interventions. However, such evidence as exists suggests some success, both in terms of outcomes for children and also increased understanding of the key process and management factors that influence the impact of interventions. Perhaps the strongest evidence emerges from interventions that are targeted at pre-school and early years education. The evaluation of the impact of a parenting programme on children aged 3–5 years showing conduct disorder (Hutchings *et al.*, 2007), revealed significant improvements in most measures of parenting (self-reported and observed competence, reduced levels of stress and depression) and reductions in problem behaviour among children (parents' reports and direct observation). Another study of early intervention (Evangelou *et al.*, 2008) looked at a project supporting a total of 12 different approaches, trialled by nine voluntary organisations across the country. The key findings were that the initiative developed both skills and understandings among practitioners; identified and brought about important changes in organisational practices; demonstrated that it was possible to reach and engage with vulnerable families in disadvantaged communities and help them to support their children as learners.

The evaluation (DfES 2004, 2006) of the Children's Fund initiative reinforces many of these findings. It reported that local initiatives had often been able to respond to previously unmet needs of children and their families. Valuable learning about the organisation, commissioning and delivery of services to children had taken place, and there were measurable gains in school attendance and performance. Breakfast and homework clubs proved popular with socially disadvantaged groups, though after-school activities attracted children from more comfortable environments, and some innovative ways to involve users in service planning and delivery were developed. However, sustaining parental involvement and breaking down barriers to social inclusion in the wider community proved more problematic.

But sometimes findings are contradictory, as is the case of evaluations of the early years' numeracy and literacy strategies. Here some studies show positive results, indicating improvements in teacher effectiveness and pupil outcomes, whilst others are sharply critical of the limitations of these strategies, seeing them as encouraging impoverished teaching, being based on poor and limited evidence of what constitutes effective classroom practice, and leading to greater divergence between low and high achieving students (Smith and Hardman, 2000; Wyse, 2003; Earl *et al.*, 2003; Millett *et al.*, 2004) A problem here – for the researcher – is the variation in approaches used in the different interventions, which makes it difficult to identify those factors to which learning gains might be attributed.

Similar problems are associated with the evaluation of programmes to offset learning loss; while some targeted 'one-hit' summer schools have been shown to reduce learning loss, there are doubts about whether such impact can be sustained. The main body of evidence available is from the USA, and while there have been calls for a radical restructuring of the school year – there is some evidence that simply eliminating the long summer break would itself reduce learning loss – the NFER (2004) review suggested that evidence for the impact of the school calendar itself on learning progress is weak. Indeed, it can be argued that the availability of evidence relating to the sorts of initiatives outlined above is generally disappointing because, in part, the methods used in evaluations have themselves been weak. Consequently, specific evidence of the impact such interventions have on breaking the link between poverty and achievement is scarce, and the scant evidence that is available is not always encouraging. Looking at new models, in the case of Federations, an analysis of national student- and school-level datasets found little difference between student attainment levels in Federated schools and comparable non-federation schools.

But the new arrangements have a second major implication for schools; they brought the opportunity to incorporate the wider children's services agenda – *Every Child Matters* – into school-level planning and practices. This might be significant, because structures and processes can be developed that may bring local communities into schools. Trust schools also have the potential to bring in partners involved in the wider children's services agenda, although as yet there has been little research into their potential to do so.

In England, the government has maintained that Academies are more successful in improving attainment standards in socially deprived communities than local authority schools. However, this is not always supported by research findings, with some studies finding that Academies do not perform any better than local authority schools. Even where there are clear increases in attainment levels, it may be that this is related to factors other than improvements in teaching quality. For example, in Academies up to 10 per cent of the student intake can be 'selected' (though not formally on ability); some Academies have deliberately 'widened' their intake of students to include 'a more diverse pupil profile', while others attract a wider profile of students due to initial success or increased parental confidence, so it is hard to make true comparisons without looking at overall system performance. Indeed, some argue that improved outcomes may be attributed as much to a fall in the proportion of students eligible for free school meals (FSM) as to any improvements in teaching and learning. However, the impact of this factor is hard to gauge, as student numbers in Academies typically increase – not surprising since they have typically replaced failing schools. While the numbers qualifying for FSM also increase, the increase is not proportional, making it hard to refute even this claim. This indicates that the social mix in Academies may change both rapidly and dramatically, not in itself a bad thing, but a confounding variable, nonetheless, when trying to evaluate impact on children from particular socio-economic backgrounds.

Despite these examples, the apparent lack of overall impact from so many initiatives is somewhat surprising, particularly if the contention that schools make a difference is true. There are, however, a number of possible explanations for this, some of which relate to methodological matters. For example, many of the evaluations carried out to date are based on relatively short-term output data, perhaps completed too soon for any effect to show. Among policy makers there is often an expectation that interventions will have an immediate impact. However, most of the school improvement research suggests that at least three to five years are needed for an intervention to lead to measurable changes in output at the school level (Muijs and Reynolds, 2003).

But, methodological issues aside, there do seem to be grounds for raising questions about the sorts of interventions that have been made and the assumptions driving them. For example, interventions do not always seem to draw sufficiently on the effectiveness and improvement knowledge bases, leading to attention being focused at the wrong level and on low leverage approaches. In particular, there is clear evidence that teachers' classroom practices are the single most important factor in improving the performance of disadvantaged students (Muijs and Reynolds, 2003). There is also strong evidence as to which strategies work and which do not. Specifically, this evidence supports the use of direct instruction (see for example Schug *et al.*, 2001), peer-tutoring (HMI, 2003), the development of meta-cognitive strategies and collaborative small group activities (Johnson *et al.*, 1998), particularly where these are used skilfully. There is also clear evidence that when it comes to the development of pedagogy and behaviour management a consistent approach across the school is most effective (Kyriakides and Creemers, 2008), and that teachers need to be encouraged to experiment with new ways of reaching those learners who are not responding to existing teaching strategies (Petty, 2009). Powerful staff development strategies, such as lesson study, have a role to play here. By and large, the evidence is that the various national school improvement interventions have not adopted such school-level development strategies, rather electing to offer one-size-fits-all, formulaic approaches, such as the so-called 'three-part lesson plan'.

It should also be noted that many of the school improvement interventions have suffered from weak implementation arrangements. Research indicates that effective programme implementation requires extensive support (OECD, 2008), including effective staff development activities, as well as careful monitoring of impact and findings. Building support for the intervention in schools is essential, and forms of co-construction have been found to be particularly useful in this respect. Indeed, case studies of individual school successes all confirm the benefits of such approaches, not least in terms of sustainability. Unfortunately, the simultaneous imposition of too many interventions over recent years has challenged the capacity of individual schools to manage the expected changes effectively, and led to inconsistencies and contradictions, as elements of the different interventions have often seemed to contradict one another.

Ironically, even where the intention is to reduce disadvantage, the differential capacity of schools to implement interventions effectively can lead to increased differences in performance between schools, causing further equity problems. This points to an important limitation of individual school-focused approaches, which is that too often improvements in one school in an area of social disadvantage are achieved at a cost to surrounding schools. The research provides examples of how, as a school improves, it will tend to attract a greater number of students from more motivated families. Sometimes, too, a school that becomes oversubscribed may also decide to become more selective. As a result, other schools in the area are left with less motivated students from less ambitious backgrounds, locking them into a spiral of decline.

What have we learned? Some implications for policy, practice and research

All of these interventions see the school as the primary focus for national improvement efforts. In this way they also imply a central role for the school in improving equity within education systems. This has led to a strong emphasis on accountability of individual schools for the performance of their students, leading to what some have seen as unreasonable pressure on schools (Muijs and Chapman, 2009).

Emphasis is also placed on support for schools through the involvement of expert advisers and consultants, professional development opportunities, targeted financial support and support in terms of human resources. Different interventions vary with respect to the degree of emphasis on support as opposed to accountability, and can be placed along a continuum, from those that are generally supportive (e.g. centrally resourced school improvement programmes) to those that are essentially punitive (e.g. various forms of school reconstitution and closure).

Interventions have also differed in terms of the degree of prescriptiveness. Some, such as those provided through the National Strategies, come with very detailed guidelines and teachers are required to undergo training to learn how they are to be implemented. Others have allowed rather more discretion and encouraged schools to innovate, as happened to some extent as a result of the Networked Learning Communities developed by the National College for School Leadership, and through the collaboratives established under the Leadership Incentive Grant (LIG).

As noted earlier, an important strand within several national school improvement efforts has been an emphasis on various forms of school-to-school collaboration. On the surface this may seem strange, within a policy context in which competition between schools remains the key strategy for 'driving up standards'. On the other hand, there is increasing evidence that collaboration between schools has untapped potential for fostering system-wide improvement, particularly in challenging contexts (e.g. Ainscow and West, 2006). It does this by both moving around existing knowledge and, more importantly, by generating new, context-specific knowledge.

At the same time, as we build a greater understanding of the power of school-to-school collaboration as a strategy for addressing issues of equity across education systems, there is also a growing awareness of how schools can work effectively with other agencies and representatives of the wider community, although this issue needs much more attention. This period of policy overload has also thrown some light on the things that national governments need to do to encourage more effective collaboration and networking, as well as pointing to the dangers of trying to 'micro-manage' the processes involved from the centre. Too often, government's desire to prescribe not just 'what' but also 'how', has limited the space essential for effective local action in response to local challenges and opportunities.

This brief analysis suggests a number of lessons that can inform future policy and practice:

1   While schools cannot by themselves solve the problems of inequity of student experiences and inequality of student outcomes, the evidence clearly suggests that they can make some impact, and that school-focused actions remain an important part of wider solutions.

2   School improvement interventions must be designed more carefully, based on the available evidence about what generates effective schooling, but also on what we know about how successful schools develop. This means being clearer about the outcomes expected – and let us not continue to delude ourselves that any combination of GCSEs and 'equivalent' qualifications will ever be more than a proxy for effective schooling – while permitting greater latitude for specific ends and means to be determined at school level by those most acquainted with the needs and interests of their students.

3   School improvement efforts need to better reflect the local contexts within which schools work. As we have seen, initiatives that lead some schools to improve at the expense of others in their neighbourhood will not lead to overall improvements. This means that policy makers must recognise that the details of policy implementation are not amenable to central regulation. Rather, these have to be dealt with by those who are close to and, therefore, in a better position to understand particular contexts. All of this raises important questions regarding the need for effective local coordination.

4   Further, since collaboration between differently-performing schools can help to reduce the polarisation of the education system, to the particular benefit of students who are on the edges of the system and performing relatively poorly, incentives need to be provided that will encourage such processes. More efforts should also be made to understand the conditions that are needed in order to make such approaches effective. It needs to be understood that

collaboration is at least as important as competition in raising overall attainment levels.

5   At the same time, we need to pay more attention to what we know does not work. In particular, there is a need to focus on those aspects of disadvantage and under-attainment that schools can influence, and not attempt to make schools responsible for solving problems that evidence suggests they influence only marginally. Too many responsibilities given to schools distract them from concentrating on what they can do well.

6   The political desire for 'quick fixes' notwithstanding, there is a need to allow initiatives time to have an impact. The constant imposition of new initiatives is destabilising and also hinders development of the consistency in learning and teaching practices that research suggests leads to positive outcomes for learners from disadvantaged backgrounds.

Finally, these observations themselves point to several areas of doubt and uncertainty. This confirms the need to ensure that rigorous procedures for the evaluation of impact are built into future efforts to improve the ways in which schooling alleviates social inequality.

6 Educational effectiveness and school improvement in Northern Ireland

Opportunities, challenges and ironies

Anthony Kelly

Introduction

Northern Ireland (NI) poses an interesting challenge for educational effectiveness research (EER). Its schools 'continue to outperform their counterparts in England and Wales' (DENI, 2007: 7), yet any historical attempt to describe the system as 'effective' would raise a wry smile among those for whom intolerance was not a desired outcome. NI schools are disproportionately ranked among the top performers in UK state examinations and although PISA[1] 2009 showed that in reading, mathematics and science its scores were similar to those of England and Scotland (Bradshaw *et al.*, 2010: xi), this represents a decline for NI. In 2003 only three countries had significantly higher reading scores, its mathematics score was significantly above the OECD average (only six countries did better), and in science just two countries had significantly higher scores (Bradshaw *et al.*, 2007; DENI, 2007: 8). The declining trend has been noted by policy makers and politicians, who have higher aspirations for NI that merely coming top of the 'domestic' league:

> There are two notes of caution which must be sounded when forming assessments of quality [of education in NI]. The first relates to our tendency to compare ourselves with England and Wales, partly because they have similar school systems. Such comparisons certainly show our education system in a generally positive light – but there is an argument that we should be benchmarking ourselves rather more ambitiously and in an international context. It is after all from across the globe that our young people will have to face challenges and compete in tomorrow's economy.
>
> (DENI, 2007: 8)

On the ground things are changing too: for practitioners as a result of the Good Friday (Belfast) Agreement 1998 and the Northern Ireland (St Andrew's Agreement) Act 2006; and more prosaically for effectiveness and improvement researchers since NI no longer publishes pupil attainment data at the school level. When Martin McGuinness as Education Minister announced the abolition of school performance tables in January 2001 – that instead schools would provide

their own information on examination results to parents – he brought NI into line with the Republic of Ireland but broke with long-standing[2] practice in the rest of the UK. The move was welcomed by all the teacher unions and headteacher associations. John Dunford, general secretary of the (then) Secondary Heads Association, acknowledged that the tables had 'tended to polarise selective and non-selective schools' in NI and hoped that their abolition would be 'a forerunner to major changes to league tables on the mainland'.[3]

Historical and political context

The NI state was created in 1921 following the partition of Ireland: 'a Protestant parliament and a Protestant state', according to its then prime minister Lord Craigavon (1934),[4] though more than one-third of its population at the time was Roman Catholic. NI had its own autonomous parliament/government until 1973 when it was abolished because the (then Conservative) government in London did not trust it to act indiscriminately in the interests of all its citizens. Devolved government in the form of the NI Assembly/Executive was re-established in 1998 under the terms of the Good Friday Agreement with the power to legislate in a wide range of areas, including education, not explicitly reserved for the UK parliament in London. Today the Assembly operates on a consociational (power-sharing) principle whereby consensus among the parties is required to confirm majority rule, and ministerial portfolios are allocated to the different political parties using the d'Hondt method.[5] Since then, all education ministers have come from Sinn Fein, which predominantly among the political parties regards education as a critical portfolio.

NI has an unfortunate proclivity for violent conflict (euphemistically known as 'Troubles') between 'nationalists' who are almost exclusively Roman Catholic and 'unionists' who are almost exclusively Protestant. In the tribal nomenclature of the region, ultra-nationalists are 'republicans' and ultra-unionists are 'loyalists'. Traditionally, the middle-class unionist community is represented by the Ulster Unionist Party (UUP); the working-class loyalist community is represented mainly by the Democratic Unionist Party (DUP); middle-class nationalist voters are represented by the Social Democratic and Labour Party (SDLP); and the working-class/small farming republican community is represented overwhelmingly by Sinn Fein (SF).[6] Figure 6.1 shows the changing voting patterns for

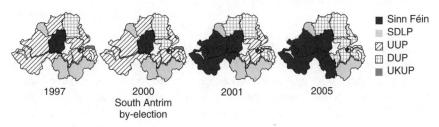

1997   2000   2001   2005
         South Antrim
         by-election

■ Sinn Féin
▨ SDLP
▨ UUP
▦ DUP
■ UKUP

Figure 6.1 Voting patterns in general elections to the UK (London) parliament

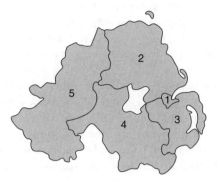

Figure 6.2 The five Education and Library Boards (1. Belfast; 2. North Eastern; 3. South Eastern; 4. Southern; 5. Western)

these political parties since 1997, the year prior to the Good Friday peace accord. It shows how the 'extremes' have over time squeezed the more moderate centre-ground parties so that incongruously the end to armed conflict has meant a more polarised political establishment.[7]

The Northern Ireland Office represents the UK government on reserved matters and also conversely represents NI interests within the UK government. It is led by the Secretary of State, who sits in the UK cabinet. At provincial level, the distribution of the 108 seats in the NI Assembly currently reflects almost precisely the various pro- and anti-union allegiances within the community: 55 are unionists/loyalists; 44 are nationalists/republican; the remaining nine are 'other'.

The education system reflects this political context. Education is the responsibility of the Department of Education Northern Ireland (DENI)[8] and at local level is administered by five Education and Library Boards[9] covering different geographical areas and therefore different political allegiances, as a comparison between Figure 6.1 and Figure 6.2 reveals. All schools follow the Northern Ireland Curriculum, which is based on the National Curriculum of England and Wales. The structure of schooling is similar too, but not identical. Primary education starts at age four and lasts for seven years ('Primary 1' to 'Primary 7'). Pupils then transfer at age 11, under various procedures, to second-level (either 'Grammar' or 'Secondary' school), which lasts for five years initially ('Year 8' to 'Year 12'), at the end of which GCSE examinations are taken.

A system divided by selection

In 'Primary 7' pupils sit various high-stakes entrance examinations, the results of which determine whether they attend one of the (approximately) 70 Grammar schools[10] or one of the (approximately) 170 Secondary schools. Until recently, the transfer test used by all schools was the 'Eleven Plus' (11+), but this was abolished in 2008 (for 2009 entry) amid widespread controversy,[11] with the exception of Craigavon and Armagh where the so-called Dickson Plan is in operation (SELB, 2011).[12] There is little consensus about academic selection in the province, with general agreement that it puts too much pressure on young people and creates a sense of failure among too many (Gardner and Cowan, 2000) balanced by the widespread feeling that there should be selection *at some stage* and that those who do not get into Grammar schools still receive a first-class education (Gallagher and Smith, 2003). Successive ministers, all of whom have been SF, have chosen *not* to turn the system into a Comprehensive one, although that is SF party policy, because the evidence from outside NI suggests (to SF ministers, at least) that it does not facilitate social mobility or redress historical inequalities.

Since the 'open enrolment' reforms of 1989, Grammar schools in NI have been required to fill every place, and that number of places has been increasing. In 2009/10, the sector educated 62,444 pupils or 42 per cent of the total, although only ten per cent of Grammar schools took *all* pupils from the top 30 per cent by prior attainment (Ruane, 2008). The percentage of pupils in selective education in NI is very high compared to England and Wales, which according to support-ers is a factor in the province's success, though PISA 2009 reveals that NI has the largest achievement gap in the UK between those from well-off and those from poor backgrounds (Bradshaw *et al.*, 2010: xi), which as the OECD (2004: 5) notes probably means that 'students from disadvantaged backgrounds do not achieve their full potential'.

Seventeen per cent of school pupils in NI are entitled to free school meals (FSM): 26 per cent in Secondary and six per cent in Grammar schools (DENI, 2011a; b). As in the rest of the UK, FSM entitlement is disproportion-ately concentrated among lower-attaining pupils – the mean score of candidates from schools with high FSM entitlement is significantly lower in NI (Gardner and Cowan, 2000) – but relative to England the percentage of FSM in the selecting sector is high, suggesting some element of advancement on the basis of merit as official school improvement policy recommends and claims (DENI, 2009:iii), though several ethnographic studies in Belfast suggest that local-ity and habitus limit that advancement (Connolly and Healy, 2004; Connolly *et al.*, 2007).

In EER as a discipline, the assumption that schools are autonomous units acting independently of each other (Goldstein and Woodhouse, 2000) privileges school-based characteristics as acceptable indicators of effectiveness, and in NI this is a particularly acute problem as the interaction between schools in the same sector is so strong. For example, Catholic Maintained schools have very close sporting and cultural links with each other – as do 'Protestant' Grammar schools, say – so that a 'sub-systemic' (or 'meta-school') level exists, unrecognised, in the model. Large-scale research (e.g. Gallagher and Smith, 2000) suggests that 'the systemic con-straints on school improvement are less evident in' the selective system, but that selection restricts improvement, especially for schools 'located in urban areas and serving economically disadvantaged communities' (Byrne and Gallagher, 2004:

161). EER has also been poor historically at incorporating system-wide structural inequalities into its models (Gewirtz, 1998; Gibson and Asthana, 1998) and this poses an additional challenge for researchers in NI in relation to compliance with international testing standards and the provision of reliability and validity information (Gardner and Cowan, 2000). A large-scale analysis in 2005 (Gardner and Cowan) using practice scripts found, as earlier research had done (Gardner and Cowan, 2000), that the results of the 11+ had the potential to misclassify up to two-thirds of any cohort by as many as three grades, and that essentially the tests were 'too easy'.[13]

A system divided by religious affiliation

In addition to the division of schools by academic selection, there are divisions in the extent to which they are controlled by the state, which itself was established along ethno-religious lines. State or 'Controlled' schools are in practice attended overwhelmingly by those from the Protestant community; and there is a separate publicly funded 'Maintained' system for Roman Catholics. 'Integrated' schools, which attempt a balanced enrolment of pupils from both traditions, are becoming increasingly popular, notwithstanding the falling demographics, but the sector remains very small. It is a moot point, of course, the extent to which different communities have a right to separate faith-based schools, even ones that are in theory (if not in practice) open to all (Berkeley, 2008: 5): on the one hand they are perceived to perpetuate division and sectarianism (Hayes and McAlister, 2009; Hughes, 2010: 1); on the other it is suggested from research in France (Dronkers, 2004), the US (Coleman and Hoffer, 1987), the Netherlands (Driessen, 1997) and elsewhere that they are more effective than comparable public schools, even for low socio-economic groups (Corten and Dronkers, 2006; Dronkers and Levels, 2007: 436). In any case, early EER studies in NI suggest that the religious affiliation of a school has little or no impact on pupil attainment once pupil intake and 'selective status' has been taken into account (Daly, 1991), which finding undermines the anecdotal narrative that schools in the Protestant sector perform better (e.g. Osborne and Cormack, 1989).

Controlled schools

Controlled schools are under the management of Boards of Governors, though staff are employed by the local Education and Library Board. Although open to those of all faiths and none, most Controlled schools were originally church schools whose control was transferred to the NI state in the first few decades of its existence. Since that state was explicitly Protestant in both outlook and intent, the 'transferors' were naturally the main Protestant churches – Presbyterian, Church of Ireland and Methodist – which still maintain links with their former schools through statutory church representation on their governing bodies.[14] This right of representation for transferors on Controlled schools was recently re-examined under the Review of Public Administration, which proposed its removal on the grounds that it contravened the equality requirements of the Northern Ireland Act 1998, but this reform was never implemented.

Maintained schools

There are more than 500 Catholic-managed schools in NI and they educate approximately 51 per cent of all pupils.[15] Like Controlled schools they are under the management of Boards of Governors, but the employing authority is the Council for Catholic Maintained Schools (CCMS), the largest employer of (8,500) teachers in NI. In EER terms it is another meta level as responsible as schools themselves for effectiveness. CCMS includes DENI representatives, trustee representatives, and parent and teacher representatives. Established under the 1989 Education Reform (NI) Order, its primary aims are to provide an upper tier of management for schools, improve standards and plan effective delivery.

Education through the medium of Irish takes place within this sector. The Education (NI) Order 1998 obliges DENI to support and facilitate its development in the same way as the 1989 Education Reform Order obliged DENI to support Integrated education. Irish-language schools can apply for stand-alone Maintained status or (where a free-standing school is not viable) for support as units within existing schools. Some researchers (e.g. Wright and Scullion, 2007) regard education through the medium of Irish as cross-cultural and as a convenient starting point for EER in the Integrated sector, but given that 'Gaelscoileanna' (as Irish language schools are known) are almost completely supported by parents from the nationalist tradition, they are not 'integrated' in any meaningful sense, though they do represent an accommodation within the NI state of 'the other' tradition and testify to a growing cultural confidence among NI's Roman Catholic population.

Although research on pupil perception in NI by Wright and Scullion (2007) showed a small but significant difference in attitude between Irish-medium and English-medium pupils, with the former having 'highly instrumental views of schooling' (p. 57), assessing the effectiveness of Gaelscoileanna and Catholic Maintained schools generally is challenging since any multi-level model needs to cater for bi-lingual and socio-cultural motivational aspects not found elsewhere in mainstream (UK or other) models, and there are multicollinearity issues regarding language, culture, level of parental education and socio-economic status.

Integrated schools

Although Integrated education is expanding – there are approximately 40 primary and 20 second-level schools in the sector – NI remains a religiously segregated system, with in excess of 90 per cent of pupils attending either a Maintained (Catholic) or a Controlled (Protestant) school *with their co-religionists* (DENI, 2007). Teaching and leading schools in NI has over the years required a secure learning environment and no small degree of subtlety, but various stakeholders and practitioners have risen to the challenge. Fresh-start Integrated schools[16] were established by the voluntary efforts of parents (unsupported by the churches) under the 1989 Education Reform (NI) Order, which obliged DENI to 'facilitate and encourage the development of integrated education where there is parental demand' (HMSO, 1989).[17] In some ways they were a forerunner of 'Charter schools' in the US and 'Free schools' in England, and the absence of politico-religious support in the early days was not necessarily a bad thing as many advocates were anxious not to be identified with any one particular outlook (see Moffatt, 1993). This is not to imply that the only objection to Integrated schooling came from established religious and political interests; there is the view, as there is with Academies and Charter schools, that the continued growth in the sector has 'complex ramifications' (Morgan and Fraser, 1999: 364) for, and negative effects on, other schools in the system. It is claimed that Integrated schools have had a positive impact on community relations, but it is difficult to isolate their effect from that of curriculum initiatives like 'Education for Mutual Understanding' and 'Cultural Heritage' (Harland *et al.*, 2002; NICED, 1988; NICC, 1990; NICC, 1992; Smith and Robinson, 1996; Watling and Arlow, 2002) and EER in other jurisdictions suggests that impact is probably limited anyway by the 'privileged' (Gallagher, 2005: 440) and self-perpetuating nature of difference. Others (e.g. Hughes, 2010) have urged caution in relation to the extent to which education can ever change societies like that in NI, though the importance of *individual teachers* in breaking the cult of acquiescence that makes it difficult to explore (remaining) difference should not be underestimated (Donnelly, 2008).

> The nation-building role of education does raise the question of whether or not the discourse of citizenship speaks equally to all people living within the state. The harsh reality, of course, is that this is not so, especially when . . . education has been used as an instrument for assimilation. Such an approach relies on the assumption that there is a unitary culture or identity within mainstream society. . . . In fact, of course, societies are heterogeneous . . .
>
> (Gallagher, 2005: 430)

A system united by the need for improvement

In January 2008, DENI undertook a comprehensive consultation in relation to school improvement policy. The consultation received responses from more than 200 organisations (DENI, 2010: Annex A) and the resulting policy document, *Every School a Good School: A Policy for School Improvement*, was launched a year later by the Education Minister Caitriona Ruane (DENI, 2009). While acknowledging the excellent provision 'that currently exists' and 'of which we can and should be proud' (p. 1), the Minister set out the vision for the future as one 'that sees schools as vibrant, self-improving communities of good practice' (p. i). The document is unambiguous and ambitious, but the tensions inherent in having powerful and competing interest groups bubble up occasionally; for example, the Minister promises strongly to 'intervene to deal with schools where there is not a clear and enthusiastic focus on improvement' (p. ii), but can only '*recommend strongly*' that schools do not provide a transfer test for Grammar schools or prepare children for such a test (p. iii).

Given the Minister's (republican) background, the issue of selection is never far away, and abolishing it is one of the mainstays of the policy:

> We cannot continue with arrangements for transfer . . . that fail the vast majority of our children and that consign our Secondary sector to carry alone the challenges associated with demographic decline and to deal with the devastating consequences of children being branded as failures at the age of ten or eleven. . . . One of the main aims behind all of these recommendations is to put an end to the distortion of the curriculum in primary schools that has resulted from the practice of academic selection at 11.
>
> (DENI, 2009: ii–iii)

It is not clear from this whether or not the Minister's condemnation of selection *at age 11 specifically* implies support for selection *at a later age*, as with the Dickson system say, but the Minister has confirmed in conversation with the author that this is not the case.

Self-evaluation and *self*-improvement are also central, as is the aspiration that professionals – those 'best placed to identify areas for improvement and to implement change' – will 'use effectively the wide range of data and information available' (p. 1).

Underpinning principles of school improvement in NI

School improvement in NI is based on a belief that equity of access and provision are critical, that all schools are capable of improvement and that schools themselves are best placed to sustain it, that inspection and intervention are necessary evils, and that good communication and co-operation within schools and between schools and communities are essential.

Characteristics of successful schools in NI

Irrespective of sector or religious affiliation, DENI is clear about the characteristics of successful schools and (in the best traditions of school improvement research) lists the salient features. It is very similar to standard school improvement models from around the world and contains no culture- or context-specific (or contentious) elements.

Characteristic 1 – child-centred provision:

- Decisions reflect at all times the needs and aspirations of pupils and there is a commitment to involve them in decision-making.
- There is a clear commitment to promoting equal opportunity for all and a respect for diversity.

- There is a culture of achievement and ambition.
- Effective interventions and support mechanisms are in place.
- There are collaborative arrangements with other schools and providers.

Characteristic 2 – high-quality teaching and learning:

- There is a broad and relevant curriculum with an emphasis on literacy and numeracy.
- Teachers are enthusiastic and use flexible teaching strategies.
- Assessment data informs teaching and learning.
- Rigorous self-evaluation is carried out using objective data.
- Teachers are reflective practitioners.

Characteristic 3 – effective leadership:

- An effective school development plan is in place, providing clear and realistic targets for improvement.
- Teachers are given the opportunity to share in the leadership of the school.
- Resources are managed properly and effectively.
- School leaders regularly monitor and evaluate outcomes, policies and practices.

Characteristic 4 – connectedness to the local community:

- There is a good relationship and clear communications internally, and between the school and external stakeholders.
- The school and its teachers are respected in the community.
- The school meets the needs of the community and other nearby schools.

Performance indicators, attainment targets and actions

Policy documents list the performance indicators and actions in six key improvement areas (DENI, 2009: 17–33, 41), and long-term attainment targets for improving educational outcomes are clearly set out (see Table 6.1):

- Effective leadership and an ethos of aspiration and high achievement – to make school governance a rewarding experience and to make school headship an attractive career.
- High-quality teaching and learning – to ensure that the teaching profession in NI is equipped and empowered to enable high-quality learning.
- Tackling barriers to learning – to ensure that strategies and programmes are in place to support children with special needs and those who face other barriers to learning.
- Embedding a culture of self-evaluation and self-assessment, and of using

Table 6.1 Long-term targets for educational attainment in NI

Level	Actual performance		Milestone targets	Long-term targets
	2005–06	2006–07	2011–12	2020
Key Stage 2 Literacy (% pupils at expected levels)	78.0%	78.0%	80%	85%
Key Stage 2 Maths (% pupils at expected levels)	80.0%	79.5%	82%	86%
Key Stage 3 Literacy (% pupils at expected levels)	76.6%	78.2%	80%	85%
Key Stage 3 Maths (% pupils at expected levels)	72.9%	74.4%	76%	85%
% pupils achieving 5 GCSEs A*–C including English and Maths	52.6%	53%	55%	70%
% FSM pupils achieving 5 GCSEs A*–C including English and Maths	26.4%	27.1%	30%	65%

performance data to effect improvement – to promote self-evaluation and the use of performance data in determining priorities.

- Focusing on support and intervention to help schools improve – to target support, intervention and inspection.
- Increasing engagement between schools, parents, families and local communities – to ensure that pupils are given a voice and that there are strong and effective links between the school and its stakeholders.

The similarities with the rest of the UK – in the lexicon, the phraseology and the aspirations – are striking, as is the importance assigned to economic imperatives (DENI, 2009: 1). However, the extent to which school improvement policy in NI is demanding *of policy makers* is different. There is no sense, as there is in England for example, that the Executive is passing responsibility for education failure onto parents and communities. The progress report on school improvement for 2009/10 revealed several areas of progress, but there were also major logjams in relation to getting primary legislation through the Assembly[18] and these were openly acknowledged (DENI, 2010). In light of recent history, this represents astonishing progress. Politics in NI may still be tribal and combative (as it is more subtly in the rest of the UK and Ireland), but the future looks much brighter today for the large vein of cultural and intellectual talent that exists there among young people.

Challenges and opportunities for EER in NI

Research in NI has found, as elsewhere, that the size of the school effect is of the order of ten per cent of total variance after adjusting for intake, which finding was surprising at the time 'given the selective nature of the school system and the extent of voluntary school provision' in NI (Daly, 1991: 319).[19] Much like PLASC in England and Wales, DENI gathers performance data by gender, year group, religion, ethnicity and special educational needs, and schools are classified according to management type to enable analysis at sectoral level. Yet much as all this sounds identical to findings and processes in the rest of the UK, the province faces peculiar challenges and opportunities in addition to the obvious difficulty of research capacity (Gardner and Gallagher, 2007).

The unusually nested and 'meta' nature of the data

In NI, there are more levels and variables at work nested within the different politico-religious traditions; too many one suspects to enable sensible comparisons to be made with Britain, and limiting the extent of school and sectoral analysis possible within the province. Advocacy groups like CCMS and NICIE act in a way that is *not* equivalent to local authorities in England – or indeed to Education and Library Boards in NI where no significant differences have been found in 11+ attainment (Gardner and Cowan, 2000) – and constitute a meta level in EER modelling that is not yet fully understood or accommodated. Additionally, schools in the same sector have unusually close cultural, sporting and academic links *below* the level of system but *above* the level of the individual school.

Different measures of prior attainment

Although Grammar schools use transfer tests (to replace the old 11+) to assess prior attainment, the sector has now split (along religious lines) into two groupings which set different examinations: the Post-Primary Transfer Consortium[20] and the Association for Quality Education. This will have a bearing on any attempt to measure and compare contextual value added (CVA), a situation further complicated by the UK minister's commitment to abolish CVA and the NI Minister's commitment to retain it!

> The absence of an agreed set of quantitative and contextual value-added measures that would allow more meaningful comparison of performance within, across and between schools is also a weakness in current policy that needs to be addressed. Along with this comes the challenge of explaining to parents, pupils and the wider public the purpose of such measures in a way that brings clarity and makes sure that value-added outcomes cannot be misinterpreted or manipulated inappropriately or distort the work of schools. It is also important to be clear that the development of such measures would not mean a return to published league tables.
>
> (DENI, 2009: 11)

Differentially improving socio-economic status within the nested politico-cultural data

Any sector analysis using NI census data is unlike the rest of the UK in that it is very closely related to political and cultural allegiance, and in one sector at least (the Catholic Maintained sector) is differentially improving in socio-economic and cultural terms since the Good Friday Agreement. The effect of this on pupil attainment, whether compounding or attenuating, is unknown. Research in NI also suggests a complicating differential effect in terms of teacher qualifications between sectors with unqualified teachers less likely to be found in Grammar schools (Eaton *et al.*, 2006).

The organisation of the school year and the urban–rural divide

The length and organisation of the school year, which in many ways is a proxy for the province's rural bias, differentiates NI somewhat from Britain, as does the relatively high number of pupils in boarding schools and the high percentage of pupils in selective schools. In 2009/10, Secondary schools educated 18,435 rural pupils and 66,880 from urban backgrounds. Grammar schools educated 3,535 rural and 58,090 urban pupils (DENI, 2011a, b). Reference to Figure 6.1 suggests a socio-cultural and political significance to this data since areas in the west of the province are 'green' in every sense, being both *rural* and *republican*.

The border

Unionists (in exasperation) and nationalists (in aspiration) agree that the border between NI and the Republic of Ireland is porous: it follows few geographical features, divides farms and villages in a nonsensical way, and is ignored by everyone who lives close to it. Although the education systems are very different in the two jurisdictions, a significant number of pupils from both communities in NI choose to be educated in the Republic of Ireland: nationalists locally in their traditional hinterland; unionists, following family tradition[21] or as a means of getting away from conflict, in Protestant boarding schools in Dublin and elsewhere. It introduces an 'out-of-system' factor to any attempted model. Interestingly, NI school improvement policy now makes reference to crossing the border – something that would never have been mentioned 20 years ago – 'to tackle educational underachievement, an area of co-operation and concern across this island' (DENI, 2009: ii).

The absence of ethnicity; the presence of religiosity

Ethnicity is not a sensible variable in any EER or CVA model in NI since 99.15 per cent of the population is white and Christian (McWhirter, 2002; NISRA, 2001), which is not to say that racism is unknown, especially in relation to Irish travellers[22] (Connolly and Keenan, 2000), or that anti-racist strategies are irrelevant (Connolly and Keenan, 2002). It would be interesting to substitute 'Christian denomination' for 'ethnicity' in the standard multi-level model to see which theological interpretation had spawned the higher attainment, but such a move would be unlikely to receive official sanction.[23]

Socio-cultural and linguistic factors

Irish-language schools are supported solely by parents from the nationalist tradition so they are not 'integrated' in the official sense, but the schools do represent an integration of sorts; namely, the accommodation of the national- ist cultural identity within the unionist state. They also testify to a growing prosperity among NI's Catholic population, which in theory at least may be linked to improved educational outcomes. Therefore, assessing the effectiveness of Gaelscoileanna (and Catholic schools generally) over time is challenging and any multi-level model would need to cater for socio-linguistic and socio-cul- tural motivational factors (Wright and McGrory, 2005) not included in existing models. Of course, the difficulty of researching effectiveness across cultures and in relation to *affective* variables generally is well known in EER (see Reynolds and Teddlie, 2000) and is not unique to NI, but it usually refers to problems *between national contexts* rather than *between indigenous factions within the same system* as is the case in NI.

School size and effectiveness across type

School size is generally thought to be irrelevant in EER, but research by Barnett *et al.* (2002) suggests that in NI larger post-primary schools tend to outperform smaller ones in both effectiveness (of outputs) and efficiency (of input and cost) across a range of educational outcomes, when schools are grouped according by type, gender and the absence/presence of a sixth form, so that unlike the rest of the UK, it may be unsound to assess the performance of schools in NI without taking account of size.

Competition and competition spaces

NI provides an opportunity to examine competition and cooperation in a quasi- open system – i.e. a system in theory open to all, but in practice closed to those from 'the other' tradition – and to investigate whether or not one sector's gains are mirrored by another sector's loses. More than 20 years ago, Daly (1991) sug- gested that the grammar school effect may be a contextual one, with 'zero sum implications' (p. 320) within a wider debate about the goals of education in a democracy. However, the presence now of a significant Integrated school sector adds a complexity to the analysis that did not exist substantially at the time, and the importance of education to improving community relations, and the over- powering necessity of getting that right, means that partnerships and joint activi- ties between schools, within and across sectors, make the isolation of the school effect more difficult in NI. For this reason, findings from previous research need to be considered carefully in terms of evidencing change over time. And within the Integrated sector there are important differences between schools that are fresh-start and those that have transferred from the Controlled sector, so NI pro- vides an opportunity for EER, as it shifts its attention to more affective factors, as it must, to examine the impact (if any) of initiatives like Integration on social cohesion and non-cognitive outcomes generally.

Some contextual ironies

While there is a discernable political spectrum from Right to Left in NI and communities are still polarised along traditional lines, the fall-out from recent political developments has thrown up interesting juxtapositions in relation to education and schooling.

Traditional middle-class aspiration in the unionist camp is represented by the UUP, and being the party of government for the first 75 years of the state's existence, the education system was structured to advantage its constituency. The UUP remains in favour of Grammar schools and selection at age 11 (UUP, 2010). The Protestant working class was education fodder in this middle-class system, condemned to take advantage (so to speak) of blue-collar jobs reserved for them in the shipyards. On the Twelfth of July, in celebration of King William's defeat of King James in 1690, they were feted as part of the ascendancy, but the next day sent to work the docks for a fraction of what the equivalent jobs were being paid in Liverpool and Glasgow. The Controlled Secondary sector was their lot, providing an education just basic enough to keep the recipients compliant. They have no love today for 'selection' or for the 11+, and feel no sentimental attachment (other than self-loathing) for Grammar schools, yet for many years this community has been represented by the DUP, which seeks 'to preserve and promote Grammar schools' believing that 'the ending of academic selection in Great Britain has coincided with a marked fall in intergenerational mobility' (DUP, 2011).

On the other side of the political divide, working-class nationalists were denied access to the better-paid industrial jobs so they had little incentive to migrate from rural areas to the larger conurbations. Along with those from deprived Catholic areas in Belfast and (London) Derry, they constitute the republican heartland, generally supportive of militancy and represented by Sinn Fein. The Controlled sector was never an option for them. The few who were academically able *and* were supported in their endeavours by parents who themselves had not gone to post-primary school, progressed through the Maintained Grammar system . . . and out of NI. The remainder left school as soon as they could to obtain underpaid employment in the locality or elsewhere. Sinn Fein, which overwhelmingly represents this constituency, opposes the Grammar school system in favour of 'all-ability 11–18 comprehensive schools' to 'redress generational disadvantage' (Sinn Fein, 2011), though significant effects in relation to socio-economic status in NI (treated as a school contextual variable) are thought to be 'more likely to emerge' in such a system (Daly, 1991: 320).

Middle-class nationalist families, the aspirational element within the Catholic community, used and profited from the Maintained Grammar school system, not always to stay in NI but nearly always to progress to and through the professions. Insofar as anyone can profit from a system that is inherently discriminatory against one, the nationalist middle classes did well from their engagement with selection and the Grammar schools, though they are represented by the SDLP which supports the decision to abolish the 11+ (SDLP, 2011a) and like SF favours an end to academic selection (SDLP, 2011b).[24]

The irony then is that the views of middle-class *nationalist* families regarding schooling and selection are now more accurately represented *by the UUP* than by their own political parties, while the views of working-class *loyalists* are represented *by Sinn Fein*! In the absence of class politics in NI and notwithstanding the view of Walsh (2006) and others that EER and the growth of prescription themselves generate inequality, these juxtapositions may do more to bring the communities together than the political polarisation represented on Figure 6.1 would suggest. The political spectrum in NI might be linear, but the education spectrum is becoming decidedly two-dimensional!

Acknowledgement

Thanks to colleagues Alison Williamson and Anna Lyon for their help in preparing this manuscript.

Notes

1 The Programme for International Student Assessment (PISA) is a survey of the educational achievement of 15-year-olds organised by the Organisation for Economic Cooperation and Development (OECD). The 2009 results were published in 2010.
2 England and Wales have been publishing annual league tables since 1993.
3 Ironically the phrase 'on the mainland' is guaranteed to produce near hysteria among those (like the Minister) not of the unionist persuasion, although no such offence was intended by Dunford.
4 The commonly cited phrase 'a Protestant parliament for a Protestant people' is a misquotation, though it expresses the same sentiment.
5 As they are in the London Assembly and in the European Parliament.
6 The DUP is aligned with right-wing groups in Scotland and elsewhere; the UUP is allied to the UK Conservative Party; the SDLP has fraternal links with the UK Labour Party; SF has links with left-wing interests in the UK and elsewhere.
7 In the 2010 general election, the UUP lost its one and only seat at Westminster when Lady Sylvia Harmon was returned as an Independent.
8 Except for Higher and Further education, which is the responsibility of the Department for Employment and Learning.
9 The proposed Education and Skills Authority (ESA, 2011) replacing the Boards has not yet come into being.
10 NI with its 70 Grammar schools contains only 3 per cent of the UK population. There are approximately 160 Grammar schools in England, which has 84 per cent of the UK population.
11 A provision in the Education Order (NI) 1997 allowed DENI and the Minister to 'issue and revise guidance' for the 'admission of pupils to grant-aided schools', so to avoid the need for her proposals to be passed by the Assembly where lack of cross-party support would have meant it failed, the Minister (Ruane) passed the new guidelines as regulation rather than as legislation.
12 The Dickson Plan is a two-tier transfer system in which pupils can sit transfer tests at age 11 or 14. This is interesting from a school effectiveness viewpoint, even if it is unwitting, since research by Marks (2006) using PISA 2000 data suggests that the

younger students are when selection takes place, the stronger is the effect of parental background. Other research (e.g. Alexander *et al.*, 1998) indicates that the Dickson system is popular, though comparing pupil attainment under Dickson with attainment in the rest of NI is difficult because there is so much pupil movement.

13 In fact, children with 70 per cent correct answers could be awarded the bottom grade (Gardner and Cowan, 2005)!

14 Schedule 4 and Schedule 5 of the Education and Library Board (Northern Ireland) Order 1986.

15 Pupils do not have to be Roman Catholic to attend.

16 Sometimes called 'grant maintained integrated schools'.

17 Other Integrated schools, which were originally Controlled (and therefore Protestant) but which opted through parental ballot to switch to the Integrated sector, have since come on steam. These are sometimes called 'transformed' Integrated schools in the literature.

18 For example, in setting up the Education and Skills Authority.

19 Daly also found that the impact of family background was smaller than expected, but generally in line with comparable findings from England and Scotland, after allowance had been made for prior attainment.

20 Representing mostly Roman Catholic Grammar schools.

21 Many 'southern' Protestants re-settled in NI after partition in 1921, but retain strong links with schools there.

22 Defined by the Race Relations (NI) Order 1997 as a community 'who are identified (both by themselves and by others) as people with a shared history, culture and traditions including, historically, a nomadic way of life on the island of Ireland'.

23 Previous research suggests that there is no mean difference in performance at sector level (Gardner and Cowan, 2000).

24 The Northern Ireland Commission for Catholic Education (NICCE) accepts selection only as a temporary measure. According to (RC) Bishop Donal McKeown, chair of NICCE, 'academic selection at age eleven has no place in a modern education system' and parents have nothing to fear from its abolition as 'the new arrangements will not damage excellence in any of our schools' (NICEE, 2009). However, not everyone in the Catholic sector agrees, as the loud protests from Catholic Grammar schools demonstrate (BBC, 2008).

7 School effectiveness in Scotland

Challenging the orthodoxy

John MacBeath

Introduction

There is a Scots saying 'Whau'rs like us?' It is, in fact, a rhetorical question not a desire for some comparative indices of effectiveness. It is founded in 'myth' (in the Platonic sense of that word) that Scottish education is the envy of the world. Scotland has long nurtured the boast that 'the lad o' pairts' (no mention of the lassies) can achieve just as highly as his more privileged counterpart.

It may, therefore, be little comfort to discover that scientists have discovered another Scotland. In November 1998 the *Daily Record* ('Scotland's national newspaper') reported that 'US experts were stunned when their latest multi-million-pound cameras unearthed a "Scotland" – 7000 light years away'. The article concluded 'Scots have always known their country is out of this world – and now scientists have proved it'.

Scotland is, however, in some ways unique and does differ significantly in some crucial respects from its southernmost neighbour. The following are key and influential differences:

- 97 per cent of children in Scotland go to state schools.
- All state schools are comprehensive and have been since 1970.
- Scottish state schools do not have governors but some have advisory bodies called School Councils.
- There is no Ofsted. HMI continue in their traditional role although the form of inspection is changing.
- There is no National Curriculum, no Key Stages and no SATs.
- In the last two elections there were either no Conservative MPs or less than three.
- The employers are local authorities (LAs) not schools.

The mediating role played by local authorities, in all cases either Labour or SNP controlled, is a critical aspect of the Scottish scene. As the employers, around half of all decision making rests with local authorities compared with around 5 per cent in England. A new partnership between the Scottish Government and local government was set out in the Concordat agreed in November 2007. Single Outcome

Agreements set out goals and targets aimed at creating a fairer Scotland, developed between the Scottish Government and each local authority or Community Planning Partnership. This is the much-vaunted 'vertical relationship', which is, in theory, a partnership of schools, LAs and government working together.

However, in practice, in many cases LAs present an obstacle to initiative, decision making and flexibility at school level. These issues came to the fore in the recent study of recruitment and retention of head teachers (MacBeath *et al.*, 2009), in which successful schools found themselves as 'dumping grounds' for ineffective teachers who continue to be shuffled around the system.

The strength of Scottish unions is an important ingredient in the mix as sacking any teacher is generally a fraught and contested process. The Education Institute of Scotland (the EIS), the oldest teaching union in the world, is described by Forrester (2008: 3)) as the 'default organisation', speaking as it does for the vast majority of Scottish teachers. It describes itself 'as one of the most respected voices in education in Scotland', integrally involved in policy development for all stages of education from nursery, through to further and higher education. Its politicised stance brings it into constant tension with the GTC (the General Teaching Council) whose official role is 'advocacy and regulation of the teaching profession in Scotland'. Unlike its counterpart in England, which enjoyed a brief life, the GTC, now half a century old, sees itself as the guardian of professional standards in schools and colleges.

Both the GTC and EIS welcomed the introduction of chartered teachers. Following the McCrone agreement in 2001, this initiative was designed to provide teachers with an alternative career path, keeping them in the classroom as 'leaders of learning' rather than ascending through the management hierarchy. Critiques of the programme (Reeves, 2007; Connelly and McMahon, 2007), however, suggest that it has often had a divisive influence and that rather than keeping teachers in the classroom the professional development involved can actually change their career aspirations.

Flexible Routes to Headship

The introduction of Flexible Routes to Headship (FRH) in 2008 provided an alternative pathway to headship through the highly demanding and time intensive SQH (Scottish Qualification for Headship). By late 2006, the possibility of an alternative had crystallised around the idea that aspiring head teachers would benefit from more focused support provided by a dedicated coach. Thus, 'an individual aspiring head teacher would benefit from an opportunity to reflect on their own practice, to share their self-evaluation to engage in quality dialogue with an individual whose clear purpose was to support, but to support and challenge' (Davidson *et al.*, 2008: 8). The programme (in common with the SQH) is managed through universities in collaboration with local authorities and the Scottish Executive. This was a deliberate decision by the Scottish Government not to go down the National College route as in England, retaining the arms-length relationship of the universities with national policy.

While the Scottish National Party, the party with the largest number of seats, is keen to preserve Scotland's uniqueness, the character of the system is not impervious to global pressures. In their treatise on education and nationalism under the SNP, Arnott and Ozga (2009) describe the policy discourse as 'combining "inward" references to fairness and equality with global economic policy in a distinctive way'.

> Outward comparison and referencing has also been used to align Scotland with comparators in education beyond the UK. Discursive strategies are highly important as a way of governing within the constraints and complexities of global and UK pressure.
>
> (Arnott and Ozga, 2009: 2)

As Keating (2005) has argued, the extent to which the Scottish Government could pursue its own distinctive policies is questionable. Comparative measures provided by PISA, TIMMS, TALIS and other transnational data weigh heavily with policy makers and politicians. These data rely to a large extent on school effectiveness assumptions and measures of student attainment, and while PISA has tried to include other more creative measures these do not merit the headlines and tend to be bypassed by newspaper editors and are a cause of concern for politicians, academics and school leaders alike.

The effectiveness tradition in Scotland

Policy makers in Scotland were quick to embrace the effectiveness movement and they have maintained a constant presence at ICSEI at which there is an annual revisiting of the movement's essential tenets. Throughout the 1970s and 1980s the Scottish Office kept a close watching brief on seminal school effects research being undertaken by the Centre for Educational Sociology (CES) at Edinburgh University (Gray *et al.*, 1983). While highly influential in laying the groundwork for future effectiveness studies, researchers were careful to signal that performance data should be used judiciously. One of the key findings was that if you were a pupil of average ability you would be more likely to succeed in a school where your peers were of high ability than in schools in which many students were of low ability. CES researchers also found that parental choice on the basis of exam results would often lead to the wrong choice. The poignant testimony from school leavers in Gow and Macpherson's *Tell Them from Me* (1980) illustrated the imperative of taking account of young people's perceptions of their schools and argued for ethnographic approaches to be married with quantitative measures. In similar vein Riddell and Brown, in their 1991 publication *School Effectiveness Research: Its Messages for School Improvement,* add important caveats. They underline the dangers of reducing school experience to quantitative measures and making 'invidious comparison' on that basis.

The Riddell and Brown volume commissioned by the Scottish Office followed two prior Scottish Office publications *Effective Secondary Schools* (1988) and

Effective Primary Schools (1989) which put into the hands of head teachers and teachers the rationale and criteria by which schools were judged as more or less effective. Reviewing the field in 1994, John Tibbitt, Senior Researcher Officer in the Scottish Office, set out the parameters for a major Scottish study, whose three key foci – Development Planning, Ethos and Learning, and Teaching – would bring effectiveness closer to current policy priorities. The inclusion of 'ethos' is explained by the publication in the early 1990s of 'ethos indicators', derived from perceptions and expectations of parents, pupils and teachers as to what made a good school. *How Good is Our School?*, a self-evaluation framework followed, and since then has been revised many times, imitated by other countries and translated into other languages (e.g. *Wie gut ist unsere Schule?*).

Improving school effectiveness

Awarded the contract in 1997, teams from the University of Strathclyde and the Institute of Education in London gathered data from a representative sample of 80 Scottish primary and secondary schools, 24 of which were designated case study schools, and each of those schools allocated a researcher and critical friend.

While the research employed a fairly orthodox effectiveness methodology, collecting value-added achievement and attitudinal data together with individual and focus group interviews, the critical friend was a less traditional element. On an ongoing basis he or she fed back data to school staff to help them address key issues – in learning and teaching, the ethos, which enhances teaching and learning, and the form of transformational planning, which arises from new ways of seeing. A change profile instrument and a behavioural event interview were used to take staff through key events, a dialogic process in which the challenges of change were explored and documented. Feedback sessions, with small groups and sometimes a whole staff, problematised the data, its very ambiguity providing the space for differing interpretations and understandings. As David Bridge writes:

> 'Understanding' needs always to be replaced by 'understandings'. Members of the same community will, notwithstanding this identity, have different understandings of the community's experience. Not only that, but any one individual will, at different times and places and for different purposes, construct different understandings of the same experience or social situation. Any attempt to understand the other, therefore, has to be interpreted in terms of a collection of understandings engaging with another collection of understandings – and this is an encounter in which the differences between insider and outsider understandings become very blurred.
>
> (Bridges, 2007: 1)

Bridges argues that understanding is richer and fuller by virtue of the extent to which internal stakeholders engage with an outsider's view, enriching both insider and outsider perspectives. In the language of interpretive research it is the *verstehen* that comes through the attempt to understand the life of schools and classrooms from the inside, with a focus on the lived experience of people, place and activity.

In this sense the ISEP study went beyond the conventions of effectiveness to follow where the dialogue led and began to open up questions as to the limitations of school effectiveness orthodoxy and its continuing relevance for the future.

> In short, schools and other formal organisations for learning will just be seen as one element of learning in the future (Watkins and Mortimore, 1999). The implications of this for future research are that studies comparing schools in their effectiveness or improvement will need to take much greater account of the multiplicity of learning experiences which children and young people have outside schools. We will have to take greater account of contexts, opportunities, and constraints on learners. More fundamentally, if schools are only one element of a learner's potential learning encounters, detailed longitudinal case studies of learners, rather than schools, are likely to be more helpful in understanding what combinations of experiences best promote the learning of different people.
>
> (Stoll *et al.*, 2001: 195)

This presents a challenge to the ever increasing attempts to quantify aspects of school effects in which we reach the *ad absurdam* position of John Hattie's 2007 meta study which was able to identify effects sizes of classroom environment (0.56), parent involvement (0.46), homework (0.43), teacher style (0.42), affective attributes of students (0.24) among many other such correlations.

Data such as these may make sense to researchers working within the effectiveness tradition, but they are baffling and impossible to make sense of in the real world of classrooms, schools and communities. No one could dispute the importance of classroom environment but it covers a range from sitting under a tree (as in many African countries) to a resource-rich space with individual computers, hand-held devices, internet access, interactive whiteboards and music keyboards for example. 'Affective attributes of students' may be higher in the class under a tree and 'teacher style' ranging from story-telling to peripatetic facilitator is clearly driven to a large extent by context, culture and resource (the internal resource of children themselves as well as the material world of learning that surrounds them).

How to capture 'parental involvement'? It may refer to a parent, or parents', communication with the school, supportive or confrontative, proactive or reactive, through letters, phone calls, parents' meetings, workshops, membership of the PTA, individual visits, lobbying or fund raising. Or it may refer to a very much bigger concept – the process through which a parent, parents or extended family engage with their children's learning – a process largely invisible to, and inaccessible by, researchers but immensely complex and powerful in determining the social capital which children bring, or fail to bring, with them into the classroom.

The depth and complexity of parental influence was illustrated in a Scottish study published as *Home from School* (MacBeath *et al.*, 1986), in which researchers spent anything from an hour to three and half hours in conversation with a parent or parents in their home surroundings. The meeting ground of the living room or kitchen, with children coming in or out, the tenor of the adult–child exchange, encouragement and reprimand, lent another layer or texture to the interview. Following on from a previous Scottish study of homework (*Learning out of School*, 1991) it revealed the extent to which 'home work' could not be isolated from the encouragement, reward or direct tuition offered by parents, in some cases both parents themselves school teachers. Nor could the quantitative data easily capture the influence of older brothers and sisters who coached their younger siblings, directly teaching them or initiating them into the dark arts of tactical achievement.

The attempt to isolate and quantify school effects is further bewildered by the pervasive and growing use of private tuition, highly variable in quality and impact but largely the preserve of middle-class and/or ambitious parents. Crediting the school with value-added was problematised by Strathclyde's Director of Education a decade or so ago when he visited the Region's highest achieving school and asked children to raise their hand if they had a private tutor. More than 90 per cent confessed to that source of added value.

That children from the most privileged background benefit most from private tutoring is exemplified in a business that appears to be expanding at an exponential rate. Kumon Centres are one example. Their website (http://www.kumon. co.uk/private-tutors/find-your-local-centre/scotland.htm) contains the truism 'Behind every successful child is a parent', together with personal testimony from children as to the benefits of Kumon. A mapping of Kumon centres conveys a graphic picture of provision. In Glasgow, for example, Kumon centres are located in the seven league table-topping post code areas.

The nesting of children's learning

In her prize-winning book *The Nurture Assumption*, Judith Harris (1998) took to task conventional assumptions about the nurture effect of parents and teachers. That the peer effect, particularly in adolescence, weighed much more heavily in shaping attitudes and achievement was not entirely news to school effectiveness researchers who have identified what is termed the compositional, or contextual, effect (Gray *et al.*, 1983; Mortimore, 1998). Thrupp (1999), however, contends that 'the social mix' is too slippery to be so easily quantified or treated as a troublesome variable. It constitutes a critical mass of motivation or disinclination, engagement or disengagement, a precarious balance, and tipping point into either order or anarchy. Four decades of school effectiveness simply confirm what most parents already know – that who your children go to school *with* is the strongest determining factor of achievement and attitudes.

The weaker the social and intellectual capital in the family the stronger the influence of peers which, as Harris shows, tends to the lowest common denominator – particularly in areas of deprivation. Added into this mix is the 'neighbourhood effect' (Wacquant, 2001). He found that different neighbourhoods establish different norms, which are observed by insiders and present hazards for the outsiders. While Wacquant's push and pull factors derive from studies in Paris banlieus, the same factors are found in 'schools on the edge' (MacBeath *et al.*, 2007), in Scottish cities, towns and rural neighbourhoods. These were graphically described by head teachers in a recent study for the Scottish Government (MacBeath *et al.*, 2009). One head in an outside-Glasgow estate characterised many of the children in that area as 'crawling out of hell to come to school', children so highly disturbed ('affective attributes'?) that they could not engage with what their teachers took as their impatient priorities. In Wacquant's litany the interlocking force field includes one or all of the following:

- economic and social disenfranchisement;
- insularity and disillusionment;
- transience and instability;
- erosion of work-based identity;
- racism, violence and intimidation;
- media images, rumour and disinformation;
- lack of mobility and navigational know-how.

These are not separate sources of influence on children's well-being or learning dispositions, nor should they be treated as variables, which can be accounted for in an effort to determine the black box effect. They are dynamically inter-related. As David Berliner argues, we need to understand with greater clarity the 'nesting' of children's lives and learning and tell the story with richer texture.

> Children and young people live nested lives, so that when classrooms do not function as we want them to, we go to work on improving them. Those classrooms are in schools, so when we decide that those schools are not performing appropriately, we go to work on improving them, as well. But those young people are also situated in families, in neighbourhoods, in peer groups who shape attitudes and aspirations often more powerfully than their parents or teachers.
>
> (Berliner, 2005: 3)

Navigational know how, claims Tom Wylie, former Director of the Youth Agency, is the differentiating factor between children who fail and those who succeed. In school it is often a tactical and strategic process to succeed with minimal emotional investment, for many children a legacy from backgrounds in which the cultures of home and school coincide. In disadvantaged neighbourhoods lack of navigational know how of parents can have disastrous consequences for their children. The inability of parents to deal with institutional authority whether in respect of schools, hospitals, police or welfare services can often compound the impact of disadvantage for their children.

Effective for whom and effective for what?

This is the question posed by Bogotch *et al.* (2007: 93) in their critique of an effectiveness movement which, they say, has claimed 'legitimacy by attribution' but has been unable to provide insights into the deep structure of the school experience for children. How can it account for, or take account of, the disturbing 2007 UNICEF finding that the UK ranks in last place among 21 countries on three of six key dimensions – subjective well-being, behaviour and risks, family and peer relationships? As the introduction to the UNICEF report contends:

> The true measure of a nation's standing is how well it attends to its children – their health and safety, their material security, their education and socialization, and their sense of being loved, valued, and included in the families and societies into which they are born.
>
> (UNICEF, 2007: 3)

In Scottish urban and rural communities the impact on children's ability to cope with school relies on the ability to address a basic hierarchy of needs – health, safety and well-being. Scottish Government's data reveals that 17 per cent of Scotland's population – 210,000 children and 440,000 working-age adults are below the poverty line – requiring interventions which tackle causes of underachievement lying outside schools, accounting in large part for the disaffection of young people and the lack of adequate support ('parental involvement'?) they receive from their families.

The *Fairer Scotland Fund* worth £435 million over three years promises investment in alleviating poverty with targeting of families in the three lowest income deciles with an average weekly income of around £220 (as compared with those in the highest three deciles receiving around £630 per week). This group includes highly vulnerable unemployed lone mother households with dependent children. Workshops for parents, offered by a number organisations and local authorities, aim at helping parents to help themselves and their children through a range of programmes focused on literacy, behaviour management, child care and employability. Adding 'value' in the arena before and beyond the school.

A Place for Success

In recognition of the widening achievement gap a number of parallel out-of-hours learning (OHSL) initiatives have been created to cater for the most disadvantaged of children and most marginalised of neighbourhoods. In the early 1990s Strathclyde Region invested substantially in supported study, with grants to schools to provide after-hours access and tuition for children on a voluntary basis. The greatest bonus was for teachers, who saw learning and children's lives in a new light. The evidence from the two Strathclyde University evaluations (*Learning for Yourself,* 1992 and *A Place for Success,* 1994) was clear – supported study added value to the attainment scores of children who attended in comparison with the control group of non-attenders. These data have not, however, been factored into school or teacher effectiveness studies. Ironically it was, in some cases, the weakest teachers who benefited from the improved outcomes of their class, achieved despite, (rather than because of) their teachers.

An extension of study support is *Playing for Success* (PfS), a nationwide initiative to exploit places for out-of-hours-learning which would prove more attractive to children than a school environment. The starting point was with football clubs, places where children could meet players, lure their fathers with promises of free tickets, with most of the major, and some of the minor, clubs in Scotland involved. Much of the success of the PfS is explained by conditions for learning, an ethos that could hardly be more different from school.

An allied initiative bound to confound conventional measures of effectiveness is The Children's University, also targeting children from more disadvantaged backgrounds. With over 70 centres in the UK, the 2010 evaluation (MacBeath) showed significant gains for children who participated in C.U. activities as against the non-participant control group. Aberdeen Children's University runs in local primary schools and in one secondary school and exploits learning destinations such as the Satrosphere, the Natural History Centre and Aberdeen University. As learning destinations expand to airports, stations, docks, at galleries and museums, children are furnished with a learning passport stamped only on completion of validated activities in hallmarked learning destinations.

In Glasgow, Kelvingrove Museum and Art Gallery has built a dedicated space, The Centre for New Enlightenment (TCONE), which children visit initially as a school class or on a return visit with their parents or friends. The Centre grew out of the Hunter Foundation's ambition for children and young to 'find the hero inside themselves', to believe that they were not victims of circumstance but architects of their own futures. It was recognised that Scotland's achievements were owed to the much vaunted 'canny' Scot but that the 'cannae' (can't) Scot was a much more familiar figure to teachers in Scottish schools. In interviews leading to the design of TCONE it was reported that young people found it much easier to talk about failure than success. Failure in exams was the most frequent theme, with unemployment, addiction and dependency recurring as salient aspects of thediscourse. Inevitability and fatalism were prevalent themes in these conversations.

These findings gave impetus to confronting the 'cannae' and bringing out the buried sense of agency, which lies at the centre of the TCONE's purpose. Problem-solving activities around the various exhibits involve children working in pairs with a hand-held PDA immersing them in a learning experience so engaging and so different from school that in the evaluation of TCONE children wrote fulsomely about the new lease of life it had given them as to their capacity as learners. The navigation with the hand-held PDA was integral to the experience – no paper and pencil, no adult direction or supervision, but a demonstration of trust – that you are capable of learning on your own, capable of helping your partner, capable of looking after expensive technology and behaving considerately in a public space.

Twenty years ago, before the invention of the virtual world, the 'real world' beyond the school offered an alternative arena for lifelong learning. Parkway in Philadephia was an iconic demonstration of a powerful alternative to desk-bound learning. Parkway, the central artery that runs through the heart of the city, offered the learning space for a whole curriculum centred on the agencies that compose the life of a city. This not only saved millions on school buildings, textbooks, administration and all the paraphernalia that consumes the lion's share of the education budget, but also showed that young people have a much greater capacity for initiative and agency than schools give them credit for. The Parkway model inspired an initiative in the 1970s in two Renfrewshire second-ary schools. Two classes of young people enjoyed the experience of learning in the city for the whole of the third term of their third secondary school year, never touching down at school but trusted to make journeys on their own across the city to their chosen learning destinations. These were young people from the bottom stream, the most expendable, ones whom teachers admitted they had simply failed to reach.

Every student had an individualised highly varied five-day timetable which met his or her expressed interest in places they saw as learning destinations. What was both surprising and highly gratifying was the willingness of the Royal Navy, Glasgow University Observatory, the AA, the ambulance service, The Scottish National Orchestra, St Andrew's Ambulance service, the Chrysler factory, Cal-derpark Zoo, Glasgow Museum, hospitals, car workshops and car markets, manu-facturers, shops and farms, not only to take on young people but to help build a coherent educational programme to broaden their horizons. Seminars were arranged with tutors and small student groups in parks and cafes to debrief and share experiences, probing their learning and relating it to a broader educational agenda.

While much of the content learned did not fit easily within a school curricular framework, many of the insights and skills gained exceeded what might have been gained by a third term spent in the classroom. The greatest impact was, however, the enhanced self-esteem of these young people, their new found sense of agency and their re-engagement with learning.

These experiments in alternative 'construction sites' (Weiss and Fine, 2000) remind us again of the power of different kinds of behaviour settings and alterna-tive models of peer and adult-child relationships. Weiss and Fine's collection of essays chronicles how young people construct meaning from their experience in differing situations and through the interplay of the various sites in which they struggle to find meaning and coherence. The more we venture into this territory the more complex and contested becomes our knowledge of children's learning, its social and emotional character and the precarious path that young people have to tread to make sense of what schools promise them. How to help children and young people bridge their learning across these disparate construction sites con-tinues to elude effectiveness research.

Nearly a century ago the visionary educator, Henry Morris, had a vision of the village college, one that would 'provide for the whole man, and abolish the duality of education and ordinary life'.

> It would not only be the training ground for the art of living, but the place in which life is lived, the environment of a genuine corporate life. The dismal dispute of vocational and non-vocational education would not arise in it. It would be a visible demonstration in stone of the continuity and never ceasingness of education. There would be no 'leaving school'! – the child would enter at three and leave the college only in extreme old age.
>
> (Morris, 1925, Section IV)

A question of purpose

The Henry Morris idyll returns us to the question of purpose. What purposes do schools serve in this brave new world? What purposes are served by comparing schools' effectiveness? What are the purposes in continuing to differentiate internal effects within the black box? How will we address the current malaise in schools by replicating effects studies in the hunt for the unicorn?

These are not intended as rhetorical questions. Rather they suggest an agenda for dialogue as to the potential gains and possible drawbacks of comparative and quantitative data. Peter Mortimore, who might be described as the father of school effectiveness in the UK, questions the purposes and use to which much current data collection is put. In relation to PISA, he argues for shifting the aims of PISA from a snapshot of national achievements to more nuanced interpretations of countries' strengths and weaknesses in their development of lifelong learning; for a refocusing on how schools and school systems may promote achievement; for disposing of league tables which both oversimplify and mislead, with a plea for more contextually sensitive longitudinal studies and the involvement of teachers in the framing and conduct of what is measured (Personal interview, November 2009).

Andreas Schleicher, Director of PISA, agrees that the problem in comparative studies is the sacrifice of validity gains for efficiency gains. He calls for broader spectrum studies, which are more 'dialogue orientated'.

> We try and do things cheaply, on a mass scale and, therefore, we lose relevance. There is also another dilemma. We know that when you do evaluation to make a trade-off between objectivity and relevance. When I want to do something, to get the same results; I choose a very simple question, a multichoice question, and I can test you twenty times and get the same answers. When I have a more dialogue-orientated question, when I ask students to actually create an answer, or draw conclusions, or explain something, it's less objective but probably more relevant. This is a broad spectrum.
>
> (Personal interview, September 2009)

Hedley Beare (2007: 27) with four decades' involvement in school effectiveness and improvement (SESI) argues the need for 'a giant step' away from current approaches. The incremental development of effectiveness over four decades has surely reached saturation point and hopefully through challenges to orthodoxy, we can begin to chart the path to some radical reframing of purpose and protocols which bridge construction sites and help the research field to provide richer thicker description.

8 School effectiveness in *The Learning Country*

Wales and school improvement

David Egan

Introduction

Over the last 13 years the advent of devolved government has enabled Wales to fashion for the first time its own educational system. The policies, practice and systemic architecture of the education system in Wales are now very different to those of its neighbours in the rest of the United Kingdom (Egan and James, 2001a, 2001b, 2001c, 2002, 2003; Daugherty *et al.*, 2000; Institute of Welsh Affairs, 2006). The seminal exhibits of this transformation have been two documents published by the Welsh Assembly Government: *The Learning Country* in 2001 and *The Learning Country: Vision Into Action* in 2006 (Welsh Assembly Government, 2001 and 2006a).

In the former it was recognised that significant progress had been made in the previous decade in the attainment of schools and students in Wales, but that there continued to exist a 'long tail' of achievement, which was strongly associated with socio-economic disadvantage (Welsh Assembly Government, 2001). The 2006 publication recorded the progress that had been made in meeting the objectives of *The Learning Country* after five years. It also recognised, however, that assessment data indicated that school improvement appeared to have stalled particularly in secondary education. It therefore committed the Assembly Government to a greater use of the 'body of knowledge on how schools can transform themselves using the outcomes of research on school effectiveness and improvement' (Welsh Assembly Government, 2006a: 7).

More recently, the publication late in 2010 of a second set of disappointing PISA results for Wales has led the Minister of Education to question both the actual extent of progress that has been made under devolution and the degree to which this results from systemic weaknesses within the education system (Bradshaw *et al.*, 2010; Andrews, 2011). The second decade of devolution promises at least initially to be one where further significant reform will be promoted with increased emphasis on policy delivery and system improvement.

This chapter considers the extent to which absolute and comparative improvements have been achieved in Wales' schools over the last 20 years and the extent to which a body of Wales-specific knowledge on school effectiveness and improvement has emerged during that period. It also reports on the ambitious programme – the School Effectiveness Framework (SEF) – that has been developed in recent years to develop a system-wide approach to school effectiveness. It considers finally the challenges that face the educational system in Wales in introducing this programme.

The performance of the education system in Wales

Table 8.1 below presents evidence on the expected levels of performance of students in Wales at ages 7, 11 and 14 from 1998 to 2010.

These are outcomes based on teacher assessment. Wales abandoned national tests for 7 year olds in 2001 and, following the recommendations of a Government-commissioned review (Daugherty, 2004), for 11 and 14 year olds in 2005. The outcomes achieved by 15/16 year olds in GCSE and other level 1/2 qualifications point to a similar trend as is revealed in Table 8.2 below:

When these figures are compared to similar ones for England, other interesting trends emerge. Tables 8.3 below presents comparative outcomes for age 7, 11 and 14 in two core subject areas and the attainment of 16 year olds at level 1 and level 2.

Comparative performance at age 7 shows little variation between the two countries. At age 11 Wales is slightly ahead, although that gap has narrowed in recent years. In secondary education, the trend moves strongly in the direction of a gap in attainment that favours England. This is apparent by the age of 14 and

Table 8.1 Percentage of students attaining expected levels of performance in the national curriculum core subjects, 1998–2010

	1998	*2003*	*2010*
Key stage 1	77	79	82
Key stage 2	57	70	78
Key stage 3	47	54	64

Table 8.2 Percentage of students attaining level 1 (equivalent of 5 GCSEs at *A–G or better) and level 2 (equivalent of 5 GCSEs at *A–C or better), 1992–2010

	1992	*1999*	*2010*
Level 1	75	85	89
Level 2	33	49	64

Table 8.3 Comparative student attainment in England and Wales: percentage attaining key indicators at ages 7, 11, 14 and 16 in 2008

	English (expected level)			*Maths (expected level)*				
	KS1	*KS2*	*KS3*	*KS1*	*KS2*	*KS3*	*KS4 Level 1*	*KS 4 Level 2*
England	82	79	76	90	79	79	91	64
Wales	80	80	69	87	81	72	87	58

continues through to 16. More recent figures on the attainment of level 2 out-comes by 16 year olds in 2009 confirm that trend. They show that the gap has widened to one where ten per cent more students reach this level in England compared to their peers in Wales.

The outcomes of the Programme for International Student Assessment (PISA) paint a far less rosy picture. In 2006 Wales participated in PISA for the first time. The outcomes published in 2007 revealed that 15 year olds in Wales on average did less well in assessments for literacy, numeracy and science than their counter-parts in the other four countries of the United Kingdom and were also below the OECD country mean (Bradshaw *et al.*, 2007). The recently published outcomes of the 2009 PISA tests are even more concerning for Wales. In absolute and rela-tive terms, the performance of 15 year olds in reading, mathematics and science have declined against international and UK benchmarks (Bradshaw *et al.*, 2010).

It would, therefore, appear that despite overall improvements in student achieve-ment in Wales over the last 20 or so years that this progress has slowed over time and that Wales lags behind the rest of the UK and many international countries. National curriculum assessment and Key Stage 4 examination data suggests that this is more apparent in the secondary than the primary phase of education. The PISA outcomes, however, which measure the skills of students, reveal that based on their cumulative experience of education by the age of 15 young people in Wales are not as accomplished as their peers elsewhere in the UK and many parts of the OECD.

Inevitably this general picture includes a good deal of complexity. It is impor-tant to recognise that figures for Wales are depressed by the significant amount of socio-economic disadvantage that exist within Welsh society and the low levels of educational performance that are associated with this. In the context of child poverty this phenomenon has attracted particular attention in recent times (Egan, 2006, 2007 and 2010; Kenway *et al.*, 2005; Kenway and Palmer, 2007), it is in fact a feature that has deep roots within the educational history of Wales and has long been both recognised and debated (Loosmore, 1981; Jones, 1997; Gorard, 2000; Gorard and Rees, 2002; Jones and Roderick, 2003). The link between disadvantage and low attainment is as strong as it ever has been within the educa-tion system in Wales. Figure 8.1 below represents this in relation to the GCSE achievement, where it can be seen most starkly.

Whilst the associations between disadvantage and relatively low educational performance is a feature of many, but certainly not all, education systems, it is particularly prominent in Wales (Whelan, 2009; Mourshed *et al.*, 2010).

Significant variations exist in Wales in what schools are able to achieve for their students. The largest gap is that which exists between schools in more advantaged and disadvantaged areas. Whilst a number of schools situated in disadvantaged areas have bucked the trend, generally these are the strongest locations of rela-tively low student achievement. Where schools do 'succeed against the odds' it has proved difficult for them to sustain improvement over a number of years. More tellingly, the education system in Wales has not generally been successful in making this effect 'viral' whereby schools that do succeed in these challenging

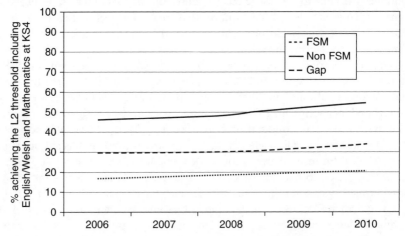

Figure 8.1 Achievement of the level 2 outcome (5 GCSEs at *A–C or equivalent) by 16 year olds in Wales, 2006–2010, in relation to receipt of free school meals

circumstances are able to positively influence the performance of similar schools and thereby contribute significantly to overall improvement.

This is demonstrated in Figure 8.2 below. This presents evidence on the percentage of students in schools in Wales who attain level 2 outcomes at the age of 15/16 in relation to their predicted performance. It clearly exemplifies that in many cases in Wales the school that a child attends has a significant bearing on

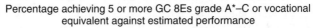

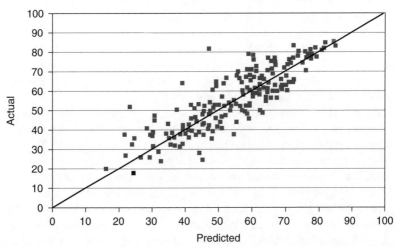

Figure 8.2 Performance of cohorts in secondary schools in Wales at level 2 in relation to predictions about the ability of their cohorts, 2008

what they achieve against what is expected of them and which they have the innate capability to achieve.

What, therefore, can be said in summary about educational performance in Wales over the last 20 or so years:

- Overall levels of student attainment have increased considerably.
- In the last decade the rate of improvement has slowed compared to the earlier period.
- This is particularly the case in secondary education although it is likely that the roots of this are to be found in the later years of the primary phase.
- It is likely, thereby, that a pattern of declining achievement by some students begins in the later years of primary education and accelerates in their early years in secondary schools.
- The outcomes of PISA in 2007 and 2010 suggest that in relation to the use of skills in literacy, numeracy and science, students in Wales are behind in their accomplishment compared to young people of this age in the other UK countries and in many parts of the world.
- Whilst this evidence is not incompatible with the overall improvements being measured through National Curriculum teacher assessment and examination courses, it does reveal that in relation to the use of generic skills that students in Wales do not perform as well as might be expected of them. It is also likely that as these tests are taken by 15 year olds, that they pick up the decline in achievement that affects many students in the 8–14 phase of their education.
- A wide range of factors can be seen to contribute to this pattern of performance. They include issues to do with: ethnicity; gender; literacy; the influence of a range of factors on student aspirations; within and between school variations; and the influence of parental choice in relation to Welsh-medium and faith education.
- The single biggest contributor, however, to low performance within the education system in Wales is the enduring association between being born into a socio-economically disadvantaged home/community and relatively low levels of educational attainment.

The school improvement tradition in Wales

The school improvement movement in Wales can be seen to have evolved through four distinct phases. The first three are considered in this section and the most recent – the SEF – is the focus of the following section.

The first phase of school improvement work in Wales was focused around the work of David Reynolds and other colleagues at Cardiff University and represented some of the first studies undertaken in the academic field in the United Kingdom (Reynolds, 1976; Reynolds and Sullivan, 1979; Reynolds, 1982; Reynolds *et al.*, 1987; Reynolds and Cuttance, 1992).

Based on innovative research in secondary schools in South Wales it established:

- that schools themselves strongly influence student achievement;
- the factors that contribute to this;
- the close association between cognitive (academic) and affective outcomes (such as attendance, participation, behaviour, etc.) for students in effective schools;
- the close link between socio-economic background, school perceptions of the ability of their student intake and low achievement.

In a second phase of school effectiveness activity in Wales this knowledge began to be exploited by individual schools and local authorities, much of which has neither been written up nor evaluated. A concerted initiative of this type was the *Improving the Quality of Education for All* (IQEA) project, which undertook work with a number of schools and local authorities in Wales from the early 1990s up to recent times. The association with that work of two leading researchers born and educated in Wales – David Hopkins and Alma Harris – provided both a specifically Welsh connection to IQEA and a lineage that has extended up to the development of the SEF.

Although the work of IQEA in Wales has not been independently evaluated, it is known in a number of instances at school and local authority level to have contributed to the achievement of improved outcomes, particularly through the knowledge it has created on the importance of:

- staff development;
- the involvement of students in their own learning;
- the development of school-level strategies for learning and teaching;
- the need for monitoring and development of school performance based on review, inquiry and reflection;
- distributed leadership;
- the need to coordinate and highlight improvement;
- the importance of collaborative planning for improvement and the allocation of specific resources to support this (Hopkins *et al.*, 1994).

In the mid-1990s a group of schools in Neath, Port Talbot became involved in the *High Reliability Schools* (HRS) Project led by David Reynolds, Sam Stringfield and Eugene Schaffer (Reynolds *et al.*, 2006; Stringfield *et al.*, 2008). This achieved significant improvement in level 2 outcomes for 16 year olds in all of the schools with an overall increase of level 2 outcomes about 10 per cent above the Wales average. The project leaders identified the following factors as having contributed to this success (Stringfield *et al.*, 2008):

- the importance of a finite number of goals that are evolved and shared school-wide;
- the centrality of, and an evolving sophistication with, data and data analysis for practical improvements;

- standard Operating Procedures for dealing with problems that might impact on student achievement;
- seeking best practice;
- holding off-site residentials to consider best practice;
- skilfully managed leadership succession;
- cyclical phases of sustained improvement.

This represented the first fully evidenced example of the effects of a school improvement project on schools in Wales and its originators were able to claim that 'the substantial rise in academic achievement within the project is the clearest evidence to date that substantial change-bearing reform of secondary schools is possible at scale' (Stringfield *et al.*, 2008: 21).

One of the major themes of the HRS project and of other recent work in the school effectiveness field is the importance of within-school variation in student performance (Reynolds, 2006). The extent to which this can be associated with variations in teacher quality was one of the outcomes of a study undertaken by two researchers in ten secondary schools in South Wales over a five-year period in the mid-1990s (Morgan and Morris, 1999). Based on the interviews they undertook with teachers and students in these schools they reported the following implications for effective learning and teaching pedagogy:

- The need for teachers to have significantly more belief in themselves regarding the amount of difference they can make to student learning.
- The need for a wider range of activity methods together with more open discussion of these between students and teachers.
- The desirability of there being stronger interpersonal strategies between the affective and technical aspects of learning and teaching.
- The importance of students taking more responsibility for their own learning.

These messages have also been a consistent theme in reports from Wales' school inspectorate. A major survey of inspection evidence undertaken in 1988 concluded that effective schools had 12 characteristics: good leadership; clear aims; high academic standards; good relationships with students; a coherent curriculum; concern for students' development; well-qualified staff; suitable and respected working accommodation; good relationships with the community; and a capacity to manage change (HMI, 1988).

Subsequent reports between 1996 and 2007 have also stressed the importance of learning and teaching, assessment policies, the learning environment, relationships between a school and its community, the importance of leadership and planning, monitoring and evaluation as the key characteristics of success (OHMCI, 1996; Estyn, 2002 and 2007). Estyn reports are the major evidence source on the role of Wales' local authorities in school improvement. A survey in 1999 (OHMCI, 1999: 2) found that whilst their work was contributing to the general improvements in standards that were occurring in schools, they were not:

- exerting the appropriate balance of pressure and support in those schools most in need of improvement;
- drawing on and disseminating the good practice that exists in the most successful schools;
- securing the necessary range of administrative functions and other services for schools.'

More recent evidence points to considerable variability in the performance of local authorities in Wales in supporting school improvement (Estyn, 2008a; Estyn, 2009a). In particular the inspectorate has pointed to the limited capacity possessed by local authorities in attempting to effectively support and challenge their schools (OHMCI, 1999; Estyn, 2009a). As a result of a review of local government service delivery in 2006 (Welsh Assembly Government, 2006b) funding has been provided for the four regionally based local authority consortia in Wales to develop stronger collaboration. This has not, however, led to the strengthening of local authority school improvement capacity and therefore the development of the SEF in Wales has placed considerable emphasis on strengthening consortia working in this area particularly through the development of system leadership (Egan and Marshall, 2007; Higham *et al.*, 2009).

Local authorities did play a significant part in partnership with the Welsh Assembly Government in shaping the national agenda for school effectiveness and improvement during a third period of school improvement development in Wales. This began in 2000 with the creation of a Task and Finish Group to examine gaps in performance between secondary schools in Wales, particularly those located in prosperous compared to deprived areas, that drew the following conclusions (Welsh Assembly Government, 2002):

- A wide variation in the performance of schools existed in Wales.
- At secondary level the gap appeared to be constant.
- Schools differed greatly in the rate of progress made by students compared to their prior attainment.
- Developing the community focus of schools appeared to bring benefits to learners, schools and communities.
- The relationship between disadvantage and performance was particularly strong for secondary schools.
- Three key factors could be identified in schools in disadvantaged areas that improve their performance. They were:
  - Clear leadership roles to drive school improvement.
  - Monitoring of learning and teaching and the promotion of effective practice.
  - Effective use of data.
- Other important factors included:
  - Effective transition from primary to secondary school.
  - The development of literacy.
  - Behaviour strategies.

-    Improvements in attendance.
- Local authorities have a key responsibility for supporting schools in difficult circumstances and needed, therefore, to review their strategies in this respect.
- The Assembly Government and other national organisations needed to support developments in this area through ensuring appropriate funding was in place, that a framework for teacher professional development existed, promoting the community role of schools and sharing good practice.

In 2005, a report commissioned by the group on primary schools where there was high levels of disadvantage but also relatively high levels of performance pointed to the importance of:

- 'A productive, strong and highly inclusive culture that focused on effective learning and teaching for all pupils'.
- Six characteristics that supported this:
  -    Leadership at head teacher, governing body and distributed levels.
  -    A positive culture and mindset.
  -    The collaborative working and sharing of teachers.
  -    The engagement and commitment of pupils and parents.
  -    Efficient and effective organisation and management.
  -    Support, validation and valuing from all those connected with the school.

(Welsh Assembly Government, 2005: 2; James et al., 2006)

In 2008 a case study of five secondary schools in Wales, undertaken as part of a wider international study of effective schools (Caldwell and Harris, 2008) came to similar conclusions (Egan, 2008). In this case the schools were drawn from a wider range of socio-economic backgrounds, with examples from both the most privileged and disadvantaged communities in Wales. The studies drew on a theoretical framework based around the use of various forms of capital (intellectual, financial, social and spiritual) aligned through leadership and governance as being the likely critical factors that would lead to and sustain highly effective outcomes.

The research in Wales revealed that the schools used the various forms of capital in an individual way that was aligned to both context and the extent to which the forms of capital were available to them. In the cases of the schools serving the most disadvantaged areas, particularly strong use was made of forms of social and spiritual capital. This could be seen to validate both the importance of schools having a moral purpose and the need for a focus upon affective as well as cognitive factors in contributing to improved outcomes. In all of the schools, the various forms of capital were seen as the pre-conditions on which the key aspects of leadership and high quality teaching could be exploited in order to sustain effectiveness and continuing improvement.

Returning to an earlier theme, it is interesting that these two school based studies on school effectiveness in Wales draw different conclusions on the role of local authorities in supporting schools. The James *et al.* research points to a significant role being played by local authorities in Wales, although the lack of 'systemic leadership for schools' is also noted (James *et al.*, 2006: 144). The work on secondary schools, however, notes that these successful schools believed that whilst support from local authorities was welcomed when it was available, that the extent and value of such support was variable in quality and that in general these schools did not premise their school improvement strategies on the assumption that it would be a resource they could draw upon (Egan, 2008).

The outcomes from these national studies also resonate with the experience of the most extensive national school improvement initiative thus far undertaken in Wales. This is RAISE (Raising Attainment and Individual Standards in Education), which commenced in 2006 and completed its final year of funding in 2009–10. Immediately prior to it being introduced a number of reports had once again highlighted the relatively low levels of educational attainment of students in the most disadvantaged schools and communities in Wales (Kenway *et al.*, 2005; Estyn, 2005). RAISE provided approximately £14 million in each of the three years 2006–08 and a diminishing amount in 2009, for schools where the free school meals quotient was 20 per cent or above and in proportion to the amount of actual disadvantage within the school (Davidson, 2006). The final independent evaluation of the RAISE programme is awaited, but it seems clear that its achievements have been mixed. Two reports from Estyn (2008b, 2009b) and a series of interim reports by the independent evaluation team (Holtom, 2008a, 2008b, 2009a, 2009b) have pointed to variable outcomes.

These reports point, however, to a series of weaknesses in the way the scheme has worked, particularly the tendency of schools to focus on remediating the low attainment of students but not in addressing the causative effects of disadvantage, the limited collaboration that has existed between schools receiving funding and variability in the quality of coordination by local authorities.

Perhaps the major weakness of RAISE has, however, been its failure to utilise approaches that are known to be successful and effective in situations where there is low achievement associated with disadvantage, drawing upon the outcomes of school effectiveness research. In this sense it reflects the enervating tendency that is so often a feature of such major intervention programmes of allowing the recipients of hard-won funding to make their own decisions – good and bad – about its utilisation rather than drawing upon evidence-informed practice as was intended to be the case for RAISE (Davidson, 2007).

The knowledge gained from these three overlapping 'phases' of school effectiveness and improvement work in Wales up to 2007 can, therefore, be seen to have established:

- the clear existence of a 'school effect';
- the close interrelationship between cognitive and affective aspects of student achievement in schools;

- that what has variously been identified as 'mindset' (James *et al.*, 2006) or 'spiritual capital' (Egan, 2008) plays a significant role in creating the 'moral purpose' that appears to be a pre-condition for schools being able to successfully undertake improvement work;
- that whilst school (and local authority) effect is significant, the greatest variations in effective learning and teaching occur within schools and, therefore, this is where the greatest gains can be made;
- achieving the gains required to reduce variations between classrooms and teachers is best done through purposeful school leadership and the collaborative endeavour of teachers to share effective practice;
- a growing awareness that factors outside of the immediate control of schools also have a critical influence on student achievement and school effectiveness;
- the profound effect that high quality teaching and distributed forms of leadership have as the key internal ingredients for achieving and sustaining improvement;
- the ongoing challenges faced in achieving school improvement and effectiveness in the most disadvantaged communities and schools in Wales and the evidence that additional funding, if it is not accompanied by evidence-informed and effective strategies, will not succeed in overcoming these problems;
- the work of local authorities in Wales in leading school improvement and effectiveness in their areas is variable in its success and is unlikely to improve unless their capacity to support and challenge schools is increased.

The school effectiveness framework

In 2006 the Welsh Assembly Government committed itself to making greater use of the knowledge produced by work in the field of school effectiveness and improvement in Wales and internationally (Welsh Assembly Government, 2006a). The appointment in that year of Steve Marshall, formerly Chief Executive of the Department of Education and Children's Services in South Australia, as the new head of the Welsh Assembly Education Department strengthened that resolve (Caldwell, 2006).

Marshall became convinced that a national school effectiveness programme was required to lead further improvements in educational performance in Wales. In 2006–07 with the assistance of Michael Fullan and others he promoted this idea with politicians, local authorities and school leaders and in the summer of 2007 commissioned three researchers to undertake an initial scoping study. They worked with a group of head teachers from highly effective schools in Wales to identify the following factors that had been critically important to their success:

The researchers used this and other evidence in proposing the development of a National School Effectiveness Programme for Wales established on the premise that whilst many societies had tried to improve their education systems over the last decade, with varying results, for the following reasons it was possible that Wales could do better (Egan *et al.*, 2007):

Table 8.4 Factors leading to school effectiveness identified by successful head teachers in Wales in 2007

Strong leadership
- Distributed throughout the school
- Involving the governing body
- Setting high expectations
- Putting learning and teaching first
- Providing vision and purpose
- Empowering staff and pupils
- Leading planning for effectiveness
- Developing new leaders.

A rich and balanced curriculum
- Providing transformative experiences for students
- Personalised to meet student need
- Developing creativity
- Utilising ICT
- Exploiting outdoor learning and visits.

High quality teaching
- Providing models of successful practice
- Reducing internal variations in quality
- Exploiting shared knowledge gained from curriculum tours
- Common approaches to lesson planning and delivery
- Reducing 'teacher talk'
- Maximising the use of support staff.

A strong focus on learning
- Behaviour policies related to learning pedagogy
- A focus on literacy
- Developing skills and independence
- Use of mentoring support
- Appropriate subject knowledge and expertise
- Assessment for learning
- Developing thinking skills
- Links between primary and secondary phases
- Appropriate use of learning styles
- Importance of learner voice.

The importance of data
- Appropriate for purpose
- High quality
- Rigorous analysis, use and deployment.

Internal accountability
- Based on self-evaluation
- Linked to performance management
- Departmental reviews
- Use of responsibility posts to lead learning and teaching.

The importance of continuing professional development
- Available on demand
- Linked to a national funding strategy
- For all teaching and support staff
- Within the workplace

Table 8.4 Continued

- Utilising action research
- Professional learning communities.

Networks
- Enabling teachers and schools to share and access good practice.

External partnerships
- With parents
- With outside agencies
- Family learning
- Community schooling.

A rich environment for learning
- Fit for purpose buildings
- Sufficient resources
- A feeling of ownership by students.

(Egan and Marshall, 2007)

- Firstly, the very results of the attempts made by other countries, and their often indifferent results, tell us what not to do and what to do. We know, for example, that 'prescription' of what goes on in schools and classrooms was not enough, but also that leaving practitioners free to 'invent the wheel' wasted time and commitment. The answer was clearly to specify 'what works' but to maximise the contingencies so as to ensure the specification is owned and taken into practice.

- Secondly, we now have knowledge about 'what works' that we did not have before. We have successful school improvement initiatives – some built by those who have helped design this initiative. We have knowledge about where improvement should be 'aimed' – at the classroom, where most pupil variance is explained. We have understanding of issues to do with leadership of the how to vary approaches in accordance with the contexts of school and of the need for high quality data that we did not have before. And we have knowledge of whole new areas – cognition neuroscience particularly – that we did not even know we did not know.

(Egan *et al.*, 2007: 2–3)

Following further development work, in February 2008 the *School Effectiveness Framework* for Wales was launched at a series of conferences across Wales addressed by the Minister, Steve Marshall and others (Welsh Assembly Government, 2008). Interdependent areas of activity that would need to be developed within the Framework were represented in a diagram (see Figure 8.3), which became known as 'the Pizza'.

The School Effectiveness Framework was piloted in about 180 of Wales' 1,800 schools in 2008–09. In the spring of 2009 a 'pause and review' period was undertaken, drawing upon the report of independent evaluators of the pilot

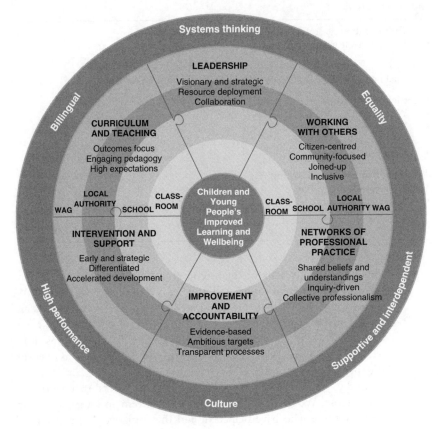

Figure 8.3 The School Effectiveness Framework

Source: Welsh Assembly Government, 2008: 9

(Holtom and Lloyd-Jones, 2009) and also the continued involvement of some of the researchers who had undertaken the original scoping work for SEF (Egan and Hopkins, 2009). This led to an agreement that the SEF should be further developed in 2009–10 ready for national implementation beginning in September 2010. The main features of the finalised SEF were to include:

- A strong emphasis on school self-evaluation aligned to the new common inspection framework that has been in place in Wales since September 2010.
- The availability to schools of extensive datasets that will assist them in undertaking self-evaluation and strengthen the accountability process.
- A National Model for School Improvement that flows from the national purposes for schools set out above and which draws upon the corpus of research on school improvement and effectiveness.
- Differentiated approaches to SEF that would enable schools at different stages

of the improvement journey to deploy appropriate strategies and that would also strengthen accountability.

- An extensive programme of developing Professional Learning Communities across Wales (Jones and Harris, 2010).
- The strengthening of local authority capacity to support SEF through consortia working between the 22 existing authorities and the development of system leadership within the consortia.

(Higham *et al.*, 2009; Egan *et al.*, 2009)

Conclusions and challenges

From the evidence presented in this chapter it is clear that whilst it has made good progress over the last 20 or so years, Wales faces significant challenges in further raising the educational performance of its students, particularly those who live in its most disadvantaged communities. Whilst they need to be viewed alongside other indicators, the 2009/10 PISA outcomes for Wales provide a clear illustration of this.

As a response to these challenges the Welsh Assembly Government has drawn upon a developing tradition of school effectiveness and improvement from within and outside Wales in order to fashion SEF as a system-wide approach to school effectiveness. It is too early to judge either the efficacy of this approach or its outcomes, but it is already clear that – as is generally the case in introducing systemic change programmes – considerable additional challenges will be faced.

In the first place there is a problem of *leadership*. If SEF is to be successful then the highest quality leadership will be needed at national, local authority and school level. It could be suggested that currently there are major weaknesses in Wales at each of these levels. Second, there is the issue of *impact*. SEF can only succeed if it influences the practice of every teacher, in each classroom across Wales. It is well known in the field of school effectiveness and in education reform more generally that achieving such an impact represents a veritable 'holy grail' (Elmore, 1996; Hattie, 2009). SEF is at the early stages in attempting to achieve such penetration and it is still not entirely clear what precisely it is attempting to achieve at the level of each teacher and the students they work with. In this respect the mixed outcomes of the RAISE programme reported above appear to be both a spectre and a warning.

Third, there is the matter of *fitness for purpose*. New work in the field of education recognises both the importance of effective schools and the limitations of school effectiveness approaches. We are increasingly aware of the influences that affect students in relation to their aspirations, their self-efficacy and self-esteem both inside and outside of school and that these are not factors which can easily, if ever, be controlled by schools, or by schools alone. New bodies of work are pointing also to the impact that 'place' has on student and school achievement (Egan, 2010; Ainscow, 2009; Lupton and Kintrea, 2008; Gutman and Ackerman, 2008; Cuthbert and Hatch, 2009). This evidence makes it increasingly clear that school effectiveness is a necessary but *not* sufficient requirement for educational success and that we need more holistic area-based approaches that build upon the experience of programmes such as the 'Challenges' in England (Ainscow, 2009).

Wales has a number of communities and indeed regions where the nature of low educational performance and its association with disadvantage will not be tackled by interventions that are narrowly school focused. Time moves on and it is self-evident that SEF cannot alone be a panacea for all that ails our education system. The next decade of devolution will require that Wales draws upon both the extensive experience it now has of traditional school improvement and effectiveness work and newer paradigms of educational change if it is to create the high achieving and egalitarian educational system it desires.

9 Educational quality, effectiveness and evaluation

Perspectives from China, South America and Africa

Sally M. Thomas, Massoud M. Salim,
Bernardita Munoz-Chereau and
Wen-Jung Peng

Introduction

Since the recent worldwide economic downturn, the key aim of almost all countries to improve the quality of children's education has greatly intensified in order to counteract the impact of the crisis on economic growth, prepare for economic recovery and alleviate poverty (UNESCO, 2004; Zhang and Minxia, 2006; Thomas, 2010). In this context, competition for the best educational provision and resources will increase, especially in developing countries and for students and schools in disadvantaged and poor rural areas. Moreover, there is increasing influence from international legislation promoting education quality and the principles of relevance, equity and rights such as the world declaration of universal basic education for all and Millennium Development Goals (UNESCO, 2000; World Bank, 2005). If developing countries are to meet the challenge of delivering good quality and relevant education to all learners in the twenty-first century they need to undertake major reforms in their education systems, including ensuring that both access and quality are enhanced for those generally excluded by poverty, ethnicity, gender, and other factors. Thus, the need to identify and evaluate good policy and practice to feed into new educational reforms in developing countries has reached a critical point. China, for example, has recently announced a new long-term programme of reforms to enhance educational quality, fairness and equity as well as specifically teacher quality, which policy makers and the public see as one of the key levers to improve student outcomes (NPC, 2009). China has also recently announced a considerable increase in education funding to 4 per cent of GDP, much nearer to the funding levels of developed countries. Similarly, new educational reforms are in progress, to a greater or lesser extent, across many developing countries in Africa and South America.

In this chapter, we aim to review the potential for successful new reforms in developing countries but first provide an overview of international perspectives on educational quality and effectiveness, and the important role of context specificity in defining quality and understanding 'what works' in different educational contexts. Three case studies are then provided from China, South America (Chile) and Africa (Zanzibar) of new educational effectiveness research to illustrate the direction of new reforms and in particular new approaches to educational evaluation. To what extent these approaches can feed into and enhance school self-evaluation and improvement processes, as well as teacher development and teaching quality are key questions. Finally, we consider the implications of the research reported and future potential for improving educational quality and effectiveness in developing country contexts.

Defining educational quality

Although many would agree that educational quality is important, it is much more difficult to agree on how educational quality should be defined and measured. OECD has highlighted this issue and argued that the definition of educational quality 'depends on the selection of relevant elements, the assessment of the character of these elements and the weighting given to their relative importance. The assessment of quality is thus complex and value laden' (OECD, 1989). In other words, how educational quality is defined depends on the priorities, context and perspectives of the persons or organisation creating the definition. Nevertheless, in spite of these difficulties some consensus has been reached at the international level. For example, in 2004 UNESCO published an influential report on educational quality which emphasised in particular the crucial importance of student outcomes and also made the distinction between first, cognitive outcomes – that is traditional academic skills but also vocational qualifications – and second, values, attitudes and citizenship which are acknowledged to be more difficult to measure. In the UK there have also been policy developments to emphasise a broader range of outcomes for children and the UK Children's Act 2004 now requires schools to work with other professionals to ensure five key outcomes for all children: being healthy; staying safe; enjoying and achieving; making a positive contribution; and economic well-being.

There have been contributions from many perspectives to these policy developments; however, School Effectiveness Research (SER) conducted since the 1960s has been a primary influence in how educational quality is understood and measured as well as the kind of strategies, levers or educational reforms likely to improve quality (Reynolds and Creemer, 1990). For example, the basic conceptual model of school effectiveness reported by Scheerens (1992) has four interrelated aspects (inputs, context, process and outcomes), which are clearly linked to the educational quality frameworks subsequently proposed by UNESCO (2004) and UNICEF (2007), as well as emerging SER in developing countries (e.g. Heneveld, 1994; Heneveld and Craig, 1996). More recent models have developed specific aspects of these initial frameworks such as the Dynamic Model of Educational Effectiveness which emphasises the need to measure effectiveness factors operating at different levels using five dimensions (frequency, focus, stage, quality, and differentiation) and the importance of examining changes over time (Creemers and Kyriakides, 2006), as well as new teacher effectiveness models (see for example Campbell *et al.*, 2004). In particular, SER has emphasised educational outcomes and how these are influenced by inputs invested in education, the local and national context, and teaching and learning processes in classes and schools and this evidence has been used to design strategies for improving educational quality in different contexts. Drawing on this evidence base, researchers have attempted to summarise 'what works' in terms of promoting educational quality and rapid increases in schooling outcomes in different country contexts (Barber and Mourshed, 2007). However, it could be argued that this comparative approach has not gone far enough in recognising the educational priorities, cultures and challenges in different countries. If local priorities emphasise a need to focus on specific educational quality objectives, such as equity, relevance, sustainability, inclusion, democracy or transformation (Adams, 1993), then clearly, improvement strategies and the focus of evaluation systems need to be tailored to fit these circumstances.

Moreover, it is important to note that most SER has been mainly conducted in the west and a key requirement of future SER is to test out the relevant theories and concepts in different international contexts, particularly in developing countries where the SER knowledge base is very limited. Interestingly the 2005–10 UKAID research programme explicitly reflected this gap in the literature on educational quality and effectiveness by funding separate research consortiums to focus on three aspects: access (inputs, learners, and resources); quality (teaching and learning process); and outcomes (qualification, employment and attitudes) (Tikly and Barrett, 2007). Morley and Rassool (1999) provide support for this approach and have rightly questioned the transferability of Western education policies in diverse global contexts. They emphasise that SER needs to be 'be contextualised within particular societies and specific conditions that exist' (p. 134) and also the need to look more closely at issues of power, poverty, deprivation and social exclusion when evaluating educational quality; as well as a broader range of educational outcomes. Fertig (2000) similarly has argued that the conceptualisation of school effectiveness should be based on the contextual factors (social, economic, cultural and political) and internal processes of a country where it is exercised because these conditions are likely to influence how stakeholders understand educational effectiveness concepts as well as the role stakeholders play in exercising school effectiveness results and in designing strategies for improving educational quality. Other researchers have similarly argued that 'context matters' and cautioned on the issue of uncritical international transfer of educational theory, policy and practice from one context to another (Fosket and Lumby, 2003; Crossley and Watson, 2003).

Of course, in spite of gaps in the international SER evidence base and the importance of considering context and culture, it is also important to recognise that the SER field is constantly developing. As outlined by several chapters in this volume which have reviewed the SER evidence base in the UK and elsewhere, it is proposed that a fundamental rethinking of effectiveness and improvement is required, moving to a position where school effectiveness and school improvement is reconceptualised as educational effectiveness and improvement. This shift is important, giving recognition to different levels within education systems

– student, classroom, department, region or local authority, national as well the school level – and to how a variety of factors at these different levels can influence students' educational achievements and progress. Thus it is crucial that alongside strengthening the SER base in developing countries, the evidence for educational effectiveness is also considered in different international contexts in terms of:

- How can educational effectiveness and improvement research and practice support the development of more equitable education systems?
- What are the key indicators of educational effectiveness and improvement and what key theories, methods and practices are required to promote educational effectiveness and associated improvement processes?

Evidence to address these questions is sought by academic researchers, international organisations and crucially by individual countries or regions through locally implemented research studies and monitoring and evaluation systems. Thus a first step in addressing these questions and in reviewing 'what works' in different country contexts is to examine the local research findings, infrastructures and methods used to evaluate educational quality and new reform efforts.

Improving evaluation of quality: value-added measures of school and educational effectiveness

Many developing countries are worried about the performance of their education systems (Morley and Rassool, 1999) and new improved approaches to school evaluation and pupil assessment are seen as key levers to improve educational quality (Gipps, 1998). Largely this is because measures of educational quality and effectiveness are considered to have two critical purposes in raising educational standards. First, to inform accountability mechanisms that hold education systems, schools and teachers accountable for their functioning and performance and also to support democracy in education. Second, to inform improvement strategies as a mechanism to stimulate improvement in educational outcomes and organisational learning (Scheerens *et al.*, 2003). The twin strategies of accountability and a continuous focus on improvement, alongside enhanced quality evaluation and student assessment processes, often within a context of decentralisation, are approaches favoured by many Western countries aiming to improve educational quality (OECD, 2008). Moreover, valid, reliable and fair student examination and assessment systems play a key role in accreditation – that is to formally regulate desired levels of quality of educational outcomes and provisions – as well as providing critical data to feed into accountability and improvement evaluation systems (Scheerens *et al.*, 2003).

So, irrespective of the particular focus of new educational policy in developing countries in terms of accountability, improvement or accreditation, innovative methods to evaluate quality schooling are needed to provide alternative frameworks for teachers and policy makers to identify best practice in teaching and learning in a variety of contexts. Moreover, similar to the situation in the UK in the early 1990s, alternative approaches are needed to reduce the common practice of evaluating school performance on the basis of raw examination scores (Thomas and Mortimore, 1996; Thomas *et al.*, 2007). Using raw performance scores alone, schools with disadvantaged intakes tend to be judged unfairly, while complacency is possible amongst schools with more able pupils, and it is difficult to identify best practice. However, the UK and some other countries worldwide have moved forward in developing value-added measures, drawing on SER paradigms and methods, to provide a fairer and more accurate approach to evaluating school performance than raw examination results. This has involved the establishment of comprehensive and longitudinal datasets and use of sophisticated statistical analysis techniques (multilevel modelling) to create estimates of the relative progress made by pupils in a school, in comparison to pupils in other schools. It is clear that SER has fed directly into identifying new methods to evaluate school performance, and more broadly educational effectiveness at different levels of the system. As a result, wide-ranging policy developments in educational evaluation have been introduced in the UK and elsewhere (e.g. DFES and Ofsted, 2004; Ray, 2006). For example, from 2006 contextualised value-added measures have been included in the Department for Education and Skills (DFES) school performance tables for all English schools and school self-evaluation is a central element of the new national inspection framework. Thus the concept of 'value-added' measures of school effectiveness as an indicator of school performance, and related school and educational effectiveness research in the UK, has played a very significant role in focusing the attention of educational policy makers on the potential for raising student achievement. The impact of new approaches to evaluation and accountability has been linked to improved student outcomes (Miliband, 2004).

As indicated by the examples from China, South America (Chile) and Africa (Zanzibar) outlined below, there is now growing evidence from several countries (at different stages of development) that the potential for new educational evaluation systems to enhance educational quality and effectiveness is being actively investigated. However, it is important to emphasise that if these methods are to be useful to evaluate quality in different contexts then it is crucial to be aware of both the limitations of the methodology (e.g. mainly a quantitative perspective) and the issues of context specificity. In particular, Harber and Davies (1997) have stressed that the contexts for education in developing countries are very different from those of the developed world since they do not have universal enrolment. They contend that, developing countries face little expenditure on education as well as health challenges and poverty, which affects capacity to study and learn, especially in rural areas where the majority of people live. It should therefore be acknowledged that there are important priorities in developing countries such as adequate teacher training, school buildings and teaching materials as well as the need to address inequitable distribution of educational resources and insufficient leadership and expertise to bring about improvements (Stephens, 2007).

Nevertheless, many commentators have argued strongly regarding the need for more robust quantitative evidence about the range and extent of school effectiveness in different country contexts. Indeed, the application and results of value added methods in different countries may underline important aspects of context specificity such as the underachievement of particular student groups or inequity in the distribution of resources. In other words, in spite of key contextual differences, SER methodology remains important as it allows normative within country (or region) comparisons and may help to improve equity in the distribution and provision of quality education through improving evaluation processes and the identification of best practice. Such evidence is vital to inform rapidly changing education reforms and initiatives aiming to raise student outcomes, particularly in rural and socio-economically disadvantaged areas (e.g. DFID Gansu basic education project; Chu and Liu, 2005) as well as to promote innovative longitudinal quantitative research methods that will enhance the validity of international comparative research (Goldstein and Thomas, 2008) and increase the SER international knowledge base (Teddlie and Lui, 2008). As noted previously there are gaps in school effectiveness literature which need to be addressed by providing comparative data and evidence from different contexts, particularly China, South America and Africa where little evidence exists. Therefore in the following sections we present case studies of new SER from these three regions to highlight aspects of context specificity as well as point to potential common features in terms of 'what works', focusing on the role of innovative evaluation methods to enhance educational quality.

China

Policy and research context

New educational reforms in China over the last ten years have put a strong emphasis on raising educational quality, particularly in rural areas and for girls. As part of these initiatives systematic transformation of curriculum goals, structure and content, teaching and learning approaches, and assessment and administrative structures has occurred and control has increasingly been devolved from the centre to provincial, district and school levels (Chinese Ministry of Education, 1996). At the 2009 National People's Congress, the Chinese Premier Wen Jiabao reiterated the need to prioritise educational development and outlined an initial focus on five key areas: (1) promote fairness in education; (2) optimise the education structures to develop vocational education; (3) improve the quality of teachers; (4) advance well-rounded education; and (5) implement a programme to ensure that all primary and secondary school buildings are safe and promote standardisation in the construction of rural primary and secondary schools (NPC, 2009).

The issue of fairness in education is crucial and relates to equal opportunities but also to fair assessment of both students and schools. Therefore, one important strand of the new reforms centres on improving pupil assessment as well as the methods used to evaluate quality and improvement in schools. Moreover, this has been an outstanding issue for over fifteen years: in the Ninth Five-Year Plan for China's Educational Development the Chinese government made explicit the need to improve performance measures as well as reduce performance differences between schools (Chinese Ministry of Education, 1996). In addition there are particular concerns about the exam-oriented nature of the education system in China, the need for curriculum and examination reform, and the lack of systematic methods evaluate education quality, highlighted by the substantial variations in university admission rates across different areas (Xie, 2007; Jiang, 2008; Jiang and Ma, 2008).

In spite of the Chinese government's desire for new methods to evaluate quality in education, SER is just beginning in China. Raw measures of pupils' academic outcomes and entrance levels to higher education are still viewed as the key indicators of school quality. However, some Chinese researchers have reviewed SER undertaken in the Western context (Chen, 2003; Cheng, 1994; Yu, 2005) and others have sought to contextualise the meaning, definition and methodology of school and educational effectiveness in China (Sun and Hung, 1994; Wang and Zheng, 1997). Of the few relevant empirical SER studies that currently exist some have examined class and school effects on raw student attainment at one point in time (e.g. Zhou and Wu, 2008; Xue and Min, 2008; Jiang *et al.*, 2005), but these studies are limited because the data employed are cross-sectional rather than longitudinal (Scheerens *et al.*, 2003). Also due to the small-scale nature of most of these studies and unsatisfactory operational definitions of student ability, Chinese researchers have called for further empirical research, and emphasised the need to introduce prior attainment baseline measures such as Entrance Examination to Senior Secondary School (EESSS) and to systematically establish student databases across cities, provinces and even at national level to enable a fairer evaluation of school effectiveness (Jiang *et al.*, 2005; Tang and Liang, 2005; Sun *et al.*, 2010). This is not the case in Hong Kong and Taiwan where several significant studies of school effectiveness have been conducted (see Cheng, 1999), although given the substantial differences in the education and assessment systems, SER outside mainland China is viewed as a different case.

Mainland China is also largely missing from international comparative studies of school effects (Scheerens, 2001), although results for one highly affluent region (Shanghai) have recently been included (OECD, 2011). Moreover, currently there are no contextualised school evaluation criteria or an established indicator system in mainland China, and there is a lack of technical expertise to use and adapt appropriate methodological tools for educational evaluation (Yang and He, 2008). These issues, as well as a lack of relevant empirical research on school effectiveness in China to inform policy development (Tang and Liang, 2005; Ding and Xue, 2009), has led to new SER outlined below which provides the first rigorous estimates of the range and extent of school effects in China as well as providing a useful model to support the development of new educational evaluation systems.

Improving educational evaluation and quality in China

Two new linked research projects have been funded by the UKAID/ESRC programme to examine the issue of educational evaluation in China (IEEQC,

2009), in collaboration with China National Institute for Educational Research, Beijing (CNIER). The first project 'Improving Educational Evaluation and Quality in China (IEEQC)' was recently completed and this research has been extended in a new project 'Improving Teacher Development and Educational Quality in China (ITDEQC)'. The IEEQC project aims are twofold. First, to extend current knowledge concerning the definition and measurement of secondary school effectiveness across a range of regional contexts in China, using a value-added approach for different pupil outcomes. Second, to explore how 'value-added' approaches to evaluating school performance and educational quality may have been adapted and developed by policy makers and practitioners in China to take account of local contexts and priorities. For example, in terms of the type of student learning and outcomes valued such as citizenship versus academic, preference for qualitative versus quantitative approaches, and the kind of contextual features that impact on student and school performance. Broadly, the aims of the new project are to enhance understanding of school effectiveness in China – but crucially a more fundamental question has been examined – how local context may play a key role in determining definitions of educational effectiveness and quality. Moreover, school effectiveness and improvement research would be very much enhanced by a clearer understanding of why concepts of education quality, and approaches and methods of educational evaluation largely developed in the UK, Europe and the USA, may be viewed differently by policy makers and practitioners in different social, economic and political cultures such as mainland China (Teddlie and Reynolds, 2000; Scheerens, 2001). Comparative evidence of this kind is also essential to understand how contextual and cultural issues may impact on educational values and priorities of both schools and individual students.

The IEEQC project involved two complimentary research strands: the first strand collected new qualitative data – interviews and focus groups were conducted with 90+ key stakeholders including head teachers, teachers, students, national and local policy makers – to explore the way educational quality is defined and evaluated in China as well as how international research on school effectiveness, evaluation and self-evaluation may have been applied and adapted in the Chinese context. The second strand has investigated school effectiveness in China by using innovative quantitative methodology (multilevel modelling) to analyse examination, prior attainment and other pupil, class and school background data, collected from the 2009 cohort of 90,000+ students in 120+ senior secondary schools in three district education authorities (LEAs) across western and eastern China. The findings so far indicate that although international definitions of educational quality are acknowledged in the views of stakeholders, there is very much a concern to take account of and emphasise the specific educational priorities in China where issues of equity and all-round development of students are major quality objectives (Thomas *et al.*, 2011). Moreover, some stakeholders also recognised that educational evaluation methods were not scientific and that improving evaluation processes was a necessary condition for improving policy and practice. With regard to estimates of school effectiveness in China, the findings indicate that in terms of students' raw Total Higher Education Entrance Examination (HEEE) outcome scores, differences between schools account for 24–27 per cent of the total variance in student scores, across the three LEAs investigated. However, the apparent performance of senior secondary schools changed significantly when comparing raw and value-added measures. After controlling for student prior attainment on entry to senior secondary school and other student and school context factors outside the control of the school, 43 to 57 per cent of the total variance and 70 to 91 per cent of the school variance in students' Total HEEE scores was explained. Of the remaining total variance, 5–15 per cent was attributable to differences between schools thereby demonstrating a school effect, particularly in western China where the largest school effects were observed (Thomas *et al.*, 2011). These findings are largely supported by similar comparable results from previous studies in China (Peng *et al.*, 2006; Ma *et al.*, 2006; Ding and Xue, 2009) and in comparison to the UK it seems that at least two Chinese LEAs indicate school effects larger than equivalent results in UK (e.g. see Thomas, 2001). Interestingly, out of a wide range of school input and process variables additional tested in the value-added models for the three Chinese LEAs, only a few (such pupil–teacher ratio, head teacher training and head teacher observation of class teaching) were found to be statistically significant. These input and process variables were found to explain a further 7–30 per cent of the school variance in students'. Total HEEE scores indicating that almost all of the remaining differences between schools were explained. The findings also revealed that in all three LEAs investigated within school differential effects were identified for different groups of students in terms of prior attainment and for different curriculum subjects. These results indicate that the issue of differential school effectiveness may be concealed if only one overall measure is used to evaluate value-added performance and is especially pertinent in the Chinese context where almost all senior school students are taught in mixed ability classes. For example, evidence of differential effects within a school may help schools and teachers identify when less able students are struggling and/or when more able students are not being sufficiently challenged by their academic work.

In conclusion, the IEEQC project provides a useful illustration of the kind of large-scale school effectiveness research projects that would be possible if the appropriate datasets were comprehensively available at regional or national level in China. One important finding of the research is the apparent differences in the value-added model results between regions in China, indicating that contextual factors may operate in different ways and that separate regional evaluation systems may be more appropriate than a national evaluation system. Further details of the IEEQC project findings are reported elsewhere (Thomas *et al.*, 2011), but nevertheless it is important to emphasise that only three LEAs were examined in this research and it is clear that across a landscape as huge as China, more large-scale and representative educational effectiveness studies are needed, including further examination of the contribution of different levels within the education system to educational quality and effectiveness (Thomas, 2005; Thomas and Peng, 2009).

Chile

Policy and research context

A largely macro-orientated policy to improve quality and equity in education has been implemented in Chile since the 1990s. These reforms were implemented through the advocacy of democracy and were essentially in response to perceived failures of neo-liberal principles applied to education in the 1970s and 1980s, which encouraged private education provision. The reforms focused on three areas of action: (1) increase in public spending from 2.6 per cent in 1990 to 4.4 per cent of GDP in 2000 and significant improvements to teachers' income and labour rights; (2) direct interventions in schools regarding quality and equity; (3) structural changes regarding the length of the school day and the curriculum (Cox, 2003). However, in spite of these far-reaching reforms, the school administration system introduced in the 1980s remained unaltered, arguably acting as a strong barrier against change by imposing restrictions on the autonomy of schools. Subsequently, many studies have shown minimal increases in average test scores over this period (Bellei, 2001) and of more concern, increasing inequality in the distribution of school effects between low-income and high-income students, thereby generating a school system extremely stratified by socio-economic level which may be not just perpetuating but also magnifying social inequalities within the country (McEwan and Carnoy, 2000; Bellei, 2001; Hsieh and Urquiola, 2006; Carnoy, 2007). International comparative studies have also pointed out that in Chile inequalities in education remain present (OECD, 2002; OECD, 2007). PISA has been systematically reporting that Chile stands out by presenting one of the highest between schools variance in students' raw attainment outcomes from the participant countries. Specifically in the best performing countries, such as Finland, New Zealand and Canada 12 per cent, 16 per cent and 18 per cent of total variance respectively was attributable to school differences; in comparison the equivalent figure for Chile was 57 per cent and a large part of Chilean pupils' performance variation is still attributable to their socio-economic background. At the same time, its quality, defined as raw student educational achievements, is also low: PISA has reported that Chile has a below average student performance, in comparison with other countries within the OECD.

Yet not everything is discouraging in the Chilean educational system. There is a shifting focus from macro-policy to a school-based policy. The challenge the Chilean educational system is facing today is how to empower schools in order to help them to become effective. Shifting the focus from a macro-policy (heavily based on inputs and resources), towards a micro-policy that conceives schools as organisations that prioritise improving the quality of teaching and learning, has been identified locally as a promising way of action (Raczynski and Munoz-Stuardo, 2007). Indeed, a recent qualitative case study conducted in 14 effective schools located in poor areas in Chile (Raczynski and Munoz-Stuardo, 2005) identified the presence of the following factors:

1   institutional and pedagogic leadership;
2   management team focused on learning;
3   nothing is left to chance;
4   responsible evaluation;
5   handling and specific responses to student diversity;
6   clear and shared rules as regards the use of discipline;
7   high expectations and demands as regards knowledge acquired by students;
8   school-family alliance;
9   efficient use of human resources;
10 use of external support;
11 student learning is the priority;
12 emphasis on significant learning;
13 constant updating and adaptation to changes;
14 high level of structuring and anticipation of learning conditions;
15 intense use of time, sustained pace;
16 good teacher-student relationship;
17 didactic materials with teaching qualities.

Although similarities with effectiveness factors previously identified in Western countries are evident (Sammons *et al.*, 1995; Scheerens *et al.*, 2003), Chilean researchers argue that the belief in the universal validity of SER still needs to be examined (Murillo, 2007). Perhaps one of the key conclusions of the Chilean case study is that the identified factors needed to be simultaneously present (Raczynski and Munoz-Stuardo, 2007), which might explain why there are so few truly effective schools. As well as examining school-based policy developments as a fruitful strand of potential reforms for improving educational quality there has also been a focus on the professional development of teachers in Chile. Different strategies oriented to support the professional development of teachers at their initial stages, as well as in-service (LEM, AEP, Network Master of Masters) have been developed in recent years by the Ministry of Education. Unfortunately, its evaluations have not been put under public scrutiny. However, with regard to supporting efforts to empower practitioners to identify and apply best practice as well as providing relevant evidence to evaluate teacher development and other educational quality reforms, efforts have been made to improve the way education quality is evaluated to enhance accountability systems. As in China, new approaches are needed to provide better estimates of school effects and how these vary across Chile by using more sophisticated methods than raw examination scores. New research on this aspect is examined below.

A value-added approach to complement the school accountability system

Over the last 30 years the school external accountability system SIMCE (National System of Measurement of Educational Quality) has been based on raw results of students' educational achievements. Tests are administered annually for the whole population of 4th grade students in maths, language and science and every two years in the same subjects for 8th and 10th grade students. Results are made public via annual league tables of each school's raw performance scores. Not at all surprisingly, privately funded schools have better raw achievement levels than state funded schools or those with a mix of state and private funding. Many researchers have argued that school mean examination results unadjusted for school differences in student background seriously bias the perception of the effectiveness of Chilean schools (McEwan and Carnoy, 2000; Bellei, 2001; Hsieh and Urquiola, 2006; Carnoy, 2007; Valenzuela *et al.*, 2009).

Interestingly, the last two Chilean governments have appeared more favourably disposed towards attempts to complement SIMCE with contextualised value-added approaches. For example, in 2006 the Ministry of Education hosted an international conference on this topic and also commissioned MIDE-UC – a research organisation within Pontificia Universidad Católica – to study and develop a value-added model using SIMCE data. During the last five years, a team of Chilean academics and policy makers have been working jointly in order to try different models, assess different datasets and software and the results have recently started to be under public scrutiny. In May 2010 MIDE UC hosted an international conference in Santiago, called 'Educational Progress and Value Added' in which academics from USA, England and Belgium reflected on key issues to take into account when educational measurements of progress are used to elaborate educational policies. Nevertheless, so far, the Ministry of Education has not developed a school accountability system to assess the school effect using value-added methodologies. Undoubtedly, it is necessary to build on the capacity of the researchers, policy makers and educational practitioners in Chile in order to develop methodological approaches that can take into account complexities derived from the strong selection bias that operates in the country. But bearing in mind that the creation of high-quality frameworks for assessing value added takes time and needs support (Gray and Wilcox, 1995), the road towards complementing raw league tables with value-added approaches in Chile is only just starting.

However, pilot research has been conducted by Munoz-Chereau (2010), which analysed 10th grade (16 year old) students' language and mathematics attainment scores matched to their previous attainments at age 14 and other student background and school context data. The data was collected as part of a nationally representative survey of 2,283 Chilean secondary schools carried out by the Chilean Ministry of Education in order to assess students' learning of the national curriculum in 2004 and 2006. Preliminary findings indicate that in terms of students' raw 10th grade outcome scores in language and mathematics, differences between schools and classes account for 44 and 9 per cent of the total variance in students' maths scores, respectively. The equivalent figures for language scores are 34 and 8 per cent, slightly lower. However, after controlling for student prior attainment two years earlier (i.e. 8th grade scores) and other relevant student and school context factors outside the control of the school, 67 per cent of the total variance and 88 per cent of the school variance in students' maths scores were explained. The equivalent figures for language scores are 79 and 93 per cent, slightly higher. Of the remaining total variance, 16 and 9 per cent (maths) and 7 and 5 per cent (language) was attributable to differences between schools and classes respectively. These pilot findings are therefore intriguing, suggesting that having adjusted for relevant factors outside the control of schools, the range and extent of school effects in Chile are considerably reduced when comparing schools' raw and contexualised valued added performance scores (Munoz-Chereau, 2010). Indeed the variance in school effects, at least for language outcomes, seems to be similar to the UK (Thomas, 2001), although the time period examined in Chile is shorter (two years vs. five years). Further large-scale research is clearly needed and is being conducted by Munoz-Chereau to extend these initial findings and provide a detailed explanation of the implications for policy and practice in Chile.

In summary it can be concluded that to some extent 'what works' in terms of promoting Educational Quality in Chile cannot be derived from its previous success, but from its failure. From the neo-liberal reforms it can be inferred that: (1) school competition and school choice generated in Chile the opposite to the originally intended effects claimed by the vouchers' advocates (i.e. Friedman): it provided less educational opportunities for the most disadvantaged students; and (2) the transference of school organisation to unprepared local authorities or private entities did not improve education. From the macro-policy reform it can be concluded that although significant input resources, material and technical support was provided to schools, there was insufficient attention and understanding of how teachers in fact received these reforms (Avalos, 2007). 'Reform results are mediated by organisational characteristics and teaching practices that prevail in the schools' (Raczynski and Munoz-Stuardo, 2007: 655). This conclusion has been echoed in the last decades by the growing recognition that top–down approaches to whole school development and change have limited impact in raising pupil performance and achievement (Harris, 2001). Chile is now facing a complex challenge – revert the situation by improving equity and quality inside schools. The current evidence points to the combination of a value-added approach to complement the school accountability system, a new focus on a micro school-based policy, school self-evaluation and a strong emphasis on the professional development of teachers as potentially the most fruitful reform innovations in future years.

Zanzibar

Policy and research context

It is clear that in many African countries, including Zanzibar, the quality of education provision is low in relation to the Education for All goals to increase access to education and improve educational quality and outcomes (UNESCO, 2000). This is indicated, for example, by SACMEQ – the cross-national study on measuring the quality of primary education in sub-Saharan African countries (Nassor *et al.*, 2005; Nassor and Mohammed, 1998). In Zanzibar, students' performance in secondary schools is similarly low as the proportion of students qualified to join the next education level (A-level) is minimal (MoEVT, 2007) and the government's view is that the delivery of basic education is unsatisfactory and improvement is essential (RGZ, 2006).

Recently, there have been some remarkable improvements particularly at primary level, but nevertheless there are several critical constraints, challenges and contextual issues affecting educational development in Zanzibar (Salim, 2011). These include low participation rates particularly at secondary education level and the abrupt change in language of instruction, from Kiswahili in primary schools – which most students speak at home – to English in secondary schools. This results in access and assessment difficulties across the whole curriculum for students with inadequate English language skills (Rea-Dickens *et al.*, 2008). Moreover, students generally have a relatively heavy educational workload given that the majority additionally attend Quranic religious schools, especially at primary levels. There is also insufficient capacity to maintain and extend quality in learning and teaching as the number of pupils accessing schooling increases. Generally, the teaching force remains inadequate and many secondary school teachers are either under-qualified or unqualified. However, there is also an oversupply of teachers, they are poorly distributed and many lack subject competence. This is exacerbated by the fact that many primary-trained teachers are now teaching in secondary schools. Double-shift schools still operate in Zanzibar, limiting class time, and school facilities including textbooks for some social science subjects and other teaching and learning materials are inadequate, particularly at secondary education level. Management and administration of the education system is centrally controlled but regional and district education officers and their supporting staff lack the capacity and professional skills necessary for the management of education in their respective regions and districts. The budgetallocation at regional, district and school levels to support the development of education is also low and inadequate.

However, these constraints and challenges are being addressed in the short term and long term by Zanzibar Ministry of Education and Vocational Training (MoEVT) through its education policy and various donor supported programmes and projects. For example, the new Education Act among other things has defined clearly the roles and responsibilities of the National Education Council, regional and district education offices and education boards (MoEVT, 2010). Also ZEDP, the first comprehensive education sector strategic plan in Zanzibar, has identified and established substantial targets for the education system that are achievable and sustainable, both in terms of equitable access and quality (MoEVT, 2009). A World Bank funded project *Basic Education Improvement Programme in Zanzibar*, on the other hand, aims at improving access to good quality secondary education so as to achieve universal lower secondary education by 2015. The project focuses on five key components, namely: (1) increasing enrolment and improving quality in secondary education through the provision of infrastructure; (2) improving quality of education through provision of teacher training in order to upgrade teacher competences and skills, provision of textbooks for secondary school students, and improving science education for girls; (3) improving the capacity of inspectorate services; (4) curriculum reforms; and (5) training on life skills education (World Bank, 2007). These multifaceted efforts highlight the critical importance of not only funding and implementing new strategic plans and programmes but also the need to evaluate and monitor subsequent improvements in the effectiveness of schooling. In particular, more sophisticated approaches and methods are needed than just monitoring raw examination scores in order to demonstrate 'what works', to guide the distribution of limited resources and as a first step towards improving accountability as well as educational evaluation and feedback systems to support improvement initiatives in Zanzibar.

Previous research by Yu and Thomas (2008) has highlighted the lack of empirical evidence of school effects in the African context and the need to use more sophisticated methods to evaluate and contextualise educational quality. They used cross-sectional methods to re-analyse the SACMEQ dataset and proposed 'interim' measures of school and regional effects to evaluate educational quality. They also identified a range of school process factors that are associated with better student performance (such as teacher attendance and competencies) that support the direction of new reforms in Zanzibar. However, this research was limited by not having access to longitudinal datasets in order to estimate value-added measures. Importantly, this limitation has been addressed in new research, outlined below, which estimates school effects in Zanzibar and illustrates a potentially fruitful approach to improve evaluation methods.

A pilot value-added study in Zanzibar

Salim (2011) has recently conducted a study that aimed to examine the applicability of value-added measures in the context of Zanzibar and investigated for the first time in this region the range and extent of senior secondary school effectiveness using a longitudinal methodological approach. He also explored the possible explanations of any differences observed in school effects and the relevance and potential for using value-added measures of school effectiveness to enhance evaluation processes. The study collected student background characteristics and school process and contextual data including head teachers' views on various school effectiveness and improvement factors thought to be enhancing or hindering effectiveness of their schools. These data were matched with students' national assessment outcome data (Form 4 examination results taken at age 18 years) and their prior attainment (Form 2 examination results taken at age 16 years). The purpose was to carry out a longitudinal analysis using multilevel modelling techniques to calculate 'value-added' measures of relative student progress to estimate schools' effect on student outcomes. These value-added measures were then tested against head teachers' views on educational processes and other school factors in order to determine whether these factors could explain some of the observed differences in school effects. Interviews were also conducted with education stakeholders (policy makers, school inspectors and head teachers) to explore their perceptions and experiences on educational quality, effective schooling and school evaluation processes, in particular whether value-added approaches could be applied to improve external evaluation and school self-evaluation processes. A total of 7,356 students, 110 secondary school head teachers and eight stakeholders participated in the study.

The study findings indicated that not surprisingly statistically significant differences do appear to exist between Zanzibar secondary schools in terms of effectiveness. Across ten different Form 4 academic outcomes, 7–39 per cent of the total variance in students' performance was estimated to be attributable to schools, after adjusting for factors outside the schools' control including students' Form 2 prior attainment and their background characteristics (such as gender, age and family income indicators) and school context factors. These findings indicate a substantial influence of schooling on some student outcomes, somewhat higher than countries such as the UK (Thomas, 2001) and China (Peng *et al.*, 2006) and somewhat lower than some sub-Sahara African countries such as South Africa, Kenya, Namibia and Uganda (Lee *et al.*, 2005). Within individual schools there is also evidence of differential effectiveness for students of different levels of prior attainment as well as by gender across a range of student outcomes. Furthermore, the findings indicated that many Zanzibar secondary schools are not consistently effective across all curriculum subject areas.

Importantly, head teachers' views on school effectiveness, improvement and other factors were subsequently found to explain some of the differences in schools' value-added results. School process factors (measured via a head teacher questionnaire) that were positively associated with higher value-added scores included: regular marking and monitoring of homework; good monitoring of student assessment; regular monitoring of student achievement and progress; and a good proportion of experienced and well-qualified teachers. Interestingly, head teachers reporting that 'poor quality teaching' was less of a hindering factor in creating effectiveness of their secondary schools was also associated with higher value-added scores, most likely reflecting the unequal distribution of qualified teachers in Zanzibar. Moreover, it was evident that in schools where the head teacher is more qualified (i.e. with Bachelor's Degree), students make better progress than in other schools. In contrast, other statistically significant school process factors reported by head teachers were found to be negatively associated with schools' value-added scores, including: low teacher morale; insufficient emphasis given to students on academic matters; little support from School Management Committee (SMC); and little support from parents and community members. SMC and parent/community support are likely to be related to issues such as supporting schools in dealing with student absence and financial contributions.

The evidence from the quantitative analyses was generally substantiated and extended by the qualitative research results where stakeholders' interview accounts revealed that, from their perspective, more effective secondary schools in Zanzibar tend to demonstrate good policy and practice in terms of one or more of the following aspects: leadership skills of the head teacher; participation and cooperation of all stakeholders in a school; collaborative arrangements with other schools; professional development support programmes for teachers; support for girls' education; adequate student assessment system; self-evaluation practice; and better resources via community and parental financial support. Also, stakeholders indicated that more effective head teachers are likely to have been trained in management and leadership, be better qualified and focus specifically on aspects of teaching and learning. In contrast, less effective schools are considered to have one or more of the following features: severe shortage of resources; little time allocated to classroom teaching; poor quality teaching; and low motivation and commitment of some teachers. Stakeholders' interview accounts also suggested that, if adapted to local context and priorities such as equitable provision of teaching and learning resources and funding, self-evaluation approaches could help in improving educational quality in Zanzibar. This is because by itself self-evaluation is a form of teacher development since it gives a way to reflect on teacher practices. Moreover, if a value-added evaluation system was implemented in Zanzibar, it could provide important information for accountability and assist policy makers in identifying where to focus improvement efforts and limited resources, as well as provide detailed feedback data to schools and teachers and promote systematic record keeping of student attainment and progress. In terms of other specific approaches to promote education quality, stakeholders indicated: the need to ensure well-qualified teachers as well as good teacher professional development support are in place; development of a more responsive curriculum which reflects the Zanzibar context; and decentralisation of powers and authorities to lower levels of education management and administration in order to promote ownership, commitment and distributed leadership.

Crucially, one aspect of the study findings regarding the quality of student assessments should be emphasised, and it has important implications for other similar developing country contexts. Surprisingly, the quantitative results indicated that, in contrast to previous value-added studies in Western contexts, there were weaker than expected correlations between students' Form 2 prior attainment and their Form 4 CSEE outcomes (Salim, 2011). For reason of continuity and consistency it would normally be expected in typical educational situations that a student's previous attainment in a specific curriculum area would be fairly closely related to later attainment in the same subject so that progress can be estimated and this is the essential rationale for using 'value-added' approaches and comparisons. However, if this is not the case then the possible reasons need to be carefully explored. In Zanzibar, stakeholders' interview accounts suggested possible explanations for this finding including in relation to Form 2 examinations: (1) quality of assessment instruments; (2) quality of teacher assessments; (3) record keeping of assessment results; (4) problem with examination design and purpose; and (5) language of instruction and assessment. Given student examination results are key indicators of student outcomes used in most national educational evaluation systems, these findings underline the issue that fit-for-purpose student assessment is a critical area for development and improvement in Zanzibar and most likely also for other similar developing countries. Clearly, educational quality cannot be monitored and evaluated very meaningfully if the reliability and validity of key measures cannot be clearly demonstrated.

In conclusion this study indicates that the SER methodologies employed mostly in Western contexts can be replicated and usefully applied in Zanzibar so as to contribute to the international knowledge base. As in China and Chile, the methods employed may also be usefully seen as a national pilot for developing a value-added school evaluation framework to inform better evaluation policy and practices in Zanzibar and support less effective schools in achieving equitable learning outcomes between different schools, groups of students and for different curriculum subject areas. The evidence highlights several key issues that need to be further examined and suggest fruitful areas to investigate regarding the question: what are teachers in more effective schools and departments actually doing in the classroom given the limited contact time they have in comparison to other education systems in Africa and worldwide? Evidence of school effects has been demonstrated, but nonetheless the findings should be seen as provisional given this is the first large-scale longitudinal study of school effectiveness in Zanzibar and any interpretation of the results requires careful consideration of the validity and reliability of national assessments used, as well as the developing country context.

Conclusions

We have reported three case studies, which highlight new investigations into the range and extent of school effectiveness in different developing country contexts. We have also explored in the different contexts the relevance of using value-added measures to enhance processes of educational evaluation and self-evaluation as a key lever to improve educational quality as well as other potentially successful educational reforms. One strength of research reported is that it is fairly unique because longitudinal value-added studies are rare in the three countries examined. Other strengths of the research include:

- The size of the sample/datasets used whereby a complete or representative national or regional cohort of students was employed.
- The range and longitudinal nature of data collected whereby students' prior and outcome attainments were collected in two or more curriculum subjects, as well as additional student background characteristics and school context variables in order to create 'value-added' measures of school effectiveness.
- The collection of school process variables, which were used to explore possible explanations of differences observed in school effects.
- The recognition of educational as well as school effects in terms of modelling or analysing (where possible) different levels in the system to recognise the effects of class and region, as well as school and student effects.
- The use of mixed methodology and evidence from both quantitative and qualitative research methods to provide complimentary sources of explanations and illustrations of 'what works' in promoting educational quality in different contexts.

As for limitations, it is of course important to acknowledge that value-added measures used in the studies reported can only provide *estimates* of school and other educational effects and their value is defined by the quality, reliability and validity of the data analysed. In particular, the quality of the student assessment data employed needs to be carefully considered, especially given the developing country contexts. Moreover, technical data issues, such as measurement error and possible imperfections in the data, emphasise the importance of considering the statistical significance of the results (Goldstein, 1997).

Improving internal and external educational evaluation systems

A key conclusion of this chapter is that one important approach to improve school and educational effectiveness is through improving educational evaluation systems. The evidence indicates that the development of data feedback systems to policy makers and practitioners will improve evaluation processes at all levels of the education system – national, regional, local, school, class, learner – but particularly in terms of school and teacher self-evaluation. Importantly, the case studies provide insight into and illustrations of the usefulness of value-added indicators as a powerful alternative methodology to monitor and evaluate the effectiveness of schooling irrespective of the context in which it is applied, and this method could be seen as a universal instrument for improving the quality of education. However, clearly these methods need to be adapted and tailored to the specific educational objectives, priorities and stage of development of the country concerned. For example, a national/regional value-added system is feasible in countries with the same national/regional examinations in all secondary schools, as in our three case studies. Nonetheless, the specific focus of the analysis may differ according to the context and availability of expertise and resources that are often limited in developing countries. Differences may be manifested in terms of the types of assessment outcomes examined, the variables controlled for in the analysis and the level of sophistication of the analysis (Scheerens *et al.*, 2003). Whatever the focus, if appropriate value-added systems were in place schools and teachers could collaborate in self-evaluation to provide a mutually beneficial stimulus for identifying and evaluating the key processes of educational improvement and equity. Moreover, external evaluation via school inspection and accountability systems could also be enhanced through the use of improved evaluation methodology as well as through examining to what extent schools and teachers have the capacity to self-evaluate (e.g. DFES and Ofsted, 2004; Schildkamp and Visscher, 2009). Interestingly, decentralisation of power and autonomy to schools is seen as a key strategy by some governments to enhance ownership and engagement. However, as noted by Scheerens and colleagues (2003) this strategy also requires more rigorous evaluation systems of the kind outlined above.

In addition to improved evaluation methods, the research has highlighted two related areas of reform, which are also likely to contribute to educational quality improvement in developing countries. First, reforms which aim to improve school and classroom pedagogical practices alongside strengthening in-service training and teachers' continuing professional development, including improving teachers' assessment practices. Second, reforms which aim to improve and broaden student assessment systems and instruments to maximise reliability and validity of outcome measures and to reflect more fully the wider objectives of education. In China, Chile and Zanzibar the evidence suggests, not surprisingly, that student achievement and progress is related to what teachers are actually doing inside the classroom. The implication is that in all three contexts improving the quality of classroom teaching and learning processes is seen as a key strategy of 'what works' in raising overall educational standards, as well as promoting equitable access between different schools, student sub-groups and different academic subject areas. However, again the particular focus of strategies to improve teaching and learning need to be tailored to countries' specific educational objectives and priorities. For example, an emphasis on teacher collaboration and professional learning communities to improve teaching quality may be highlighted, or not, depending on the cultural practices or degree of teachers' autonomy. Moreover, contextual issues may also apply to the priorities or need for more comprehensive training and professional development to enhance teachers' knowledge and skills. A particular concern is also raised by the research in Zanzibar, stemming from the relatively weak association between prior and subsequent assessment outcomes revealed by the value-added methodology, which may indicate inadequate student assessment systems are currently in place. Establishing improved formative and summative student learning assessment systems would clearly support practitioners' and policy makers' understanding of students' achievement and mastery of the curriculum.

Understanding context specificity and further research

We have outlined three different areas – evaluation policy and practice, pedagogical practices and student assessment – that have the potential for successful educational reforms in developing countries. However, it is clear that some reforms may be more relevant in particular country contexts depending on the educational objectives, priorities and stage of development. Overarching educational goals such as EFA are likely to be fairly similar or even universal across the world but, as indicated by the case studies, the priorities and strategies for improvement reform will be influenced by where a country or education system lies in relation to particular contextual conditions or dimensions. Mourshed *et al.* (2010) have examined improving education systems around the world and summarised a useful framework for categorising the type of reforms and interventions likely to be successful in different contexts. We have interpreted their framework as comprising four contextual dimensions in terms of: (1) performance stage and local priorities for cross-stage interventions; (2) local priorities, culture and decisions made about whether a particular intervention is mandatory or voluntary; (3) local priorities, culture and decisions made about how sustainable improvements can be achieved; (4) the existence of a critical incidence to stimulate new reforms. These contextual dimensions are a relevant starting point but further research is needed to explore in detail how well successful reforms in different country contexts map onto these dimensions.

In conclusion, we hope the case studies in different developing country contexts have demonstrated some common benefits of more sophisticated educational evaluation methods in raising educational quality as well as highlighted some pertinent issues of context specificity. Through these examples we hope to have provided food for thought regarding the kind of key indicators, methodologies and reforms needed to promote equity, educational effectiveness and improvement processes in different contexts – the key questions raised in the introduction of this chapter as well as other chapters in this volume. Clearly, educational quality has multiple meanings in different educational contexts. The evidence calls for countries to prioritise their objectives and resources and strive to design the best strategies suited a particular country's socio-cultural context and economic realities so as to enable young people to acquire the necessary skills, competencies, values, knowledge and experience they need for lifelong learning and to be active and productive citizens.

Part III

Recent developments and future perspectives

10 The potential of continuing professional development

Evaluation and 'impact'

Jim O'Brien

Introduction

For some time now, the underpinning policy fuelling education reform internationally has been that schools and teachers require reform in order that school students become creative, flexible, problem-solving team players for the new knowledge economy. Do components and approaches exist in the School Effectiveness and School Improvement (SESI) milieu that, if combined together, might facilitate the perceived reforms of teaching and schooling? Where might this lead the SESI movement and with what effect? What components are around? Have they been trialled successfully? Are elements scaleable and what would or could be combined?

Teacher quality

A key focus for the SESI movement has to be on improving the quality of teaching. This is not a new focus, but it is in changes in the practice of teaching and the related learning of students in which we should see the fruits of effective dissemination, manifestation and influence of any SESI-related research. We seem more than capable of conducting research in systems and across schools that identifies both problematic issues and effective practices. However, a major issue involves the translation of such practices into other cultural milieus even within the same political and policy context. Certainly, from such research, the SESI 'movement' has promoted particular approaches that policy makers have adopted such as the focus on school leaders, manifested in the United Kingdom and primarily in my own context, Scotland, by an emphasis until relatively recently on the role and preparation of school head teachers or principals (Bush *et al.*, 2006; MacBeath, 2011). While leadership of a school is recognised as a very important element in whether it is a successful school or not, teacher quality equally is a key variable.

Internationally, research confirms the quality of teaching as one of the most critical school factors that influences student achievement. Darling-Hammond *et al.* (2001: 10) in their review of projects and studies of student achievement in the USA concluded that teachers' qualifications – based on measures of knowledge and expertise, education, and experience – account for a larger share of the variance in students' achievement than any other single factor, including poverty, race, and parent education.

Teacher standards

Educational policies across the world (OECD, 2005) strive to offer insights into how to enhance teacher quality so that student achievement and attainment increase. So how do we ensure quality teachers for schools? Various jurisdictions initially in Western societies have developed and adopted teacher standards and created series or a 'framework' of such standards in the past 15 years as a mainstay of policies claiming to make schools and teachers more professional and thus more effective with a prime purpose being to raise the attainment of student learners in schools (Bates, 2004; Christie and O'Brien, 2005; Mahoney and Hextall, 2000).

Of course such standards may have a duel purpose. Sachs (2003: 175) indicates the introduction of standards aims

> to improve educational performance of educational systems and to improve the practices of teachers in classrooms. In some settings, professional standards have been imposed by governments and are used as regulatory frameworks and bureaucratic controls over teachers, particularly as they relate to licensing and certification procedures. In other instances, they are used as an initiative for teachers to gain professional control over what constitutes professional work . . .

While Darling-Hammond (1999: 39) issued a clear warning about the potential limitations of standards:

> Teaching standards are not a magic bullet. By themselves, they cannot solve the problems of dysfunctional school organizations, outmoded curricula, inequitable allocation of resources, or lack of social supports for children and youth. Standards, like all reforms, hold their own dangers. Standard setting in all professions must be vigilant against the possibilities that practice could become constrained by the codification of knowledge that does not significantly acknowledge legitimate diversity of approaches or advances in the field; that access to practice could become overly restricted on grounds not directly related to competence; or that adequate learning opportunities for candidates to meet standards may not emerge on an equitable basis.

Nevertheless, clearly securing a shared understanding and commitment by teacher employers, policy makers and the profession on how best to develop and support teacher quality may be viewed positively. Identifying and publicly recognising what it is that effective teachers know, do and value can be an important step in enhancing the public profile and standing of the profession and therefore go some way to ensuring both quality and the necessary teacher numbers. Teachers often report feeling undervalued by the community while historically their status in society is perceived to have been eroded. Teaching is a demanding and increasingly complex activity, and government expectations and parental demands are mounting in most systems. A recent report (Jensen, 2010) from the Grattan Institute in Australia, based on the OECD's Teaching and Learning International Survey (TALIS: OECD, 2009, 2010), noted

> that with an excellent teacher, a student can achieve in half a year what would take a full year with a less effective teacher, and the impact is cumulative. Students with effective teachers for several years in a row outperform students with poor teachers by as much as 50 percentage points over three years.

Much of this report focuses on teacher assessment/appraisal and while important and worthy of consideration, this chapter addresses elements of the third bullet point contained on (p. 10).

There are four main mechanisms to improve the quality of teachers and the effectiveness of teaching:

- Improve the quality of applicants to the teaching profession;
- Improve the quality of initial education and training;
- Develop teachers' skills once they enter the profession and are working in our schools; and
- Promote, recognise and retain effective teachers and move on ineffective teachers who have been unable to increase their effectiveness through development programs.

Continuing professional development (CPD) policy

Various reform efforts and associated CPD for teachers based on how students may learn best have been tried and found wanting over the decades. However, research (Desimone *et al.*, 2002; Harris *et al.*, 2006) continues to suggest strongly that teacher professional development is the key to enhancing teachers' content knowledge and improving their classroom practices, which in turn issues in the belief expressed above by Jensen. Teacher CPD, like much else in education and schooling, has long been subject to political vagaries but it was clear that when New Labour came to power in the UK in 1997 that teacher professional development would be central and necessary. Given their overall 'modernisation' of public services project, the government published a Green Paper shortly after coming to power – *Teachers Meeting the Challenge of Change* (DfEE, 1998) and subsequently outlined the importance of CPD (DfEE, 2000a). This was a strand in the overall process now known as 'Remodelling the School Workforce' (including all those not qualified as teachers) within the UK, ostensibly in an attempt to promote standards and free up the time of teachers for teaching and importantly accepting the premise that formal school leaders not be required to be qualified teachers but focus on administration not learning and teaching (Gunter, 2008; Ozga, 2005).

One of the key proponents and architects of this period of reform was Michael Barber and in 2005 he published a chapter that 'examines the potential of central and local government to change radically what happens in schools and classrooms and, simultaneously considers the limits on that potential' (p. 73). Recognising school-based staff development as a factor in effective schools, he proposed as a principle that 'school improvement is a task for the schools' (p. 86) and called for investment in teacher development 'partly because the pace of technological and social change and the increased expectations of education mean that ever more is demanded from teachers' (p. 88) and opined (p. 84):

> A school's policy for professional development needs to make effective use of limited resources, and to be seen to be fair. Similarly, local and national systems need to invest in teacher development. The idea of a learning profession and, at school level, a learning staff among whom professional development and reflection are a constant feature of practice is a powerful but as yet underdeveloped notion. In an era of change unless all staff are learning there is considerable risk that an organisation will stagnate or slide. The problem for publicly funded schools in the Western world is that this growth on the demand for teachers to learn has occurred at a time of public expenditure constraint.

A number of commissioned research reports (Hustler *et al.*, 2003; Robinson *et al.*, 2008; Opfer *et al.*, 2008) and policy statements (Ofsted, 2006; TDA, 2009) help to form a contemporary picture of the state of teacher professional learning in England and how successfully CPD is overtaking policy objectives and enhancing the quality of teachers and subsequently student standards. A new CPD strategy was published after consultation with the General Teaching Council (England) [GTCE] – now to be consigned to history by the Coalition Government – which promised to 'carry out robust and reliable research and evaluation into professional development opportunities and their impact on teaching and learning to provide evidence of successful practice' (DfEE, 2001). Following on from this, research was commissioned to produce a 'baseline' reporting on teacher CPD experience during 2001; the key findings of Hustler and his colleagues confirmed what much of the CPD research literature illustrated, especially in relation to what professional development teachers considered worthwhile and effective viz. CPD:

- is relevant and applicable to school and classroom settings;
- recognises teachers' existing skills, knowledge and experience;
- is school-based when appropriate but other activities such as secondments and higher education award-bearing courses are available.

While the downside illustrated that CPD:

- involves for many teachers, traditional courses, conferences, and INSET days;
- take-up is inhibited by costs, distance and teacher workload;
- for school development needs and national priorities dominates at the expense of individual needs and this needed re-balancing;
- coordination and management can affect teachers' response to provision.

The most recent 'State of the Nation' (Opfer *et al.*, 2008) teacher survey report and other related research by the report's authors has resulted in a series of journal articles which *inter alia* consider how teachers access CPD and suggest that the promise of the strategy and CPD initiatives has not materialised (Opfer and Pedder, 2010, 2011). It is perhaps ironic, given other political imperatives, that part of the problem, according to this survey, lies with choice and the individualised nature of much teacher CPD, so teachers are faced with 'a number of options available from a highly disparate set of providers' (2011: 4). Despite evidence that school-based and sustained development was key, respondents continued to 'report professional development that has few effective features' (2011: 13). Episodic and transmission models of professional development appear to continue to dominate the landscape. Collaboration, participation, networking and active learning seem to be at a premium and this leads to the suggestion that middle- or low-achieving schools 'tend to have low levels of support for the professional learning of teachers' (2011: 17). Opfer and Pedder conclude that 'the professional development of teachers in England is generally ineffectual and lacks school level systems and supports, but that the professional development and supports for teachers in high performing schools display many of the characteristics associated with positive changes in teaching and learning' (2011: 21). The issue remains how those schools that are not high performing can raise their awareness and practice and become so and if CPD can provide an answer to this problem.

Research into CPD leadership was conducted on behalf of the Teacher Development Agency (Robinson *et al.*, 2008) and investigated how CPD 'is led in schools today, how it is supported, and the barriers and challenges faced by CPD leaders' (p. i). The results suggest 'school CPD leaders recognise and seek to strengthen the links between CPD, school improvement planning and performance management, while also acknowledging barriers to implementation' (p. vi), which once more recognised issues such as workload, time and the release of staff. Reconciling individual and whole-school needs continued to be problematic and while identifying and evaluating the impact of training and development was regarded as critical there was evidence that leadership capacity and approaches to evaluation and impact of CPD adopted while almost universal were less than optimal.

In an unpublished synthesis of TDA-funded projects Bubb and Earley (2009: 8) address the questions about the evaluation of CPD and indicate that CPD organisers

recognised their measurement of the impact of staff development as a weakness, and welcomed advice on effective systems. Impact evaluation was conducted mainly through discussions with staff, evaluation forms, lesson observation and performance management reviews. The CPD Leadership research found that evaluation was most commonly made as part of the performance review/appraisal process for support staff and the PM [performance management] process for teachers.

Bubb and Earley (p. 9) conclude that 'In all the research projects people found it hard to prove that development activities were making a positive difference to pupils'. This is the crux of the matter and we shall return to this later. At best, while recognising that CPD in certain schools is having significant impact, overall the evidence suggests that CPD policies in England have proved patchy in their execution and the degree to which teacher quality has been enhanced remains questionable and the links with student standards are generally unmade.

The emergence of teacher standards in the UK

Integral to recent CPD policy within the UK has been the development of standards that gained ground when New Labour came to government. Standards for teachers emerged quickly in England (Reynolds, 1999) and were related again to ideas associated with 'workforce remodelling' which included the introduction of a system of annual appraisal or staff development and review subsequently developing into 'performance management' (Reeves *et al.*, 2002), complete with threshold arrangements which limited pay for teachers at particular career points to certain in-school evidence-based processes which became the responsibility of head teachers. Overall this policy approach sought to transform the management of schools, career progression and the basis of remuneration for teachers (DfEE, 2000b; DfES, 2001). Standards or competence lists were also developed for 'expert' or advanced skills teachers and school head teachers themselves. Through the introduction of similar standards in Australia, teacher 'professionalism' was likened to being an educational operative (Smyth and Shacklock, 1998). This was also the opinion of Mahony and Hextall (2000: 91) who examined developments in England:

> Paradoxically, this restrictive formulation (model of tight regulation and surveillance) is presumed to provide a sense of purpose, value and progression for practising teachers, and a motivational inducement for people considering entry to the occupation. Thus what many would see as symptomatic of the *de*-professionalisation [authors' emphasis] of teaching – namely the increasingly dominant machinery of regulation – becomes re-defined within the language of 'professional standards' as the very foundation of professionalism.

In England, the Teacher Development Agency (TDA) [http://www.tda.gov.uk/teachers/professionalstandards.aspx] revised the framework of teacher standards in 2007 indicating that the purpose of such was to bring 'coherence to the professional and occupational standards for the whole school workforce' recognising that the

> framework of professional standards for teachers will form part of a wider framework of standards for the whole school workforce. This includes the Training and Development Agency for Schools' (TDA) review of the occupational standards for teaching/classroom assistants and the professional standards for higher level teaching assistants in consultation with social partners and other key stakeholders and a review of leadership standards informed by the independent review of the roles and responsibilities of head teachers and the leadership group.

What do the English teacher standards cover? The following career stages are highlighted:

Q – qualified teacher status
C – core standards for main scale teachers who have successfully completed their induction
P – post-threshold teachers on the upper pay scale
E – excellent teachers
A – advanced skills teachers (ASTs)

For each career stage the associated professional standard for teachers defines the characteristics expected of teachers; these are usually designed to build on the prior standard that must be satisfied before progression to the next standard can be undertaken. It is widely held that the professional standards articulate a teacher's professional *attributes,* professional *knowledge and understanding,* and professional *skills.* The standards thus set out clearly the expectations at each career stage and government claims such standards enhance the status and professional standing of teachers.

England is the largest educational system within the UK but the period that has witnessed standards emerge has also experienced a new devolved structure of government within the UK. The other educational systems of Northern Ireland (Montgomery and Smith, 2006), Wales (GTCW, 2006; Reynolds, 2008a) and Scotland (O'Brien, 2007; Ozga, 2005) are increasingly developing in similar but different ways with differing emphases and priorities from England. This can be seen especially in the development of the Scottish standards where while there are many striking similarities with the English equivalent (Arnott and Menter, 2007) there is much more emphasis on professional values.

The development of teacher standards in Scotland

Christie and O'Brien (2005) suggest that the Continuing Professional Development (CPD) framework in Scotland attempts to provide a coherent structure for quality professional learning at all levels of a teacher's career. The framework is underpinned by four Standards and is part of a series of changes in Scottish teachers' conditions of service designed to raise the status and enhance the professionalism of teachers and presumably student achievement and attainment. In Scotland, the Standards cover Initial Teacher Education (ITE) (Quality Assurance Agency for Higher Education [QAAHE], 2000), Full Registration, generally achieved after one year's service (SEED, 2002a), expert teacher, known as Chartered Teacher (SEED, 2002b) and Headship (Scottish Office Education and Industry Department [SOEID], 1998; SEED, 2005). A framework for the professional development of educational leaders was also published (SEED, 2003). The principal difference in Scotland was that the Standards 'were conceived of as having a developmental rather than a regulatory function' (Reeves, 2007: 58).

As in other systems and countries, part of the rationale for these changes designed to transform teachers' pre- and in-service learning into a developmental 'continuum' stemmed from the realisation that for many teachers the reality of professional development had been episodic and unsatisfactory. Pre-service, student teachers often struggled to integrate the school placement and university-based components of their undergraduate degrees or PGCE courses and, as newly qualified teachers (NQTs), they found difficulty in linking their early experiences of teaching to their pre-service courses. Some were a number of years into their careers before they could see the point of elements of their ITE, and any induction, which ideally would help beginning teachers make connections between theory and practice, had often been cursory, concerned merely to socialise teachers into the life of the school. In Scotland, the standard associated with beginning teacher induction has renewed, formalised and revitalised the experience of NQTs (Draper and O'Brien, 2006; O'Brien, 2009).

As they proceed through their careers, teachers may experience in-service provision as 'a set of disconnected and decontextualised experiences' (Feiman-Nemser, 2001: 1041), which operate on an ineffective 'deficit-training-mastery model' (Clarke and Hollingsworth, 2002: 948). In short, what Feiman-Nemser (2001: 1049) calls the 'connective tissue' linking the different phases of a teacher's career has been missing from the experience of many and there have been deficiencies in the professional development available to teachers at every stage. A framework of Standards may be viewed as an attempt to provide such 'connective tissue', however some standards are voluntary (Chartered Teacher and Headship) and many teachers will elect not to seek to achieve these. Indeed, most CPD that Scottish teachers undertake throughout their career may be unrelated to the Standards unless a renewable 'licence to teach' system is introduced and in Scotland this is now under discussion under the auspices of the General Teaching Council Scotland (GTCS). Indeed, while it may be accepted that teacher education has to improve there is no general agreement on how or why this can be realised (Cochran-Smith and Fries, 2005).

Recently, in Scotland, the former Chief Inspector conducted a wide-ranging review (Donaldson, 2010) to consider the best arrangements for the full continuum of teacher education in Scotland. The review focused on initial teacher education, induction and professional development and the interaction between them. The process involved examining evidence about effective approaches to teacher education within the UK and internationally. Stakeholders were actively involved through a call for evidence, a teacher survey and a series of meetings with interested parties. The report suggests measures to strengthen a career-long focus on professional learning, including the development of new standards, the opening of Master's-level accounts, systematic recording of training and a national online one-stop shop for resources. The development and delivery of a greater quantity and quality of provision in CPD to enhance teacher quality, leadership and management in education seems sensible but the review's conclusions and recommendations are wide-ranging and ongoing discussion will determine what and how specific recommendations and proposals can be overtaken. However, the Donaldson Review acknowledges that specific CPD approaches and initiatives including the development of Standards have not resulted in the outcomes of a collectively enhanced teaching workforce with related impact on student outcomes. Greater investment in CPD was called for by Barber (2005) in response to the degree of change evident in England in 2005 but the budgetary outlook is even more unfavourable today. The economic crisis and the UK's resulting budget deficit will inevitably have a part to play on the shaping of educational policy and, invariably in financially stringent times, teacher CPD finds itself an easy casualty. As Gamble (2010: 708) concludes:

> Managing the competing demands and interests of the markets and of citizens will test the robustness of many democracies, and the way in which these conflicts are resolved will shape the context in which future education policy is determined, and in particular the size, the funding and the ethos of education as a public service.

Despite advice from its own Council of Economic Advisers to expand the CT programme as a means of rewarding excellence in teaching and raising standards, the Scottish Government has agreed a deal with local councils to freeze entry to the programme for the next two years as a moneysaving measure.

Nevertheless, internationally, improving teacher quality remains a political imperative designed to deal with the continuing stubborn patterns of underachievement of students. Recognising the important relationship between teachers and learners suggests the need to better define and express what good teaching means. Understanding what constitutes quality teaching is a necessary element in designing approaches and providing context. This can go some way to guarantee the provision of quality teachers, and to encourage a common understanding of what may be needed across the range of stakeholders involved with teachers including government, universities and schools engaged in teacher preparation, prospective employers and increasingly teacher professional associations. Teacher unions and associations have moved to recognise that industrial trade unionism (while it has its place) is not the only approach and trade union interest in influencing and promoting teacher CPD has taken on a new lease of life in Scotland

(Alexandrou and O'Brien, 2007). Of course some more sceptical analysts would suggest that bringing trade unions into the policy-making process commits them to ensuring the success of such policies.

Success and impact of the Scottish Standards

Despite the current and hopefully temporary concerns over the cost of CT status, the initial processes of consultation that resulted in the publication of the Standard For Full Registration (SfFR) and Standard for Chartered Teacher have been reviewed positively. Generally, there is agreement that consultation on the Chartered Teacher standard was wide-ranging and thorough (Christie, 2003; Kirk *et al.*, 2003), although perhaps as Purdon (2003) suggests this was only because it was going to have to prove its value in the market place as it is not a compulsory standard. Consultation on the Standard for Full Registration was much more limited, controlled and less transparent, with few changes being made to the draft following the consultation and the final version delivered to schools as a *fait accompli* (Purdon, 2004). More importantly, there was no consultation on the *concept* of a standards-based reform of CPD. For some observers this indicates a tacit acceptance by the Scottish teacher profession that ultimate political control of CPD rests with SEED (Purdon, 2003) and there remain important questions associated with the purposes of the framework (O'Brien, 2007) that may or may not be dealt with in the post-Donaldson Review period.

The Scottish induction scheme has been described as world class by policy makers and there is some evidence to substantiate this claim (O'Brien and Draper, 2008; O'Brien, 2009). Certainly the Standard and associated support provided in schools has made a significant difference although there remain questions about the use of a formal standard and assessment juxtaposed with a developmental supportive induction approach. With respect to Chartered Teachers there is as yet less evidence (Connelly and McMahon, 2007) to access. To date, voluntary numbers coming forward to undertake or to demonstrate the professional learning necessary to be awarded Chartered Teacher status have been much less than initially expected. Recently, GTCS commissioned a report (McMahon *et al.*, no date) outlining the views of participants who had achieved CT status by May 2007. The report indicates (p. 8) that Chartered Teachers themselves believed the following typical of their classroom practice (many felt they already had such characteristics prior to seeking the status):

- self-confidence;
- knowledge and understanding that supports the exercise of effective professional judgement and decision-making;
- empathy, flexibility and responsiveness towards learners;
- the capacity to draw on a wide repertoire of teaching approaches;
- the capacity to continue to develop their practice; and
- a disposition to test and adopt innovative and creative approaches to addressing problems in teaching and learning.

Such evidence does suggest the Chartered Teacher Standard and associated programmes have a degree of efficacy and have confirmed or enhanced the professionalism of participants. This appears to substantiate Reeves' comments (2007: 62) when considering the Chartered Teacher Standard in Scotland:

> The clear commitment in this Standard to criticality and independence of judgement as a characteristic of teacher excellence in Scotland is both heartening and surprising, given that the Scottish system is as swamped with paper, performance indicators and targets as anywhere else in the UK. What this Standard affords for both providers of Chartered Teacher programmes and those teachers who wish to achieve the status is a space in which to assert a form of teacher professionalism which is in marked contradiction to the educational operationalism model.

However, MacDonald (2004) suggests that the framework for CPD and new approaches to school leadership and management based on more collegiate arrangements has made little difference to the compliance approach common to many Scottish teachers especially those in primary schools. It is far too early to make an assessment of the extent to which CTs raise the attainment of students, but to date there is scant evidence both of impact on student attainment and the desire to secure such evidence.

CPD for teachers and student attainment: the missing link?

We have noted above the apparent limitations in the English experience of reforming CPD especially with regard to enhanced classroom practice. The 2007 HMIE Report confirms that despite the Standards and CPD initiatives in Scotland that there was only very limited evidence of any impact on students' learning. While an underlying belief exists that raising the quality of teachers and teaching will result in improved student learning outcomes, the systematic and sustained evidence to substantiate this belief is in short supply across most education systems. All CPD whether it be Standards related and/or district- or school-based, personal or systems-led has not as yet been subjected to rigorous evaluation to provide the evidence of genuine impact on student outcomes. Is this perhaps because we lack the tools? There is a rich literature on evaluation propounding theories, models and techniques. Combining appropriate elements with a clear focus on the evaluation of the connections between CPD and student attainment may provide a way forward which will enhance and confirm teaching quality practice with purpose.

Harris *et al.* (2006: 92) discuss the possibilities and practicalities of evaluating CPD based on their report (Goodall *et al.*, 2005) and suggest that 'most useful evaluations combine methods, marrying the rigour of quantitative measures to the deeper formative information provided by qualitative methods, a process sometimes known as "holistic" evaluation'. They stress the role of feedback to participants as integral to effective evaluation that essentially has to be embedded in school processes. In a discussion of the limitations of evaluating CPD they identify lack of focus on cost effectiveness and agree with Guskey's views (2000) of the major weaknesses apparent in current approaches to the evaluation of CPD. When discussing the evaluation of CPD, Coldwell and Simkins (2011: 278–9) 'conclude that the complexity of CPD processes and effects and, crucially, of the social world requires a range of approaches, and that – therefore – an approach based on any single model is not enough.' While recognising this reservation, and the weaknesses identified above, two particular approaches have been highly influential of late in the evaluation of CPD, namely the work of Guskey (2000) and Kirkpatrick (1998) who identified four levels of outcome for interventions:

1   participants' reactions;
2   participants' learning;
3   changes in participants' behaviour; and
4   desired results.

Within the UK, Muijs and Lindsay (2008) suggest there is efficacy in the Guskey model of evaluating CPD. There is clearly a need to follow-up and follow-through CPD interventions so that clear links are established between CPD provision for teachers leading to enhanced teacher quality and the attainment and achievement of students. This should be an imperative not only for those systems that have adopted standards frameworks but also for those only now considering them. This need not be supportive of managerialism and operationalism approaches but can clearly also underpin developmental and professionally enhancing programmes of personal and professional learning. Guskey's 5 Level Model of Evaluation (Table 10.1) offers a number of insights and can generate substantial useful data.

Table 10.1 Guskey's 5 Level Model of Evaluation

Evaluation level	*Crucial questions*
1 Participants' reactions to an intervention or event	– Did they like the provision or intervention? E.g. training provided – Will it be useful? E.g. skills developed – Were the domestic arrangements OK?
2 Participants' learning	– Did the participants actually acquire the intended knowledge and skills? – Evidence of this?
3 Organisational support and change	– What was the impact on the organisation? – Was implementation advocated, facilitated and supported? – Were sufficient resources made available?
4 Participants' use of new knowledge and skills	– Did participants effectively apply the new knowledge and skills?
5 Student learning outcomes	– What was the impact on students/pupils/organisation? – Did it affect student performance or achievement? – Are students more confident as learners?

Guskey suggests (pp. 8–10) that there are serious limitations in existing CPD evaluation practices which Muijs and Lindsay (2008) summarise:

a   Most 'evaluation' encompasses a summary of the CPD activities undertaken. E.g. what courses were attended, and similar limited statistical data. In such approaches there is no attempt to provide an indication of the effectiveness of any CPD intervention.

b   When evaluation occurs, it usually involves the completion of participant satisfaction questionnaires. This may provide indicators of how enjoyable and successful an event or programme may have been but again fails to engage with development or impact issues either on the participant or subsequently on student knowledge and outcomes.

c   Evaluations are usually brief, one-off events, often undertaken immediately after an event and rarely followed through. Evaluation to be effective and to measure impact appropriately should involve more long-term processes.

Guskey also points out that the knowledge base in education is constantly expanding and teachers like other professionals must keep abreast of the emerging knowledge base and use it to 'up-skill' and to impact positively on their practice and their students. He also emphasises that professional development for educators must ensure enduring change in their attitudes and perceptions along with how they use the new knowledge and skills they have acquired.

Borko (2004: 4) poses the questions 'What do we know about professional development programs and their impact on teacher learning? What are important directions and strategies for extending our knowledge?' She then outlines a developmental 3 Phase approach to researching the impact of CPD:

> Phase 1 research activities focus on an individual professional development program at a single site. Researchers typically study the professional development program, teachers as learners, and the relationships between these two elements of the system. The facilitator and context remain unstudied. In Phase 2, researchers study a single professional development program enacted by more than one facilitator at more than one site, exploring the relationships among facilitators, the professional development program, and teachers as learners. In Phase 3, the research focus broadens to comparing multiple professional development programs, each enacted at multiple sites. Researchers study the relationships among all four elements of a professional development system: facilitator, professional development program, teachers as learners, and context.

Borko indicates that this is not a linear process and that there is much work to be done in all 3 Phases which may cross-fertilise between them and suggests (p. 14) especially in relation to Phase 3 initiatives that:

> To conduct the large-scale, multi-method field studies needed to address these questions will require new data collection and analysis tools – for

example, instruments to measure change over time in teachers' subject matter knowledge for teaching and instructional practices, and analytic tools that can separate out the influences of various program, school, and individual factors on teacher and student learning.

While there have been UK studies about the impact of CPD (Flecknoe, 2000; Leaton Gray, 2004; Soulsby and Swain, 2003), perhaps it is time for a strong focus on a combination of approaches? The need to add to Borko's suggested Phase elements by asking questions related to Guskey's Level 5 focus seems necessary so that we can move away from levels associated with participant satisfaction and learning. Clearly we need to heed to have focused professional learning at school level about evaluation itself. As Harris *et al.* (2006: 98–9) conclude:

> evaluative practices need to be much more sophisticated and fine grained to capture the complexity of organisational and individual change. A range of evaluative approaches are needed that match Guskey's (2000) five levels and have the potential to give meaningful formative and summative feedback to schools and teachers. Without these evaluative approaches, gauging the relative effectiveness of different forms of CPD will remain elusive and by implication investing in forms of CPD that have little or no impact on the teacher and learner will unfortunately remain a real possibility.

By developing in-school evaluation we would seek to produce particular evidence that CPD does increase teacher quality *and* there are related advances in student attainment. This may result in new and more effective designs for CPD that in turn will disseminate aspects of SESI research and evidence to impact on classroom practice and student attainment.

11 What we have learned from school improvement about taking educational reform to scale

David Hopkins

Thirty years ago this summer I read a book that changed the course of my professional life. Prior to 1979, the ability of schools to make a difference to student learning was widely doubted. Michael Rutter (1979) and his colleagues, however, with the publication of *15000 Hours*, demonstrated unequivocally that schools with similar intakes had widely contrasting effects on student performance. More importantly, the factors that accounted for that difference were largely internal and open to modification by the school staff themselves. So at last research evidence was emerging on the differential effectiveness of schools that gave an impetus and direction to those, who like myself, were beginning to work in the field of school improvement. Since then, the educational scene has changed dramatically both in terms of policy and practice, we have learned a great deal more about pedagogy and school transformation, and the emphasis on globalisation, collaboration and systemic reform has increased exponentially (Hopkins, 2007b). So, thirty years later it is pleasing to be invited to contribute to this book in order to reflect on 'what we have learned from school improvement about taking educational reform to scale' – the title of this article.

In his recent chapter in *Change Wars* Sir Michael Barber (2009) reminds us that it was the school effectiveness research in the 1980s that gave us increasingly well-defined portraits of the effective school that led in the 1990s to increasing knowledge of school improvement, i.e. how to achieve effectiveness (Hopkins and Reynolds, 2001). In the same way, we have in the last decade begun to learn far more about the features of an effective educational system, but are now only beginning to understand the dynamics of improvement at system level. What is needed is a 'grand theory' of system change in education that results in relatively predictable increases in student learning and achievement over time – this chapter is a modest contribution to that worthwhile and necessary goal.

Attempts at system improvement

The equivalent of the school effectiveness research at the system level has been provided during the last decade or so by the advent of international benchmarking studies. Most probably the best known and most influential is the OECD's Programme for International Student Assessment (PISA). Since 2000 when the

OECD launched PISA they have been monitoring learning outcomes in the principal industrialised countries on a regular basis. As Andreas Schleicher (2009) who leads the PISA for the OECD recently said, 'In the dark, all institutions and education systems look the same. It is comparative benchmarking that sheds light on the differences on which reform efforts can then capitalise.' Although, as Schleicher admits, international benchmarks alone cannot identify cause and effect relationships between inputs, processes and educational outcomes, they can highlight those key features in which education systems show similarities and differences and relate them to a student performance on a variety of outcome measures.

As a result of this work we have learned a great deal about high performing educational systems over the past ten years. This is not only from PISA, but also from secondary analyses such as Fenton Whelan's (2009) *Lessons Learned: how good policies produce better schools* and the McKinsey study (2007) *How the World's Best Performing School Systems Come Out on Top.*

As we shall see in a little more detail later, there have also been ambitious attempts to reform whole systems, but these have tended to be: (i) oppressive and resulted in considerable alienation such as some of the state-wide reforms in the USA; (ii) well designed and centrally driven but with impact stalling after early success as with the literacy reforms in England; or (iii) sustained, but usually due to factors outside the immediate control of educators and policy makers such as in Finland.

Michael Fullan (2009) in his paper 'Large scale reform comes of age' reviewed the evidence on the success of large-scale improvement efforts over the past dozen years or so. He identifies three phases that such reform efforts have passed through with increasing effectiveness.

The first is the pre-1997 period where the pressure for reform was mounting. Throughout the 1960s and 70s there were examples of exemplary curriculum innovation but none produced success at scale. Similarly in the 1980s and 90s, although the impact of the international research on school improvement sponsored by the OECD (Hopkins, 1987) and national strategies for reform such as the introduction of national curricula and inspection regimes spoke of scalable ambition, but impact still remained serendipitous.

In the second period – 1997 to 2002 – there was evidence in some cases of whole system reform in which progress in student achievement was clear. Let us look briefly at the three examples referred to earlier and their limitations.

- As regards states in the USA, Leithwood (1999) and his colleagues reviewed the impact of a number of 'performance based' approaches to large-scale reform. Although there was some initial impact on test scores, this was not sustained over time. The fact that these reform strategies neglected to focus on instruction and capacity building must have contributed to their inability to impact positively on student achievement.
- The second example is that of England when in 1997 it was the first government in the world to use an explicit theory of large-scale change as a basis

for bringing about system reform (Barber, 2008). The National Literacy and Numeracy Strategy was designed to improve the achievement of 11 year olds in all 24,000 English primary schools. The percentage of 11 year olds achieving nationally expected standards increased from 63 per cent in 1997 to 75 per cent in 2002 in literacy and in numeracy the increase was 62–73 per cent. The achievements in literacy and numeracy were however not sustained post 2002, and the subsequent success was the consequence of a different strategic approach.

- Finland, now recognised as one of the top performing school systems in the world, is the third example. Hargreaves and colleagues (2007) argue in their OECD review that Finland demonstrated between 1997 and 2002 that a medium-sized country (five million people) could turn itself around through a combination of vision and society-wide commitment. However, it could also be argued that in Finland much of their success was due to factors outside the control of the educational sector, such as the degree of homogeneity in social structures and the considerable intellectual capital already existing in the country.

Fullan's third phase is 'Large-scale reform comes of age: 2003 – to present'. In reflecting on this era of more successful reform efforts, Fullan (2009: 107) comments:

> Coming of age does not mean that one has matured, but that people are de?nitely and seriously in the game. As this happens the work becomes more analytical as well as action-oriented. There is more convergence, but not consensus; debates are more about how to realize system reform, not so much what it is.

The dynamics of system change

In reflecting on how to 'realise system reform' I suggest in my book *Every School a Great School* that the key to managing system reform is by strategically re-balancing 'top-down and bottom-up' change over time (Hopkins, 2007a). This view is gaining some support. Barber (2009), for example, currently stresses the need for system leadership along with capacity building. Hargreaves and Shirley (2009) argue for a 'Fourth Way of Change' that consists of combining top-down 'national vision, government steering and support with 'professional involvement' and 'public engagement' all for the purpose of promoting 'learning and results'. The argument goes something like this:

- Most agree that when standards are too low and too varied some form of direct state intervention is necessary and the impact of this top-down approach is usually to raise standards, but only in the short term.
- But when progress inevitably plateaus – while a bit more might be squeezed out in some schools, and perhaps a lot in underperforming schools – one must question whether this is still the recipe for sustained reform.

- There is a growing recognition that to ensure that every student reaches their potential, schools need to lead the next phase of reform.
- The implication is that we need a transition from an era of Prescription to an era of Professionalism – in which the balance between national prescription and schools leading reform will change significantly.

However, achieving this shift is not straightforward – it takes capacity to build capacity, and if there is insufficient capacity to begin with it is folly to announce that a move to 'professionalism' provides the basis of a new approach. Fullan (2004: 7) also recognised early on the importance of leadership in system reform and in *System Thinkers in Action* argued that

> a new kind of leadership is necessary to break through the status quo. Systematic forces, sometimes called inertia, have the upper hand in preventing system shifts. Therefore, it will take powerful, proactive forces to change the existing system (to change context). This can be done directly and indirectly through systems thinking in action. These new theoreticians are leaders who work intensely in their own schools, or national agencies, and at the same time connect with and participate in the bigger picture.

The key question though is 'how do we get there?' We cannot simply move from one phase to the other without self-consciously building professional capacity throughout the system. It is this progression that is illustrated in Figure 11.1 (Hopkins, 2007a).

It is worth taking a little more time unpacking the thinking underlying the diagram. Four further points in particular need to be made:

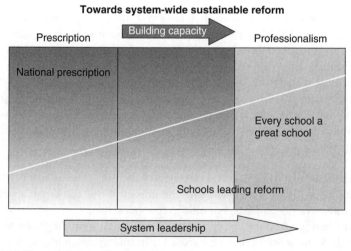

Figure 11.1 Towards large-scale sustainable reform

- The first is to emphasise that this not an argument against 'top-down' change. Neither 'top-down' nor 'bottom-up change' work just by themselves, they have to be in balance – in creative tension. The balance between the two at any one time will of course depend on context. The state reforms in the USA previously referred to employed a virtually exclusive top-down approach and failed simply because they just did not adapt the strategy over time.
- Second, it must be realised that in England in 1997, for example, it was clear that more central direction was needed initially. This reflects the balance towards national prescription as seen in the left-hand segment of the diagram, but over time the policy agenda and school practice moved towards the right-hand side of the diagram which accounts for the subsequent rise in standards.
- Third, of course there is no suggestion that one always has to start from the left-hand side of the diagram and move in some sort of uniform way to the right. Some systems, Finland for example, may well start from the middle and then move into the right-hand segment.
- Finally, it should be no surprise to realise that the right-hand segment is relatively unknown territory. It implies horizontal and lateral ways of working with assumptions and governance arrangements far different from what we know now. The main difficulty in imagining this landscape is that the thinking of most people is constrained by their experiences within the power structure and norms of the left-hand segment of the diagram.

It needs to be re-iterated that the transition from 'prescription' to 'professionalism' is not easy to achieve. In order to move from one to the other, strategies are required that not only continue to raise standards but also develop social, intellectual and organisational capital. This leads to two further and on initial appearance contradictory points:

- The first is that movement from one phase to another requires context-specific strategies that are described towards the end of the chapter.
- The second is that there are a number of continuing themes, described below, that require consistent focus throughout the improvement process.

Building capacity demands that we replace numerous central initiatives with a national consensus on a limited number of educational trends. In his paper, *Choosing the Wrong Drivers for Whole System Reform*, Michael Fullan (2011: 3) describes the wrong driver as a 'deliberate policy force that has little chance of achieving the desired result'. Whereas (Fullan, 2011: 5):

> The glue that binds the effective drivers together is the underlying attitude, philosophy and theory of action. The mindset that works for whole system reform is the one that inevitably generates individual and collective motivation and corresponding skills to transform the system.

Earlier, in *Every School a Great School* four drivers were proposed that are consistent with Fullan's analysis (Hopkins, 2007a). They are: personalised learning; professionalised teaching; networks and collaboration; and intelligent accountability, and it is these that provide the core strategy for systemic improvement. They are the canvas on which system leadership and reform is exercised. As seen in the 'diamond of reform' (Figure 11.2) the four trends coalesce and mould to context through the exercise of responsible system leadership.

Personalised learning We need to reach down into the classroom and deepen reform efforts by moving beyond superficial curriculum change to create more powerful learning pathways for our students. It is the *tasks* that students undertake that are at the heart of personalised learning. It is not what teachers think they have asked students to do, nor what the prescribed curriculum says they should be doing, but what students are actually doing and the sense they make of it that is fundamental. This is why in *Models of Learning, Tools for Teaching* (Joyce *et al.*, 2009: 4) we claimed that:

> Learning experiences are composed of content, process and social climate. As teachers we create for and with our children opportunities to explore and build important areas of knowledge, develop powerful tools for learning, and live in humanizing social conditions.

Professionalised teaching Significant empirical evidence suggests that teaching quality is the most significant factor influencing student learning that is under the control of the school (McKinsey, 2007). The phrase 'professionalised teaching' implies that teachers are on a par with other professions in terms of diagnosis, the application of evidence-based practices and professional pride. The image here is of teachers who use data to evaluate the learning needs of their students, and are consistently expanding their repertoire of pedagogic strategies to personalise learning for all students.

Intelligent accountability refers to the balance between national- or state-determined approaches to external accountability on the one hand and the capacity

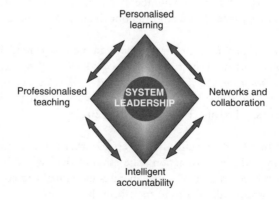

Figure 11.2 Four key drivers underpinning system reform

for professional accountability within the school that emphasises the importance of formative assessment and the pivotal role of self-evaluation on the other. There are two key purposes for accountability. The first is as a tool to support higher levels of student learning and achievement; the second is to maintain public confidence. In those situations where there is a need for more robust forms of external accountability it should always be designed to support teacher professionalism and the school's capacity to utilise data to enhance student performance.

Networks and collaboration It is clear from the prevalence of networking practice in recent years that networks have the potential to support educational innovation and change by

- keeping the focus on the core purposes of schooling in particular, the focus on student learning and enhancing the skill of teachers, leaders and other educators in change agent skills;
- providing a focal point for the dissemination of good practice, the generalisability of innovation and the creation of 'action-oriented' knowledge about effective educational practices;
- building capacity for continuous improvement at a local level, and in particular in creating professional learning communities, within and between schools;
- acting as a link between the centralised and decentralised schism resulting from many contemporary policy initiatives. In particular in contributing to policy coherence horizontally and vertically.

(Hopkins, 2001, 2002)

These key drivers provide a core strategy for systemic improvement through building capacity whilst also raising standards of learning and achievement. It is system leadership though that adapts them to particular and individual school contexts. This is leadership that enables systemic reform to be both generic in terms of overall strategy and specific in adapting to individual and particular situations. It is system leaders who reach beyond their own school to create networks and collaborative arrangements that, not only add richness and excellence to the learning of students, but also act as agents of educational transformation.

System leadership and segmentation as the basis of system transformation

One of the challenges to realising 'every school a great school' and the reason why reform efforts struggle to achieve a system-wide impact is because change is complicated by the high degree of segmentation within the school system. In any system there are a range of schools at varying stages of the performance cycle between low and high performing. For every school to be great we need to move to a new trajectory through using this diversity to drive higher levels of performance throughout the system. System transformation depends on excellent practice being developed, shared, demonstrated and adopted across and between schools.

It is important to realise, however, that this aspiration of system transformation being facilitated by the degree of segmentation existing in the system only holds when certain conditions are in place. There are two crucial aspects to this:

- First, that there is increased clarity on the nature of intervention and support for schools at each phase of the performance cycle; and
- Second, that schools at each phase are clear as to the most productive ways in which to collaborate in order to capitalise on the diversity within the system.

In both cases it is clear that one size does not fit all.

This process can continue to evolve in an *ad hoc* way as happens in most systems or it can be orchestrated by a national/regional organisation(s) with strong local roots or by networks of schools themselves. We developed this approach as a means of achieving a step change in performance of the 25,000 schools in the English school system during the mid-2000s, but the strategy has a wider applicability. As it happens, the most successful of these interventions was when a leading school partnered or federated with a school that was either facing challenging circumstances or was deemed 'failing' as a consequence of an external inspection. When the intervention design is strategic – in so far as it (a) incorporates quick wins within a medium-term approach; (b) concrete, so that successful practices are transferred rapidly from one school to the other; and (c) lubricated by extensive professional development and mentoring – the evidence suggests that the partner school can achieve national levels of performance within an eighteen-month to two-year period (Higham *et al.*, 2009). This contention has been supported by more recent empirical analyses of school improvement that has either broken the traditional link between poverty and achievement and/or sustained improvement over a three- to five-year time horizon (Day *et al.*, 2011; Hargreaves, 2010; Ofsted, 2009).

In order to be successful the 'segmentation approach' requires a fair degree of boldness in setting system-level expectations and conditions. There are five implications in particular that have to be grappled with:

1   There is a need to increase the resource of 'system leaders' who are willing and able to shoulder wider system roles. In doing so they are almost as concerned with the success and attainment of students in other schools as they are with their own.
2   All failing and underperforming (and potentially low achieving) schools should have a leading school that works with them in either a formal grouping such as a federation (where the leading school principal assumes overall control and accountability) or in more informal partnership.
3   Schools should take greater responsibility for neighbouring schools in order to build capacity for continuous improvement at the local level. This would be on the condition that these schools provided extended services for all students within a geographic area, but equally on the acceptance that there would be incentives for doing so.
4   The incentives for greater system responsibility should include significantly

enhanced funding for students most at risk. Beyond incentivising local collaboratives, the potential effects for large-scale long-term reform include

- A more even distribution of 'at risk' students and associated increases in standards, due to more schools seeking to admit a larger proportion of 'at risk' students so as to increase their overall income.
- A significant reduction of 'sink schools' even where 'at risk' students are concentrated, as there would be much greater potential to respond to the social-economic challenges (for example by paying more to attract the best teachers; or by developing excellent parental involvement and outreach services).

5   A rationalisation of national, state and local agency functions and roles to allow the higher degree of regional co-ordination for this increasingly devolved system.

It needs to be made clear however that, as was intimated earlier, for transformation, system leadership needs to be reflected at three levels:

- *System leadership at the school level* – with, at essence, Principals becoming almost as concerned about the success of other schools as they are about their own.
- *System leadership at the local/regional level* – with practical principles widely shared and used as a basis for local alignment with specific programmes developed for the most at risk groups.
- *System leadership at the national/state level* – with social justice, moral purpose and a commitment to the success of every learner providing the focus for transformation and collaboration system wide.

Operating systems and 'innovation clusters' as a means of achieving system improvement

Having described the pivotal role of the system leader it is now instructive to turn to the contribution to be made by national and local authorities in achieving system reform. A major problem here is that policy debates in many countries are often conducted with insufficient empirical evidence and policy claims are often made on the basis of tradition, aspiration or ideology. What is needed are policy frameworks that will allow countries to relate their policy choices more directly to student outcomes, to monitor the impact of changes in policy direction over time and possibly to compare policy options between countries.

In order to build the argument, it is helpful to use as an example the policy framework that underpinned the first term of New Labour's educational reforms (Hopkins, 2007a). The claim was that a national education strategy based on the principle of 'High Challenge and High Support' – that contained a complementary cocktail of policies that linked together:

- high standards but with quality materials and professional development;
- demanding targets but support for schools in the most challenging of circumstance; and
- external accountability but with increasing devolution of responsibility;

– is highly effective at raising standards in the short term.

The 'high support, high challenge' strategy proved to be successful in terms of the educational objectives of the first term New Labour government. But following the early success, standards soon began to plateau. It became clear to some that after a certain point more of the same just does not work. For learning and achievement to continue to rise into the medium to long term we need different policy arrangements because of the need to re-balance national prescription with schools leading reform. This re-balancing is necessary for building capacity for sustained improvement and leads to a transformed and re-imagined educational landscape.

The 'every school a great school' policy framework, described in this chapter, is equally sophisticated in terms of its aspiration as the 'high support, high challenge' strategy, but is more reflective of a context that has increasingly lateral responsibilities and alignments. This framework, which should be recognisable to those who have read so far, is seen below as Figure 11.3. In the centre is system leadership with the implication that it applies at a range of levels and roles within the system. The key policy drivers should also be familiar:

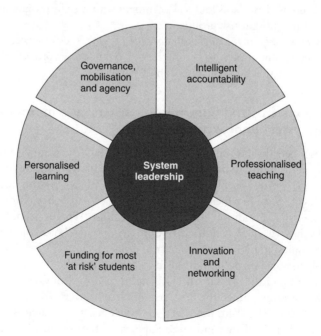

Figure 11.3 The 'every school a great school' policy framework

- The demand for personalisation requires a professional practice for teaching;
- The systemic potential of networking and collaborations requires new arrangements for governance and agency; and
- The realisation of 'intelligent accountability' within the school needs to be matched by a willingness to fund students who are most 'at risk'.

We can now locate these two contrasting policy agendas on the system reform framework discussed earlier. One can see in Figure 11.4 that on the left-hand side of the diagram the New Labour policy framework is more appropriate where standards are low and the emphasis on top-down as opposed to bottom-up change is necessary to produce rapid positive impact in the short term. The key point is that to maintain and enhance early success into the medium to long term the balance between 'national policy' and 'schools leading reform' needs to be strategically reversed over time. The proposal is that the 'every school a great school' policy framework is as appropriate for the right-hand segment of the rectangle as the original framework was to the left-hand segment in the early days of New Labour's educational reforms. This equilibrium is captured in Figure 11.4. The essential point is that different stages of reform require different strategies.

This though is not an 'either–or' issue, but more an evolutionary process that respects the wide degree of differentiation or segmentation within the system. Up until recently, however, in most systems and for most of the time, single strategies or policy initiatives tend to be worked on individually, rather than as a set of complementary and mutually supportive policies as seen in the previous discussion. What is needed is a heuristic framework to help governments (and schools) to reflect on how best to balance these various strategies in a comprehensive approach to systemic educational change.

Figure 11.5 provides an example of such a framework. It seeks to identify three key elements of a coherent approach to school change. The framework also suggests how these three elements may interact and impact on the learning and achievement of students. This idea was developed by Michael Barber (2005) based on the Thomas Friedman's analogy (1999) of a nation's economy being compared to a computer system. Originally developed for educational systems it can also apply to schools. There is the hardware – the infrastructure, funding and

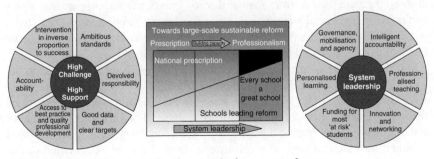

Figure 11.4 Complementary policy frameworks for system reform

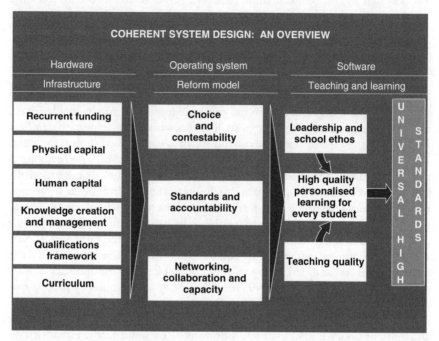

Figure 11.5 A coherent system design framework

physical resources as well as human and intellectual capital. There is also the soft-ware – the interaction between the school and the student, the process of teaching and learning infused by the leadership of the school. In between the two there is the operating system, or the strategy for change the school or system chooses, or not, to employ to develop itself as a whole.

Many schools, as well as Ministries of Education, assume that there is a direct link between the hardware and the software – as long as the resources are in place then student learning will be satisfactory. This is rarely the case and the reason is simple. We need a change strategy to link inputs to outputs: without it student and school outcomes will remain unpredictable. With it, schools will be more likely to translate their resources more directly into better learning environments and therefore enhanced learning outcomes for their children. It is also clear form the preceding argument that the set of policies or 'operating system' has to be finely tuned to the school or systems phase of development.

It is this line of thinking that has been given a greater degree of precision in the recent McKinsey (2010) report on *How the World's Most Improved School Systems Keep Getting Better*. This study is the most ambitious attempt so far to examine the improvement trajectories of educational systems. Based on their performance across a range of international benchmarking studies 20 systems were identified as either 'sustained improvers' or 'promising starts'. From an examination of this sample four stages of improvement were identified – 'poor to fair', 'fair to good',

'good to great' and 'great to excellent', In line with the research already discussed, this study identified 'stage-dependent' intervention clusters, or operating systems, that respectively were: focused on first ensuring basic standards, then consolidating system foundations, followed by professionalising teaching and leadership and finally system-led innovation.

There were, however, and in line with the four drivers previously described, six actions that apply equally across each of the phases. These are related to curriculum and standards, appropriate reward structures, building technical skill, assessing students, establishing data systems and ensuring a coherent policy framework.

The McKinsey researchers also commented in some detail on three other features of system reform. *Contextualising* refers to the way in which these intervention clusters and common policies were of necessity adapted to the specific context and cultural demands of the system. *Sustaining*, by which is meant a commitment to internalising and consistently applying a dynamic pedagogy framework as well as the positive existence of a 'mediating layer' between the centre and schools that provides support and challenge for schools. And finally the word *Ignition* captures the various ways in which change is initiated.

This is very helpful, and in two ways in particular. First it confirms the contours of this narrative; second it provides a stronger and more precise evidential base for designing system interventions. It is another step along the road of learning how to develop improvement strategies or recipes for reform from the factors or ingredients that make for successful school systems (Hopkins *et al.*, 2011).

Coda

In concluding, it is important to remember that the challenge of system reform has great moral depth to it. It addresses directly the learning needs of our students, the professional growth of our teachers and enhances the role of the school as an agent of social change. This is why I have argued that as we imagine a new educational future so we require a new operating system capable of realising a future where every school is a great one. That is why the discussion on coherent system reform is so important. The 'operating system' or 'innovation clusters' are not just technical devices for linking inputs to outputs; they are also metaphors for those strategies that when implemented lead towards 'every school a great school' as well as the 'good society'. They can be easily summarised. Below and based on the best of global experience are the principles that characterise reform efforts in high performing educational systems. Each principle has a high degree of operational practicality. The ten principles begin with:

1   Ensuring that the achievement and learning of students is at the centre of all that teachers do. This requires a focus on those strategies that have a track record of accelerating student achievement such as building student learning capability, personalising curriculum, assessment for learning and giving students a voice in their own learning.

2   As a consequence, the enhancement of the quality of teaching needs to be the

central theme of any improvement strategy. The quality of teaching is necessarily related to system goals that are likely to have a heavy emphasis in the first instance on the teaching of literacy and numeracy and the development of curiosity.

3   High levels of student learning and achievement will be partially achieved by selection policies that ensure that only the very best people become teachers and educational leaders; and then by

4   Putting in place ongoing and sustained professional learning opportunities that develop a common 'practice' of teaching and learning through blending theory, evidence and action through collaborative forms of enquiry.

5   This development of professional practice takes place in schools where the leadership has:

- very high levels of expectation for both teachers and students;
- an unrelenting focus on the quality of learning and teaching;
- created structures that ensure an orderly learning environment and that empower and generate professional responsibility and accountability;
- developed a work culture that takes pride in sharing excellence and has a high degree of trust and reciprocity; and
- when appropriate supported leadership development occurs across a locality.

6   The development of this professional practice occurs within a system context where there is increasing clarity on the standards implied by the goals set, and the generation of the most appropriate teaching strategies necessary to achieve those standards.

7   To enable this, procedures need to be in place that provide ongoing and transparent data (both assessment data and inspection evidence) on the performance of the student, school and system that facilitate improvements in learning and teaching.

8   School performance is therefore amenable to early intervention following diagnosis that reflects a range of differential strategies based on performance with targets being set that are related to implementation.

9   Inequities in student performance are addressed through:

- good early education;
- direct classroom support for those falling behind; and
- high levels of targeted resourcing.

10   Finally, system level structures are established that reflect the processes just described, that link together the various levels of the system through to the school and classroom, develop capacity by balancing professional autonomy and accountability and promote disciplined innovation as a consequence of networking. These activities combine to produce a work culture that has at its core strong pressure to improve, takes seriously its responsibility to act on and change context and that embodies a commitment to focus, flexibility and collaboration.

12 Thinking and acting both locally and globally

The future for school effectiveness and school improvement

Tony Townsend

Introduction

More than a decade ago, Paul Clarke, Mel Ainscow and myself wrote the book *Third Millennium Schools: A World of Difference in Effectiveness and Improvement* (Townsend *et al.*, 1999), which documented the thinking of scholars who had contributed to the 11th Annual ICSEI conference in Manchester in 1998. Since that time, the world has changed quite a bit. We have had terrorist attacks on the World Trade Center, we have had wars in Afghanistan and Iraq, we have had a black president elected in the United States and we have had a plethora of inventions and innovations, such as the artificial heart and liver, the hybrid car, the birth control patch, running shoes that know how firm or soft they should be for your foot, the iPod and iPhone, the memory stick for your computer, Twitter, the Wii and YouTube.

We also have massive changes in things that we knew about in the 1990s but probably didn't think that would reach the proportions they have now. We are faced with the major English-speaking country being China, closely followed by India, we have increasing concerns about global warming, we have massive increases in laptop computers being used in schools, text messaging and skype usage. An internet film of a television show in the United Kingdom is seen by millions of people and turns a dowdy Scottish spinster into the world-wide phenomenon of 'SuBo' in weeks. Then, she pretty much disappears just as quickly. What used to take decades or years to get used to now becomes popular in months or weeks. The interesting bit is how we have become so used to these changes so quickly.

So if we return to the theme of the 1998 Manchester conference, which was 'Reaching Out to All Learners', we now have to ask ourselves, what does this mean? It is interesting to recognise that this theme could equally well be the conference theme of an ICSEI today, but we may have to do it in a different way, with different speakers, different subthemes and different ways of determining success.

In the final chapter of the book that emerged from the conference we considered where SESI was headed under the title of 'Third Millennium Schools: prospects and problems for school effectiveness and school improvement' (Townsend *et al.*, 1999). In that chapter we tried to document the changes in the ways we thought about schools under the heading of 'Second and Third Millennium thinking about schools'.

It may be instructive to look again at what we said then and to consider what change, if any, has happened in education during the period since Drucker argued (1993: 209) that 'No other institution faces challenges as radical as those that will transform the school'.

It would be cause for conjecture as to whether schools in the year 2011 are more like the Second or Third Millennium schools listed above. Certainly some things have moved strongly, such as schools being subject to market forces, and others seem to not have moved at all, such as schools as we know them have been dramatically altered. The question we really need to ask is, 'How much change has happened in education and are we really keeping pace with what has happened in other aspects of life?'

Table 12.1 Second and Third Millennium thinking about schools

Second Millennium Schools	Third Millennium Schools
Schools provide formal education programmes, which students must attend for a certain minimum amount of time.	People have access to learning 24 hours a day 365 days a year through a variety of sources, some of which will be schools.
Schools offer a broad range of curriculum to prepare students for many varied life situations.	Schools offer a narrow curriculum focusing on literacy and generic technological and vocational skills.
Teachers are employed to 'know'.	Teachers are employed to match teaching to the needs of the learner.
The learner fits in with the teacher.	Schools are learning communities where everyone (students, teachers, parents, administrators) is both a learner and a teacher, depending on the circumstances.
Schools are communities of learners, where individuals are helped to reach their potential. The information to be learned is graded in a specific way and is learned a particular order.	Information is accessed according to the learner's capability and interest.
Everyone gets a similar content, with only limited differentiation based on interest.	The information will vary greatly after basic skills are learned.
Schools are still much the same in form and function as they were when they were first developed.	Schools as we know them have been dramatically altered in form and function, or have been replaced.
Schools have limited, or no, interactions with those who will employ their students or the people from the community in which the school resides.	Communities will be responsible for the education of both students and adults. Business and industry will be actively involved in school developments.
Schools are successful if they fit their students into a range of possible futures from immediate employment as factory hands and unskilled workers to tertiary education for training as professionals.	Schools will only be successful if *all* students have the skills required to work within, and adapt to, a rapidly changing employment social and economic climate.
Formal education institutions are protected from the 'market'.	Formal education institutions are subject to 'market' forces.

Changing views of education

Drucker (1993: 1) argued:

> Every few hundred years in western history there occurs a sharp transforma-
> tion. We cross . . . a divide. Within a few short decades society rearranges
> itself, its world view; its basic values; its social and political structure; its arts;
> its key institutions. Fifty years later, there appears a new world . . . we are cur-
> rently living through such a transformation.

He talks about societal transformation, the type that I have identified in the questions above. However, Drucker uses words like 'every few hundred years' and
'fifty years later', which suggest a sort of relaxed approach to change, where something that happens when I am a child permeates its way through society so that
by the time that I am fifty, we have all come to accept it. But Toffler (1971: 12),
on the other hand, suggests that this relaxed approach to change has collapsed, 'I
coined the term "future shock" to describe the shattering stress and disorienta-
tion that we induce in individuals by subjecting them to too much change in too
short a time'. He called it that feeling of 'vague, continuous anxiety', something
that I am sure many people in education today can relate to.

However, if we put these two statements together we gain an understanding that the world around us goes through substantial transformations, each of
which makes us see the world differently, and that these transformations seem
to be happening more and more frequently. As well, over time, certain changes
in our society have also changed the way in which we think about schooling.
Hedley Beare (1997) described these shifts by what he called metaphors for education that are helpful in terms of identifying when the major shifts in thinking
about schools came. From the dawn of time until the 1870s education might be
described as the 'pre-industrial metaphor' where education was 'for the few and
the privileged' (Beare, 1997: 4–5). From this time until the 1980s 'the industrial
metaphor' where 'the factory-production metaphor [was] applied to schooling'
(Beare, 1997: 5–6) was the dominant way in which education was seen and managed by 'bureaucracies which characterised factory production'. Finally he argued
that in the late 1980s we entered a time of the 'post-industrial metaphor' where
'enterprise' became 'the favoured way of explaining how education operates' and
'schools are being talked of as if they are private businesses or enterprises' (Beare,
1997: 9–13).

Using the same way of looking at the world I extended Beare's arguments into
the first decade of the twenty-first century (Townsend, 2009: 356). I argued that
up until the 1870s most education was aligned to individuals and I characterised
this as *thinking and acting individually*. But from as early as the 1870s in some
parts of the world, and up until the 1890s in others, communities started to take
responsibility for educating their people. I called this *thinking and acting locally*
(Townsend, 2009: 357). Now most people were receiving some education and
many people had education to a fairly high level.

However, by the 1980s we started to hear new terminology, 'national goals', 'national curriculum', 'national standards' and 'national testing', which was designed to adopt a more standardised approach to education across diverse state or district systems. As the opportunity to employ large numbers of people in factories diminished (the industrial age), governments (in the USA, the UK and Australia, for instance) argued there was a need for a highly skilled workforce and demanded that all students be educated for 'the knowledge age'. Education was now asked to *think nationally* but the way in which this was translated demonstrated that we were still *acting locally*.

It was at this point that the school effectiveness movement really started to have an impact on how we thought about schools. Up until this point, change had been a fairly relaxed affair with school improvement something that was done over time. However, what the school effectiveness research demonstrated quite clearly, from the 1980s onwards, is that the previous perceptions that social class could be blamed for differences in student achievement could no longer be used to the same effect. As Reynolds argued, the school effectiveness research has had the positive effect of 'helping to destroy the belief that schools can do nothing to change the society around them . . . and . . . the myth that the influence of family background is so strong on children's development that they are unable to be affected by school' (Reynolds, 1994: 2). However he also argued that it has had the negative effect of 'creating a widespread, popular view that schools do not just make a difference, but that they make all the difference' (Reynolds, 1994: 4) and it is this selective use of school effectiveness research by governments that possibly held back the progress of the field because it placed school effectiveness researchers in opposition to the social critical theorists, when in effect both groups were seeking the same outcome.

By the mid-1990s, the advent of TIMSS (then the *Third International Mathematics and Science Study,* now the *Trends in International Mathematics and Science Study*) started to create a new level of discussion. When this was joined by PISA, the OECD's *Program for International Student Assessment* which in 2009 tested in countries that make up 89 per cent of the world's economy, the international comparisons that were made in these tests led to *thinking internationally but still acting locally.* Although international comparisons were being used and countries were now sharing knowledge about curriculum, pedagogy and the administration of schools, individual schools were still seen as the locus of change. The dominant metaphor (if we use Beare's terminology) could be identified as accountability and the mechanism by which many governments have instituted this is through the use of market terminology.

Just as the rest of the world has accepted the idea of a global market, the education market has been constructed using the same underlying principles, that of privatisation and choice. Whether tacitly or not, governments, especially those in the west, seem to have accepted that they cannot afford to educate everyone to high levels of skill (despite the rhetoric that this is what is needed) and have adopted the rather facile approach of supporting private enterprise as the means of achieving this goal. Put simply (perhaps crudely), Western governments are saying 'If you don't like the school you are in, go to another one. If the government system can't provide for you, there is a private system that will'. This has allowed governments to keep education budgets within what they consider to be reasonable bounds, based on the other increasing demands for funding (from rapidly ageing and an increasingly overweight population of 'seniors' and those who will soon join them), together with a burgeoning budget for terrorism surveillance.

However, the school effectiveness research in many cases was used as a justification for some of the decisions being made by government. They argued that the more decentralised schools were, the more they seemed to be effective. Typical of this connection is the one made by Caldwell (1996: 13), who argued:

> when we do look at schools that have improved, or if we look at schools that are so-called effective schools, we've seen that in all cases, people have taken the initiative to make decisions for themselves, to solve their own problems, to set their own priorities. They've usually been schools that have been able to select their own staff in some way. So the characteristics of improving schools one can find in a system of self-managing schools.

This statement reflects the sort of leap-of-faith view that if the current practices of already successful schools are recreated for all schools, then all schools will become equally successful. This clear link between school effectiveness research, decentralisation and even a market orientation, one used by many governments to justify their policies, is a link that most school effectiveness people would disagree with. It could be argued that these are very simplistic responses to very complex problems.

What we can say is that there is ample evidence that student achievement has been hard to shift, even after all of the reforms that have occurred in recent times. The National Assessment of Educational Progress (NAEP) Reading test scores in the USA have been virtually unchanged despite over 40 years of educational reform efforts (Rampey *et al.*, 2009). There is some evidence that the gap between the socially advantaged and the socially disadvantaged has closed somewhat, but this has been confined to the elementary years of school. By the time students reach high school the level of performance is the same as it was in the 1970s. Despite all of the resources and reform efforts that have occurred since the 1980s after the *Nation at Risk* report, overall achievement is much the same as it was then.

However, an interesting study by Alexander *et al.* (2001), subsequently updated in 2007, suggests that the focus that is placed on schools for student achievement might not be as fair as we would hope. Their study, tracking students of 20 elementary schools in the Baltimore area, led them to conclude:

> cumulative achievement gains over the first nine years of children's schooling mainly reflect school-year learning, whereas the high SES–low SES achievement gap at 9th grade mainly traces to differential summer learning over the elementary years.

> (Alexander *et al.*, 2007: 1)

Poorer students, and especially those from the middle class, do better than their higher socio-economic counterparts during the school year, but the overall performance of schools is mitigated by the months that students spend away from school. This suggests that perhaps schools may have been more effective than politicians have given them credit for, and their ability to outweigh the social disadvantages of poor students is not as high as governments would have us think, because they are only in school for around 15 per cent of the year (or about 2 per cent of their lifetimes), and the rest of the time they are awake the community influence overwhelms what schools and teachers have done. In fact it could be argued that by the time that they reach the end of primary school, the amount of time spent in school is about the equivalent of the time they spend in their community, but is in many cases now considerably less than the amount of time spent in front of a computer.

The 2006 PISA Report makes the following statement:

> It is now possible to track change in reading performance over a six-year period. The results suggest that, across the OECD area, reading performance has generally remained flat between PISA 2000 and PISA 2006. This needs to be seen in the context of significant rises in expenditure levels. Between 1995 and 2004 expenditure per primary and secondary student increased by 39% in real terms, on average across OECD countries.
>
> (PISA 2006 – Executive Summary, p. 48)

This would suggest that our efforts at reforming schools might not be seen as being cost effective, or perhaps not effective in any sense. We have moved through what Beare called the Pre-Industrial, the Industrial and the Post-Industrial metaphors of education and we are currently in what I call the Accountability metaphor of education, where the market and choice programmes have been put in place as a means of promoting education for all. However, we are not yet there. Townsend (1998: 248) argued:

> We have conquered the challenge of moving from a quality education system for a few people to having a quality education system for most people. Our challenge now is to move from having a quality education system for most people to having a quality education system for all people.

Perhaps the way forward is to start *thinking and acting both locally and globally* and the metaphor for education has to change again, from accountability, which clearly has not worked, to responsibility, where we do what is necessary to deliver a quality education to the world's population. Here, the recognition is that for true education to occur, we cannot have education for the few who are rich and privileged (pre-industrial), we cannot see schools as factories (post-industrial) or businesses (enterprise), and we cannot expect the market to solve our problems (accountability), but must see education as a global experience, where people work together for the betterment of themselves, each other, the local community and the planet as a whole. To do this the focus must become universal. All people must succeed.

Townsend (2009: 364) argued that we have to do things in a different way:

> we have to move beyond accountability, which is simply a counting and sort-ing process, and seems to mostly have been designed to enable politicians to report things to communities in slick sound bites and with little or no analy-sis, and towards responsibility, where we need to respond to the needs and circumstances of the young people we serve and have an internal motivation to improve schools, not because it makes us look better, but because it is the right thing to do for the young people we interact with. Under these circum-stances communities, and governments, accept that it is both their legal and moral responsibility to ensure that all people within their communities are given the educational provision required to enable them to achieve their full potential as global citizens.

There are implications in moving towards thinking and acting both locally and globally at the policy level, for both teaching and leadership practice and for the education of both teachers and school leaders. These levels incorporate how we structure education at the system level, how leadership and classroom practices need to change in schools, which in turn affects curriculum, pedagogy and assess-ment practices. This leads to new understandings about educating both teachers and school leaders. Since these issues are briefly described in Townsend (2009), I wish to use the rest of this chapter to focus only on how thinking and acting both locally and globally will impact on our understanding of school effectiveness and school improvement and to make some tentative statements as to how SESI might move forward in ways that might support educational change on the global level.

School effectiveness and school improvement: thinking and acting both locally and globally

One of the original tenets of the school effectiveness research was a strong belief in social justice. This is perhaps best summed up by Edmonds (1978: 3) when he said:

> Specifically, I require that an effective school bring the children of the poor to those minimal masteries of basic school skills that now describe minimally successful pupil performances for the children of the middle class.

So much has happened in the time since that statement. Certainly there have been ups and downs along the way. However, overall, the field has moved forward quite substantially. At the conclusion of their book in 1999 (Townsend *et al.*, 1999: 365) made the comment:

What it means to be an effective school, given some of the scenarios we have painted, suggests that the next twenty years of research may be even more interesting than that we have identified in this book. It will be a journey worth taking.

We are now halfway through that 20-year period, so what can we say now? First, somehow, school effectiveness still manages to get itself tied to government policies which seem to pay lip-service to social justice without having the necessary strength to actually bring this about. As mentioned earlier, the ability of government to selectively use the research and then to ignore much more robust and sensitive methods of analysing the effects, because it didn't suit their needs, has been to the detriment of the movement for more than a decade. The data collected from early studies has been used as a major force in one of the sweeping reforms that have occurred in the past two decades, the movement towards self-managing schools, which now is an accepted form of school governance in many countries around the world, with the promise of more to come. The terms used may be different, but the impact is much the same. Responsibilities previous held in the centre have been moved to the school, with vastly increased forms of accountability and reporting. In the new accountability regime, countries are compared to other countries, states or provinces within a country are compared, districts or local authorities are measured against one another and individual schools are identified as being successful or not, with different consequences for unsuccessful schools, from attracting additional funds and support in some places, to being shut down in others.

Yet, there is evidence that the collection and analysis of data is much more valid and sensitive to the various factors at play. Multilevel modelling, Structural Equation Analysis and a stronger focus on the broad range of schools, rather than simply an analysis of outliers, is now able to provide a much more robust understanding of both school and classroom effectiveness than there was a decade ago. Stringfield (2010: pers. comm.) reports that

> The simultaneous evolution of both quantitative measures geared to the analysis of multi-level quantitative data, and the increasing sophistication of qualitative methods, both leading to the rapidly emerging field of mixed-methods research methods, are increasing the rate of understanding of the field.

While Creemers and Kyriakides (forthcoming) promote 'the use of a dynamic perspective of educational effectiveness and improvement stressing the importance of using an evidence-based and theory-driven approach to the improvement of teaching practice'.

Further, Bisschoff and Rhodes (forthcoming) make it abundantly clear that what might count as effectiveness in many Western countries just has no meaning in places like sub-Saharan Africa where just getting to go to school in the first place, let alone regularly and safely, is a bonus in young people's lives.

Townsend (2007: 951) suggested the need for a range of new ways of looking at the field of school effectiveness and school improvement:

- Redefining the concept of effectiveness to consider contextual issues that occur at various levels of education.

- Redefining the measurement of effectiveness to consider broad, rather than narrow, outcomes, based on the reality of people's experiences of the world.
- Redefining the structures and implementation of schooling in ways that take into account the complexity of the experience.
- Redefining the experience of schooling for students based on what we now know about learning, about the impact of context and about the changes brought about by globalisation and technology.
- Redefining teacher education to consider the issues of effectiveness identified above for the professional education and development of teachers and school leaders.

If we are to take seriously the statement 'thinking and acting both locally and globally', then we have to define what we mean by 'local' and 'global' and there are various levels that we need to think about to do this. If the student is local, then the classroom is global; if the classroom is local, then the school is global; is the school is local, then the system is global; if the system is local, then the community, or society in which that system resides is global; and finally, if the society is local, then the world is global. There are various players within each of these levels and if we are to both think and act locally and globally there are implications related to finding world's best practice and translating that into individual classrooms, schools or school systems. Since the world's best classroom practice exists in classrooms (somewhere), the trick is to find out where those classrooms are, research them well and then translate the results into some form of communication that can be heard by others. Some questions to consider, given each of the imperatives listed above, might be:

- On redefining the concept of effectiveness to consider contextual issues that occur at various levels of education, what would change if the unit of effectiveness being measured was:

    - the school system (an effective educational system)?
    - the community (an effective educational neighbourhood)?
    - the student (an effective educational student)?
    - the family (an effective educational family)?
    - the government (an effective educational government)?

- On redefining the measurement of effectiveness to consider broad, rather than narrow, outcomes, based on the reality of people's experiences of the world, how would we measure the following:

    - education for survival (the building blocks for everything else)?
    - understanding our place in the world (how my particular talents can be developed and used)?
    - understanding community (how I and others are connected)? and
    - understanding our personal responsibility (understanding that being

a member of the world community carries responsibilities as well as rights)?

- On redefining the structures and implementation of schooling in ways that take into account the complexity of the experience, where are the powerful decisions about education taken:
  - Nationally?
  - Local authority level?
  - School level?
  - Somewhere else?
  - If we are to focus our attention on every child, where *should* these decisions be made?

- On redefining the experience of schooling for students based on what we now know about learning, about the impact of context and about the changes brought about by globalisation and technology, if the situation below is the current case:

Every morning in every school in the world, there are two groups of students who bring different understandings of what their day will be like. For the first group, they are going to a place they enjoy (school) to work with people they like (teachers) to do something of value (learning) that will bear fruit in the future. The second group are going to a place that they hate, to work with people they think hate them, to do something they don't believe they can do for a future they don't have.

(Townsend, 2007: 957)

  - How do we change this so the latter group have the attitudes of the former group?

- On redefining teacher education to consider the issues of effectiveness identified above for the professional education and development of teachers and school leaders, Clinch (2001) argued 'There are two types of teachers, the tellers and the askers'.
  - Which type is more likely to lead to effective learning?
  - If we learn best when we are asked questions, what types of teachers do we need?

We still have to define school effectiveness in a way that allows all countries to understand what the term means, we need to identify first of all what we should measure when we are talking about school effectiveness and then come up with ways of doing that and then we need to build teacher and school leader education programs that will enable the highest levels of skills to be developed. That, as Townsend (2010: 15) points out, is not an easy task either, as different governments around the world focus on different aspects to develop in either teachers or school leaders: 'In Florida, the focus is firmly on the "what" of school leadership.

Victoria, on the other hand, has gone some way to not only consider the "what" but also to focus on the people issues, the "how" of school leadership'.

None of these are easy issues and to think that they are is making the mistake of trying to deal with a complex problem by using simple solutions. So, if we reconsider the issues identified above, we recognise that despite all of the progress made and especially with that in the past decade, we still have a long way to go. What we can say, however, is that if the progress of school effectiveness and school improvement over the last decade is matched by further development over the next decade, then we should be much closer to solving the complex issue of educating everyone to the level of quality that we hope for.

13 Finding balance

Cultivating a future

Paul Clarke and Anthony Kelly

I think that there are good reasons for suggesting that the modern age has ended. Today, many things indicate that we are going through a transitional period when it seems that something else is painfully being born. It is as if something were crumbling, decaying, and exhausting itself – while something else, still indistinct, were rising from the rubble.

(Václev Havel, President Czech Republic, speech in Philadelphia, June 1994)

Introduction

In 2010, the human race changed from being predominantly rural to predominantly urban. We can now legitimately claim to be an industrial, human-centric, urban species. This industrialisation shapes our economies, our societies and our cultures, and its lexicon of improvement and effectiveness determines how we collectively think and act. More than 3.3 billion people now live in urban environments; by 2030 this is estimated to increase to 5 billion of a global population predicted to peak at around 9 billion mid-century.[1] The dominant narrative of the modern urban world, which forms many of the conditions in the cities we inhabit globally, has emerged from the industrial era, and this narrative is promoted and maintained through an overwhelmingly industrial model of schooling. However, its utilitarianism is showing signs of fatigue (Chomsky, 2006); simultaneously with the rise in population, we are witnessing an unprecedented collapse in our global ecosystem and increasing dysfunction in our systems of education, health, politics, finance and agriculture. The established linear capitalist model seems no longer sufficient to provide for a changing reality, which suggests that the way we relate to our world is outdated, destructive and unsustainable, and our solutions predictable, short term and pathologically selfish.

What happens next? This largely depends upon how, and whether, we can we learn to live more sustainably in our built landscapes and communities around the planet, turning our collective genius for science, technology and the arts towards establishing new foundations for a sustainable society (Diamond, 2005). This is ultimately an *educational* challenge; a challenge of how to respond to a crisis through schooling in its broadest sense and with practical sustainable solutions.

A measure of our action

As we settle in to our new found urban mind, what will be the measure of our collective action? We already have some indicators, for industrialised nations the sum of our activity currently boils down to Gross National Product (GNP), an economic metric; in the Kingdom of Bhutan, the sum of collective worth is measured as Gross National Happiness, a measure of well-being; in China, the government have recently announced a national Talent Plan,[2] a skills measure. Yet while these different measures are important, they are trumped by one single overarching value which functions universally as a coherent measure of concern: that of ecological sustainability,[3] a life-ensuring measure. All other measures – indeed all other endeavours, whether technological, scientific, artistic or economic – are reduced to nothing if the ecological systems upon which we depend cease to function (Berry, 2005). It therefore becomes *the* significant educational question: how do we educate and school ourselves as a species in order to establish the conditions which are conducive to maintaining life on earth? It is not something we have yet established as a basis for our educational actions, and consequently, our trajectory of development has been and remains fundamentally unsustainable. As we have sought greater literacy in the traditional sense, we have become functionally illiterate ecologically.

Education for sustainable development

The focus on establishing sustainable conditions has been an international concern for some time, under the guise of 'sustainable development'. Sustainable development[4] is a term first used by the United Nations in the Brundtland Commission (UN, 1987), which coined what has become the often-quoted definition as development that 'meets the needs of the present without compromising the ability of future generations to meet their own needs'. Sustainable development ties together concern for the carrying capacity of Natural Systems with the social challenges facing humanity. As such, the field of sustainable development is broken into three constituent parts that capture critical components:

1 environmental sustainability;
2 economic sustainability; and
3 sociopolitical sustainability.

Each component is pursued through a restorative intent, and leads to restorative action, sometimes integrated, sometimes isolated.

Despite its widespread use, the idea of sustainable development is not without its critics (Ridley 2010; Jickling, 1992). James Lovelock's (2006, 2009) recent work challenged the premise of sustainable development by arguing, 'Two hundred years ago, when change was slow or non-existent, we might have had time to establish sustainable development, or even have continued for a while with business as usual, but now is much too late, the damage has already been done' (pp. 3–4). Lovelock makes a compelling case of the failings of the scientific community to confront the practical realities of the evidence that they have gathered, suggesting that 'as a cosy, friendly club of specialists who follow their numerous different stars, they are wonderfully productive but never certain and always hampered by the persistence of incomplete world-views' (ibid.).

We might apply Lovelock's critique across every sector of our societies, but it would seem to have particular resonance when applied to educational policy and practice, and of recent efforts in the field of school effectiveness and improvement. Education and schooling deal daily with uncertainty and incompleteness, but the education and schooling system could not be more differently conceived, based as it is upon operational certainties and business as usual despite evidence to the contrary. We suggest that it is this approach to education that is now causing us so many problems in our schools. Education is wedded to an industrial economic model, and measured through GNP. It teaches people to participate inside an economic system that perpetuates consumers, reliant upon continuous economic and industrial growth. This, the old order, has crumbled, its financial system is in tatters (Soros, 2008), and its associated institutions are in varying degrees of crisis. We continue to operate schools in a way that suggests there is no alternative, yet we fail to see that the damage in many schools is already done, the old formula is redundant.

Instead, we need to imagine a future beyond the existing order of things (Carson, 1962). This is the basis of a new set of measures, where the effort is focused upon a need to transform the whole idea of education as a preparation of our communities for sustainable living (Alexander *et al.*, 1977; Barth *et al.*, 2007). If we consider the role of education in this way, we can explore it on economic, cultural, personal and societal terms, through the lens of how we relate to our planet. Ecological sustainability enables us to establish the conditions to maintain the diversity of life as the basis of productivity, so:

- society must have the capability and resilience to solve and preferably prevent its major problems in a timely fashion (equity is one contributing factor);
- society's aggregate use of resources and land must be ultra-frugal;
- material flowing into and out of society must not systematically increase (the previous two conditions require a closed-cycle economy, de-materialisation, and geographical containment/land efficiency);
- the human population must be sustainable;
- actions must be timely and at an adequate scale.

To establish these capabilities people need to be able to solve and prevent major problems in a timely fashion, so these conditions might include:

- honesty/not corruption;
- participatory action;
- diverse and constant experimentation;
- inclusive, caring, cohesive, tolerant communities;

- critical skills of analysis and reflection;
- creative and skilled processes of socialisation;
- anticipatory abilities, future scoping and pattern understanding;
- conservation of valuable aspects of present and past;
- commitment to the achievement of the social good and collective well-being;
- ability to give adequate time to civic activity and community;
- adequate resource and equipment to ensure that the civic infrastructure, knowledge and skills are maintained and enhanced;
- a political system/s which can achieve these objectives.

This is a major new educational undertaking, demanding new metrics, but as we can see, elements of our existing educational system are already present in such goals. What is perhaps different is the focusing instrument of ecological need, and it is this, as Joanna Macy and Young Brown (1998) argue, that can be understood as the essential adventure for our time – a shift from the Industrial Growth Society to a life-sustaining civilisation.

This is a re-evaluation of how we live together on a grand scale and represents an awakening of an environmental consciousness. As they observe (ibid., 35),

> People are recognizing that our needs cannot be met without destroying our world. We have the technical knowledge, the communication tools, and material resources to grow enough food, ensure clean air and water, and meet rational energy needs. Future generations, if there is a livable world for them, will look back at the epochal transition we are making to a life-sustaining society . . . To see this as the larger context of our lives clears our vision and summons our courage.

A climate of change

What of the context of these observations? John Beddington, the UK Government's Chief Scientific Adviser, recently warned of difficult times ahead, to which government needed to begin to respond; where climate change, energy shortages, food shortages, water depletion all converge to create the 'perfect storm of environmental and economic collapse' (Beddington, 2009). These observations are not reserved to scientific commentators, within the corporate world Lloyds of London (2010) reported that the idea of *business as usual* is no longer a feasible way to respond to the set of global ecological challenges. In their annual analysis of risks to business, the Lloyds Group (ibid.) specifically identified water, food, energy and population as themes that have to be attended to over the next fifty years.

What is perfectly clear is that even if we are not just yet at the endgame of an old order, we are indeed in a significant period of existential and physical disequilibrium within our taken-for-granted systems of social and economic organisation. As Havel's quote at the start of this chapter illustrates, as one set of circumstances begins to fragment, a new set of circumstances begins to rise; such is the way of evolutionary change. The question is what might those be, and how well will they facilitate the required conditions for ecological sustainability?

Instructional shift

What is also clear is an underlying assumption that we will find the appropriate mode of instruction to facilitate the move from one way of living to a whole new level of living. This signals a radical overhaul of how we modify the destructive tendencies of capitalist consumer society. As Tim Jackson from the New Economics Foundation observes, we need new models of learning that render the existing ways of seeing our complex reality as obsolete (Jackson, 2009), primarily because the existing industrial models have generated the conditions that have created the global ecological and economic crisis (Soros, 2008).

The connection between the natural story and the human story therefore comes down to past, present and future measures of balance and new ideas of what we call 'growth'. Instead of simply measuring economic output, an emphasis on ecological sustainability raises the bar for communities to redefine their presence on the earth. Our defining questions become questions of harmony: Do the human and natural narratives co-exist harmoniously? Or are they in crisis? Do we currently have the wisdom to make appropriate judgments to rectify any imbalance? Do we need to learn new things to move forward? How does this translate into the school context, which has structural and cultural association to the old rather than new order?

Direct instruction has a place in establishing and communicating a knowledge base of unsustainable and sustainable practice, but not on its own. Scientific evidence over the last decade is overwhelming agreed on the view that climate change is evident across the planet,[5] yet on its own, we have seen, the general public do not respond to such data and make substantive life changes. It is in itself, an indicator that our relationship with the earth is far from harmonious and at a sufficiently significant state of disequilibrium to consider how we might change track (Kellstedt *et al.*, 2008). These concerns are by no means wishful thinking, even putting aside climate challenges, as Lloyds (2010) indicate, the convergence of water, food, and particularly in the next decade energy challenges, are sufficient to focus the collective mind to ask can we do this differently? Defining how to interpret what we might do, and how we might proceed are not simple responses to circumstance, they need reformulating educationally on the grand scale (Berry, 1999, 2009; Kirschenmann, 2010; Macy, 2006).

Cultivating (sustainable) community

Our own take on this problem was first formulated in the early 1980s (Clarke, 1983). Since that time we have been interested in the ways that human community can connect through education for collective action, self-realisation and social change.

A decade ago (Clarke, 2000), the school-based learning community concept was formulated on the notion that its integration in the education system would stimulate a progressive and systemic redesign. However, reflecting on the earlier work on the learning community we think that too much faith was put on the institution of the school as an agent of social change and too little recognition that school is in fact an agent of social conformity. Despite many valiant efforts, it is clear that the learning community concept was in this regard, fundamentally flawed, being, too insular, managerially conceived and self-referential to modify the dominant narrative of reform (Clarke, 2010a).

Instead, drawing upon lessons learnt in formulating learning communities (Jackson, 2004) we have been developing both practically and theoretically, the idea of Sustainable Community. This involves stepping beyond the constraints of the school environment and connecting to the wider community, service and business sectors, then reconnecting schools within these new configurations.

In doing this we have become interested in the way in which we might use the metaphor of growing, literally and metaphorically, as a focusing idea to develop our communities. Cultivating sustainable community through investigation of the implications of living sustainably within our places, understanding how community is formed through sustained relationship, through practical sustainable action and a fervent interest in all aspects of how we humans thrive in consort with other living things (Clarke, 2009a, 2009b, 2010a) connects people, ideas, places and actions in ways that the earlier idea of single site-based solutions seemed to restrict. In turn, a multi-site set of activities focused on growing food, which draws these disparate themes together, provides a range of different ways for people to generate assets that enhance the capability (Sen, 1999) of communities to become more resilient in a period of change. This includes responding to cultural, social, ecological, economic and spiritual needs, but in this particular example they have a specific connection to cultivating food within urban and rural settings, and an examination of how such cultivation generates work, health and well-being. The idea of the singular community is less important here than that of the connected communities that pursue issues of interest, action, place and enquiry that are commonly held. The connection between these different communities of practice (Wenger *et al.*, 2002) comes through ecological sustainability, looking at new forms of building for sustainable living and, of course, exploring how we educate all members of the community to begin to participate in what Senge (1990) calls 'metanoia' – a Greek word for a shift of mind and practice in response to a changed environment.

The sustainable community experiments with the ideas of consciousness shift (Schumacher, 1973; Damasio, 1999), from the ego-centric perspective we have at present which has accelerated as the industrial era developed to global proportions, to the eco-centric position we might adopt if we are to realign with our earth. This transition from *ego to eco* is our aide memoire, it enables us to define and then develop strategic responses in each and every aspect of our lives (see Figure 13.1).

The shift from ego to eco is more than a series of developmental steps from the modern industrial mind to a post-modern ecological mind, *it is* the

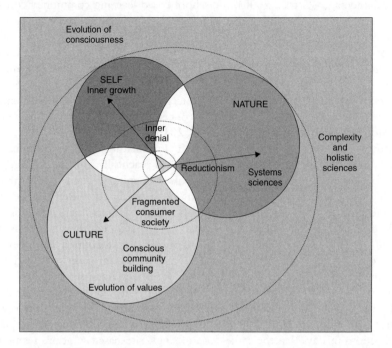

Figure 13.1 The shift from ego to eco (adapted from the original by Esborn-Hargens, S. and Zimmerman, M. (2009))

metanoia, from the reductive linear to the inclusive holistic, from the instrumental to the emancipatory, from the singular to the collective. It signals the potential for transformation of education and educational systems from the managed to the Living Systems aligned within an ecological competence, what has been called elsewhere an eco-capability (Orr, 2004, 2009; Capra, 2010; Clarke, 2009b; 2009c).

Grappling with immensity, whilst doing the day-to-day things, is at the hand, heart and mind (De Guimps, 1904) of the transformation envisaged in cultivating sustainable community. It translates itself into the practicalities of daily life (Register, 2006), through which our curricula concern these operational practicalities:

* How do we organise our world?
* How do we educate our citizens?
* How do we feed, water and clothe ourselves?
* How do we keep warm or cool?
* How do we ensure quiet places and restorative spaces for our well-being? (Prochnik, 2010)
* How do we ensure the sustainable continuation of modern civilisation and pass it on to future generations in a better state than we received it? (Scheffer, 2009).

This is the gritty stuff of learning to living together but doing so in non-destructive ways, it forms a new curriculum *of life* and *for life*, concerned with how we make our places work for our collective needs. In the past we have built these environments within an industrial mindset, and our schools served this agenda. Now we now have to make a move to incorporate the natural into the overall design so that our actions can build resilient communities, robust enough to cope with the changing climate on a warming earth.

From instrumental to emancipatory

> We still do not know one thousandth of one percent of what nature has revealed to us.
>
> (Albert Einstein)

To establish such an eco-capability, which is the basis of the new literacy, requires knowledge. For example, we already know that the consequences of climate change and pollution are going to span not decades but centuries in to the future, because of the biological characteristics and behaviours of many of the pollutants we have created and the expansive time frames that carbon science functions within (UNESCO, 2009). This is particularly important when we come to consider the way that education might play its part in a transformational narrative from an industrial to an eco-economy (Kelly, 2010). Fundamentally, the transition required is:

- a shift of hand (doing things sustainably);
- . a shift of heart (feeling the need to do things sustainably); and
- a shift of mind (thinking sustainably).

> (de Guimps, 1904)

As our education system has grown to increasingly attend only to the mind, and an industrial mind at that, it is clear that much too much emphasis is placed on short-term solutions. It is not enough to just facilitate change in behaviour; attention has to be given to values and consciousness of time as well.

For example, we cannot escape the fact that we live our lives in the cycle of birth and death, growth and decay. Facing up to this reality is going to have to become a part of the restored narrative of our century, a realisation that we are of the earth. If we are moving ever more towards living well in the built environment of the urban city, then we have to overcome the denial of nature as to fail to do so is likely to have catastrophic consequences for our shared urban futures, their distribution of wealth and their ability to ensure well-being, equity and social justice (Wilkinson and Pickett, 2009). We have not made a great start in this regard, writing of modern life Michael Cohen (1993: 14) observes,

> We live stress-filled lives full of traffic jams, busyness, noise, artificiality, and substitutes for the real thing. Our culture is riddled with stress and stress-

Table 13.1 Setting direction and action for ecological sustainability

Policy	Objectives (system conditions)	Targets (stretch goals)	Actions (generic strategies)
Society should be ecologically sustainable.	• Ecological sustainability must not be undermined by systematic: • increases in concentrations in nature of substances that come from the earth's crust or are produced by society • increases in the manipulation or harvesting of nature • failure to restore the ecological basis for biodiversity and ecological productivity. • Society must make it easy to achieve system conditions 1–3 by ensuring that: • society has the capability and resilience to solve and preferably prevent its major problems in a timely fashion • material flowing from nature into and out of society does not increase systematically • society's aggregate use of resources and land is ultra-frugal • the human population does not increase systematically. • the speed and scale of responses is adequate.	• Society should aim for: • 'zero' extinctions • 'zero' climate damage • 'zero' soil degradation • 'zero' waste • 'zero' pollution • a 90% improvement in resource use efficiency (Factor 10) (2) • 'zero' net greenhouse gas emissions. • 'zero' encroachment on nature. • 75% of land for nature.	• Society should take action to: • contain human activity (for nature) – don't encroach, boost land efficiency • tread lightly (for nature) • restore habitat (for nature) • dematerialise • create a closed-cycle economy • use renewable resources • design for no toxicity (including eco-toxicity) • protect people from environmental threats • strive for sustainable population • green up business • green up lifestyles • green up culture • boost social and economic capability • encourage 'ecological take-off' in the economy/ society • achieve results at a desirable speed and scale.

related pathologies: addictions, broken marriages, violence, and greed. More than 70% of our medical problems, costing $250 billion in the USA alone, are believed to be stress related.

The costs become ever greater, and the solutions ever more urgent.

Our view is that the educational methodology is as significant a variable in steering a new way of thinking about our relationship with the environment as is the ensuing content we might establish in the form of curricula. For example, if we have learnt through an instrumental approach, we might assume a system where: (a) the approach that is adopted is already fixed and decided; (b) the sequence of interventions are assumed to be understood and coherent.

This contrasts with what might happen if we use an emancipatory approach to learning. This design, takes it as given that learners need to participate in a formative and unfolding dialogue (Bohm, 1996), that the design is as yet unformed and uncertain, and that through an active and engaging process of learning together, people will begin to generate co-owned objectives, develop coherent and meaningful strategies in the form of concepts and practices, and begin to generate self-determined plans of action to make changes they consider desirable, and which will contribute to a more sustainable society as a whole (Wals and Blewitt, 2010; Wals, 2007).

From . . . to . . .

There is, therefore, an obvious difference between existing and desired practice, but to get to the desired practice requires action, and this action has to be rooted in existing reality. Therefore an intermediate response is required, perhaps our most pragmatic response – one which enables us to start where our schools and communities are, and then move forward from that position. To do this we have experimented with some far-reaching 'stretch targets' but have defined them within a familiar instrumental framework. The departure that is anticipated from present practice comes in what we then do to try and achieve them.

This approach mirrors the recent work of Macy (2010) who defines the possibilities of emancipatory learning as a form of community action, where the community is both localised, in the form of neighbourhood response, and collective as human community. She creates three areas of action, all of which raise interesting considerations for the school community, as to how it might respond.

1 Actions to slow the damage

Perhaps the most visible dimension of response comes through political, legislative and legal work required to reduce the destruction. This can include direct action, blockades, boycotts, civil disobedience, and other forms of refusal. A few examples:

- documenting the ecological and health consequences and effects of the Industrial Growth Society;
- lobbying and protesting against the World Trade Organisation and the international trade agreements that endanger ecosystems and undermine social and economic justice;
- blowing the whistle on illegal and unethical corporate practices;
- blockading and conducting public awareness campaigns and vigils at places of ecological destruction, such as old-growth forests under threat of clear-cutting or at nuclear dumping grounds.

Work of this kind buys some time. It saves some people's lives, and some ecosystems, species, and cultures, as well as some biodiversity, for the sustainable society to come. But it is insufficient to bring that society about on its own.

2 *Analysis of structural causes and the creation of structural alternatives*

The second dimension of response is equally crucial and engages people in greater knowledge of place, action and purpose. To liberate ourselves and our planet from the damage being inflicted by the Industrial Growth Society we have to understand its dynamics. Learning about the tacit agreements that create obscene wealth for a few, while progressively impoverishing the rest of humanity. Learning that an insatiable economic model uses our earth as supply house and sewer. This is not a pretty picture, and it takes courage and confidence in our own common sense to look at it with realism and clarity; but people are making this happen, and are slowly demystifying the workings of the global economy. When we see how this system operates, we are less tempted to demonise the politicians and corporate CEOs who are beholden to it. Instead, we begin to see how, despite its apparent power and dominance, our existing system is extremely fragile. This system depends upon compliance and obedience, and those dependencies can change.

In addition to learning how the present system works, we are also creating structural alternatives through communities who are redefining themselves through their own actions. In countless localities across the world, as in Havel's quote, green shoots are rising up through the rubble, new social and economic arrangements are emerging. These are not waiting for the organised leadership of our national or state politicians to play catch-up with us, people are getting together, taking action in their own communities and making new sense of their own places. These actions may look marginal, but their global presence is notable and significant, they hold the seeds for the future.

Some of the initiatives that illustrate this are:

- community growing projects – the single most radical thing communities might do is to grow substantial amounts of their own food because as they begin to do this they break their dependence on the established agribusiness and its associated services (I will return to this shortly);
- strategies and programs for nonviolent, citizen-based defence;
- reduction of reliance on fossil and nuclear fuels and conversion to renewable energy sources at local levels through community energy companies and small-scale community energy management;
- collaborative living arrangements such as co-housing and sheltered housing schemes for the less able. When integrated with community gardens, neighbourhood cooperatives, community-supported agriculture programmes, restoration and maintenance projects using restored and restructured buildings this can generate considerable adhesion and resilience within communities which were previously under stress and fracture (examples are globally based:

from the USA, Wisconsin growers projects, Detroit City of Hope; to the UK, Incredible Edible, Project Dirt in London; to Asia, Mai-Won Permaculture Community in Hong Kong, Chennai City farms in India and Australia, CERES, Melbourne).

3 Shift in consciousness

These structural alternatives cannot embed and survive without deeply ingrained values that become normalised in order to sustain them. This is a critical educational matter. Learning must mirror what we want and how we relate to earth and each other. They require, in other words, a profound shift in our perception of reality. The insights and experiences arise as grief for our world, giving the lie to old paradigm notions of rugged individualism, the essential separateness of the self from others. They arise in the form of positive response to breakthroughs in scientific thought, as reductionism and materialism give way to evidence of a living quantum universe. And they arise in the resurgence of traditional knowledge and wisdom, reminding us that our world is a sacred whole, worthy of adoration and service (Berry, 2009; Bohm, 1980). The many forms and ingredients of this dimension include:

- Living/Natural Systems theory: encompassing deep ecology and the long-range ecology movement where environmental consciousness is a core aspect of understanding self and situation;
- emergence theory: the realisation that letting go of old ways of seeing how we see is vital if we are to formulate new approaches to human habitation;
- spirituality: the connection of self to universal, not religious, but spiritual connectedness with other living beings;
- slow living movement, and other movements that are concerned with realisations that save us from succumbing to either panic or paralysis. They help us resist the temptation to stick our heads in the sand, or to turn on each other, for scapegoats on whom to vent our fear and rage.

Ways forward

To transcend the destructive cycle of the industrial mind we therefore need to begin to design learning experiences that promote the simple message of emancipation from the dominant pedagogic and consumerist model. The emancipation comes from the shift away from industrialised thinking towards Natural and Living Systems thinking locked to particular types of emancipatory pedagogy, and in our assertion, embedded in urban renewal programmes focused upon food growing schemes. This activity focuses on enquiry-based approaches to learning to inform a dialogue of change focused on our own place. In a school context this is the school landscape. It can be examined and investigated through specific zones around a school site that provide for the study of micro climates, soil fertility, passive solar energy, water capture and management, biodiversity, but these converge upon the production of edible produce. The enterprise of growing food generates an entire ecosystem of ecological literacy, school site by school site.

It must be noted that while we see this as absolutely focused on education for sustainable community, it is not exclusively based upon action that happens within the school grounds. Instead, we have found that such an approach gets people to participate in a conversation, leading to action, which asks what a sustainable community might be like? The sustainability objectives, targets and actions are then nurtured around connections between people (communities of kinship, new green businesses – local food purchasing, instructional programmes for cooking and baking); their ideas (communities of interest – treading lightly – looking at the local environment and redefining how it is used through new organisational arrangements such as community charities and land asset management projects, closed cycle economics); the way they go about doing what they are keen to establish (communities of action – restoring habitats, boosting land efficiency, community supported agriculture projects); and the way this enables them to redesign their relationship with the environment, built space around them (community of place, creating recycling and renewable projects, art and creativity programmes). For example: in cultivating sustainable communities we might consider what it means to be 'sustainably smart'. This question then generates a set of dialogues (Bohm, 1996) of enquiry and change modelled around some overarching themes of observation, maintenance, implementation, design, evaluation, resources and boundaries (see Figure 13.2).

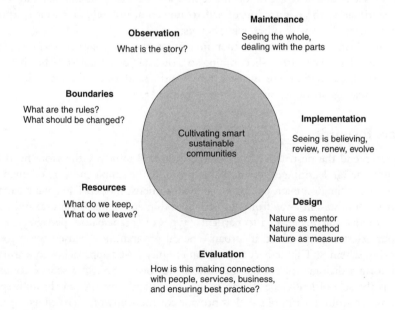

Figure 13.2 Cultivating smart sustainable communities (from Clarke, 2010b)

The design of dialogue into the process of change enables participants to steer clear of the paralysis and apathy that often results from the 'wait and see' attitude prevalent among many citizens in response to climate change. This avoids the paralysis of waiting until we are absolutely sure, and until there is agreement among the scientists and policy makers about what is happening to the earth. Instead, it encourages action and enables anyone, in any situation, to be a participant in a process of consciously defined change. School improvement therefore has a specific, ecological focus and transformational objective. It is defined for and by the community, and is used to overcome individual and systemic procrastination. It begins to generate examples of robust alternatives; that can diffuse and challenge the argument that we can afford to continue to operate under the conditions of business as usual.

As we have already indicated, this work is systemic, is conceived as longitudinal and deeply embedded practice, is widespread in its connectivity and is internationally informed. Around the world there are many such examples of innovative, transitional experiments and 'next practices' that are breaking free of the normative underpinning of the industrial growth model, and are replacing it with a broader and more inclusive agenda that is emerging around the sustainable community concept. Whilst it is understood that many of these projects and initiatives are still at the margins of mainstream society, they are beginning to be noticed within mainstream culture primarily because they are highly visible, they often demonstrate community regeneration where previous efforts from centralised planning have singularly failed to galvanise public interest and involvement. Part of the success is simply because they involve people in doing things that they are motivated to want to be involved with, and as such they are evidence of people '*doing*' rather than being '*done to*'.

Systemic considerations

However, we must ask if this way of looking at global response to ecological crisis is going to have sufficient momentum to ensure change quickly, as what happens in the next two decades is of vital longer-term significance (Wilson, 1991, 2002). A vital part of the change is participation from the grassroots level, but this poses problems for systemic practice if we conceive of their actions within the previous mindset of transferability, as the replication of a successful scheme from one place to another is not necessarily the motivational driver behind the interests to the participants.

What we are learning as we cultivate Sustainable Communities is that there is a deeper learning process taking place amongst people, one that is grounded in the everyday reality of people's lives in organisations, institutions, businesses, schools and communities. It is centered around relationship, how people relate to each other, to their problems, and to the natural space around them. These examples of 'next practices' can be extremely illuminative, not only because they can inspire and inform, but because they can serve as a source of inspiration and, equally important, illustrate that what people do in their own settings matters. As Paulo

Freire articulated so powerfully, hope has its origins in practice, it is rooted in what people do and feel they can do, it is in the struggle. If it is not, we find inaction, people begin to feel incapable of doing things in response to ever worsening circumstances and they generate hopelessness and despair (Freire, 1992). Freire described hope as an ontological need that should be *anchored in practice* in order to become *historical concreteness*. Without hope, we are hopeless and cannot begin the struggle to change. Our experience suggests this can begin with simple, small-scale projects, which have to be participatory and dialogic in design.

Conclusion

We have suggested in this chapter that in starting to formulate a substantive response to the ecological challenges of our time, we have to imagine, design and practice a different educational model. We know that projects and programmes such as Incredible Edible in the UK, or CERES in Australia, Eden Project in Hong Kong, Growing Communities in Accra, Ghana, Detroit City of Hope (Boggs, 1998) and the Edible Schoolyard (Waters, 2008) in the USA, or the urban food growing programme in Havana, Cuba, are just some examples of the way that people can begin to function within a sustainable community of learners (Clarke, forthcoming) taking the first practical steps towards sustainable living.

We know that any development of this kind requires us to live with uncertainty, as the jump to solutions is just as likely to generate further, unsustainable outcomes, than it actually resolves (Brown, 2003). In designing educational responses, therefore, our efforts should be guided towards pedagogic approaches which enable learners to experiment with different dimensions of community, working within communities of interest (things that engage them), action (participating in hands-on practices), kinship (working in teams, extended inter-generationally) and place (locally focused, that extend beyond the idea we currently hold of school).

We have learnt that a focus on food is a powerful way to begin to cultivate sustainable community, focusing on the celebration and life-affirming features that growing food can illustrate (Capra, 2010). Growing food enables us to connect to nature and to learn from nature as a mentor, design and measure. The knowledge being created is of local and universal value. We have learnt that the most conducive styles of learning that facilitate sustainable modes of community are enquiry-based and emergent. If our pedagogic experiment becomes enquiry-led, we know that the approach leads learners to think about real-time challenges, and this helps them to connect their concerns to local issues. We already know that local solutions, suited to the nuances of local knowledge of place and connectedness to place have proved to be a feature of nature's way of surviving. Nature is both global and local, and so we too must continue to make sense of the micro- to macro-level narratives of global and local human systems, this work enhances the purpose of using technology as a connector of ideas across the world.

These simple starting points provide our students and citizens with a direct link to their environment and offer them a route to redefine their urban environments based upon what they discover (Hungerford and Volk, 1990). This is the first step to an eco-capability of retrofitting what we have to suit new-found situations as this learning extends from school, to neighbourhood, to community to town, to city, reinforcing the significance of educational effectiveness and improvement, and signifying a step-change from the earlier formulation of the field (Reynolds *et al.*, 2011).

Physical school structures need not be an impediment to these new ideas, they simply have to be re-imagined for new uses and that imagination has to be continually conscious of the need to remain within Natural Systems design. The point being that cities, neighbourhoods and streetscapes are not going to go away in a hurry, they will be the places we continue to live – sustainably or otherwise over this century and beyond, and they will form the landscape which in turn will shape the mindscape of our future citizens, for good or ill. As a result, we have to reconceptualise our living place so that it serves our needs and the needs of the planet. The small act of growing a seed, one learner to the next, becomes a route map through which this new literacy will flourish.

That is why growing sustainable community is all about the measure of our relationships, being civilised and intelligent no longer pertains to the nuance of localised needs. It is at once an awareness of the self, the place, the relationships with others, the community, the consequences of our choices on our immediate and our planetary presence. Small starting points matter, whether they are growing food in the school-yard, or working as a neighbourhood to rethink the built environment as a living landscape in which we play a part alongside nature. These acts represent the first tentative steps on a journey towards full use-age of the city as a naturally thinking environment, and a direct link to the myriad of problems people face daily in their struggle to exist in cities at the present time as it enables and empowers, rather than deskills and disempowers the citizen.

Schools can be the hubs of such dialogue, forming the conversations across the world of how to do the simple things, which connect us all together through our affinity to life. This simple demonstration of new uses for existing spaces has profound possibilities.

We should continue to ensure that this work remains naturally focused (Berry, 1999). This is why, in our formative work in this field, we have tried to ensure that we have aligned our activity towards the simple act of growing food. Growing is such a powerful connector, it serves as a guide to the necessary capabilities of observation, nurture, maintenance, conservation of resource, attention to solar energy, the cropping and preparation of food as a life source, and the cyclical properties of resources once used to form waste to enrich and maintain the soil. It enables us to initiate a curriculum that is guided through a model of learning aligned to Living Systems theory, and by doing this we begin to see how the first steps into eco-capability might flourish. The lessons are learnt through collegial activity, in a spirit of celebration and connectedness to life, it is done with a clear desire to begin to reconnect with our places, each other, and our world. As Braungart and McDonough (2009: 186) so powerfully express:

Imagine what a world of prosperity and health in the future will look like, and begin designing for it right now. What would it mean to become, once again, native to this place, the Earth – the home of all our relations? This is going to take us all, and it is going to take forever. But then, that's the point.

The sum of our efforts to move from the industrial mind to the ecological mind should be the measure of our collective educational action across the planet.

Notes

1 UN Population predictions http://www.un.org/esa/population/publications/longrange2/WorldPop2300final.pdf accessed 15 December 2010

2 Measure of a country's total economic activity, or the wealth of the country. GNP is usually assessed quarterly or yearly, and is defined as the total value of all goods and services produced by firms owned by the country concerned. It is measured as the gross domestic product plus income earned by domestic residents from foreign investments, minus income earned during the same period by foreign investors in the country's domestic market. GNP does not allow for inflation or for the overall value of production. It is an important indicator of an economy's strength.

Hussain, W. (2009) "Gross National Happiness in Bhutan: A Living Example of an Alternative Approach to Progress." Wharton International Research Experience. University of Pennsylvania.

The National Medium- and Long-term Talent Development Plan (2010–2020) creates a blueprint for creating a highly skilled national work force within the next 10 years. This plan is the first major national comprehensive plan in China's history of national human resources development since the Cultural Revolution and is of vital importance to China's current and future development in the next decade and beyond. In Chinese, the plan refers to the development of rencai, which can be translated as educated and skilled individuals. (source http://www.brookings.edu/papers/2010/1123_china_talent_wang.aspx last accessed on 14 December 2010).

3 Ecological sustainability: to be maintained, the diversity of life and the basis of its productivity must not be systematically diminished, and must be restored where it has been diminished.

4 United Nations (1987) "Report of the World Commission on Environment and Development." General Assembly Resolution 42/187, 11 December 1987

5 IPCC Fourth Assessment Report, Summary for Policy makers, 2004, p. 9; B.D. Santer, "A Search for Human Influences on the Thermal Structure of the Atmosphere," *Nature* 382, 4 July 1996, 39–46; Gabriele C. Hegerl, "Detecting Greenhouse-Gas-Induced Climate Change with an Optimal Fingerprint Method," *Journal of Climate* 9, October 1996, 2281–2306; V. Ramaswamy *et al.*, "Anthropogenic and Natural Influences in the Evolution of Lower Stratospheric Cooling," *Science* 311, 24 February 2006, 1138–114; B.D. Santer *et al.*, "Contributions of Anthropogenic and Natural Forcing to Recent Tropopause Height Changes," *Science* 301 (25 July 2003), 479–483; National Research Council (NRC) (2006) *Surface Temperature Reconstructions for the Last 2,000 Years*. National Academy Press, Washington, DC; J. A. Church and N.J. White (2006), A 20th Century Acceleration in Global Sea Level Rise, *Geophysical Research Letters*, 33, L01602, doi:10.1029/2005GL024826; The global sea level estimate described in this work can be downloaded from the CSIRO website; T.C. Peterson *et al.*, "State of the Climate in 2008," *Special Supplement to the Bulletin of the American Meteorological Society* 90, 8, August 2009, S17–S18; I. Allison *et al.*, *The Copenhagen Diagnosis: Updating the World on the Latest Climate Science*, UNSW Climate Change Research Center, Sydney, Australia, 2009, p. 11.

14 Thinking the unthinkable?

The future of school effectiveness and school improvement to be realised through closer relationships with educational policies and policy makers

David Reynolds

Introduction

There is no doubt that school effectiveness and school improvement (SESI) has made substantial progress over the last twenty years, as shown in numerous reviews of the field (e.g. Teddlie and Reynolds, 2000). The sheer noise of our critics and their number tells us this, given the academic tendency for substantial achievement to evoke trenchant criticism, a situation within our field that started from the very beginning with the somewhat hostile academic reaction to the pioneering work of Rutter *et al.* (1979).

But, to ensure future progress, the argument in this chapter is that we now need a close association between SESI and the practical needs of educational policy, which necessarily involves seeking out a closer relationship between the discipline, educational policy makers and politicians, and additionally better relating to their concerns. Put simply, while SESI as it stands is clearly an 'applied' discipline more than a 'pure' or theoretical one, the argument in this chapter is that we need to be both more 'applied' and more 'problem centred' in the future even more than we have been in the past.

Working collaboratively with the world of educational policy and with educational policy makers may be difficult to envisage, and to support, after the ways in which SESI has been historically 'used' by government. The Strategies, for example, owed much in the late 1990s to thinking from SESI in such areas as their commitment to whole class interactive teaching, but political/policy maker interest in our field substantially evaporated without any attempt to bring the more complex and sensitive descriptions and analyses of effective practices from SESI research into educational policies in the early 2000s. Many findings from SESI, and from related bodies of knowledge, such as those on formative assessment for example, are well established, but have been taken little notice of because they appear to be 'inconvenient' for policy makers and politicians (see Reynolds (2010) for further discussion on this theme).

So, attempting to establish a closer relationship between SESI and policymaking may not immediately appeal to researchers and academics in the field. It would involve moving away from the focus on relating to professionals and to practition-ers that has been the concern of many in the discipline – away from the notion that SESI should stand with those who often *oppose* present policies and politicians and who often celebrate alternative world views to those of governments. This view of where SESI belongs is seen frequently within the 'critical perspectives' beloved of many within SESI and in much of the writing on school improvement and teacher development from North America, as seen in for example Hargreaves and Shirley's (2009) interesting recent manifesto. Any reorientation of the discipline could cost us valuable knowledge about the practice community if we were less involved with it. The issue is whether we would gain more than we possibly lost, which one suspects would be the case.

The benefits of a problem-centered orientation

So, there are likely to be possible blocks on any disciplinary movement towards an even more 'applied' orientation than at present that 'takes' the politicians and policy makers problems, rather than problematises them, and which erodes his-torical concerns for the developmental needs of the teaching profession in favour of a closer allegiance with policy. What benefits can there possibly be in such a reorientation?

First, any close allegiance with policy necessarily imposes a discipline upon us and stops any movement towards the metaphysical, or to possibilitarianism, or to value debates that by their nature cannot be concluded. By taking problems as 'given', we restrain ourselves from the 'what if' questions that cannot be answered because they are about ethical or philosophical judgements. Certainly there should be full discussion of the ends of education, the value choices inherent in the notion of 'education' and the careful analysis of the values implicit in, for example, the 'New Labour' educational paradigm. But a close allegiance with policy does not prevent such discussions – what it does is make it more likely that such discussions are informed by practical knowledge about the results of any commitments, ethics and value positions in terms of how these value positions are likely to be shown in different kinds of school and classroom organisation and processes.

Second, there is evidence about the intellectual power of close practical policy and/or problem involvement from those disciplines that have attempted it. To take Medicine as an example, at first Physiology was, in the nineteenth century, a largely philosophically based discipline in which there was considerable discus-sion about what was the nature of the fluid (that we now call blood) that flowed through veins. Physiology was transformed into one of the best developed of all the medical sciences through responding to the practical problem-solving needs of clinical medicine, and replaced metaphysical speculation with meeting practical health needs.

A second example is the British discipline of Sociology of Education, which made very rapid progress in the 1960s on the back of a widespread concern from politi-cians of the Left about the educational system's wastage of ability. Interestingly, what disabled it from both policy relevance and intellectual progress was the popularity of the relativist approaches pioneered by Young (1971) in which problems were to be not 'taken' but themselves analysed in terms of their values/definitions, the vested interests that they served and the deeper ideologies that they reflected. Sociology of Education marginalised itself, destroyed itself and embarked upon a period of low intellectual 'reach' because it abandoned the close links with policy, the 'taking' of policy problems and the association with policy needs.

The third example of a discipline that flourished is the early stages of our own SESI that made major progress through adopting a 'taken for granted' stance that simply accepted that certain outcomes from school (academic and social) were more desirable than others and that our job was to generate the evidence of the processes at multiple levels that were associated with these outcomes. Our own rapid development can be interestingly compared and contrasted with that of the other specialities of educational research that attempted a more 'values driven' intellectual enterprise, and/or who encountered even more 'critical perspectives' than we did.

Third, the promise of a close relationship with policy makers and politicians is huge in terms of how it would advance SESI and its thinking. The sheer range of the ongoing English educational and social interventions means that there are multiple sources of evidence about possibly effective practices, the interactions between these practices and contexts, and the effects of the interventions upon different parts of the social and economic structure of society. Indeed, there are multiple experiments of that nature ongoing in which 'before' and 'after' analyses can be explored that look at change over time in the outcomes of policies either using a school or an area, or both, as their own controls, or by taking control groups from schools or areas unaffected by the particular intervention (if that is possible). This was the methodology we followed in the well-known study, *The Comprehensive Experiment* (Reynolds *et al.*, 1987), where we looked at a part of our historic Welsh mining valley that had gone comprehensive by comparison with a part that had stayed selective, using cohorts of pupils passing through both systems. These experimental methods are not as scientifically powerful as the experiments that involve random allocation that are advocated by some (e.g. Slavin, 1996) as the gold standard of educational research, but they are a considerable improvement upon the correlational, cross-sectional studies that cannot 'control out' the influence of multiple variables in the way that experimental studies can and which also suffer from considerable problems of multi-colinearity. Policy interventions have very large sample sizes to play with too.

The argument is, therefore, that SESI attempts to intensify some of the close links it has had to policy and to the practical problem-solving needs of policy. In so doing, it frees itself from trying to answer some of the 'what if' questions in favour of taking educational outcomes, problems and policies as given. It may well be that some of the problems of any close relationship with policy that have shown themselves historically may recur of course, for example in policy makers/politicians only using the research that appeals to them, in the picking up of selective findings and in the failure to follow through consistently on any set of research findings. But at least we are forewarned that these things are likely to happen, given our experience. We look at these issues below.

It is also likely that re-establishing the discipline as 'close to policy makers' may generate a restatement of much of the criticism that emanated from mainstream educational research about SESI, and may reduce the appeal of the SESI knowledge base to practitioners, who may be 'put off' by the fear that any sponsorship of SESI by the State shows SESI as untrustworthy. Again, we know it may happen so could plan to do something about it.

The possible problems at the research/policy interface

It is best to acknowledge that there are likely to be problems relating research to policy, and in relating closely to policy makers and politicians. These have not featured much in the accounts of relevance from the political community (e.g. Blunkett, 2006) but surprisingly have not taken much space in those from the researcher community either (e.g. Barber, 2007), perhaps because of the paucity of experiences of many of the latter in the first place. The analysis and speculations about the problems here draw on my own experience from 1995 to 2006 in England (see also the Introduction to Reynolds, 2010).

The first problem concerning the interaction between the two groups is likely to be the different timelines of the two groups, policy makers and researchers. Politicians and policy makers have a short-term orientation, working to 'fix' things and then move on. So, with the English Primary Numeracy Strategy, the short-term increase in test scores that followed the Strategy indicated to them that the problem of low performance had been solved. Thus they then moved on to designing the Secondary Strategy, without noting the long-term developmental needs of the primary sector that had been explicit in the Primary Strategy, and to which they had already agreed. The commitment to the long-term curriculum up-rating of the Mathematics teaching profession in primary education was forgotten, until a decade later when the problem of teachers' subject knowledge and the need to improve it were 'rediscovered'.

The short termism reflects, more than anything, the nature of professional life in the policy maker/political communities. Whereas researchers exist to provide through their work more valid and reliable explanations and descriptions of educational matters over time, usually within one discrete research area, policy makers and politicians are moved ceaselessly between policy areas, between Ministries in the case of the politicians and in terms of ownership of different policy areas in the case of policy makers. There is, therefore, considerable pressure to deliver in the short term, because of the need to prove competence short term.

The other influence making for short termism is of course the demands of the media in an age of 24-hour news. Given the need to 'feed' a media that requires constantly changing stories to fill its multiple slots and channels, moving from one policy area to another in terms of focus is inevitable. All journalists and media correspondents have instant access through electronic means to those stories and policy announcements that have already appeared – the pressure to generate new 'focii' is clear.

Given this pressure it is not surprising that 'pilot' projects lead inevitably to full-scale implementation projects, as for example in the rapid move from the (une-valuated and very preliminary) Literacy and Numeracy pilots of the late 1990s to full-scale implementation in the 'roll out' (as it was called) to all primary schools. With media pressures, after all, how can one wait?

It is also worth noting that the pressure to appeal to the media manifests itself in the use of celebrities, actors and actresses to participate in the policy formulation and dissemination process, such as Carol Vorderman being used in the Mathematics-related policies devised both by New Labour and the present Conservative (coalition) government. To gain attention the educational stories require 'hooks' that celebrities inappropriately provide.

This pressure from the media does not just manifest itself in a need to constantly shift policy focus to appear 'new' – it actually can also determine the content of policy itself. When the Numeracy Task Force was entrusted with reforming primary Mathematics education it was made explicit that the issue of calculator usage was an area that it was thought the Task Force should look at. Calculator usage itself was unlikely to have had major effects upon the trajectory of Mathematics test scores, since they have had a substantial role in schools since the 1980s through to the present day, a role that appears to have been independent of the shifts in the international Mathematics scores of the UK for example.

But to 'New Labour' seeking to associate itself with 'traditionalist' educational views to appeal to the middle class, and particularly to win the support of *The Daily Mail* and *The Daily Telegraph* newspapers that were the preferred read of the middle-class 'swing voters', any attack on progressive educational methods that did not 'work' would be appealing. Calculator usage was therefore flagged in the media releases that reported the setting up of the Task Force. Indeed, when the Task Force was about to report, the English Education Department stated in a press release that calculator usage was to be banned, even though those writing and approving the release knew that calculator usage had only been recommended for reduction!

Many of the other problems of the 'research/policy' interface reflect the nature of politicians themselves. They are – if not simple – simply less well versed in the domain issues of education than researchers. Educational researchers' desire to present complicated, multi-layered answers to complex, complicated issues sits ill with the simple perspectives of most politicians. As an example, it always proved difficult to persuade New Labour politicians of the apparently counter-intuitive truth that successful countries educationally postpone having academic demands upon young children until relatively late, such as to age seven in the much vaunted Finnish educational system, whereas all the simple instincts of politicians were to believe that enhanced outcomes would come from very early application of academic pressure through the use of SATs and an academically based orientation.

The low level of educational knowledge among politicians also probably explains the utter failure of New Labour to move beyond simplistic, school-based policy formulations from 1997 to 2010, even though researchers have moved increasingly to a teacher-based viewpoint that reflects on the school and teacher effectiveness research studies that show teacher effects to be four or five times greater than school effects (Muijs and Reynolds, 2010). The New Labour emphasis upon school-based solutions such as Academies, without any corresponding emphasis upon the teaching level content of the schools, was probably the factor behind the early disappointing results of the first tranche of these schools, and behind the plateauing of results in international surveys.

Even though Labour politicians and their advisers knew in their heads that the key was the teacher, their hearts were involved in the school level. The school level, additionally, was easier to report on, could be press released about more easily and did not furthermore involve attention to the very complicated area of the extent to which 'teaching' was a legitimate focus for policy and prescription.

The foci of the research to establish the effectiveness of the National Literacy and Numeracy Strategies in the early 2000s, which had a 'macro' level focus upon evaluating system and school change rather than instructional or teacher level change, suggests the same inability to focus upon teachers and teaching. Ironically, it was the Conservative Party and government from 2010 that has appeared to understand that 'the teacher is the key', but that has not prevented non-rational Tory policies in multiple other areas from the use of market based choice to an embarrassing neglect of ICT.

Other, more sinister, motivations of politicians make their relationship with researchers difficult. Politicians appreciate certainty – it is after all the currency in which they publicly deal. Researchers' legitimate scientific doubt is not a trait they admire. Indeed, the only explanation for the survival of some of the earlier advisers to New Labour right through until close to the end of the 2005–10 government was their apparent certainty rather than their intellects.

Politicians also deal in the currency of 'fame', and it interesting that their decision about who to appoint as Chair of the Numeracy Task Force was influenced by a *Panorama* documentary. In recent years, the visits of senior Tory politicians and their researchers to Monkseaton Community High School in Tyne and Wear followed upon the publicity given to the school's famous 'spaced learning' experiments in national newspapers, and especially in *The Daily Telegraph*. If your own currency is 'fame' as politicians, judgements about who to relate to in the educational world may be based upon fame too. This may make for unwise choices.

Ways of handling the tensions outlined here need clearly to be found. Researchers developing their own media links and strategies to achieve their own 'take' on their research and policies helps, as does knowing that politician/policy maker 'domain' knowledge in education may be low and therefore communicating very simply helps too. Constant repetition of the same message in interaction with them also helps, as also does attempting to know politicians and policy makers outside their formal organisational roles.

But all of the above suggests that there needs to be a fairly substantial set of cautions about researchers working closer to policymaking and policy makers. In spite of this, the argument is that these closer links, a concern with policy and a desire to help in practical policymaking may have an up-side of potentially productive links too. Areas where policy needs are particularly acute and where SESI might both help to generate better policies, and help itself too, are now identified.

Researching teaching and learning

Educational policy in the UK has historically been obsessed with 'the school' as the unit of measurement, accountability, policy change and improvement. Although in the future it is currently acknowledged in general policy discourse that education will take place across multiple settings additional to schools, these settings are still viewed in terms of their macro level organisational provision and features, rather than their micro level teaching and learning processes. However:

- Young people do not learn in schools or other organisations. They learn in classrooms and in other face-to-face locations with their teachers. If policy is truly interested in meeting their needs, it needs to have educational perspectives and policies that look upward from their (probably highly variegated) experiences, rather than down from their school or 'organisational level'. A focus is needed on education as *experienced,* not as *intended* by policy, two very different things.
- It is the teacher or educator in the classroom or learning setting that is the biggest source of influence over children, not the level of the school. Indeed, in virtually all SESI analyses conducted to date, in whichever country or sector, teacher or classroom effects on achievement outcomes are four to five times greater than school effects (see Muijs and Reynolds, 2000, 2002, 2003, 2010).
- School level organisational factors do not appear to be very powerful determinants of outcomes at all, whether they are formal designation, governance, type of school or any other school level variables. Yet if one reads the number of references to 'the school' in policy documents, it is much greater than the references to the classroom. This is something that appears to be greatest in the Anglo-Saxon countries rather than others, perhaps related to the way in which 'education' in our societies has become intensely politicised and the repository of what have been historically simplistic political solutions. In most societies of the world – including the high achieving Pacific Rim and Finnish ones – discussions about education are usually about teaching and the curriculum rather than about the school unit. They are therefore linked to the most powerful 'levers'.

All this is a pity, since SESI shows that teaching as a research area is endlessly productive. There seem to be about 60 behaviours associated with student outcomes, most of which are weakly inter-correlated and with an absence of strong correlations, suggesting that good teaching is not about getting a few 'big things' right but a large number of 'little things' right. There is a relationship between the beliefs that teachers have – about themselves, their efficacy – and their students' progress, but their behaviours influence their attitudes as well as vice versa. Teaching can be modified, easily and effectively, (Hopkins and Reynolds, 2001; Slavin, 1996).

The fact that all political parties now emphasise that, to paraphrase, it is the teacher in the classroom that is the 'key' means that they are likely to be receptive to SESI material in the 'teacher effectiveness' area, and that we could collaborate with policy makers in this area. There are multiple research areas of possible importance:

- The teacher factors associated with academic, social and affective outcomes, whether behavioural and/or attitudinal;
- The potential contextual variability in those teacher/teaching factors that are 'effective';
- The programmes that optimise long-term teacher development.

Researching cognitive neuroscience

However, the biggest area where SESI could contribute to policy, and in turn learn from policy, is in assessing the prospects for educational practice offered by the cognitive neuroscience revolution now gathering pace. In its neglect of the importance of this for the future of schooling, SESI is in good company – in British educational circles generally there has been a muted response to some of the emerging findings. Educationalists seem to need to believe in improvement through the systems of education (happily linked with us of course!), rather than remediation through involvement directly with the human physiology or genotype (which heaven forbid may not need us). These latter approaches cut against the grain of our discipline because there are widespread misunderstandings that the brain is a static, self-contained unit that has a pre-determined, immutable set of attributes with high genetic heritability. In fact, the brain is at certain ages highly 'plastic' and billions of neurones in the brain are capable of connecting with each other or not (what is referred to as the 'wiring'). It is inherently social also and learners need opportunities to clarify, discuss and question to enhance memory and retrieval. It can be moulded by educational and environmental change. Interestingly, given the very positive effects for formative assessment approaches, the brain is self-referencing and so relies heavily on feedback to develop. What are the present insights that SESI could build on and learn from in cognitive neuroscience?

The first concerns the neglected role of the cerebellum. We know that skill acquisition occurs in several stages – one is the 'declarative' stage in which a person learns what to do; another is the 'procedural' stage in which a person learns how to do it, and then there is the 'automatic' stage where the skill is exercised without conscious control.

The cognitive neuroscience revolution has demonstrated that there are two circuits in the brain – one for declarative learning (the frontal lobe and hippocampus) and the other for procedural learning (the frontal lobe, cerebellum and motor areas). The cerebellum functions for physical skill and mental skill, and is central to language acquisition, temporal processing and with clear connectivity to the frontal cognitive regions.

Nicolson *et al.* (2001), have outlined a Cerebellar Deficit Theory (CDT), believing that inadequate development of the cerebellum is implicated in a wide range of learning problems such as dyslexia, dyspraxia and ADHD/ADD, because of the inability of those children affected to make their learned skills 'automatic'. They believe that Cerebellar Developmental Delay (CDD) is at the heart of much avoidable educational failure, more generally.

The thesis is controversial, and indeed our work showing considerable achievement gains from an exercise-based intervention designed to potentiate the cerebellum (the famed 'balancing on a wobble board' and the 'throwing of bean bags from one hand to the other') has been criticised by some for small sample sizes, and for inappropriate statistics (see Reynolds and Nicolson (2003, 2006) for the original studies and Nicolson and Reynolds (2003), for a defence against critics). Nevertheless, it remains possible that the educational system of the future needs to give as much attention to finding processes that can potentiate the cerebellum as to those which are aimed, more conventionally, at the 'thinking brain'. These might involve use of exercise-based regimes to improve visual functioning and regimes to improve hand-eye coordination for example. Interestingly, there are hints (Budde *et al.*, 2008) now of the positive effects of such interventions on 'normal', non-learning disabled children even when the exercise programmes are short in time exposure and standard for all children involved, not individually prescribed. Whilst those with conventional, pre-ordained views about what does and what does not belong in school in terms of acceptable practices may baulk, those of us in SESI who are more interested in improving outcomes than in the purity of school processes could begin interesting experimentation here.

The second insight from cognitive neuroscience is concerned with how to potentiate skill development for the brain as a whole. We have known for a long time that 'distributed' practice is more effective than 'massed' practice – i.e. it is better to learn a skill in six ten-minute sessions rather than in a one-hour time slot. This is probably because there are different stages in skill acquisition – from the storing in an easily alterable EEG form, to in a few more hours a more stable form (that can still be influenced) and then to a more concrete form, often produced with sleep. In the longer term still, the neural pathways get further established. In these processes, sleep is of major importance. These stages need time to operate as the brain is stimulated: simply, the brain needs space. Also the brain needs constant stimulation in the particular skill area to avoid redundancy of material learned.

However, it is massed learning and non-distributed practice that remains the conventional educational method. Subjects are taught for an hour or longer, meaning merely that the information presented later in a long lesson interferes with the acquisition of that which was presented earlier. Then – compounding error upon error – nothing is done for a day or two in the same subject so that there is no developmental 'fine tuning', and so there is much redundancy.

Existing practice contrasts with evidence from neuroscience and in particular from the long-term potentiation (LTP) paradigm. LTP has provided the theoretical basis for spaced learning (Eichenbaum and Otto, 1993; McGaugh, 2000), but in LTP the optimum spaces (intervals) between bursts of stimuli were of the order of minutes to hours. Early experiments had in fact found that the expression of key proteins required for the strengthening of synapses was optimised when the interval was ten minutes (Itoh *et al.*, 1995; Frey and Morris, 1998).

Fields arrived at the same temporal pattern of activity when investigating the intracellular switches for DNA synthesis during development (Fields, 2005). His studies suggested that the activation of CREB, a key transcription factor involved in memory, was optimised by three pulses of stimulation separated by the ten-minute intervals. (This material is taken from Kelley (2007), who reviews this literature extensively.)

The highly publicised 'spaced learning' experiments conducted at Monkseaton High School (Barkham, 2009), in which a pure spaced learning teaching session of only 90 minutes generated equivalent results to four months' conventional teaching, show the potential for radical redesign of teaching and learning. Admittedly, the 'spaced learning' material was taught by an outstanding teacher, it was 'new' and therefore interest was high, the power points were multi coloured and of high quality, and the cerebellum may also have been potentiated by the fact that the ten-minute gaps between teaching were filled with sessions involving the dribbling of a football between cones in the school gymnasium, thereby improving motor coordination. Nevertheless, there is nothing in the existing literature that could even partially explain gains of this size as due to the above factors alone. One must begin to ask very serious questions of 'mass education' if these results are shown elsewhere through experimentation. SESI could begin this, and other kinds of experimentation in this newly emerging field.

The third insight from contemporary cognitive neuroscience concerns optimising brain function through appropriate resourcing. There are the hints about the positive effects of fish oil supplements – the major dietary change of the British population since the 1950s has been the decline in per capita fish consumption of approximately two thirds, and the argument is that neural connectivity can be enhanced artificially by these supplements replacing what would have been naturally occurring through diet. Water is another important supplement argued to be implicated in improving learning outcomes.

The fourth insight from contemporary neuroscience comes in the work looking at sleeping patterns and the effects of the different patterns of circadian rhythms that are evidenced by children of different ages (Foster, 2007). Teenagers are heavily sleep deprived – they show delayed sleep and fewer hours of sleep once in bed. Sustained periods of reduced sleep generate poor performance in terms of increased errors, impaired vigilance, poor memory, reduced mental/physical reaction times, reduced motivation, reduced risk taking and increased depression. The practice of starting school early and of putting more demanding subjects in the morning timetable is disliked by teenagers and generates lower performance, which improves for this group later in the day.

Unfortunately, adult performance – of the teachers – is likely to be *higher* in the morning, which is why of course schools start early and the 'difficult' subjects are timetabled for the mornings. Ways of squaring this circle need to be found!

The dramatic gains shown by approaches influenced by cognitive neuroscience – from exercise to fish oils to spaced learning – may be because they are from enthusiasts, on often small samples in atypical situations. Alternatively, it may be that they are, simply, more powerful interventions than our conventional educational 'weak' levers. Whatever, the opportunities for SESI to study these innovations as they apparently 'ripple through' the education system are substantial. Interestingly, cognitive neuroscience has been generated as a field of study by a revolution in methodology (through MRI scanning) as SESI has been generated as a field by the multilevel methodologies that were introduced from the 1980s.

Researching variation in effective provision

Historically, education policies have been born of a belief in 'one right way' that in part reflected the early findings of SESI from the 1980s and 1990s, largely because the historic research concentration upon the education of the socially and economically disadvantaged meant that there was little of the variation in context within British SESI samples that was shown in corresponding work in the United States in the 1980s and 1990s. Unsurprisingly, studies that were conducted in the same kinds of catchment areas generated the same kinds of 'effectiveness factors'. New Labour fondness for a limited number of exemplary individuals as the blueprints for the methods of others contributed also.

These 'one right way' methods have of course historically influenced the Ofsted inspection system, although this is less in evidence now when the judgement is more being made about a school's capacity to improve itself than about its actual processes. They continue to resonate in political discussions of education and indeed practitioners' discussions have also been encouraged to focus on the development of undifferentiated 'good practice'.

However, as research in SESI has accumulated, there is more and more evidence that to be effective processes may need to vary according to the:

- cultural context of the nation (Alexander, 2000; Reynolds *et al.*, 2002);
- the socio-economic composition of the school classrooms (Wimpleburg *et al.*, 1989; Teddlie and Stringfield, 1993);
- the effectiveness level of the school (Hopkins and Reynolds, 2001);
- the trajectory of improvement that the school is on (Hopkins, 2002);
- urban or rural status of the school (Teddlie and Reynolds, 2000).

Additionally, some recent evidence is that a wide variety of programmes may be similarly effective, but that the key to effectiveness is to do something – indeed perhaps almost anything – reliably, as shown in the interesting work of Stringfield *et al.* (1997) that evaluated the American government's 'Special Strategies' improvement schemes. The precise nature of the programme chosen by a school didn't matter – what did matter was co-constructing it and doing it reliably. Interestingly, our own High Reliability Schools Project (Stringfield *et al.*, 2008a), was based not upon trying to encourage schools to put into practice 'right ways of doing things' but upon getting schools to use the right *concepts* and *systems* that enabled them to be intelligent organisations. Our rapidly improving sample of schools were, therefore, somewhat different in *what* they did, but the same in *how* they had worked out what to do differently. It is worth remembering that this project shows the most rapid improvement of any group of secondary schools where outcomes have been measured, in the world literature to date.

The important thing about variety in provision rather than 'one right way' or 'one size fits all' methods is that it opens the way to the teaching profession becoming 'rational empirical problem solvers' whose job is to diagnose their school and classroom context and to choose appropriate strategies. Such an approach, which can be furthered by SESI researchers and practitioners, is likely to lead to much more professional development than the imposition into practice of 'one right way' models that might generate only compliance and uniformity. SESI historically encouraged a 'tightness' on processes – perhaps we need to encourage more 'looseness' on processes but more 'tightness' on the systems used to generate them.

Conclusions

We have argued in this chapter for an intensification of the close historic links of SESI with policy and policymaking that were evident for a period of time in the 1990s and into the 2000s. Working in this way imposes a discipline on us and stops the 'what if' and the possibilitarianism that is often in evidence in the views of SESI's 'critical theorists'. There is evidence from our own history and from certain other disciplines that a close allegiance with practical problem solving can be intellectually highly productive. Even the semi-philosophic discussions about what 'might be' could take place informed by a greater recognition about the kinds of educational practices that might be implicated by different value positions, as the problem- and policy-centred research is likely to show. And, of course, SESI involvement in policymaking might make educational policies more rational, more effective and therefore lead to improved outcomes for children and the chance of populations of children that are able to understand their world better and therefore change it. No one doubts that the relationship may be a difficult one, but the results may be well worth it.

It is likely that the next few years will provide major opportunities – in the UK and internationally – for this to happen, in terms of an enhanced policy maker interest in what SESI has to say. It may also be the case that the practitioner community that thinks it 'did' SESI in the late 1990s may be ripe for exposure to the SESI of the 2010s, given the hugely increased quantity and quality of what SESI has to offer and the former's concerns with what it is receiving through policy currently. Simply, the rolling back of the educational 'State' in societies such as England means that there will be an increased space to forge links between SESI and the professionals who will be increasingly left alone by the abolition of the 'quangos' and retrenchment of the local authorities that supported them.

There are a number of factors that will make policymakers and politicians more receptive to SESI. First is the social, political and economic situation brought on by the international economic situation generated by the banking crisis. The sheer scale of borrowings necessary within many advanced industrial societies means that public expenditure will be under pressure in all areas of state welfare for probably the next decade. Doing 'more with less', consequent upon the inevitable expenditure cuts or restrictions in expenditure in the schools sector will become the watchword. Ensuring that the *quality* of education is optimised even though there are fewer *quantities* of resources available will be increasingly axiomatic, replacing much of the historic 'improvement through additional spend' paradigm that dominated the last decade. SESI is ideally placed to resource – intellectually and practically – what are the likely new emphases, recognising that in the UK for example many of the policies pursued in the decade of the 2000s bear a surprising resemblance (curriculum reform, enhanced expenditure, changes in the governance/organisation of schooling) to those that were the 1960s/1970s paradigm of educational change. SESI originally followed the failure of that paradigm to enhance outcomes – one suspects the same may be happening now.

The second factor that makes the situation one of immense opportunities for SESI is the arrival of many societies at precisely the time that is ripe for them to embrace the discipline. Societies such as China, India and those of Latin America such as Brazil have been showing explosive rates of growth largely on the back of the simple factors of rapid urbanisation, and the application of limited amounts of capital in that industrialisation. Extra resources have been allocated to education systems in terms of new buildings, more teachers, more technology and more time at school for students, yet across these societies there is a dissatisfaction in the policymaking community with the results of these policies, not unsurprising because it is clear from all the SESI evidence that these resource-based policy levers are weak ones in terms of affecting outcomes.

There is some evidence of increased awareness within these societies' policymaking communities and educational systems of the existence of SESI – China, for example, has its own national association for school effectiveness, with close links to the other SESI research communities of the world. Given that these societies are at 'lift off' in their search for educational quality, SESI research might become a viral force in these societies as it has been in those where it is longer established. There are 22 million teachers in China. They serve 400 million children. Were SESI to 'root', it would be a seismic event.

The third factor that is generating a favourable international policymaking situation for SESI is the clear evidence of limited outcomes from the other groups and organisations that have tried to address the issues of school quality. In the UK, governmental enthusiasm has been for use of unusually effective head teachers to advise on policy, serve on quangos and be a general repository of wisdom. But it is increasingly clear that many of these people are unusual creatures and may not necessarily be those whom an educational system can be modelled on. They are often the 'edge of the circle' innovators – truly, with some of them, 'the ego has landed'. Using them has brought considerable advantages to policy makers – they are charismatic, practical and have added usefulness in that they have actually done the business of running schools, rather than talking about it or researching those who do.

But their unusual characteristics are increasingly seen as posing problems within policymaking. They have used methods that may not be useful for all. They are a very small sample on which to base the practice of school change and transformation. In short, the SESI research may be historically done by those at one step removed from practice, with all that means, but at least SESI academics use large samples, more representative persons and at least we try to separate out the 'personal' from the 'organisational' in the search for 'what works'.

Fourth, the reactions from policymakers and politicians against the historic influence of all educational research – and also of SESI – have produced a situation where the need for 'thought leadership' has never been stronger. This plays to SESI's strengths. SESI after all 'thought' itself from the margins of academic life to be a central educational research discipline of the age.

The problem has been that 'thought leadership' has been seen as threatening, especially to those who can't think. The Department for Education in England has seen most of its original thinkers leave, happy to leave in most cases a situation in which they have been marginalised by a managerial, corporate culture. New Labour's paradigm shifts over the 2000s ended up in a focus upon improving merely the *reliability* of delivery, rather than upon original thought about the *validity* of the delivery model or the processes themselves being delivered.

The practice of using head teachers and others from the educational system has also generated a restrictive educational culture, in which 'by schools for schools' became not schools' liberation from the irrelevance of academic research work and policy maker excesses, but a restrictive culture in which only what the system thinks was regarded as worthy of use. Thought leadership from outside the system is badly needed, as is increasingly recognised. SESI can provide it.

Lastly, SESI is in a fortunate position, because whilst many other disciplines would be hard put to find much evidence of progress in their insights over the last years, SESI can show much progress. If we were to take those areas of educational research where there has customarily been the evidence of large 'effect sizes', assessment for learning approaches seem to be rather similar, in conceptualisation and practice, to the findings of a decade ago. Comparative education still seems to be a collection of individual scholars sending home their picture postcards from overseas trips. Approaches that combat learning defects seem to have changed little. Whilst there is much 'noise' in issues to do with school restructuring emanating from North America, whether there is a proven substantive body of practice and theory more than sloganising and semi-mystical invocations of moral purpose seems in some doubt. SESI by contrast has shown considerable progress, and could show even more if the position outlined in this chapter is followed.

The argument in this chapter is not that SESI should always have a close allegiance with educational policy makers and politicians, but that in its present situation it should. Much time has been wasted in radical chic critiques and semi-philosophical musings about what SESI could be doing, rather than in the expansion of the discipline's scientific base. National and international educational systems now need advice and intellectual foundations because they need new paradigms to guide them, as the old ones are somewhat exhausted. SESI needs to make the rapid intellectual progress in the next decade as it did in its first decade of existence, the 1990s. A 'trade' whereby the policy community gains knowledge, and SESI gains access to experimental situations to test out its ideas, would be in everyone's interests, even though there may be problems in maintaining the relationship.

Note

An earlier version of the second part of this chapter was given as a paper at the Invitational Seminar on The Twenty First Century School at the Department for Children, Schools and Families in London in March 2009, and a revised version of the same part is published as the final chapter in D. Reynolds (2010) *Failure Free Education? The Past, Present and Future of School Effectiveness and School Improvement.* London: Routledge. The first half of the chapter has not been published before.

15 Innovation, transformation and improvement in school reform[1]

Ben Levin

Introduction

In the current discussion of school improvement one of the main debates is about the place of innovation and transformation. We hear many calls today for the transformation of schooling; to reshape schools in some entirely new way, and for a greater role for innovation in improving schools (e.g. Cisco, 2010). The argument in this chapter is that we should be cautious about embracing transformation and its handmaiden, innovation, as the requirements for schooling. I take the view that the more promising avenue in terms of student outcomes, even broadly defined, would focus instead on improving existing school systems by focusing on better use of what we already know. This is not an argument against change but springs from the belief that a focus on innovation and transformation could distract us from what is both possible and desirable in order to pursue goals that may be desirable but are not very possible.

The case for dramatic change

There are reasons for advancing a transformation agenda. It is easy to see that many aspects of schooling are largely unchanged from a hundred years ago while many aspects of the larger society have changed dramatically. As is often pointed out, schools embody an industrial model of organization in a post-industrial world, and an authoritarian and hierarchical character in a world where networks and negotiations are increasingly prevalent. The literature on the changing nature of work (e.g. Osberg *et al.*, 1995; National Council on Economic Education, 2007) show how much workplaces are changing, with important implications for the skills people need to be economically successful.

One can also point to the dramatic changes in information technology that have altered the way people find and share information. The internet and social networking tools have changed how and when people learn. But technology has impacts in other directions as well; concepts of citizenship are also shifting as a result of population migrations and instant and pervasive communication. In light of these trends – and many others one could cite – it is tempting to argue that the institution of the school needs to be remade. Still, I am going to argue that transformation should not be our primary aim.

Exploration and exploitation

March (1991) pointed out that all organizations need a combination of what he called 'exploration' (another word for innovation) and 'exploitation' (another term for system-wide improvement based on known ways of getting results). March notes that an organization that does not innovate will die, but that too much innovation is also a bad thing. The real profits of an organization, be these financial as in businesses or improved student outcomes as in schools, come, March argues, not from innovation but from putting in place across the organizations ('exploiting') what is known to be effective. As March puts it,

> Adaptive systems that engage in exploration to the exclusion of exploitation are likely to find that they suffer the costs of experimentation without gaining many of its benefits. They exhibit too many undeveloped new ideas and too little distinctive competence.
>
> (1991: 71)

That sounds very much like a description of education policy in the last several decades – endless new ideas and not enough distinctive competence. Thus the common observation that education is subject to many fads that are imposed one year and abandoned the next. It takes very little effort to think of dozens of widely promoted and adopted innovations in education that vanished shortly afterwards or failed to have a positive impact on student outcomes – think open area, differentiated staffing, middle schools, new maths, semester systems, integrated services, magnet schools, small schools, white boards and so on.

It is in the nature of innovation to have this pattern. Most innovations will turn out to be ineffective, or very difficult to do, or very expensive. This is true in every area of innovation. Most new business, for example, fail (Pease, 2009).

Information technology is a particularly interesting example because it is one of the most frequently cited grounds for requiring significant change in schooling. For fifty years we have been hearing that changes in technology – from radio to television to computers to iPads – would fundamentally change the provision of education. But fifty years of history shows that the promise has never been achieved (Cuban, 2001; Moss *et al.*, 2007). Reviews of research have concluded that none of these have had any discernable impact on student learning (Ungerleider and Burns, 2002). One might argue that the continuing effort to implement technologies in schools has been one of the biggest wastes of time and money in the recent history of education – all in the name of transformation.

Several features of schools and innovation contribute to the poor track record of innovation. First, most systems do not have a system for judging ideas or making distinctions between those that are more likely to be effective and feasible (e.g. Coburn *et al.*, 2009; Spillane, 2006). The decision to adopt particular innovations seems to depend often on the views of an individual – perhaps a principal, a superintendent or a board member. Questions about the evidence behind the proposed policy or program tend not to be asked. Even a clear explication of the theoretical basis for the idea, its theory in action, may be missing. There is money to be made in education for both individuals and companies from promoting pet ideas to schools and school systems, and where there is a profit motive there is likely to be hucksterism. Such a cavalier process does not seem adequate when we are talking about the lives of real children.

This line of argument is not meant to suggest that all new ideas should have to meet some unreasonable test of effectiveness before being attempted. As noted earlier, some degree of innovation is essential to all organizations, including schools. And it is certainly not the case that all existing practices in schools are well supported by evidence of impact; many of them also rest on untested assumptions. One should not apply a standard of evidence to new ideas that is more stringent than what we expect from our existing practices. Still, ideas in the education system seem often to be proposed and adopted – and sometimes to become common practice – without much evidence of their value.

Evidence of value is not as available as it might be because there is insufficient evaluation of practices in education systems. Innovation requires discipline but in education we have not learned nearly as much as we could from all the innovation of the past forty years so are quite likely to adopt some of the same ideas and make some of the same mistakes as a generation or two ago. As Hattie (2009) has demonstrated, many practices that have been widely espoused turn out, based on existing evidence, to offer no advantages over doing nothing, and quite a few actually seem to produce less learning than the practices they replaced.

These problems of innovation are even worse in a highly decentralized system where each school can make program choices, because the capacity to analyze options will necessarily be quite limited in most schools. Although there is still faith expressed in some quarters about local wisdom in making program choices, it is hard to see how or why thousands of individual schools would have the capacity to make intelligent choices about every aspects of their operation. More than a decade ago we had convincing evidence (e.g. Thomas and Martin, 1996; Wylie, 1997; Leithwood and Menzies, 1998) that decentralized authority produced relatively little innovation or improvement – though this does not imply the superiority of highly centralized systems either.

The precise balance between exploration and exploitation will differ from one setting to another, but, in most cases, March's formulation suggests that making effective use of what we already know should be a much bigger element. Yet it appears that in the case of schools, innovation has been more the order of the day, but with few innovations either reaching scale or being sustained. While innovation is necessary to organizational survival and success, it also necessarily involves a substantial waste of energy and resources. Education has had a great deal of innovation and not enough exploitation.

Transformation

The discussion so far has been around innovation in schools. But what of transformation, the idea that the education system must be remade in fundamental ways?

A main distinction between innovation and transformation is scale. Innovations are changes in discrete elements of schooling – a new program or a new pedagogy or a new organizational format. But transformation implies changes in all of those. A corollary is that most innovation in education presently occurs in schools or classrooms but that transformation is a system level change.

As noted earlier, a case for the transformation of schooling as we know it has been made based on what is seen as a growing mismatch between the relatively static nature of schools and a dynamic society in which demographics, ideas, norms, structures and technologies have all shifted and continue to change in significant ways. Surely an institution cannot retain the same fundamental shape and practices and be successful in such a changed environment? Do we not have a long history of organizations that disappeared because they were no longer able to cope with a changed environment?

On further thought, though, the case is not, perhaps, as obvious as it seems when put that way. Stinchcombe (1965) suggested that institutions take on the shape of the historical period in which they were developed and find it very hard to change those fundamental organizational characteristics. Thus formal religions continue to have characteristics based on the small, tribal and largely agrarian social systems in which they were developed. Universities are still mediaeval in many ways. Many national constitutions and political systems have endured for centuries. And schools retain the features of the industrial age, their birth period. Yet all of these are institutions that continue to survive and even flourish despite the enormous changes around them. Of course they have had to adapt to changing times in many ways, but many of their essential elements are largely as they were centuries ago. Schools may turn out to be another example of the same phenomenon.

Meyer and Zucker (1989) described what they called 'the permanently failing organization'. Their argument was that some organizations could survive indefinitely even if they failed to achieve their goals. Borrowing from sociological work on 'the logic of confidence' (Meyer and Rowan, 1977) they noted that organizations that fail to achieve any goals can survive for long periods of time if there is a general acceptance that they are doing the right things in the right way. Organizations may continue indefinitely even if some see them as very far from adapted to current circumstances.

The call for transformation also implies the need to change schools to meet the demands of a future that is likely to be very different than the present. However, predicting the future is a notoriously uncertain business; the overwhelming majority of such predictions turn out to be wrong. Beniger (1986) for example, cites fifty claimed 'transforming' trends in modern societies since World War Two. These were all seen to be reasons to change various social policies or practices yet none of them came to fruition. Those who study earthquakes or other natural disasters may speak of 'forecasting' instead of 'predicting'. We know there will be major earthquakes and other natural disasters but we do not know precisely when, where, or how severe. The challenge of being prepared under those circumstances is enormous and one has to weigh the very immediate costs against an uncertain probability of future benefits.

One of the problems in responding to the call to transform schools involves understanding just what it is that is to be transformed. Does transformation refer primarily to teaching and learning activities within (or outside) the school? To the curriculum? To the governance structure? Financing? Credentials offered? All of the above? Advocates of transformation are not necessarily clear on what it is that should change. For example, the CISCO report mentioned earlier (2010) identifies four areas where transformation seems needed: supplying the increasing demand for learning in new fields, at different ages, and in more countries; new teaching methods that give learners more autonomy; a curriculum that values different skills than do most school curricula now; and decreased distance between schools and the wider society.

These different goals could presumably lead to quite different kinds of transformations. One can imagine very different sorts of transformation proposals if one wanted to focus on teaching different skills versus what might be required to reach new learners. Of course one could advocate changing all aspects of the institution. But that raises new challenges. While it is hard to generate sustained improvement in a large organization, it seems to be extraordinarily difficult to transform significant institutions in a directed way. And the broader the scope of the change, the more challenging implementation will be, both substantively and politically.

The political challenges around transformation – or innovation for that matter – are also important and generally underestimated. In a public enterprise such as schooling, public acceptability is the *sine qua non* of any change. As one of the ministers with whom I worked used to say, 'We only get to do what the public will let us'. Because everyone went to school and has ideas about what schooling is like, the public appetite for very large change in education is generally quite limited, especially if people perceive a risk to their children's futures. As Machiavelli noted centuries ago, those who stand to benefit from a future change are almost always less vocal in support than is the opposition from those who fear losing from it. It is easy to call for 'political will' on the part of leaders, but sometimes that means that we want them to invite their own political demise, and that is not a reasonable expectation for anyone to have.

That public caution about dramatic change in our institutions is one reason that many of the main changes in schooling in the past have been driven by larger social forces rather than the plans of educators. For example, the development and growth of special education came largely from changing ideas about human rights and disability in the society. So did the decision to provide equal education for girls and women, or the growing recognition of the needs of various minorities, or the move to have virtually all students complete secondary education. Of course educators played important roles in advocating and implementing these changes, but their primary impetus lay in broader social developments.

Some of these pressures have had very large effects on schools. Mass secondary – and now post-secondary – education has changed schools in very important ways. So has the growing emphasis on inclusion and the understanding that demographic diversity is not a reason for systematic differences in performance.

These ideas have affected school structures, policies, curriculum, community relations and public attitudes. Does this constitute a transformational change? If so, these are changes that have come about gradually and not in a planned way. Yet it would be hard to think of a planned change that has had a greater effect on schools than these examples.

Transformation, then, is an appealing idea in some ways but one with enormous practical problems in that it is not clear what is to be transformed, what the new system will look like, or how, if at all, the desired changes can be brought about.

Improvement

The alternative to a transformation or innovation agenda is an improvement agenda, in which we focus on wider use and application of what we already know to be effective. As a recent McKinsey report (2009: 22) put it:

> long experience around the world serving both private companies and public-sector entities teaches us that when large variations in performance exist among similar operations, relentless efforts to benchmark and implement what works can lift performance substantially.

We now have considerable knowledge about 'what works' – by which I mean practices supported by substantial amounts of empirical evidence from multiple sources all pointing in similar directions – but this knowledge is not broadly applied and we are only just learning what it takes to change school practice on a widespread basis in ways that truly produce improved student outcomes. Organizing schools so that we get much more of practices known to be effective and much less of practices known to be ineffective is highly likely to yield more results per unit of effort than is the search for further innovation or for transformation, both of which carry significant risks.

Hattie recently (2009) meta-analysed some 800 other meta-analyses of research in education and compared the relative effect sizes of more than 130 different programs, strategies and interventions – from formative evaluation to cooperative learning to class size to retention in grade. There are, of course, limitations to this kind of secondary analysis. Because each rests on different quantities and bodies of evidence, the conclusions and ranking of interventions or approaches can only be regarded as indicative. The findings are, however, highly suggestive, and many of the ideas that had the most powerful effects are still very far from common practice in our schools. For example, formative evaluation and student self-reporting of grades had among the very highest effect sizes, confirming the view of others that formative assessment has powerful positive effects on students' work while many other assessment practices, such as averaging grades or using marks to control behaviour, have negative impacts (e.g. Earl, 2003; William, 2009). Yet formative assessment is still uncommon in many, perhaps most, schools.

To take a different example, failing or retaining students in grade is associated with worse outcomes, both short and long term (Hattie, 2009; Jimerson, 2009), yet continues to be common, especially in secondary schools.

How much improvement could we generate through a serious and sustained effort, basically using what we already know? The answer to this question is that we do not know what might happen because few efforts of sufficient scope and scale have been made.

We do, however, know three things.

1   Over time, levels of education achievement have increased dramatically around the world, and sometimes in spectacular fashion over relatively short periods of time.
2   There are large differences in school performance among schools, and among classes within schools, suggesting that the right practices can have powerful effects even given the significance of external factors such as student demographics.
3   Interventions in individual schools and systems have regularly (though certainly not always) produced powerful results.

These three demonstrated facts suggest that the limits of improvement are unknown, but that there are grounds for being quite optimistic about what is possible.

Knowing what practices are effective is one step; the second element has to do with effective implementation, or knowing how to have effective practices occur much more widely in large systems. At one time it was assumed that knowledge would be taken up by professionals simply because that was the right thing to do. Few now believe that; work in many areas has shown that well-validated practices are not necessarily adopted in any profession. Witness the difficulties that medicine has had getting widespread adoption of clinical practice guidelines (Graham and Tetroe, 2007; Grimshaw *et al.*, 2004).

Without systematic efforts to evaluate alternatives based on evidence, decisions will rest on whatever grounds individuals adduce. Nor can one assume that schools or even districts have the wherewithal to make those judgments without support. What counts as accepted knowledge is controversial in every field, but in many fields there is either greater consensus or more elaborated mechanisms for answering this question than we have in the area of schooling. The 'What Works Clearinghouse' in the US or the EPPI-Centre in England are two of many examples one could cite of recent efforts to provide more guidance to school systems around what is known, with what degree of confidence, about various practices and policies. There is no education equivalent to clinical practice guidelines in medicine, or to similar practice guides in many other professions such as engineering or law.

One reason for the absence of such guidelines, and a further important barrier to greater exploitation of knowledge, is the widespread belief among many in education that schooling is an activity that is not amenable to general rules and common practices. Each teacher or school, it is argued, must find a way forward that works in that specific context and the attempt to create common approaches is an assault on professional judgment and autonomy. On reflection that argument seems indefensible (Levin, 2010). Most professions are centred around a common core of knowledge about practice. Indeed, in many cases professionals define themselves by their adherence to a particular body of knowledge. Every profession also faces similar contingencies in practice such that the application of standards depends on particular situations. There is no contradiction between the acceptance of standards of practice and the exercise of professional judgment. Indeed, these standards or practices are the very grounds for that judgment. Teaching, unlike other professions, has very few standard practices that are seen to be desirable for every member of the profession, and the norms that do exist are often at a level of generality that makes it very difficult to know if they are being observed. Yet without agreement that common practices are possible and desirable, it is hard to see how any profession can advance.

Given all the barriers and difficulties, what are the prospects for improvement as defined in this chapter – that is, wider and deeper use of principles of education known to be effective based on substantial empirical evidence? This is, in many respects, the subject of investigation of the fields of school effectiveness and school improvement over the last decades. One might say that school effectiveness research has been more (but not exclusively) about what to do or what practices and policies to adopt, and school improvement research has been more (but not exclusively) about how to get it done. Much of the attention, especially in school improvement, was focused on small numbers of schools, driven in large measure by the limitations imposed by particular research methods. So our knowledge base about system-wide improvement, not only in education but in related fields such as health, is relatively young.

Still, quite a bit has been learned (e.g. Barber, 2007; Levin and Fullan, 2008; Levin, 2008; Fullan, 2010; Hargreaves and Shirley, 2009). We can be confident that changes in organisational structures, incentive systems, governance and financing, while important, will not by themselves produce improvement (Levin, 2010). We can also have some confidence that a sustained and positive focus on building the skills and motivation of all parties, especially but not only teachers, can result in real improvements across large numbers of schools. We have learned that school improvement has a political element as well as an educational aspect; that work has to be done to build and maintain understanding and support for improvement from the main stakeholders and the public as a whole. We have learned that changing the skills of large numbers of educators requires a significant infrastructure that works in ways that are consistent with growing knowledge about how people learn and about what changes people's behaviour. Most of the elements of this framework have been known for some time, but it is only recently that they have all been brought together in a comprehensive approach. There is every reason to be optimistic about the prospects for significant improvement in educational practices and outcomes across large numbers of schools given focused attention and support.

Implications for school effectiveness research

If the reader is persuaded by the argument that most of our focus should be on improvement rather than innovation or transformation, there are some important implications for research.

First, the scope of research on school improvement needs to go beyond small groups of schools. We already know a considerable amount about improvement in these situations; the real challenge now is how to make that happen at a much larger scale, across hundreds or thousands of schools, with the kinds of resources that are likely to be available. This also means that research cannot focus solely on outlier schools; the task is to generate improvement across all kinds of schools, serving quite different populations. Given the importance of equity goals, attention is still needed to schools in challenging circumstances, but most under-achieving students are not in the highest-need schools, so those schools cannot be the main focus of research attention.

Second, school improvement and effectiveness research should pay more attention to actual teaching and learning practices. The literature on effectiveness still often stops at general characteristics of schools such as a focus on student achievement or use of data. But without better daily teaching and learning practices, these changes cannot produce improvement. Growing knowledge about both the practices needed in classrooms (as described, for example, by Hattie, 2009 or by Marzano, 2003) can mesh well with growing knowledge about effective leadership (e.g. Robinson *et al.*, 2009) but these connections are not yet well established in the literature on school improvement or school effectiveness.

Third, school effectiveness and improvement research should pay more attention to knowledge translation or knowledge mobilization – that is, how research actually connects to policy and practice. There is a large and growing literature on this issue (e.g. Nutley *et al.*, 2007; Levin, 2004; Cooper *et al.*, 2009) including some excellent examples in the UK (e.g. Cordingley, 2009; Rickinson, 2005). The issue merits at least an equivalent paper to this on its own. However, to draw just a couple of key points, this work tells us that systematic efforts to communicate research are necessary, particularly efforts around interpersonal connections on an ongoing basis. The research community needs to think about how it could do this more systematically and effectively other than through our current and rather traditional modes of standard scholarly communication.

Conclusion

I have argued in this chapter that improving educational outcomes across all schools, for large numbers of students, on a broad range of outcomes should remain the primary goal of education policy for the foreseeable future. While disciplined and careful innovation is essential to learning and further improvement, it should not be the main focus of attention. The real benefits are to be gained from deeper and wider use of existing knowledge about good teaching and learning and the supports needed for them – such as leadership and professional development. I believe that we already know a considerable amount about these questions that we do not use. Transformation of schooling may be an attractive idea in some respects, but has the potential to exact very high costs for very uncertain returns in that there is no agreement about what needs to be transformed, how that would happen, or how much benefit it would yield relative to the clearly enormous effort it would require. The more rigorous use of existing knowledge seems a surer basis for continued progress in education and for increased benefits to students.

Conclusion

*Christopher Chapman, Paul Armstrong, Alma Harris,
Daniel Muijs, David Reynolds and Pam Sammons*

Introduction

In this book we set out to draw together the thinking and themes which emerged from the ESRC seminar series. In this concluding chapter we reflect on a number of the key themes that transcend the individual chapters in this volume. We focus our attention on three key areas:

1 organisation of the discipline;
2 advances and challenges within the field;
3 key issues for the field.

We take each of these areas in turn and conclude by reflecting on where we might go from here.

Organisation of the discipline

The improvements in our capacity to make theoretical formulations, and in our methodological capacity that has come through harnessing fixed/multiple methods, has also been paralleled – as is obvious through the volume – by increases in our knowledge about the scientific properties of our field. The chapters by Sammons, Kyriakides, Muijs (1, 3 and 4) and those on the four nations of the United Kingdom (5, 6, 7 and 8) show valid and reliable knowledge bases concerning:

- the size of educational effects upon pupils, where it is clear that school and classroom processes can make a significant difference to student progress;
- the variation within schools in their effectiveness in different academic areas, between academic and social areas and between children of different background characteristics, such as gender, social class, ethnicity and special educational status;
- the primacy of teacher or classroom effects rather than of school, or district/ local authority effects.

The field is also now embracing the study of contextual variation in 'what works', particularly looking at how international country contexts may be different in these factors, in their conceptualisation and in their operationalisation. Chapman's Chapter 2 reflects on the strong rhetoric of context-specific improvement but argues that in the field context-specific approaches remain relatively simplistic. The field is also moving from the study of primary/elementary and secondary/high schools only towards study of other educational sectors including preschool and the non-compulsory settings such as colleges and, to an extent, higher education.

Indeed, some of the chapters in this volume now embrace a more holistic 'educational effectiveness and improvement research' (EEIR) perspective, which attempts to merge the historically somewhat separate traditions of school and teacher effectiveness, and the historically separate traditions of school and teacher improvement. This merger of formerly separate traditions is something that is continued in the upcoming *International Handbook of Educational Effectiveness and Improvement Research* (Chapman *et al.*, forthcoming).

It is worth noting though that the school improvement/development material in the volume seems to show a different intellectual trajectory than the EEIR material. There is, firstly, less of it in total, as there is less of it in the field as a whole. Partly this is because the school improvement community may have moved on to newer foci – to the 'system effectiveness' paradigm and interventions that are outlined in Chapter 11 from Hopkins, and also in the material from Chapman and Levin (Chapters 2 and 15). The four country case studies offer an alternative explanation, the close relationship and applied nature of much school improvement work may account for 'different' forms of knowledge being generated with school improvement efforts. Others have moved on from basic concerns of improving young people's life chances to issues to do with more philosophical discussions about which new outcomes are necessary to give children the leverage they need to be 'system' or 'societal' changers of the world around them, as seen in the paper by Townsend (Chapter 12).

The 'scientific properties' of the field of school improvement are much less well known than those of the teacher effectiveness or school effectiveness fields. It is often unclear which factors at school level are important for improvement to occur. The outcomes of pupils before and after any improvement interventions are not always measured, so effects are unclear. Interventions are often pitched at the level of the school rather than that of the classroom and its practice, so that only weak influences, directly, over student outcomes are being addressed. Also, considerable attention is given to cultural, attitudinal, social and relational factors in the understanding and improvement/remediation of schools, even though the evidence is overwhelming that children and their outcomes are related to the behaviours of those within educational organisations more than to their 'affect'.

Whereas it is clear that educational effectiveness has incorporated much thinking from the educational improvement field, in the importance of educational leadership for example, the same cross fertilisation of effectiveness constructs and methodologies into improvement does not appear to have happened, or at least to the same extent. We will consider what needs to happen to the school improvement field later on in these conclusions.

The final thing that should be clear from this brief analysis of the field is, though, that there is an organisational framework in place that has developed considerably the capacity of EEIR to make practical and intellectual progress. The original 'normal science' review of the field over a decade ago (Teddlie and Reynolds, 2000) drew on approximately 1,200 references – the upcoming *Handbook* will probably have double that number. The International Congress for School Effectiveness and Improvement has turned from its focus upon criticism of the field to a willingness to discuss the field's scientific properties in plenary sessions, both in the 2011 meeting in Cyprus and the 2012 meeting in Malmo. The European Association for Research in Learning and Instruction (EARLI) has flourishing biennial meetings of its effectiveness Special Interest Group (SIG) and the AERA effectiveness SIG has record membership.

But the organisational structure to facilitate intellectual advance is not enough. It needs new, substantive areas of the EEIR discipline to focus on. We now attempt to look at the theoretical, methodological and practical achievements and challenges associated with the field.

Theoretical advances and challenges

When reflecting on this varied set of chapters, we are led to both significant strengths and remaining weaknesses in our field. Here we will attempt to summarise some of these achievements and challenges, looking at ways to further develop EEIR.

One area where we have seen some significant developments is that of theory. In the past, the school and educational effectiveness in particular was frequently criticised for what was seen as an a-theoretical approach, often limited to the production of lists of factors associated with outcomes. In many ways this criticism was premature, as it is by no means unusual for scientific areas to develop from an empirical and empiricist perspective, with theory built, as it were, bottom up. Increasingly, though, this criticism becomes even less valid. As is clear from Chapter 3 by Kyriakides, our original empirical base has led to the development of theoretical models, culminating in the Dynamic Theory of Educational Effectiveness, the strongest theoretical base the field had ever had and the first to take into account the dynamic interaction of factors and levels. This is, of course, not to say that the Dynamic Theory provides us with the definitive 'Grand Theory' of educational effectiveness. As in all scientific fields, theories are always provisional and subject to change, and variables in the model may be more or less applicable depending on context. However, that we now possess a theory that allows us to do this key job of testing across different contexts is a major advance for research in educational effectiveness, for which all involved in its development deserve great credit.

The situation in the area of improvement is somewhat different in that in many ways improvement research showed a greater interest in theoretical models from the outset, but has possibly developed less in this area than the field of effectiveness. Models of improvement have long existed in the field, both in terms of phases of improvement and types and levels of improvement, as is clear in Chapter 2 by Chapman. However, little attempts have been made so far to make the leap from meso-level heuristics and models for improvement to a more encompassing theory of improvement as a process. It is clear that this is an urgent task for researchers in the field.

A further task for all of us working in effectiveness and improvement research and practice is to integrate and relate our respective theoretical frameworks and models to one another. Here, those of us working in effectiveness need to be sure not to repeat the errors of earlier effectiveness researchers, who simply tried to apply effectiveness factors in schools without a thorough understanding of the processes of change and improvement in schools. We cannot assume that theoretical development simply means applying our theories of educational effectiveness to school improvement. Rather, colleagues need to develop theoretical models that draw on the insights of the two distinct but symbiotic sisters of effectiveness and improvement.

Methodological advances and challenges

Some of the most significant achievements in SESI and more recently in EEI research and practice can be found in the methodological advancements made over recent decades. As Chapman notes in Chapter 2, SE and SI come from very different roots, each with their own separate histories, traditions and associated methodologies. School effectiveness research has tended to focus on large-scale quantitative methodologies, while school improvement research and practice's roots are far more applied, with researchers and practitioners producing small-scale case studies often based on qualitative methods and involving action research techniques.

The distinctiveness of these traditions has been both a major strength of the field and a challenge to further development. The methodological contribution of school effectiveness research has included the advancement of quantitative methodologies designed to identify significant relationships and interactions relating to effectiveness at the pupil, teacher, school and system level. Some of the techniques outlined by Muijs in Chapter 4, such as multilevel modelling, have been taken up by other disciplines such as health sciences and biology to assess key relationships associated with effective performance in the social sciences and beyond. The most recent advances in SER have involved randomised controlled trials. This methodological advancement indicates a new direction for the future of pure SE research.

For the most part, school improvement's methodological contribution has involved the development of qualitative methodologies to provide detailed case studies into the inner workings of the school. This tradition can be traced back to, amongst others, David Hargreaves' (1967) ethnography of social relationships in a school setting. The action research approach adopted by many school improvement activists can be traced back even further to Kurt Lewin's work in 1946. The main methodological challenges for school improvement research is to develop

finer-grained analyses of the interactions and processes playing out in schools and to gain a deeper understanding of the relationship between different actors experiences of the schooling processes. This will require drawing on new methods from elsewhere in the social sciences as well as developing new approaches that make use of emerging technologies.

The separate methodological strengths of SE and SI have ensured a strong, if at times tense set of relationships between SESI researchers. On the one hand, school effectiveness researchers have focused on an input-output model and been confident they have identified the significant factors or key characteristics associated with more or less effective schools and classrooms across a population without venturing into what might be done inside the 'black box' to improve a school or classroom. In contrast, SI researchers and activists have been interested in the structures and processes associated with the milieu of the black box; and for the most part have attempted to make analytical rather than statistical generalisations.

The methodological advancements and challenges of each tradition have also challenged the field's development; each methodological perspective is underpinned by a philosophical position located in an opposing paradigm. The positivist nature of SER combined with the constructivist perspective of SI have often illuminated two very different and at times contrasting views of schools and classrooms. These alternative lenses helpfully provided differing insights but also presented challenges in the interpretation of what the emerging knowledge base was indicating and what action was needed to improve matters.

The mid-1990s saw a bringing together of the individual strengths and more research involving combined teams of SE and SI researchers. This Merging of Traditions (Gray *et al.*, 1995) enabled a significant methodological advancement. For the first time serious attempts were made to develop mixed methods designs incorporating the strengths of both SE and SI research. In practice, many of these early attempts, and some contemporary efforts are better termed as 'multiple methods' research, where the quantitative and qualitative strand of inquiry occur in parallel and are drawn together in a final analysis or where the quantitative strand is used to 'map the terrain', identifying key relationships and then the qualitative strand attempts to provide explanations for their existence.

It would seem the next phase of methodological advancement for EEIR should involve a commitment to develop 'real' mixed methods approaches where each strand of data collection and analysis is more fully integrated and has the power to inform the substance and direction of the research. As noted above, a further challenge is to incorporate a broader range of methods into the qualitative strand of research. There are opportunities through technological advancement to develop more versatile approaches that support the collection of different types of visual and audio data and to access a wider range of participants.

Practical advances and challenges

SESI and latterly EEIR can point to a number of successes over the past 30 years or so. The first, and possibly the most significant, is the contribution the field has made to raising awareness that schools, classrooms and teachers do matter and can make a difference to the educational outcomes achieved by young people. This has bought the debate on educational standards to the fore in many education systems. Socio-economic disadvantage is no longer an excuse for low educational achievements in many systems. Schools do succeed against the odds. However, raised awareness is a necessary but insufficient ingredient for making a significant contribution. While some schools succeed against the odds, after decades of raised awareness and intervention many more still do not.

The universals of SESI are well understood. We have an understanding about what improving and effective schools look like over time. For example, Gray *et al.* (1999) utilised pupil level achievement data taken from public examination results, obtained from the workings of the educational monitoring systems of two local authorities in England, and followed cohorts of tens of thousands of pupils each year with matched 'intake' and 'outcome' data in over 80 secondary schools, over five years. Data upon school processes were gathered through multiple visits using multiple instruments, by observers who were 'blind' to school performance. Results showed associations between various school-level and classroom-level factors and pupil gain over time.

There is also a growing knowledge base around what effective teaching and learning looks like. There is evidence to inform a whole range of school-level strategies for improvement, from home-school partnerships, to effective networking and collaboration with other organisations and targeted interventions with specific groups of children. For example, elements of the influential *Improving the Quality of Education for All* approach (Hopkins *et al.*, 2004) dealing with these issues can be found in government improvement initiatives in England and have also been taken up in diverse contexts including Hong Kong and Iceland.

A second example where the SESI knowledge base has influenced and impacted on practice is the High Reliability Schools programme (Stringfield *et al.*, 2008). This programme involved intervention with secondary schools in three British LEAs, comparing the gain over time of schools participating in the programme with gain of the national totality of secondary schools in England, and in Wales, utilising public examination results at age 16. An analysis was also undertaken across the entire sample of schools – approximately 25 in total – of the relationship between the adoption of the 60 individual component parts of the improvement programme, and gain over time on the achievement data. A further example of EEIR making a contribution is Houtveen and colleagues' (2004) report on an evaluation of the Mathematics Improvement Programme (MIP), which used an experimental and comparison group. This indicated both significant benefits for the MIP on pupil progress in Grade 3, and a reduction in the percentage of struggling learners. On top of this, the study revealed important school level variance in improvement trajectory and also identified five out of ten implementation features studied that significantly contributed to differences in pupils' results.

In addition to the key issues discussed in the next section of this chapter there are a number of other challenges associated with EEIR and practice. First, the issue of scaling up – EEIR interventions seems to work when schools that are 'ripe' for change can opt into initiatives and interventions. However, when EEIR interventions are mandated or forced on schools they are often become diluted or lose their impact. This is not surprising if one understands improvement as a social as well as technical process – unfortunately this is not always the case with politicians and policy makers. Second, there has tended to be a lack of audit about specific contexts. This means we understand less about context. This compounds the situation whereby we have a strong grasp of the universals but less understanding about what works and why in particular settings. This is particularly acute for schools serving the extremes of society. Put simply, we know less about schools serving the most socially advantaged and disadvantaged communities. We now move on to discuss four emerging key issues for EEIR.

Key issue 1: the problems of take-up

A major issue across the area of both effectiveness and improvement is that of ensuring better take up of findings and results within the practitioner and policy maker communities. Practitioners have been influenced by the climate that 'schools make a difference', and of course in many societies State educational policies have used EEIR insights to measure and evaluate schools, train leaders and develop their teachers, but there is little evidence of major take up of findings. Some take up happens through the participation of teachers in Higher Education courses on effectiveness and improvement, through use of EEIR material in CPD, through public and private improvement consultancy efforts and no doubt through individual teacher interest in the field through book and journal readership.

But little *direct* translation of findings into practice has taken place thus far. Why is this and what might we do about it?

First, the teaching profession is not necessarily well versed in the 'rational-empirical' research methodology that is used in EEIR. The methods of training are still largely 'craft' based, at which a trainee soaks up knowledge about effective practice from an HE 'master craftsman', and then applies the knowledge under practical supervision from others in classrooms. Knowledge about research methods, the language of research, the quantitative language used and even the importance of issues such as reliability and validity are rarely part of the professional training process.

Second, the meagre proportion of total EEIR work that has been done on classroom teaching means that one of teachers' main focal concerns has been rarely addressed.

Third, the historic concentration upon academic measures in EEIR, which has of course been slowly changing, may not have endeared the field to a profession which has often been attracted to the social and more affective pupil outcomes in their own day-to-day professional lives.

Fourth, the absence of theories that can link the disparate findings of a field together in ways that *explain* patterns of relationships may have meant that the profession sees our field as little more than the lists of good practice so beloved of the early EEIR pioneers (Reynolds, 2010).

Lastly, the way in which the policy community has picked up some of the 'mood music' of EEIR to generate policies that the profession commonly regard as controversial may also have had the effect of putting professionals off heavy involvement in the field. EEIR persons have worked for the UK inspection agency Ofsted (Sammons, 1995), have used EEIR to design the primary Numeracy Strategy (Reynolds, 2010) and have participated extensively in advising activities, all of which may have had the effects of painting it as a governmentally approved set of persons and knowledge, making it suspicious.

Take up by policy makers – as will be clear from the above – has been seen at certain times in certain settings but has again not been extensive over time. It is clear from Chapters 5–8 on the four United Kingdom countries that EEIR has come and largely gone from the policy-making community in England after the high water mark of the late 1990s/early 2000s. In Scotland, the sponsorship of EEIR through the Scottish Office of the 1990s has also gone, and in Northern Ireland there has been little more than the use of the 'effectiveness check lists' that have simplistically marred the attractiveness of the discipline over time. Only in Wales, with its databank of EEIR bodies of knowledge and its School Effectiveness Framework, generated in part by persons from the EEIR community, is there evidence of substantial current involvement with the policy-making community.

The way in which EEIR has slipped in and out of policy maker take up is difficult to explain. Chapter 14 by Reynolds speculates that the policy-making community has a short-term, politically- and media-driven timescale, which means it 'picks up' fields and then drops them with speed. Politicians and policy makers may not have the 'domain knowledge' about research, and EEIR research in particular, to embrace it. They may also prefer to trust their own judgements, rather than rely on occasionally inconvenient truths from effectiveness researchers.

But, of course, these well-known limitations on the possible policy maker reach of the field have not stopped productive relationships at certain times in the countries of the UK, nor in the Ontario Province of Canada as Levin's Chapter 15 notes, so we need to understand *why* in certain contexts, at certain times, a close relationship can be formed.

Key issue 2: context specificity

Context specificity is not a new issue for the field. Much has been written about the importance of context in relation to SESI. For the most part this has tended to focus on matching school improvement interventions to specific contexts. Some work has explored the importance of school types in relation to improvement (Hopkins *et al.*, 1997), some has focused on particular contexts such as urban and challenging circumstances (Reynolds *et al.*, 2002), and school context, improvement and leadership (Chapman, 2006; Day *et al.*, 2011), while other work has examined matching interventions to different levels of school effectiveness (Hopkins, 2008).

However, despite prolonged interest and a general acceptance that SESI ignores the 'context issue' at its peril, the recent focus on achieving systemic change highlights a major fault-line between attending to the complexity of context and 'scaling up'.

Where sensitive context-specific interventions have been attempted, it is rare have they been successfully scaled up across the system. For example, the Schools Facing Extremely Challenging Circumstances Project in England (Harris *et al.*, 2006; MacBeath *et al.*, 2007) involved a SESI team of researchers developing context-specific approaches to stimulate capacity building, teaching and learning and leadership development in eight of the most challenging schools in the country. This initiative was unable to be taken to scale because of the costs involved in supporting an intensive contextually specific intervention.

It is not only cost which limits the potential of scaling up context-specific improvement. The complexity of developing and implementing context-specific interventions is also a barrier to moving to scale. Such programmes require a detailed understanding of the locality, organisational and classroom characteristics. This requires critical friends and consultants with wide-ranging and sophisticated skill sets to get under the surface of what is happening. Those working in these environments require high order analytical skills to provide insightful diagnoses of the setting, a detailed knowledge of what works and why in different contexts and a sense of the universals and specifics associated with school improvement. Furthermore, an ability to build strong relationships in difficult circumstances, combined with excellent communication skills and a detailed understanding of the phases of change, from initiation to institutionalisation is required (Fullan, 1992).

Conversely, system-wide initiatives often lack the potency or nuance to serve a wide range of contexts. For example, in Chapter 5 Mel West outlines some of the recent experiences of the literacy and numeracy strategies in England. These initiatives touched every school in the country but failed to recognise the importance of individual contexts. This initiative was adapted by some schools to serve their own contexts – perversely, these tended to be the more effective schools which were confident enough to adapt, reject and subvert elements of centrally mandated strategies while weaker schools, often serving the most challenging communities, slavishly went through the prescribed motions of the initiative failing to adapt the materials or practices to their own complex and challenging circumstances, ironically, where context-specific solutions were most needed.

The field urgently requires a more sophisticated understanding about what types of improvement approaches are more or less likely to work for schools in different contexts. In Chapter 2, Chapman argues low capacity settings with low effectiveness, schools may need to draw in external capacity to 'kick start' improvement and focus on more *mechanistic* approaches that minimise variations in practice and generate collective confidence and capacity for change. As confidence rises, less external input is likely to be needed and the task becomes more focused on *organic* approaches, which encourage inquiry, experimentation and risk-taking, and move knowledge around the school. At the later stages of this phase external partnerships are likely to come to the fore again. However, in contrast to the early stages of development where the school drew in external capacity now the school is likely to be providing system leadership to generate capacity elsewhere.

Understanding school context is more than getting to grips with improvement approaches and school development phases. It is also more than understanding locality and organisational culture. In an attempt to deepen our understanding we have broken down the complexity of school context into four key dimensions:

1 institutional;
2 social;
3 geographical;
4 political.

We suggest each dimension has a number of key elements. The mix of each of the elements within each context combines to offer an overarching school context with a unique *culture and capacity for change*. Understanding the specific overarching school context and the composition of its dimensions and elements will serve to identify resources, opportunities and barriers to improvement. Table 16.1 outlines the key dimensions and elements that we believe come together to provide an overarching school context.

At the institutional level, arrangements within the school and the characteristics of the staff are of primary importance – how the school is organised and the relationships that underpin these arrangements determine the nature of the institutional context. The social context in which the school exists is the second dimension. Here, the student, family and wider community arrangements interact to determine the nature of the social context. The nature of the geographical context in which the school is located will also serve to shape the school context. The regional environment also plays a role. The history of working traditions, industrial development and relative isolation of the area will all contribute to the geographical context of a school. Finally, the school operates in an overarching political context where policy serves to shape the modus operandi of schools.

The blend of these factors and dimensions create what is a unique overarching school context for every school. We suggest high leverage school improvement requires a detailed understanding of these individual factors and dimensions. However, this is a necessary but insufficient prerequisite. The key to understanding overarching school context is based on understanding the interaction between and influence of each of the four dimensions. Furthermore, it would seem that as one moves from left to right across the taxonomy the potency of each dimension decreases. This would suggest the institutional and social dimensions are the most powerful and have the largest sphere of influence. If this is the case, school improvers should focus their attention on understanding the relationship between the institutional and social dimensions, for this is where high leverage school improvement is most likely to be achieved.

Key issue 3: new outcomes and linkages

The need to study a wider range of outcomes than academic achievement has long been acknowledged by researchers in educational effectiveness and

Table 16.1 A taxonomy of school context

OVERARCHING SCHOOL CONTEXT

Institutional	*Social*	*Geographical*	*Political*
School arrangements Phase (age range), size, co-ed/single sex, selective/non-selective, type (e.g. faith), governance, physical resources	**Student** SES background, race, gender, prior attainment, culture, self-esteem, disposition to learning	**Local context** Inner city/ urban/ suburban/ rural	**Policy decisions** National and local policy imperatives, political vision, values aims and objectives
Academic and pastoral arrangements Curriculum, academic faculty structures, groupings, identification and intervention for support, extra-curricular provision, SEN provision	**Family** Parental income and qualifications, expectations, family/ career characteristics and support network, housing, aspiration	**National and regional context-** Economically developing/ developed, centre of commerce and industry, coastal/isolated upland/isolated lowland	
Student arrangements Gender balance, cohort characteristics	**Community** Culture, crime, welfare provision, economic prosperity, social facilities, community cohesion, employment opportunities, FE and HEI provision		
Staffing characteristics Leadership and teacher: culture, vision and values, experience, capacity, CPD, staffing mix and turnover, structure, quality assurance, financial and legal understanding, non-teaching and administrative data management staffing			

improvement, and has, as is evident in Chapter 1 by Sammons, led to a broad-
ening of studies to include outcomes such as (amongst others) well-being and
capability (De Fraine *et al.*, 2005; Kelly, 2007), self-concept (De Fraine *et al.*,
2007), attitudes to school (Van de Gaer *et al.*, 2009), mental health (Modin
and Ostberg, 2009), physical health (West *et al.*, 2004), and problem behaviour

(Sellstrom and Bremberg, 2006). However, it is true that the majority of studies still focus on attainment. This of course is not entirely unnatural or unreasonable, as, first, attainment remains a prime goal of schooling in all education systems and forms a necessary, if not sufficient, condition to improving the life chances of young people; second, most studies continue to show greater school effects on attainment than on affective outcomes; and, third, that in many education systems (such as those discussed by West and Egan) attainment is the outcome for which schools are primarily held accountable. These points notwithstanding, it is clear that effectiveness and improvement need to continue to expand their work in the area of non-cognitive outcomes, particularly in those areas, like health outcomes, where significant school effects have been found.

An area in which very little work has so far occurred in our field is that of environmental sustainability. Clarke and Kelly, in Chapter 13, rightly point to this area as being absolutely central to our future, and also point to some interesting work being done in addressing some of the issues at school and local community levels. That neither effectiveness nor improvement researchers have to date taken much account of these factors is a serious omission that relates directly to the relevance of the field in what may become an increasingly challenging environmental context. We would, therefore, encourage and indeed exhort researchers to develop programmes of research in this area, building, for example, on the work of Eco-schools in Flanders which has been evaluated from an effectiveness perspective (Van Petegem, 2011).

Another area that requires further development is exploring the linkages between schools, classrooms and communities. We have too frequently treated schools as isolated units that can be studied as if operating outside of their contexts. In part, as Muijs pointed out in Chapter 4, this is due to the methodological constraints of methods like multilevel modelling, which tend us towards looking at levels separately. In part too, as MacBeath points out in Chapter 7, this is due to us ignoring key external variables, such as private tutoring, which may confound estimates of school effects with those of tutoring. In effectiveness, in particular, there has also been a tendency to treat the community the school works in as an exogenous factor that can be 'modelled out' rather than as a core constituent of school effectiveness itself. The latter is particularly problematic in light of what we know about the importance of peers and parents in developing aspiration and 'readiness to learn' in pupils, something acknowledged in programmes that have aimed to extend the role of schools in the community through outreach and extended services. That these appear to be only partially effective (e.g. Cummings *et al.*, 2008) strengthens the need for more development and research in this area.

By focusing too strongly on schools as individual entities, effectiveness and improvement also risk being left behind by changes in the system itself, which have in many cases had the effect of limiting the individual autonomy of schools. As Chapman points out in Chapter 2, in many countries there have been moves towards encouraging between-school networking and collaboration. This is not only the case in England as described in this volume, but is also a strong driver of policy in, for example, the Netherlands and Flanders. Schools are encouraged to form networks which, in their strongest form, may result in a group of schools being managed by one 'executive' head teacher and a joint governing body, with frequent cross-school professional development and teachers working in more than one school. In these cases it will be hard to limit the locus of causality to any one school, and research (and accountability measures) will need to consider the network as a whole rather than as a collection of individual schools. Another development, which was highlighted by Mel West in Chapter 5, is related to the development of academies in England in particular. This is the formation of chains of academies, run by single sponsors, several of which now control a large group of schools across the country. In some cases these are run very much along the lines of a business franchise, with many processes in teaching, learning and management run along centralised lines, and individual schools expected to follow 'corporate' strategies. Here again it makes sense to study the chain as a whole as much as the individual schools, in the same way that a business franchise would not be studied as simply a set of separate entities rather than a whole.

That so far the field has made little inroads into this area is in all likelihood mainly a result of a certain inertia that may lead us to continue on well-travelled roads, rather than any major methodological and practical constraints, as quantitatively this type of structure can be modelled quite easily, while qualitative research by definition lends itself to the study of complex contexts. As pragmatists (see Teddlie and Tashakkori, 2003) we need to study reality as it is, rather than as it may exist in theoretical models or ideals.

Key issue 4: systemic learning

The opportunities for systemic learning have greatly increased over recent years, as the number, scale and frequency of international research programmes has risen exponentially. The same is true of the influential PISA studies conducted by OECD. Data on the characteristics of education systems, such as that collected by the European Union's Eurydice programme, are also ever more available and common.

The influence of these international studies is clear, as illustrated in Egan's Chapter 8 on Wales, which shows the reaction of the Welsh Assembly Government to disappointing PISA results, as well as in major school reforms undertaken in countries such as Germany (in the past decade) and Denmark (in the 1990s) for similar reasons. This influence is, however, almost entirely based on comparison of the test results and, while important, these are by no means the only data collected as part of these studies. It is surprising that much of the other data on education systems that is available in the international studies themselves and in other international databases is largely ignored by policy makers. PISA, for example, contains data on school choice, classroom environments and school policies, while TIMSS contains quite detailed data on classroom teaching. A wealth of other data on systems is available elsewhere. However, what is typically done following disappointing test results are visitations to successful countries, where policy makers and, it has to be said, education academics, pick out aspects that suit their prior convictions as being those that have made the visited country more successful.

Key issue 5: the need to understand the school level

Even a cursory glance at the contents of this volume and at other relevant reviews of the field (Teddlie and Reynolds, 2000; Townsend, 2007) shows that our understanding of the level of 'the school' has not increased as much as that in various other areas. We know considerably more about the 'scientific properties' of the field in terms of the size of effects, in terms of the international range of variation in achievement scores and in terms of the importance of the teacher and classroom 'level' in generating outcomes. We have seen research move from the compulsory years of education to the non-compulsory, but the volume of research, and the quality of it in terms of its insights, into the school has been much less than in those areas.

No doubt reductions in funding opportunities for research have had an effect, given that research into the school 'level' needs to be broad, encompassing as it must a school's relationship with its community hinterland, the multiple levels of provision within schools and the interactions between those levels, such as between the school and classroom teachers. Research into the scientific properties can be done utilising existing national datasets (e.g. the English PLASC one) or additional local authority ones, at minimal cost. Research into the school level necessitates considerable data collation.

But many of the intellectual sources of ideas that facilitated the growth of 'school level' understanding in the 1990s also appear to have run their course in the 2000s. The insights from the British sociology of the school that were so influential from the work of Bernstein, Hargreaves and Lacey have not been supplemented except to a limited extent from the more recent qualitative work done on classrooms.

The result of all these factors is that research in EEIR has continued to adopt a 'whole school' view of what is being measured at school level, which does not disaggregate the school to investigate the processes actually experienced by the varying populations of children within it. Pupils do not experience a 'whole school' – they experience a particular niche within it, yet in virtually all EEIR research schools are seen as a common and constant factor.

There have been some attempts to look at these issues, but these have been limited in scope theoretically and methodologically. In a number of the American school effectiveness studies there have been attempts to study the 'range' or 'dispersal' of the scores at the level of the school, when aggregating together the results from the study of factors such as the expectations of teachers, the use of rewards or the nature of the classroom environment, say, yet this work is based upon the relatively one dimensional and simple views of the school level that were surfacing 20 years ago (e.g. Teddlie and Stringfield, 1993).

There has been work into the differences between Departments within UK secondary schools (Harris, 1997; Sammons *et al.*, 1997; Reynolds, 2010), but little attempt to understand the school-level factors implicated in the production of variability. The interactions between the school and departmental 'levels', and the factors responsible for variation in their quality, are not studied in detail any more than are the interactions between the school and the classroom level that generates a wide variability between teacher effectiveness in some schools and lesser variability in others.

Additionally, we don't have enough understanding of which school-level factors may be responsible for the differential school effects by ethnicity, socio-economic status and gender that is now one of the established scientific properties of the field. Schools will vary considerably in the 'gender achievement gap' between boys and girls for example – are the usual collections of school-level factors able to explain this? In all likelihood, the gender differential effects are a product of specific factors at school level that may not be the usual 'school' factors – perhaps the gender composition of the staff, the school's emotional tone, the school's role models it offers its boys and the like may need to be measured to capture this school effect.

There will be variation in academic achievement by social class too – more in some schools than others. Children from more disadvantaged backgrounds are likely to be more affected by their schools than other groups across all schools, but there will be variability in this within schools, reflecting perhaps factors such as the strength of school structuring, and school disciplinary climate.

Lastly, there will be differential effects of schools upon their different kinds of outcomes, with schools differing upon their 'value added' in cognitive, affective, social, relational and other areas, yet the precise explanations for variation in the non-cognitive areas may be difficult given that our conventional school-level factors have been designed to explain variation in academic/cognitive achievement outcomes. In one of the earliest studies in the British field (Mortimore *et al.*, 1988), the school-level factors associated with the non-cognitive outcomes were different from the cognitive, and there were many fewer of them, even where the variance explained by the school level was the same, suggesting that whatever it was that affected children's self-esteem, self-conception and attitudes to school was not being tapped by the conventional school-level factors. It is extraordinary that we are no closer to understanding these issues today than we were two decades ago.

The effect of this 'whole school' perspective has not just been the impoverishment of our understanding – it has encouraged corresponding 'whole school' policies, interventions and systems of accountability. The Ofsted inspection regime, for example, is clearly based upon a whole school model, notwithstanding recent attempts to look at the experience of particular groups in the classroom and recent acknowledgement of within school variation in academic subject performance. Interventions such as the Academies programme or the National Challenge likewise assume that school-level interventions may help to raise overall standards, but there is less evidence that they have reduced within school variation or narrowed equity gaps in performance (Sammons, 2008). Given our lack of knowledge about the school-level levers to pull it is not surprising that we appear to be unable to design programmes that do this.

Conclusion

The five key issues we outline above highlight a number of important areas for further development. This will involve the field building on the work of the BERA SIG, ESRC seminar series and recent ICSEI State of the art reviews and debates presented at Cyprus and Malmo.

It would seem to us, focusing on challenging the orthodoxy that has emerged within the field remains a priority if these key issues are to be addressed. This will involve developing new and creative approaches to foster theoretical and empirical advances in our understanding about the key factors and processes associated with educational effectiveness and improvement. The on-going discussions within ICSEI and other arenas signal a commitment to rising to this challenge. The progress made on this front will be documented in contributions in the forthcoming *International Handbook of Educational Effectiveness Research* to be published in 2013. In the meantime, we must continue to build a robust and insightful knowledge base about what works and why in educational settings.

References

Adams, D. (1993) *Defining Educational Quality*. IEQ Publication No. 1: Biennial Report.

Ainscow, M. (2009) Local Solutions for Local Contexts: The Development of More Inclusive Education Systems, in R. Alenkaer (ed.) *Leadership Perspectives in the Inclusive School*. Frydenlund: Copenhagen.

Ainscow, M. and West, M. (eds) (2007) *Improving Urban Schools*. Maidenhead: Open University Press.

Aitkin, A. and Longford, N. (1986) Statistical Modelling Issues in School Effectiveness Studies, *Journal of the Royal Statistical Society* A, 149(1): 1–43.

Alexander, C., Ishikawa, S., Silverstein, M., with Jacobson, M., Fiksdahl-King, I. and Angel, S. (1977) *A Pattern Language*. New York: Oxford University Press.

Alexander, J., Daly, P., Gallagher, A.M., Gray, C. and Sutherland, A. (1998) *An Evaluation of the Craigavon Two-Tier System – DENI Research Report Series No. 12*. Bangor: Statistics and Research Branch DENI.

Alexander, K.L., Entwisle, D.R. and Olson, L.S. (2001) Schools, Achievement and Inequality: A Seasonal Perspective, *Educational Evaluation and Policy Analysis*, 23: 171–191.

Alexander, K.L., Entwisle, D.R. and Olson, L.S. (2007) Lasting Consequences of the Summer Learning Gap, *American Sociological Review*, 72: 167–180.

Alexander, R. (2000) *Culture and Pedagogy*. Oxford: Basil Blackwell.

Alexandrou, A. and O'Brien, J. (2007) *Union Learning Representatives: Facilitating Professional Development for Scottish Teachers*. IEJLL: University of Calgary, 11(19). Available online at: http://www.ucalgary.ca/iejll/vol11/brien

Allison, I., *et al.* (2009) *The Copenhagen Diagnosis: Updating the World on the Latest Climate Science*. UNSW Climate Change Research Center, Sydney, Australia, p. 11.

Andrews, L. (2011) *Teaching Makes A Difference*. Cardiff: Welsh Assembly Government.

Arnott, M. and Menter, I. (2007) The Same but Different? Post-Devolution Regulation and Control in Education in Scotland and England, *Educational Research*, 6 (3): 250–265.

Arnott, M. and Ozga, J. (2009) *The Discourse of Education and Nationalism: Education Policy and the SNP Government, Working Paper 2*. Edinburgh: Centre for Educational Sociology, University of Edinburgh.

Avalos, B. (2007) School Improvement in Latin America: Innovations over 25 Years (1980–2006), in T. Townsend (ed.) *International Handbook of School Effectiveness and Improvement*. Dordrecht, The Netherlands: Springer. Part I, pp. 183–303.

Barber, M. (2005) National Strategies for Educational Reform: Lessons from the British Experience since 1988, in M. Fullan (ed.) *Fundamental Change*. Dordecht, The Netherlands: Springer, pp. 73–97.

Barber, M. (2007) *Instruction to Deliver*. London: Politicos Publishing.

Barber M. (2008) *Instruction to Deliver* (Revised Paperback). London: Methuen.

Barber, M. (2009) From System Effectiveness to System Improvement, in A. Hargreaves and M. Fullan (eds) *Change Wars*. Bloomington, IN: Solution Tree.

Barber, M. and Fullan, M. (2005) Tri-level Development: It's the System, *Education Week*, March 2005.

Barber, M. and Mourshed, M. (2007) *How The World's Best-Performing Schools Systems Come Out On Top*. London: McKinsey and Company.

Barkham, P. (2009) Can You Really Do a GCSE in Just Three Days? *The Guardian, G2 Section*. 13 February, pp. 4–7.

Barnett, R., Glass, J., Snowdon, R. and Stringer, K. (2002) Size, Performance and Effectiveness: Cost-Constrained Measures of Best-Practice Performance and Secondary-School Size, *Education Economics*, 10(3): 291–311.

Barth, R. (1990) *Improving Schools from Within: Teachers, Parents and Principals Can Make a Difference*. San Francisco, CA: Jossey-Bass.

Barth, M., Godemann, J., Rieckmann, M. and Stoltenberg, U. (2007) Developing Key Competencies for Sustainable Development in Higher Education, *International Journal of Sustainability in Higher Education*, 8(4): 416–430.

Bates, R. (2004) Regulation and Autonomy in Teacher Education: Government, Community or Democracy? *Journal of Education for Teaching*, 30(2): 117–130.

Baxter-Jones, A., Mirwald, R., McKay, H. and Bailey, D. (2003) A Longitudinal Analysis of Sex Differences in Bone Mineral Accrual in Healthy 8–19-year-old Boys and Girls, *Annals of Human Biology*, 30(2): 160–175.

BBC (2008) Resignation Call over School Test, 1st April. Available online at: http://news.bbc.co.uk/1/hi/northern_ireland/7323818.stm Accessed 21 February 2011.

Beare, H. (1997) Enterprise: The New Metaphor for Schooling in a Post-Industrial Society, in T. Townsend, *The Primary School in Changing Times: The Australian Experience*. London and New York: Routledge.

Beare, H. (2007) Four Decades of Body-Surfing the Breaker of School Reform, in T. Townsend, *International Handbook of School Effectiveness and Improvement*. Dordrecht, The Netherlands: Springer, pp. 27–41.

Beddington, J. (2009) World Faces Perfect Storm of Environmental Problems by 2030. *The Guardian*. 18 March 2009.

Bellei, C. (2001) *¿Ha tenido impacto la Reforma Educacional Chilena?* Santiago: Ministerio de Educación. Proyecto Alcance y Resultados de las Reformas Educativas en Argentina, Chile y Uruguay.

Beniger, J. (1986) *The Control Revolution*. Cambridge, MA: Harvard University Press.

Berkeley, R. (2008) *Right to Divide: Faith schools and Community Cohesion*. London: Runnymede Trust.

Berliner, D. (2005) Our Impoverished View of Educational Reform, *Teachers College Record*, April.

Berry, T. (1999) *The Great Work: Our Way into the Future*. New York: Crown Publishing.

Berry, T. (2005) Personal correspondence.

Berry, T. (2009) *The Sacred Universe*. Columbia, NY: Colombia University Press.

Bisschoff, T. and Rhodes, C. (forthcoming) Good Schools for Some but why not Better Schools for all? Sub-Saharan Africa in transition, in C. Day (ed.) *International Handbook on Teacher Education*. Dordrecht, The Netherlands: Springer.

Blunkett, D. (2006) *The Blunkett Tapes – My Life In The Bear Pit*. London: Bloomsbury.

248   References

Boggs, G.L. (1998) Living for Change. Minneapolis, MN: University of Minnesota Press.

Bogotch, I., Miron, L. and Biesta, G. (2007) Effective for who? Effective for what? Two Questions SESI Should Not Ignore, in T. Townsend, *International Handbook of School Effectiveness and Improvement*. Dordrecht, The Netherlands: Springer, pp. 93–111.

Bohm, D. (1980) *Wholeness and the Implicate Order*. London: Routledge.

Bohm, D. (1996) *On Dialogue*. London: Routledge.

Borko, H. (2004) Professional Development and Teacher Learning: Mapping the Terrain, *Educational Researcher*, 33 (8): 3–15.

Borman, G., Hewes, G., Overman, L. and Brown, S. (2003) Comprehensive School Reform and Achievement: A Meta-Analysis, *Review of Educational Research*, 73(2): 125–230.

Bosker, R. (2011) *From Educational Effectiveness to Evidence Based Education*, Keynote presentation at the International Congress for School Effectiveness and Improvement, Cyprus, January 2011.

Bradshaw, J., Sturman, L., Vappula, H., Ager, R. and Wheater, R. (2007) *Achievement of 15 Year Olds in Wales: PISA 2006 National Report*. Slough: National Foundation for Educational Research (NFER).

Bradshaw, J., Ager, R., Burge, B. and Wheater, R. (2010) *PISA 2009: Achievement of 15 Year Olds in Wales*. Slough: National Foundation for Educational Research (NFER).

Braungart, M. and McDonough, W. (2009) *Cradle to Cradle: Remaking the Way We Make Things*. London: Vintage Books.

Bridges, D. (2007) *Education and the Possibility of Outsider Understanding*. Von Hugel Institute, St. Edmund's College, Cambridge.

Brighouse, T. (2000) *How to Improve your School*. London: Routledge.

Brookover, W., Beady, C., Flood, P., Schweitzer, J. and Wisenbaker, J. (1979) *School Social Systems and Student Achievement. Schools Can Make a Difference*. New York: Praeger Publishers.

Brophy, J. and Good, T.L. (1986) Teacher Behavior and Student Achievement., in M.C. Wittrock (ed.) *Handbook of Research on Teaching*. New York: Macmillan. 3rd ed., pp. 328–375.

Brown, B.W. and Saks, D.H. (1986) Measuring the Effects of Instructional Time on Student Learning: Evidence From the Beginning Teacher Evaluation Study, *American Journal of Education*, 94: 480–500.

Brown, L. R. (2003) *Plan B: Rescuing a Planet Under Stress and a Civilisation in Trouble*. New York: W.W. Norton and Company.

Bryk, A., and Raudenbush, S. W. (1992) *Hierarchical Linear Models for Social and Behavioral Research: Applications and Data Analysis Methods*. Newbury Park, CA: Sage.

Bubb, S. and Earley, P. (2009) *What Do We Know About School Workforce Development? A Summary of Findings from Recent TDA-funded Research Projects*. Unpublished Report. Available online at: http://eprints.ioe.ac.uk/2842/ Accessed 30 March 2011.

Budde, H., Voelcker-Rehage, C., Pietrask-Kendziorra, S., Ribiero, P. and Tidow, G. (2008) Acute Coordinative Exercise Improves Attentional Performance in Adolescents, *Neuroscience Letters*, 441: 219–223.

Bush, T., Briggs, A. and Middlewood, D. (2006) The Impact of School Leadership Development: Evidence From the New Visions' Programme for Early Headship, *Journal of In-Service Education*, 32(2): 185–200.

Byrne, G. and Gallagher, T. (2004) Systemic Factors in School Improvement, *Research Papers in Education*, 19(2): 161–183.

Caldwell, B. (1996) Factors Associated with Improved Learning Outcomes in the Local

Management of Schools: Early Findings from Victoria's *Schools of the Future*. A paper presented at the Annual Conference of the British Educational Management and Administration Society, Coventry (October).

Caldwell, B. (2006) *Re-Imagining Educational Leadership*. London: Sage.

Caldwell, B. and Harris, J. (2008) *Why Not the Best Schools?* Victoria: ACER Press.

Campbell, R.J., Kyriakides, L., Muijs, R.D. and Robinson, W. (2004) *Assessing Teacher Effectiveness: A Differentiated Model*. London: Routledge Falmer.

Capra, F. (2010) *Schooling for Sustainability: Making Teaching and Learning Come Alive*. Lecture series at Berkeley, California, June 23–25, 2010.

Carnoy, M. (2007) Improving Quality and Equity in Latin American Education: A Realistic Assessment. La mejora de la calidad y equidad educativa: una evaluación realista. *Rev. Pensamiento Educativo*, 40(1): 103–130.

Carroll, J.B. (1963) A Model of School Learning, *Teachers College Record*, 64: 723–733.

Carroll, J.B. (1989) The Carroll Model: A 25 Year Retrospective and Prospective View. *Educational Researcher*, 18: 26–31.

Carson, R. (1962) *Silent Spring*. New York: Fawcett Crest.

CCMS (2011) *Council for Catholic Maintained Schools*. Information available online at: http://www.onlineccms.com Accessed 28 January 2011.

Chapman, C. (2006) *School Improvement through External Intervention?* London: Continuum.

Chapman, C. (2004) Leadership in Schools Facing Challenging Circumstances, *London Review of Education*, 2(2): 95–108.

Chapman, C. (2008) Towards a Framework for School-to-School Networking in Challenging Circumstances, *Educational Research*, 50(4): 403–420.

Chapman, C., Ainscow, M., Bragg, J., Hull, J., Mongon, D., Muijs, D. and West, M. (2008) *Emerging Patterns of School Leadership: Current Trends and Future Directions*. Nottingham: National College.

Chapman, C., Ainscow, M., Mongon, D., Muijs, D. and West, M. (2009) *Emerging Patterns of School Leadership: A Deeper Understanding*. Nottingham: National College.

Chapman, C. and Gunter, H.M. (eds) (2009) *Radical Reforms: Public Policy and a Decade of Educational Reform*. London: Routledge.

Chapman, C. and Hadfield, M. (2010) Reconnecting the Middle Tier: Local Authorities and School-Based Networks, *Journal of Educational Change*, 11(3): 221–247.

Chapman C. and Harris, A. (2004) Strategies for School Improvement in Schools Facing Challenging Circumstances, *Educational Research*, 46(3): 219–228.

Chapman, C., Lindsay, G., Muijs, D. and Harris, A. (2010) The Federations Policy: From Partnership to Integration for School Improvement? *School Effectiveness and Improvement* 21(1): 53–74.

Chapman, C., Mongon, D., Muijs, D., and Williams, J., Maria Pampaka, M., Wakefield, D. and Weiner, S. (2011) *A National Evaluation of the Extra Mile*. London: DfEResearch Report DFE-RR133.

Chapman, C., Muijs, D., Reynolds, D., Sammons, P. and Teddlie, C. (forthcoming) *International Handbook of Educational Effectiveness Research*. London: Routledge.

Chen, F.W. (2003) Review on External Schools Effectiveness, *Jianxi Educational Research*, 10: 33–34 and 42.

Cheng, J.K. (1994) Theory and Practice of American Effective Schools, *Global Education*, 3: 58–63.

Cheng, Y.C. (1993) Profiles of Organizational Culture and Effective Schools, *School Effectiveness and School Improvement*, 4(2): 85–110.

Cheng, Y.C. (1999) Editorial, Special issue on recent educational developments in South East Asia, *School Effectiveness and School Improvement*, 10(1): 3–9.

Chinese Ministry of Education (1996) Notification of State Council on printing and distributing the Ninth 5-Year Plan for China's educational development and the development outline by 2010. Retrieved 15 July 2009, from http://210.28.182.158/edu/1/law/12/law_12_1082.htm

Chomsky, N. (2006) *Failed States: the Abuse of Power and the Assault on Democracy*. London: Penguin.

Chu, H., and Liu, X. (2005) *Independent Review of the Gansu Basic Education Project (GBEP) on Impacts on Management*: Cambridge Education (CE) and Gansu Provincial Education Department (GPED).

Christie, D. (2003) Competences, Benchmarks and Standards in Teaching, in T. Bryce and W. Humes (eds) *Scottish Education Post Devolution* (2nd edition). Edinburgh: Edinburgh University Press, pp. 952–963.

Christie, F. and O'Brien, J. (2005) A CPD Framework for Scottish Teachers: Steps or Stages, Continuity or Connections?, in A. Alexandrou, K. Field and H. Mitchell (eds) *The Continuing Professional Development of Educators: Emerging European Issues*. Oxford: Symposium, pp. 93–110.

Church, J.A. and White N.J. (2006) A 20th Century Acceleration in Global Sea Level Rise, *Geophysical Research Letters*, 33, L01602, doi:10.1029/2005GL024826.; The global sea level estimate described in this work can be downloaded from the CSIRO website

Cisco, Inc. (2010). *The Learning Society*. Available at cisco.com.

Clarke, D. and Hollingsworth, H. (2002) Elaborating a Model of Teacher Professional Growth. *Teaching and Teacher Education*, 18(8): 947–967.

Clarke, P. (1983) *Community, Living and Learning*. Unpublished undergraduate thesis. London University Library.

Clarke, P. (2000) *Learning Schools, Learning Systems*. London: Continuum.

Clarke, P. (2009a) *Incredible Edible: Growing Community*. Todmorden: IET publications.

Clarke, P. (2009b) A Practical Guide to Radical Transition: Framing the Sustainable Community, *Education, Knowledge and Economy*, 3(3): 183–197.

Clarke, P. (2009c) Sustainability and Improvement: A Problem 'of' Education and 'for' Education, *Improving Schools*, 12(1): 11–17.

Clarke, P. (2010a) Community Renaissance, in M. Coates (ed.) *Shaping a New Educational Landscape*. London: Continuum.

Clarke, P. (2010b) Incredible Edible: How to Grow Sustainable Communities, *Forum*, 52 (1): 69–79.

Clarke, P. (forthcoming) *Finding Balance: Sustainable Communities, Sustainable Schools*. London: Routledge.

Clinch, R. (2001) *Secret Kids' Business*. Melbourne: Hawker-Brownlow.

Coates, D. (2003) Education Production Functions Using Instructional Time as an Input, *Education Economics*, 11(3): 273–292.

Coburn, C., Honig, M. and Stein, M. (2009) What's the Evidence on Districts' use of Evidence? in J. Bransford, D. Stipek, N. Vye, L. Gomez and D. Lam (eds) *The Role of Research in Educational Improvement*. Cambridge, MA: Harvard Education Press, pp. 67–87.

Cochran-Smith, M. and Fries, K.M. (2005) The AERA Panel on Research and Teacher Education: Context and Goals, in M. Cochran-Smith and K. Zeichner (eds) *Studying Teacher Education: The Report of the AERA Panel on Research and Teacher Education*. Washington, DC: American Education Research Association, pp. 1–37.

Coe, R. (2009) School Improvement: Reality and Illusion, *British Journal of Educational Studies*, 57(4): 363–379.

Cohen, L., Manion, L. and Morrison, K. (2007) *Research Methods in Education* (6th edition). London: Routledge.

Cohen, M. (1993) Integrated Ecology: The Process of Counseling with Nature, *The Humanist Psychologist*, 21, 3.

Coldwell, M. and Simkins, T. (2011) Level Models of CPD Evaluation: A Grounded Review and Critique, *Professional Development in Education*, 37(1): 143–157.

Coleman, J. S. and Hoffer, T. (1987) *Public and Private High Schools: The Impact of Communities*. New York: Basic Books.

Connelly, G. and McMahon, M. (2007) Chartered Teacher: Accrediting Professionalism for Scotland's Teachers: A View From the Inside. *Professional Development in Education*, 33(1): 91–105.

Connolly, P. and Healy, J. (2004) Symbolic Violence, Locality and Social Class: The Educational and Career Aspirations of 10–11 Year Old Boys in Belfast, *Pedagogy, Culture and Society*, 12(1): 15–33.

Connolly, P. and Keenan, M. (2000) *Racial Attitudes and Prejudice in Northern Ireland* (Reports 1 and 2). Belfast: Northern Ireland Statistics and Research Agency.

Connolly, P. and Keenan, M. (2002) Racist Harassment in the White Hinterlands: Minority Ethnic Children and Parents' Experiences of Schooling in Northern Ireland, *British Journal of Sociology of Education*, 23(3): 341–355.

Connolly, P., Muldoon, O. and Kehoe, S. (2007) *The Attitudes and Experiences of Children Born in 1997 in Northern Ireland*. Belfast: BBC Northern Ireland.

Cools, W., De Fraine, B., Van den Noortgate, W. and Onghena, P. (2009) Multilevel Design Efficiency in Educational Effectiveness Research, *School Effectiveness and School Improvement*, 20(3): 357–373.

Cooper, A., Levin, B. and Campbell, C. (2009.) The Growing (But Still Limited) Importance of Evidence in Education Policy and Practice, *Journal of Educational Change*, 10(2–3): 159–171.

Cordingley, P. (2008) Research and Evidence-Informed Practice: Focusing on Practice and ractitioners, *Cambridge Journal of Education*, 38(1): 37–52.

Corten, R. and Dronkers, J. (2006) School Achievement of Students From the Lower Strata in Public, Private Government-Dependent and Private Government-Independent Schools: A Cross-national Test of the Coleman-Hoffer Thesis, *Educational Research and Evaluation*, 12: 179–208.

Cox, C. (2003) *Politicas educacionales en el cambio de siglo: La reforma del sistema escolar en Chile*. Chile: Editorial Universitaria.

Craigavon, Lord (Prime Minister NI, aka Sir James Craig) (1934) *Debate in the Parliament of Northern Ireland on 24 April*. Northern Ireland House of Commons Official Report, Vol. 34, col. 1095.

Creemers, B.P.M. (1994) *The Effective Classroom*. London: Cassells.

Creemers, B.P.M. and Kyriakides, L. (2006) Critical Analysis of the Current Approaches to Modelling Educational Effectiveness: The Importance of Establishing a Dynamic Model, *School Effectiveness and School Improvement*, 17(3): 347–366.

Creemers, B.P.M and Kyriakides, L. (2008) *The Dynamics of Educational Effectiveness: A Contribution to Policy, Practice and Theory in Contemporary Schools*. London: Routledge.

Creemers, B.P.M. and Kyriakides, L. (2009) Situational Effects of the School Factors Included in the Dynamic Model of Educational Effectiveness, *South African Journal of Education*, 29: 293–315.

Creemers, B.P.M. and Kyriakides, L. (2010a) School Factors Explaining Achievement on Cognitive and Affective Outcomes: Establishing a Dynamic Model of Educational Effectiveness, *Scandinavian Journal of Educational Research*, 54(3): 263–294.

Creemers, B.P.M. and Kyriakides, L. (2010b) Explaining Stability and Changes in School Effectiveness by Looking at Changes in the Functioning of School Factors, *School Effectiveness and School Improvement*, 21(4): 409–427.

Creemers, B. and Kyriakides, L. (forthcoming) Using Educational Effectiveness Research to Improve the Quality of Teaching Practice, in C. Day (ed.) *International Handbook on Teacher Education*. Dordrecht, The Netherlands: Springer.

Creemers, B.P.M. Kyriakides, L. and Sammons, P. (eds) (2010) *Methodological Advances in Educational Effectiveness Research*. London: Routledge.

Crossley, M. and Watson, K. (2003) *Comparative and International Research in Education: Globalisation, Context and Difference*. London: RoutledgeFalmer.

Cuban, L. (2001). *Oversold and Underused: Computers in the Classroom*. Cambridge, MA: Harvard University Press.

Cummings, C., Dyson, A., Fay, L., Muijs, D. (2008) *Evaluation of the Full Service Extended Schools Pilot*. London: DCSF.

Cuthbert, C. and Hatch, R. (2009) *Educational Aspiration and Attainment Amongst Young People in Deprived Communities*. London: Centre for Research on Families and Relationships.

Daily Record (1998) Scotland in Space: Where's Like us? Glasgow: 2 November.

Daly, P. (1991) How Large Are Secondary School Effects in Northern Ireland? *School Effectiveness and School Improvement*, 2(4): 305–323.

Damasio, A. (1999) *The Feeling of What Happens*. London: Heinemann.

Darling-Hammond, L. (1999) *Reshaping Teaching Policy, Preparation and Practice: Influences on the National Board for Teaching Professional Standards*. Washington, DC: AACTE Publications.

Darling-Hammond, L., LaFors, J. and Snyder, J. (2001) Educating Teachers for California's Future, *Teacher Education Quarterly* (Winter).

Davidson, J. (2006) Pathways Out of Poverty, *Agenda: Journal of the Institute of Welsh Affairs*, Summer 2006.

Davidson, J. (2007) The Importance of Evidence-Informed Policy Research in Education: A Perspective From Wales, in OECD (2007) *Evidence in Education: Linking Research and Policy*. Paris: OECD.

Davidson, J., Forde, C., Gronn, P., MacBeath, J., Martin, M. and McMahon, M. (2008) *Towards a 'Mixed Economy' of Head Teacher Development: Evaluation Report to the Scottish Government on the Flexible Routes to Headship Pilot*. Edinburgh: The Scottish Government.

Daugherty, R., Phillips, R. and Rees, G. (eds) (2000) *Education Policy-Making in Wales*. Cardiff: University of Wales Press.

Daugherty, R. (2004) *Learning Pathways Through Statutory Assessment: Key Stages 2 and 3*. Cardiff: Welsh Assembly Government.

Day, C. *et al.* (2011) *Successful School Leadership*. Maidenhead: Open University Press/McGraw-Hill.

Day, C., Sammons, P. and Gu, Q. (2008) Combining Qualitative and Quantitative Methodologies in Research on Teachers' Lives, Work, and Effectiveness: From Integration to Synergy, *Educational Researcher*, 37(6): 330–342.

Day, C., Sammons, P., Hopkins, D., Harris, A., Leithwood, K., Gu, Q., Brown, E., Ahtaridou, E. and Kington, A. (2009) The Impact of School Leadership on Pupil Outcomes, *DCSF Research Report–RR108*. London: DCSF.

Day, C., Sammons, P., Leithwood, K., Hopkins, D., Gu, Q. and Brown, E., with Ahtari-dou, E. (2011) *Successful School Leadership: Linking with Learning and Achievement.* Maidenhead: McGraw-Hill/Open University Press.

Day, C., Sammons, P., Stobart, G., Kingston, A., and Gu, Qing (2007) *Teachers Matter.* Milton Keynes: Open University Press.

Day, C., Stobart, G., Sammons, P and Kington, A. (2006), Variations in the Work and Lives of Teachers: Relative and Relational Effectiveness, *Teachers and Teaching: Theory and Practice*, 12(2): 169–192.

De Fraine, B., Van Damme, J. and Onghena, P. (2007) A Longitudinal Analysis of Gender Differences in Academic Self-Concept and Language Achievement: A Multivari-ate Multilevel Latent Growth Approach. *Contemporary Educational Psychology*, 32(1): 132–150.

De Fraine, B., Van Landegem, G., Van Damme, J. and Onghena, P. (2005) An Analysis of Well-Being in Secondary School with Multilevel Growth Curve Models and Multilevel Multivariate Models. *Quality & Quantity*, 39: 297–316.

De Guimps, R. (1904) *Pestalozzi, His Life and Works.* New York: Appleton and Company.

De Jong, R., Westerhof, K.J. and Kruiter, J.H. (2004) Empirical Evidence of a Compre-hensive Model of School Effectiveness: A Multilevel Study in Mathematics in the 1st year of Junior General Education in the Netherlands, *School Effectiveness and School Improve-ment*, 15(1): 3–31.

Dedrick, R., Ferron, J., Hess, M., Hogarty, K., Kromrey, J., Lang, T., Niles, J. and Lee, S. (2009) Multilevel Modeling: A Review of Methodological Issues and Applications, *Review of Educational Research*, 79(1): 69–102.

DENI (2007) *Pupil Religion Series.* Available online at: http://www.deni.gov.uk/pupil_religion_series Accessed 3 March 2010.

DENI (2009) *Every School A Good School: A Policy for School Improvement.* Available online at: http://www.deni.gov.uk/index/85-schools/03-schools_impvt_prog_pg/03-every-school-a-good-school-a-policy-for-school-improvement.htm Accessed 21 February 2011.

DENI (2010) *Every School a Good School, A Policy for School Improvement: Implementation Plan Progress Report 2009/10.* Available online at: http://www.deni.gov.uk/index/85-schools/03-schools_impvt_prog_pg/03-every-school-a-good-school-a-policy-for-school-improvement.htm Accessed 18 February 2011.

DENI (2011a) *Statistics and Research.* Available online at: http://www.deni.gov.uk/index/32-statisticsandresearch_pg/32-statistics_and_research_statistics_on_educa-tion_pg/32_statistics_and_research-numbersofschoolsandpupils_pg/32_statistics_and_research-northernirelandsummarydata_pg.htm Accessed 12 February 2011.

DENI (2011b) Compendium of Northern Ireland education statistics, 1996/97 to 2008/09. Available online at: http://www.deni.gov.uk/index/32-statisticsandresearch_pg/32_statistical_publications-indexofstatisticalpublications_pg.htm Accessed 14 Feb-ruary 2011.

Department for Education and Employment (DfEE) (1998) Green Paper: *Teachers Meet-ing the Challenge of Change.* London: HMSO.

Department for Education and Employment (2000a) *Professional Development: Support for Teaching and Learning.* London: HMSO.

Department for Education and Employment (2000b) *Performance Management in Schools: Performance Management Framework.* London: DfEE.

Department for Education and Employment (2001) Green Paper: *Learning and Teaching: A Strategy for Professional Development.* London: HMSO.

Department for Education and Skills (2001) *Teachers' Standards Framework*. London: DfES.

Department for Education and Skills (2004) *The National Evaluation of the Children's Fund (NECF): Annual Report 2004*. London: DfES.

Department for Education and Skills (2007) *Excellence in Cities. National Evaluation of Excellence in Cities 2002–2006 Research Report DCSF-RR017*. Nottingham: DfES.

Department For Education and Skills and ofsted (2004) *A New Relationship with Schools: Improving Performance Through School Self-Evaluation*. Nottingham: DfES.

Desimone, L., Porter, A., Garet, M., Yoon, K. and Birman, B. (2002) Effects of Professional Development on Teachers' Instruction: Results From a Three-Year Longitudinal Study, *Educational Evaluation and Policy Analysis*, 24(2): 81–112.

D'Haenens, E., Van Damme, J. and Onghena, P. (2010) Multilevel Exploratory Factor Analysis: Illustrating its Surplus Value in Educational Effectiveness Research, *School Effectiveness and School Improvement*, 21(2): 209–235.

Diamond, J. (2005) *Collapse: How Societies Choose to Fail or Succeed*. London: Viking.

Diez-Roux, A. (2000) Multilevel Analysis in Public Health Research, *Annual Review of Public Health*, 21: 171–192.

Ding, Y.Q. and Xue, H.P. (2009) A Study on the Education Production Function with High School Data, *Journal of Huazhong Normal University (Humanities and Social Sciences)*, 48(2): 122–128.

Donaldson, G. (2010) *Teaching Scotland's Future: Report of a Review of Teacher Education in Scotland*. Edinburgh: Scottish Government.

Donaldson, L. (2001) *The Contingency Theory of Organizations: Foundations for Organisational Science*. Thousands Oaks, CA: Sage.

Donnelly, C. (2008) The Integrated School in a Conflict Society: A Comparative Analysis of Two Integrated Primary Schools in Northern Ireland, *Cambridge Journal of Education*, 38(2): 187–198.

Doyle, W. (1986) Classroom Organization and Management, in M.C. Wittrock (ed.) *Handbook of Research on Teaching* (3rd edition). New York: Macmillan, pp. 392–431.

Draper, J. and O'Brien, J. (2006) *Induction – Fostering Career Development at All Stages*. Edinburgh: Dunedin Academic Press.

Driessen, G. (1997) Islamic Primary Schools in the Netherlands: The Students' Achievement Levels, Behaviour and Attitudes and their Parents' Cultural Backgrounds, *The Netherlands' Journal of Social Sciences*, 33: 41–66.

Driessen, G. and Sleegers, P. (2000) Consistency of Teaching Approach and Student Achievement: An Empirical Test, *School Effectiveness and School Improvement*, 11(1): 57–79.

Dronkers, J. (2004) Do Public and Religious Schools Really Differ? Assessing the European Evidence, in P.J. Wolf and S. Macedo (eds) *Educating Citizens: International Perspectives on Civic Values and School Choice*. Washington, DC: Brookings Institution Press.

Dronkers, J. and Levels, M. (2007) Do School Segregation and School Resources Explain Region-of-Origin Differences in the Mathematics Achievement of Immigrant Students?, *Educational Research and Evaluation*, 13(5): 435–462.

Drucker, P.F. (1993) *The Ecological Vision: Reflections on the American Condition*. New Brunswick, N.J.: Transaction Publishers.

DUP (2011) *DUP Policy Priorities: Education*. Available online at: http://www.dup.org.uk/Meducation.asp Accessed 15 February 2011.

Earl, L. (2003) *Assessment as Learning*. Thousand Oaks, CA: Corwin.

Earl, L., Watson, N., Leithwood, K. and Fullan, M. (2003) *Watching and Learning 3: Final Report of the External Evaluation of England's Literacy and Numeracy Strategies*. Toronto: Ontario Institute for Studies in Education.

Eaton, P., Bell, I., Greenwood, J. and McCullagh, J. (2006) Who is Teaching Your Child? The Issue of Unqualified Subject Specialists in Northern Ireland, *Cambridge Journal of Education*, 36(4): 549–564.

Edmonds, R. (1977) *Search for Effective Schools. The Identification and Analysis of City Schools That Are Instructionally Effective for Poor Children*. Washington, DC: National Institute of Education.

Edmonds, R. (1978) *A Discussion of the Literature and Issues Related to Effective Schooling*. A paper presented to National Conference on Urban Education, CEMREL, St Louis, USA.

ESA (2011) Convergence. Available online at: http://www.esani.org.uk/convergence/index.asp Accessed 22 February 2011.

Egan, D. (2006) Educating for Social Justice, *Agenda: Journal of the Institute of Welsh Affairs*, Spring 2006.

Egan, D. (2007) *Combating Child Poverty in Wales: Are Appropriate Education Policies in Place?* York: Joseph Rowntree Foundation.

Egan, D. (2008) *Why Not the Best Schools: the Wales Report*. Victoria: ACER Press.

Egan, D. (2010) Educational Equity and School Performance in Wales, in *Poverty and Social Exclusion in Wales*. Ebbw Vale: the Bevan Foundation.

Egan, D., Hopkins, D., Reynolds, D. and Mackay, T. (2007) *National Education Effectiveness Programme for Wales – School Strand: Final Proposal*. Cardiff: Welsh Assembly Government.

Egan, D. and Hopkins, D. (2009) *The School Effectiveness Framework in Wales: Ways Forward*. Cardiff: Welsh Assembly Government.

Egan, D., Hopkins, D. and Matthews, P. (2009) *System Leadership and the School Effectiveness Framework in Wales*. Cardiff: Welsh Assembly Government.

Egan, D., and James, R. (2001a) A Promising Start: The Pre-16 Education and Early Years Committee, in B. Jones and J. Osmond (eds) *Inclusive Government and Party Management*. Cardiff: Institute for Welsh Affairs.

Egan, D., and James, R. (2001b) Driving a Policy Agenda: The Post-16 Education and Training Committee, in B. Jones and J. Osmond (eds), *Inclusive Government and Party Management*. Cardiff: Institute for Welsh Affairs.

Egan, D., and James, R. (2001c) Watching the Assembly: The Subject Committees and Educational Policy in Wales, *Welsh Journal of Education*, 10(1): 4–20.

Egan, D., and James, R. (2002) Open Government and Inclusiveness, in B. Jones and J. Osmond (eds) *Institutional Change, Policy Development and Political Dynamics in the National Assembly for Wales*. Cardiff: Institute for Welsh Affairs.

Egan, D., and James, R. (2003) Education, in B. Jones. and J. Osmond (eds) *Birth of a Welsh Democracy: The First Term of the National Assembly for Wales*. Cardiff: Institute of Welsh Affairs.

Egan, D. and Marshall, S. (2007) Educational Leadership and School Renewal in Wales, *Australian Journal of Education*, 51: 3, November 2007.

Eichenbaum, H. and Otto, T. (1993). LTP and Memory: Can we Enhance the Connection? *Trends in Neurosciences*, 16(5): 163–164.

Elberts, R.W. and Stone, J.A. (1988) Student Achievement in Public Schools: Do Principals Make a Difference? *Economics Education Review*, 7: 291–299.

Elliot, K. and Sammons, P. (2004) Exploring the Use of Effect Sizes to Evaluate the Impact of Different Influences on Child Outcomes: Possibilities and Limitations, in I. Schagen and K. Elliot (eds) *What Does it Mean? The Use of Effect Sizes in Educational Research.* Slough: NFER.

Elmore, R. (1996) Getting To Scale With Good Educational Practice *Harvard Educational Review*, 66(1): 1–26.

Esborn-Hargens, S. and Zimmerman, M. (2009) *Integral Ecology: Uniting Multiple Perspectives on the Natural World.* Boston: Integral Books.

Estyn (2002) *Excellent Schools: A Vision for Schools in Wales in the 21st Century.* Cardiff: Estyn.

Estyn (2005) *Low Performing Secondary Schools.* Cardiff: Estyn.

Estyn (2007) *Transforming Schools: A Discussion Paper.* Cardiff: Estyn.

Estyn (2008a) *Annual Report of Her Majesty's Chief Inspector of Education and Training in Wales.* Cardiff: Estyn.

Estyn (2008b) *The Impact of RAISE.* Cardiff: Estyn.

Estyn (2009a) *Local Authorities and Schools Causing Concern.* Cardiff: Estyn.

Estyn (2009b) *The Impact of RAISE 2008–09.* Cardiff: Estyn.

Evangelou, M. *et al.* (2008) *What Makes a Successful Transition From Primary to Secondary School* (RR 019). London: DCSF.

Fairman, S.R. and Quinn, R.E. (1985) Effectiveness: The Perspective from the Organization Theory, *Review of Higher Education*, 9: 83–100.

Feiman-Nemser, S. (2001) From Preparation to Practice: Designing a Continuum to Strengthen and Sustain Teaching, *Teachers' College Record*, 103(6): 1013–1055.

Fertig, M. (2000) Old Wine in New Bottles? Researching Effective Schools in Developing Countries, *School Effectiveness and School Improvement*, 11: 385–403.

Fielding, A. and Goldstein, H (2006) *Cross-Classified and Multiple Membership Structures in Multilevel Models: An Introduction and Review.* Research report 791, London: DfES.

Fielding. M. (ed.) (2001) *Taking Education Really Seriously: Four Years Hard Labour.* London: Routledge.

Fields, R.D. (2005) Making Memories Stick, *Scientific American*, 292: 58–65.

Flecknoe, M. (2000) Can Continuing Professional Development for Teachers be Shown to Raise Pupils' Achievement? *Professional Development in Education*, 26(3): 437–457.

Forrester, F. (2008) Teachers' Professional Organisations, in T.G.K. Bryce and W.M. Humes, *Scottish Education: Third Edition, Beyond Devolution.* Edinburgh: Edinburgh University Press, pp. 881–886.

Fosket, N. and Lumby, J. (2003) *Leading and Managing Education: International Dimensions.* London: Paul Chapman.

Foster, R.G. (2007) Teenagers, Body Clocks, Health and Learning, *The Times Higher Educational Supplement,* 5 January.

Fox, J.P. (2004) Applications of Multilevel IRT Modelling, *School Effectiveness and School Improvement*, 15(3): 261–280.

Freiberg H.J. (1999) (ed.) *School Climate: Measuring Improving and Sustaining Healthy Learning Environments.* London: Falmer.

Friedman, T. (1999) *The Lexus and the Olive Tree: Understanding Globalization.* New York: Anchor Books.

Freire, P. (1992). *A Pedagogy of Hope.* Chippenham: Continuum Publishing.

Frey, U. and Morris, R.G.M. (1998) Weak Before Strong: Dissociating Synaptic Tagging and Plasticity-Factor Accounts of Late-LTP, *Neuropharmacology*, 37: 545–552.

Fullan, M.G. (1992) *The New Meaning of Educational Change.* London: Cassell.

Fullan, M. (2004) *System Thinkers in Action: Moving Beyond the Standards Plateau*. London/Nottingham, DfES Innovation Unit/NCSL.

Fullan, M. (2009) Large-Scale Reform Comes of Age, *Journal of Educational Change*, 10(2): 101–113.

Fullan, M. (2010) *All Systems Go: The Change Imperative for Whole System Reform*. Thousand Oaks, CA: Corwin.

Fullan, M. (2011) *Choosing the Wrong Drivers for Whole System Reform*, CSE Seminar Series 204, April, Melbourne, Australia.

Gallagher, T. (2005) Balancing Difference and the Common Good: Lessons From a Post-conflict Society, *Compare: A Journal of Comparative and International Education*, 35(4): 429–442.

Gallagher, T. and Smith, A. (2000) *The Effects of the Selective System of Secondary Education in Northern Ireland: Main Report*. Bangor: Department of Education for Northern Ireland.

Gallagher, T. and Smith, A. (2003) *Attitudes to Academic Selection in Northern Ireland: Research Update 16*. Belfast: Ark NI, Social and Political Archive.

Gamble, A. (2010) After the Crash, *Journal of Education Policy*, 25(6): 703–708.

Gardner, H. (1991) *The Unschooled Mind: How Children Think And How Schools Should Teach*, New York, Basic Books

Gardner, J. and Cowan, P. (2000) *Testing the Test: A Study of the Reliability and Validity of the Northern Ireland Transfer Procedure Test in Enabling the Selection of Pupils for Grammar School Places*. Belfast: QUB.

Gardner, J. and Cowan, P. (2005) The Fallibility of High Stakes '11-plus' testing in Northern Ireland, *Assessment in Education: Principles, Policy and Practice*, 12(2): 145–165.

Gardner, J. and Gallagher, T. (2007) Gauging the Deliverable? Educational Research in Northern Ireland, *European Educational Research Journal*, 6(1): 101–114.

Gewirtz, S. (1998) Can All Schools Be Successful? An Exploration of the Determinants of School 'Success', *Oxford Review of Education*, 24(4): 439–457.

Gibson, A. and Asthana, S. (1998) Schools, Pupils and Examination Results: Contextualising School Performance, *British Educational Research Journal*, 24(3): 269–282.

Gipps, C. (1998) Student Assessment and Learning for a Changing Society, *Prospects*, XXVIII(1): 31–44.

Goldstein, H. (1987) *Multilevel Models in Educational and Social Research*. New York: Oxford University Press.

Goldstein, H. (1995) *Multilevel Statistical Models* (2nd edition). London: Edward Arnold; New York: Halsted Press.

Goldstein, H. (1997) Methods in School Effectiveness Research, *School Effectiveness and School Improvement*, 8(4): 369–395.

Goldstein, H. (1998) *Models for Reality: New Approaches to the Understanding of Educational Processes*. London: Institute of Education, University of London.

Goldstein, H. (2003) *Multilevel Statistical Models* (3rd edition). London: Edward Arnold.

Goldstein, H., Browne, M. and Rasbash, J. (2002) Multilevel Modelling of Medical Data, *Statistics in Medicine*, 21(21): 3291–3315.

Goldstein, H., Burgess, S. and McConell, B. (2007) Modelling the Effect of Pupil Mobility on School Differences in Educational Achievement, *Journal of the Royal Statistical Society, Series A*, 170(4): 941–954.

Goldstein, H. and Noden, P. (2004) A Response to Gorard on Social Segregation, *Oxford Review of Education*, 30(3): 441–442.

Goldstein, H. and Thomas, S.M. (2008) Reflections on the International Comparative Surveys Debate, *Assessment in Education: Principles, Policy and Practice,* 15(3): 215–222.

Goldstein, H. and Woodhouse, G. (2000) School Effectiveness Research and Education Policy, *Oxford Review of Education,* 26(3/4): 353–363.

Goldstein, H., Yang, M., Omar, R., Turner, R. and Thomson, S. (2000) Meta-Analysis Using Multilevel Models with an Application to the Study of Class Size Effects, *Applied Statistics,* 49(3): 399–412.

Goodall, J., Day, C., Lindsay, G., Muijs, D. and Harris, A. (2005) *Evaluating the Impact of Continuing Professional Development.* London: Report for Department for Education and Skills.

Gorard, S. (2000) *Education and Social Justice.* Cardiff: University of Wales Press.

Gorard, S. (2006) Value Added is of Little Value, *Journal of Education Policy,* 21(2): 233–241.

Gorard, S. (2010) Serious Doubts about School Effectiveness, *British Educational Research Journal,* 36(5): 745–766.

Gorard, S. and Rees, G. (2002) *Creating A Learning Society.* Bristol: Policy Press.

Gow, L. and Macpherson, A. (1980) *Tell Them from Me.* Aberdeen: Aberdeen University Press

Graham, I and Tetroe, J. (2007) Some Theoretical Underpinnings of Knowledge Translation, *Academic Emergency Medicine,* 14: 936–941.

Gray, J. (1981) A Competitive Edge: Examination Results and the Probable Limits of Secondary, *Educational Review,* 33(1): 25–35.

Gray, J., Goldstein, H. and Thomas, S. (2001) Predicting the Future: The Role of Past Performance in Determining Trends in Institutional Effectiveness at A level, *British Educational Research Journal,* 27(4): 391–405.

Gray, J., Goldstein, H. and Jesson, D. (1996) Changes and Improvements in Schools' Effectiveness: Trends Over Five Years, *Research Papers in Education,* 11(1): 35–51.

Gray, J., Hopkins, D., Reynolds, D., Wilcox, B., Farrell, S. and Jesson, D. (1999) *Improving Schools: Performance and Potential.* Buckingham: Open University Press.

Gray, J. and Jesson, D. (1990) Estimating Differences in the Examination Performances of Secondary Schools in Six LEAs: A Multi-level Approach to School Effectiveness, *Oxford Review of Education,* 16(2): 137–158.

Gray, J., McPherson A.F. and Raffe, D. (1983) *Reconstructions of Secondary Education: Theory, Myth and Practice Since the Second World War.* London, Routledge and Kegan Paul.

Gray, J. and Wilcox, B. (1995) *Good School, Bad School: Evaluating Performance and Encouraging Improvement.* Buckingham: Open University Press.

Grimshaw, J., Eccles, M., and Tetroe, J. (2004) Implementing Clinical Guidelines: Current Evidence and Future Implications, *Journal of Continuing Education in the Health Professions,* 24: S31–S37.

GTCW (2006) *A Professional Development Framework for Teachers in Wales, Advice to the Welsh Assembly Government.* Cardiff: GTCW.

Gu, Q., Sammons, P. and Mehta, P. (2008) Leadership Characteristics and Practices in Schools with Different Effectiveness and Improvement Trajectories, *School Leadership and Management,* 28(1): 43–63.

Guldemold, H. and Bosker, R. (2009) School Effects on Students' Progress: A Dynamic Perspective, *School Effectiveness and School Improvement,* 20(2): 255–268.

Gunter, H.M. (2008) Policy and Workforce Reform in England, *Educational Management Administration and Leadership,* 36(2): 253–270.

Guskey, T.R. (2000) *Evaluating Professional Development*. Thousand Oaks, CA: Corwin.

Gutman, L. and Akerman, R. (2008) *Determinants of Aspirations*. London: Centre for the Research on the Wider Benefits of Learning.

Hallinger, P. and Heck, R. (2010) Collaborative Leadership and School Improvement: Understanding the Impact on School Capacity and Student Learning, *School Leadership and Management*, 30(2): 95–110.

Handy, C. (1994), *The Age of Paradox*. Boston: Harvard Business School Press.

Hanushek, E.A. (1986) The Economics of Schooling: Production and Efficiency in Public Schools, *Journal of Economic Literature*, 24: 1141–1177.

Hanushek, E.A. (1989) The Impact of Differential Expenditures on Student Performance, *Educational Research*, 66(3): 397–409.

Harber, C. and Davies, L. (1997) *School Management and Effectiveness in Developing Countries: The Post-bureaucratic School*. London: Cassell.

Hargreaves, A. and Shirley, D. (2009) *The Fourth Way*. Thousand Oaks, CA: Corwin.

Hargreaves, A., Hala'sz, G. and Pont, B. (2007) *School Leadership for Systemic Improvement in Finland*. Paris: OECD.

Hargreaves, D. H. (1967) *Social Relations in a Secondary School*. London: Routledge & Kegan Paul.

Hargreaves, D.H. (2010) *Creating a Self Improving School System*. Nottingham: NCSL.

Harland, J., Moor, H., Kinder, K. and Ashworth, M. (2002) *Is the Curriculum Working? The Key Stage 3 Phase of the NI Curriculum Cohort Study*. Berkshire: NFER.

Harms, T., Clifford, R. and Cryer, D. (1998) *Early Childhood Environment Rating Scale Revised*. New York and London: Teachers' College Press.

Harris, A. (1997) *The School Improvement Resource Pack*. London: Kogan Page.

Harris, A. (2001) Department Improvement and School Improvement: A Missing Link?, *British Educational Research Journal*, 27(4): 477–486.

Harris, A. (2003) *School Improvement: What's In It for Schools?*, London: RoutledgeFalmer.

Harris, A., Chapman, C., Muijs, D., Russ, J. and Stoll, L. (2006) Raising Achievement in Schools in Challenging Contexts, *School Effectiveness and School Improvement*, 16(3): 409–424.

Harris, A., Clarke, P., James, S., Gunraj, J. and James, B. (2006) *Improving Schools in Exceptionally Challenging Circumstances: Tales from the Frontline*. London: Continuum.

Harris, A., Day, C., Goodall, J., Lindsay, G. and Muijs, D. (2006) What Difference Does it Make? Evaluating the Impact of Continuing Professional Development in Schools, *Scottish Educational Review*, 37, Spring: 90–8.

Harris, A., Jamieson, I. and Russ, J. (1995) A Study of Efective Departments in Secondary Schools, *School Organisation*, 15(3): 283–299.

Harris, A. and Jones, M. (2010) *Leading Learning for School Effectiveness*. Paper delivered at ICSEI 2010, Kuala Lumpur.

Harris, J.R. (1998) *The Nurture Assumption*. London: Bloomsbury.

Hattie, J. (2007) *Developing Potentials for Learning: Evidence, Assessment, and Progress*, EARLI Biennial Conference, Budapest, Hungary.

Hattie, J. (2009) *Visible Learning*. London: Routledge.

Havel, V. (1994) Speech given in Philadelphia, June 1994.

Hayes, B. and McAlister, I. (2009) Education as a Mechanism for Conflict Resolution in Northern Ireland, *Oxford Review of Education*, 35(4): 437–450.

Heck, R. (2009) Teacher Effectiveness and Student Achievement: Investigating a Multi-level Cross-classified Model, *Journal of Educational Administration*, 47(2): 227–249.

Hedges, L.V., Laine, R.D. and Greenwald, R (1994). Does Money Matter? A Meta-analysis of Studies of the Effects of Differential School Inputs on Student Outcomes (An Exchange: Part 1), *Educational Researcher*, 23(3): 5–14.

Hegerl, G.C. (1996) Detecting Greenhouse-Gas-Induced Climate Change with an Optimal Fingerprint Method, *Journal of Climate*, 9, October, 2281–2306.

Heneveld, W. (1994) *Planning and Monitoring the Quality of Primary Education in Sub-Saharan Africa*. Washington, DC: World Bank, Human Resources and Poverty Division.

Heneveld, W. and Craig, H. (1996) *School Count: World Bank Project Designs and the Quality of Primary Education in Sub-Saharan Africa*. Washington, DC: World Bank.

Higham, R., Hopkins, D. and Matthews, P. (2009) *System Leadership in Practice*. Maidenhead: Open University Press.

Hill, P. and Rowe, K. (1998) Modeling Student Progress in Studies of Educational Effectiveness, *School Effectiveness and School Improvement*, 9(3): 310–333.

Her Majesty's Inspectors of Schools (HMI) (1988) *Secondary Schools: An Appraisal*. London: HMSO.

Her Majesrty's Inspectors of Schools (HMI) (2003) *Thinking Together*. Ofsted.

HMIE (2007) *Teaching Scotland's Children: A Report on Progress in Implementing 'A Teaching Profession for the 21st Century'*. Livingston: HMIE.

HMSO (1989) *Education Reform (NI) Order*. Belfast, HM Stationery Office.

Holtom, D. (2008a) *Evaluation of RAISE: Interim Report*. Abergavenny: People and Work Unit.

Holtom, D. (2008b) *Evaluation of RAISE: Thematic Report on the Work of Regional Coordinators*. Abergavenny: People and Work Unit.

Holtom, D. (2009a) *External Evaluation of RAISE: Thematic Report on Options for Sustaining the Impact of RAISE*. Abergavenny: People and Work Unit.

Holtom, D. (2009b) *Evaluation of RAISE: 2nd Interim Report*. Abergavenny: People and Work Unit.

Holtom, D. and Lloyd-Jones, S. (2009) *Development and Implementation of an Evaluation Programme for the Piloting in Schools of the School Effectiveness Framework for Wales*. Abergavenny: People and Work Unit.

Hopkins, D. (ed.) (1987) *Improving the Quality of Schooling*. Lewes: Falmer Press.

Hopkins, D. (2001) *School Improvement for Real*. London: Routledge/Falmer.

Hopkins, D. (2002) *Improving the Quality of Education for All: A Handbook of Staff Development Activities* (2nd edition). London: David Fulton Publishers.

Hopkins, D. (2007a) *Every School a Great School*. Maidenhead: Open University Press/McGraw-Hill

Hopkins, D. (2008) *Realising the Potential of System Leadership*, in B. Pont, D. Nusche and D. Hopkins (eds), *Improving School Leadership, Volume 2: Case Studies on System Leadershi*. Paris: OECD.

Hopkins, D. (ed.) (2007b) *Transformation and Innovation: System Leaders in the Global Age*. London: Specialist Schools and Academies Trust.

Hopkins, D., Ainscow, M. and West, M. (1994) *School Improvement in an Era of Change*. London: Cassell.

Hopkins, D., Harris, A., Stoll, L. and Mackay, A. (2011) *School and System Improvement: State of the Art Review*, Keynote presentation prepared for the 24th International Congress of School Effectiveness and School Improvement, Limassol, Cyprus, 6 January 2011.

Hopkins, D. and Reynolds, D. (2001) The Past, Present and Future of School Improvement: Towards the Third Age, *British Educational Research Journal*, 27(4): 459–475.

Hopkins, D., West, M. and Ainscow, M. (1996) *Improving the Quality of Education for All.* London: David Fulton.

Houtveen, A.A.M., van de Grift, W.J.C.M. and Creemers, B.P.M. (2004) Effective School Improvement in Mathematics. *School Effectiveness and School Improvement,* 15(4): 337–376.

Hox, J., and De Leeuw, E. (2003) Multilevel Models for Meta-analysis, in S.P. Reise and N. Duan (eds) *Multilevel Modelling: Methodological Advances, Issues and Applications.* Mahwah, NJ: Lawrence Erlbaum Associates.

Hsieh, Ch. and Urquiola, M. (2006) The Effects of Generalized School Choice on Achievement and Stratification: Evidence from Chile's School Voucher Program, *Journal of Public Economics,* 90: 1477–1503.

Hughes, J. (2010) Are Separate Schools Divisive? A Case Study from Northern Ireland, *British Educational Research Journal,* 37(5): np.

Hungerford, H. and Volk, T. (1990) Changing Learner Behavior Through Environmental Education, *Journal of Environmental Education,* 21(3): 8–21.

Hussain, W. (2009) *Gross National Happiness in Bhutan: A Living Example of an Alternative Approach to Progress.* Wharton International Research Experience. University of Pennsylvania.

Hustler, D., McNamara, O., Jarvis, J., Londra, M. and Campbell, A. (2003) *Teachers' Perceptions of Continuing Professional Development.* Research Report No. 429. Nottingham: DfES.

Hutchings, J., Bywater, T., Daley, D., Gardner, F., Whitaker, C., Jones, K., Eames, C. and Edwards, R. (2007) *Parenting Intervention in Sure Start Services for Children at Risk of Developing Conduct Disorders. BMJ,* 334 (7595), March 2007.

IEEQC (2009) Improving Educational Evaluation and Quality in China. Available online at: http://ieeqc.bristol.ac.uk Accessed 20 July 2009.

IPCC (2004) *4th Annual Assessment Report, Summary for Policymakers.* Paris: International Panel for Climate Change.

Itoh, K., Stevens, B., Schachner, M. and Fields, R.D. (1995) Regulation of Expression of the 4 Neural Cell Adhesion Molecule L1 by Specific Patterns of Neural Impulses, *Science,* 270: 1369–1372.

Jackson, D. (2004) Networked Learning Communities: Characteristics of 'Networked learning' – What Are We Learning? Paper prepared for the International Congress for School Effectiveness and Improvement (ICSEI) conference, 'Building Bridges for Sustainable School Improvement', Rotterdam.

Jackson, T. (2009) *Prosperity without Growth: Economics for a Finite Planet.* London: Earthscan.

James, C., Connolly, M., Dunning, G. and Elliot, T. (2006) *How Very Effective Primary Schools Work.* London: Paul Chapman Publishing.

Jang, E., McDougall, D., Pollon, D. Herbert, M. and Russell, P. (2008) Integrative Mixed Methods Data Analytic Strategies in Research on School Success in Challenging Circumstances, *Journal of Mixed Methods Research,* 2(3): 221–247.

Jayasinghe, U., Marsh, H. and Bond, N. (2003) A Multilevel Cross-classified Modelling Approach to Peer Review of Grant Proposals: The Effects of Assessor and Researcher Attributes on Assessor Ratings, *Journal of the Royal Statistical Society A,* 166(3): 279–300.

Jensen, B. (2010) *What Teachers Want: Better Teacher Management.* Australia: Grattan Institute.

Jiang, L., Yang, Z.-M. and Yao, S.-Q. (2005) Analysis of Influencing Factors on the

Chinese Achievement Test in the College Entrance Examination: A Hierarchical Linear Model, *Chinese Journal of Clinical Psychology,* 13(4): 414–416 and 419.

Jiang, S.J. (2008) Institutional Analysis of the Phenomenon of the Immigrants for NCEE, *Research in Educational Development,* 17: 16–20 and 30.

Jiang, W. and Ma, Z.Y. (2008) Inquiry of the First Litigation Case of Immigration for Entrance Examination for Higher Education, *Government Legality,* 12: 16–17.

Jickling, B. (1992) Why I Don't Want My Children To Be Educated for Sustainable Development, *Journal of Environmental Education,* 23(4): 5–8.

Jimerson, S.R. (2009) Meta-analysis of Grade Retention Research: Implications for Practice in the 21st Century, *School Psychology Review,* 30(3): 420–437.

Johnson, D.W, Johnson, R., and Smith, K.A. (1998) Cooperative Learning Returns to College: What Evidence is There That it Works? *Change,* July 1998: 27–35.

Jones, G.E. (1997) *The Education of A Nation.* Cardiff: University of Wales Press.

Jones, K. and Duncan, C. (1996) People and Places: The Multilevel Model as a General Framework for the Quantitative Analysis of Geographical Data, in P. Longley and M. Batty (eds) *Spatial Analysis: Modelling in a GIS Environment.* New York: John Wiley, pp. 79–105.

Jones, M. and Harris (2010) A. Professional Learning Communities and System Improvement, *Improving Schools,* July 2010: 172–181.

Jones, G.E. and Roderick, G.W. (2003) *A History of Education in Wales.* Cardiff: University of Wales Press.

Joyce, B., Weil, M. and Calhoun, E. (2000) *Models of Teaching.* Boston, MA: Allyn and Bacon.

Institute of Welsh Affairs (2006) *Time To Deliver: The Third Term and Beyond: Policy Options for Wales.* Cardiff: Institute for Welsh Affairs.

Joyce, B. R., Calhoun, E. F. and Hopkins, D. (2009) *Models of Learning: Tools for Teaching* (3rd edition). Maidenhead: Open University Press/McGraw-Hill Education.

Keating, M. (2005) *Government of Scotland: Public Policy After Devolution.* Edinburgh: Edinburgh University Press.

Kelley, P. (2007). *Making Minds.* London: Routledge.

Kellstedt, P.M., Zahran, S. and Vedlitz, A. (2008). Personal Efficacy, the Information Environment, and Attitudes Toward Global Warming and Climate Change in the United States, *Risk Analysis,* 28(1): 113–126.

Kelly, A. (2010) Personal correspondence.

Kelly, A. and Downey, C. (2010) Value-added Measures for Schools in England: Looking Inside the 'Black Box' of Complex Metrics, *Educational Assessment, Evaluation and Accountability,* 22(3): 181–198.

Kenway, P., Parsons, N., Carr, J. and Palmer, G. (2005) *Monitoring Poverty and Social Exclusion in Wales 2005.* London: Joseph Rowntree Foundation/New Policy Institute.

Kenway, P. and Palmer, G. (2007) *Monitoring Poverty and Social Exclusion in Wales 2007.* York: Joseph Rowntree Foundation.

Kerr, K. and West, M. (eds) (2011) *Social Inequality: Can Schools Narrow the Gap?* London: British Educational Research Association.

Kirk, G., Beveridge, W. and Smith, I. (2003) *The Chartered Teacher.* Edinburgh: Dunedin Academic Press.

Kirkpatrick, D. (1998) *Evaluating Training Programmes: The Four Levels* (2nd edition). San Francisco, CA: Berrett-Koehler.

Kirschenmann, F.L. (2010) *Cultivating and Ecological Conscience.* Kentucky: University Press of Kentucky.

Ko, J. and Sammons, P. (2011) *Effective Teaching: A Review*. Slough: CfBT.

Kyriakides, L. (2005) Extending the Comprehensive Model of Educational Effectiveness by an Empirical Investigation, *School Effectiveness and School Improvement*, 16(2): 103–152.

Kyriakides, L. (2008) Testing the Validity of the Comprehensive Model of Educational Effectiveness: A Step Towards the Development of a Dynamic Model of Effectiveness, *School Effectiveness and School Improvement*, 19(4): 429–446.

Kyriakides, L., Campbell, R. J. and Gagatsis, A. (2000) The Significance of the Classroom Effect in Primary Schools: An Application of Creemers' Comprehensive Model of Educational Effectiveness, *School Effectiveness and School Improvement*, 11(4): 501–529.

Kyriakides, L. and Creemers, B.P.M. (2008) Using a Multidimensional Approach to Measure the Impact of Classroom Level Factors Upon Student Achievement: A Study Testing the Validity of the Dynamic Model, *School Effectiveness and School Improvement*, 19(2): 183–205.

Kyriakides, L. and Creemers, B.P.M. (2009) The Effects of Teacher Factors on Different Outcomes: Two Studies Testing the Validity of the Dynamic Model, *Effective Education*, 1(1): 61–85.

Kyriakides, L., Creemers, B.P.M., Antoniou, P. and Demetriou, D. (2010) A Synthesis of Studies for School Factors: Implications for Theory and Research, *British Educational Research Journal*, 36(5): 807–830.

Kyriakides, L. and Luyten, H. (2009) The Contribution of Schooling to the Cognitive Development of Secondary Education Students in Cyprus: An Application of Regression Discontinuity with Multiple Cut-offs, *School Effectiveness and School Improvement*, 20 (2): 167–186.

Kyriakides, L., and Tsangaridou, N. (2008) Towards the Development of Generic and Differentiated Models of Educational Effectiveness: A Study on School and Teacher Effectiveness in Physical Education, *British Educational Research Journal* 34(6): 807–883.

Leaton Gray, S. (2004) *An Enquiry into Continuing Professional Development for Teachers*. Cambridge: Centre for Applied Research in Educational Technologies (CARET).

Leckie, G. (2009) The Complexity of School and Neighbourhood Effects and Movements of Pupils on School Differences in Models of Educational Achievement, *Journal of the Royal Statistical Society*, 172, Part 3: 537–554.

Lee, V.E., Zuze, T.L. and Ross, K.N. (2005) School Effectiveness in 14 Sub-Saharan African Countries: Links with 6th Graders' Reading Achievement, *Studies in Educational Evaluation*, 31(1): 207–246.

Leithwood, K., Jantzi, D. and Mascall, B. (1999) *Large Scale Reform: What Works?* Unpublished manuscript, Ontario Institute for Studies in Education, University of Toronto.

Leithwood, K. and Menzies, T. (1998) Forms and Effects of School-Based Management: A Review, *Educational Policy* 12(3): 325–346.

Levin, B. (2004). Making Research Matter More, *Education Policy Analysis Archives*, 12(56). Retrieved 15 November 2008, from http://epaa.asu.edu/epaa/v12n56/

Levin, B. (2008) *How to Change 5000 Schools*. Cambridge, MA: Harvard Education Press.

Levin, B. (2010) Leadership for Evidence-Informed Education, *School Leadership and Management*, 30(4): 303–315.

Levin, B. and Fullan, M. (2008) Learning about System Renewal, *Journal of Educational Management, Administration and Leadership*, 36(2): 289–303.

Levin, H.M. and Lockheed, M.E. (eds.) (1993) *Effective Schools in Developing Countries*. London: Falmer.

Levine, D.U. and Lezotte, L.W. (1990). *Unusually Effective Schools: A Review and Analysis of Research and Practice*. Madison, WI: National Center for Effective Schools Research and Development.

Lewin, K. (1946) Action Research and Minority Problems, *Journal of Social Issues*, 2: 34–46.

Lindsay, G., Harris, A., Muijs, D., Chapman, C. *et al.* (2007) *Final Report on the Evaluation of the Federations Programme*. London: DCSF.

Lloyds of London (2010) *360 Degree Insights: Globalisation and Environment*. London: Lloyds of London.

Loosmore, F. (1981) *Curriculum and Assessment in Wales: An Exploratory Study*. Cardiff: Curriculum Council for Wales.

Lovelock, J. (2006) *The Revenge of Gaia*. London: Allen Lane.

Lovelock, J. (2009) *The Vanishing Face of Gaia*. London: Allen Lane.

Lupton, R. and Kintrea, K. (2008) *Community-Level Influences on Educational Attainment: A Review for the Social Exclusion Task Force*. London: London School of Economics/Glasgow University/Cabinet Office.

Luyten, H. and Sammons, P.(2010) Multilevel Modeling, in B.P.M Creemers, L. Kyriakides and P. Sammons, *Methodological Advances in Educational Effectiveness Research*. London: Routledge.

Luyten, H., Tymms, P. and Jones, P. (2009) Assessing School Effects without Controlling for Prior Achievement, *School Effectiveness and School Improvement*, 20(2): 145–165.

Ma, X., Peng, W.-J. and Thomas, S. (2006) School Effectiveness Evaluation with Value Added Method: Case Study of Senior High Schools of Baoding Hebei Province, *Educational Research*, 10: 77–84.

MacBeath, J. (1999) *Schools Must Speak for Themselves: The Case for School Self-Evaluation*. London: Routledge.

MacBeath, J. (2010) *Evaluation of the Children's University*. Cambridge: University of Cambridge.

MacBeath, J. (2011) No Lack of Principles: Leadership Development in England and Scotland, *School Leadership and Management*, 31(2): 105–121.

MacBeath, J. and Dempster, N. (2009) *Connecting Leadership and Learning: Principles for Practice*. London: Routledge.

MacBeath, J., Gray, J.M., Cullen, J., Frost, D., Steward, S. and Swaffield, S. (2007) *Schools on the Edge: Responding to Challenging Circumstances*. London: Paul Chapman.

MacBeath, J., Gronn, P., Forde, C., Howie, Lowden, K., and O'Brien, J. (2009) *Recruitment and Retention of Headteachers in Scotland*. Edinburgh: Scottish Government.

MacBeath, J., Mearns, D. and Smith, M. (1986) *Home for School*. Glasgow: Jordanhill College.

MacBeath, J. and Mortimore, P. (2001) *Improving School Effectiveness*. Buckingham: Open University Press.

MacDonald, A. (2004) Collegiate or Compliant? Primary Teachers in post-McCrone Scotland, *British Educational Research Journal*, 30(3): 413–433.

McEwan, P. and Carnoy, M. (2000) The Effectiveness and Efficiency of Private Schools in Chile's Voucher System, *Educational Evaluation and Policy Analysis*, 22(3): 213–239.

MacGilchrist, B. (2000) Improving Self-Improvement? *Research Papers in Education*, 15(3): 325–338

Macy, J. and Young Brown, M. (1998) *Coming Back to Life: Practices to Reconnect Our Lives, Our World*. Stony Creek, CT: New Society Publishers.

Maguire, M., Wooldridge, T. and Pratt-Adams, S. (2006) *The Urban Primary School*. Maidenhead: Open University Press.

Mahony, P. and Hextall, I. (2000) *Reconstructing Teaching: Standards, Performance and Accountability*. London: RoutledgeFalmer.

March, J. (1991) Exploration and Exploitation in Organizational Learning, *Organization Science*, 2(1): 71–87.

Marsh, H.W. (1984) Self-Concept: The Application of a Frame of Reference Model to Explain Paradoxical Results, *Australian Journal of Education*, 28: 165–181.

Marsh, H.W. (1993) Relations Between Global and Specific Domains of Self: The Importance of Individual Importance, Certainty, and Ideals. *Journal of Personality and Social Psychology*, 65(5): 975–992.

Marsh, H.W. and Craven, R. (1997) Academic Self-Concept: Beyond the Dustbowl, in G. Phye (ed.) *Handbook of Classroom Assessment: Learning, Achievement and Adjustment*. Orlando, FL: Academic Press, pp. 131–198.

Marsh, H.W., Trautwein, U., Lüdtke, O., Köller, O. and Baumert, J. (2005) Academic Self-Concept, Interest, Grades and Standardized Test Scores: Reciprocal Effects Models of Causal Ordering, *Child Development*, 76: 297–416.

Marzano, R. (2003) *What Works in Schools: Translating Research into Action*. Alexandria, VA: Association for Supervision and Curriculum Development. Available online at: http://www.mckinsey.com/clientservice/Social_Sector/our_practices/Education/Knowledge_Highlights/Economic_impact.aspx

Maslowski, R. (2003) *School Culture and School Performance: An Explorative Study into the Organisational Culture of Secondary Schools and Their Effects*. Enschede: Twente University Press.

McGaugh, J.L. (2000) Memory: A Century of Consolidation, *Science*, 287(5451): 248–252.

McKinsey (2007) *How the World's Best Performing School Systems Come Out on Top*. London: McKinsey.

McKinsey (2009) *The Economic Impact of the Achievement Gap in America's Schools*. London: McKinsey.

McKinsey (2010) *How the World's Most Improved School Systems Keep Getting Better*. London: McKinsey.

McMahon, M. *et al.* (no date) *Evaluating the Impact of Chartered Teachers in Scotland: The Views of Chartered Teachers, Final Report*. Glasgow: University of Glasgow for GTCS.

McWhirter, L. (2002) *Health and Social Care in NI: A Statistical Profile*. Belfast: Department of Health, Social Services and Public Safety. Available online at: http://www.dhsspsni.gov.uk/hsc_stats_profile.pdf Accessed 12 February 2011.

Melhuish, E., Sylva, K., Sammons, P., Siraj-Blatchford, I., Taggart, B., Phan, M. and Malin, A. (2008) Preschool Influences on Mathematics Achievement, *Science*, 321: 1161–1162.

Meyer, J.W. and Rowan, B. (1977) Institutionalized Organizations: Formal Structures as Myth and Ceremony, *American Journal of Sociology*, 83: 340–363.

Meyer, M. and Zucker, L. (1989) *The Permanently Failing Organization*. Newbury Park, CA: Sage.

Meyers, J.L., and Beretvas, S.N. (2006) The Impact of the Inappropriate Modeling of Cross-classified Data Structures. *Multivariate Behavioral Research*, 41(4): 473–497.

Miliband, D. (2004) Using Data to Raise Achievement. Speech at a Conference of the Education Network, London, 11 February 2004. Retrieved 21 May 2007, from http://www.teachers.gov.uk/_doc/6280/Miliband%20speech%20at%20TEN%20Conference%2011Feb04.doc

Millett, A., Askew, M. and Brown, M. (2004) The Impact of the National Numeracy Strategy in Year 4(I): Attainment and Learning, and (II): Teaching, in O. McNamara and R. Barwell (eds) *Research in Mathematics Education*, 6: 175–206.

Mintzberg, H. (1979) *The Structuring of Organizations*. Englewood Cliffs, NJ: Prentice Hall.

Modin, B. and Östberg, V. (2009) School Climate and Psychosomatic Health. A Multi-level Analysis of Nearly 20,000 Ninth Grade Students in the Larger Stockholm Area. *School Effectiveness and School Improvement*, 20(4): 433–455.

MoEVT (2010) Zanzibar Education Act (First Draft): Author.

MoEVT (2009) Zanzibar Education Development Programme (ZEDP: 2008/2009 – 2015/2016). Author.

MoEVT (2007) Ripoti ya uchunguzi kuhusu matokeo ya mtihani wa kidato cha sita 2007 (Investigation Report on 2007 Form 6 Examination Performance). Author.

Mourshed, M., Chijioke, C. and Barber, M. (2010) *How the World's Most Improved School Systems Keep Getting Better*. London: McKinsey and Company.

Moffatt, C. (ed) (1993) *Education Together for a Change: Integrated Education and Community Relations in Northern Ireland*. Belfast, Fortnight Educational Trust.

Moller, J., Pohlman, B., Koller, O. and Marsh, H. (2008) A Meta-Analytic Path Analysis of the Internal/External Frame of Reference Model of Academic Achievement and Academic Self-Concept, *Review of Educational Research*, 79(3): 1129–1167.

Monk, D.H. (1992) Education Productivity Research: An Update and Assessment of Its Role in Education Finance Reform, *Educational Evaluation and Policy Analysis*, 14(4): 307–332.

Montgomery, A. and Smith, A. (2006) Teacher Education in Northern Ireland: Policy Variations Since Devolution, *Scottish Educational Review*, 37: 46–58.

Morgan, C. and Morris, G. (1999) *Good Teaching and Learning: Pupils and Teachers Speak*. Buckingham: Open University Press.

Morgan, V. and Fraser, G. (1999) When Does 'Good News' Become 'Bad News'? Relationships between Government and the Integrated Schools in Northern Ireland, *British Journal of Educational Studies*, 47(4): 364–379.

Morris, H. (1925) *The Village College: Being a Memorandum on the Provision of Educations and Social Facilities for the Countryside, with Special Reference to Cambridgeshire* (Section XIV).

Mortimore, P. (1998) *The Road to Improvement*. London: Routledge.

Mortimore, P., Sammons, P., Stoll, L., Lewis, D., and Ecob, R. (1988) *School Matters*. Berkeley, CA: University of California Press.

Mortimore, P., Sammons, P., Stoll, L., Lewis, D. and Ecob, R. (1988) The Effects of School Membership on Pupils' Educational Outcomes, *Research Papers in Education*, 3(1): 3–26.

Moss, C., Jewiitt, C., Leavcic, R., Armstrong, V., Cardini, A. and Castle, F. (2007) *The Interactive Whiteboards, Pedagogy and Pupil Performance Evaluation: An Evaluation of the Schools Whiteboard Expansion Project*. London: Department for Education and Skills. Research Report 816.

Morley, L. and Rassool, N. (1999) *School Effectiveness: Fracturing the Discourse*. London: Falmer Press.

Mourshed, M., Chijioke, C. and Barber, M. (2010) *How the World's Most Improved School Systems Keep Getting Better*. London: McKinsey and Company.

Muijs, D. (2004) *Doing Quantitative Research in Education*. London: Sage.

Muijs, D. (2006) New Directions for School Effectiveness Research: Towards School Effectiveness without Schools, *Journal of Educational Change*, 7: 141–160.

Muijs, D. (2008) Educational Effectiveness and the Legacy of Bert P. M. Creemers, *School Effectiveness and School Improvement*, 19 (4): 463–472.

Muijs, D. and Chapman, C. (2009) Accountability for Improvement: Rhetoric or Reality? in C. Chapman and H. Gunter (eds) *Radical Reforms: Perspectives on an Era of Educational Change*. London: Taylor and Francis.

Muijs, D., Harris, A., Chapman, C., Stoll, L. and Russ, J. (2004) Improving Schools in Socioeconomically Disadvantaged Areas: A Review of Research Evidence, *School Effectiveness and School Improvement*, 5(2): 149–175.

Muijs, D., Harris, A., Lumby, J., Marrison, M. and Sood, K. (2006) Leadership and Leadership Development in Highly Effective Further Education Providers: Is there a Relationship? *Journal of Further and Higher Education*, 30(1): 87–106.

Muijs, D., Kelly, T., Sammons, P., Reynolds, D. and Chapman, C. (2011) The Value of Educational Effectiveness Research: A Response to Recent Criticism, *Research Intelligence* 114, Spring 2011: 24–25.

Muijs, D. and Lindsay, G. (2008) Where Are We At? An Empirical Study of Levels and Methods of Evaluating Continuing Professional Development, *British Educational Research Journal*, 34(2): 195–211.

Muijs, D. and Reynolds, D. (2000) School Effectiveness and Teacher Effectiveness: Some Preliminary Findings from the Evaluation of the Mathematics Enhancement Programme, *School Effectiveness and School Improvement*, 11(3): 323–337.

Muijs, D. and Reynolds, D. (2001) *Effective Teaching: Evidence and Practice*. London: Sage.

Muijs, D. and Reynolds, D. (2002) Teacher Beliefs and Behaviours: What Matters? *Journal of Classroom Interaction*, 37(2): 3–15.

Muijs, D. and Reynolds, D. (2003) Student Background and Teacher Effects on Achievement and Attainment in Mathematics, *Educational Research and Evaluation*, 9(1): 289–313.

Muijs, D. and Reynolds, D. (2005) *Effective Teaching: Evidence and Practice*. (2nd edition). London: Sage.

Muijs, D. and Reynolds, D. (2010) *Effective Teaching: Research and Practice*. (3rd revised edition). London: Sage.

Munoz-Chereau, B. (2010) *Pilot Study on School Effects in Chile*. Paper presented to the GSOE Second Quantitative Methods Forum, 15 December 2010. Bristol: Author.

Murillo, J. (2007) School Effectiveness Research in Latin America, in T. Townsend (ed.) *International Handbook of School Effectiveness and Improvement (2007)*. The Netherlands: Springer. Part I, pp. 75–92.

Nassor S.M., Saleh, M., Ali, O.S. and Salim, M.M. (2005) *The SACMEQ II Project in Zanzibar: A Study of the Conditions of Schooling and the Quality of Education*. SACMEQ Educational Policy Research Series. Paris: UNESCO – IIEP Publishing, p. 244.

Nassor S. and Mohammed K. (1998) *The Quality of Education: Some Policy Suggestions Based on a Survey of Schools: Zanzibar*. SACMEQ Policy Research: Report No. 4. Paris: UNESCO – IIEP Publishing.

National Council on Economic Education (2007) *Tough Choices or Tough Times?: The Report of the New Commission on the Skills of the American Workforce*. Washington, DC: NCEE.

National Commission on Excellence in Education (1983) *A Nation At Risk: the Imperative for Educational Reform*, Washington, DC: U.S. Government Printing Office.

National Medium- and Long-term Talent Development Plan (2010–2020) People's Republic of China. Accessed at http://www.brookings.edu/papers/2010/1123_china_talent_wang.aspx on 14/12/2010.

National Research Council (NRC) (2006) *Surface Temperature Reconstructions for the Last 2,000 Years.* Washington DC: National Academy Press.

NCSL (2011) National Teaching Schools http://www.nationalcollege.org.uk/index/professional-development/teachingschools.htm Accessed 21 June 2011

NFER (2004) *Review of Evidence Relating to the Introduction of a Standard School Year.* Slough: NFER.

NICC (Northern Ireland Curriculum Council) (1990) *Cross Curricular Themes: Guidance Materials.* Belfast: NICC.

NICC (Northern Ireland Curriculum Council) (1992) *Education for Mutual Understanding: A Cross Curricular Theme.* Belfast, NICC.

NICED (Northern Ireland Council for Educational Development) (1988) *Education for Mutual Understanding.* Belfast: NICED.

NICCE (Northern Ireland Commission for Catholic Education) (2009) *Statement by the NICCE on Post-Primary Transfer Policy for Catholic Schools in Northern Ireland.* Released 30 March. Available online at: http://catholiceducation-ni.com/content/view/109/36/ Accessed 21 February 2011.

NISRA (2001) Northern Ireland Census 2001, Table KS07a: Religion. Available online at: http://www.nisranew.nisra.gov.uk/census/Excel/KS07a%20DC.xls And Table KS07b: Community Background: Religion or Religion Brought up in. Available online at: http://www.nisranew.nisra.gov.uk/census/Excel/KS07b%20DC.xls

Nicolson, R. and Reynolds, D. (2003). Science, Sense and Synergy: Response to Commentators, *Dyslexia*, 9(3): 167–176.

Nicolson, R., Fawcett, A. and Dean, P. (2001) Developmental Dyslexia: The Cerebellar Deficit Hypothesis, *Trends in Neuroscience*, 24(9): 508–511.

NPC (National People's Congress) (2009) The Report on the Work of the Government delivered by Premier Wen Jiabao at the Second Session of the Eleventh National People's Congress on March 5, 2009 Retrieved 14 June 2010 http://www.xinhuanet.com/2009lh/090305a/wz.htm

Nutley, S., Walter, I., and Davies, H. (2007) *Using Evidence: How Research Can Inform Public Services.* Bristol: Policy Press.

Nuttall, D., Goldstein, H., Prosser, R. and Rasbash, J. (1989) Differential School Effectiveness, *International Journal of Educational Research*, 13(7): 769–776.

O'Brien, J. (2007) Control or Empowerment? The Professional Learning of Scottish Teachers in the Post McCrone Era, in J. Pickering, N. Pachler and C. Daly (eds) *New Designs for Teachers' Professional Learning.* London: Bedford Way Papers No. 27: Institute of Education.

O'Brien, J. (2009) *Teacher Induction: Does Scotland's Approach Stand Comparison? Research in Comparative and International Education*, 4 (1): 42–52, http://www.wwwords.co.uk/rcie/content/pdfs/4/issue4_1.asp.

O'Brien, J. and Draper, J. (2008) Leadership for Learning or Learning for Leadership? The Role of Teacher Induction and Early Professional Development in England and Scotland, in J. MacBeath and Y.C. Cheng (eds) *Leadership for Learning: International Perspectives.* Rotterdam: Sense Publishers, pp. 229–240.

OECD (1989) *Schools and Quality: An International Report.* Paris: OECD.

OECD (2002) PISA 2000: Reading For Change: Performance And Engagement Across Countries. Retrieved 1 June 2011 http://www.oecd.org/dataoecd/43/54/33690904.pdf

OECD (2004) Policy Brief (February) *Education and Equity.* Available online at: www.oecd.org/dataoecd/17/10/29478774.pdf Accessed 29 December 2010.

OECD (2005) *Teachers Matter: Attracting, Developing and Retaining Effective Teachers.* Paris: OECD.

OECD (2006) *Social Disadvantage and Educational Experiences.* Paris: OECD.

OECD (2007) *Knowledge Management: Evidence and Education: Linking Research and Practice.* Paris: OECD.

OECD (2007) *PISA 2006: Science Competencies for Tomorrow's World.* Vol. 1. Retrieved 7 December 2009 http://www.pisa.oecd.org/dataoecd/30/17/39703267.pdf

OECD (2008) *Measuring Improvements in Learning Outcomes: Best Practices to Access the Value Added of Schools.* www.oecd.org/publishing/corrigenda.

OECD (2008) *Addressing the Challenges of Policy Implementation in Education:* http://www.oecd.org/document/7/0,3746, en_2649

OECD (2008) *Education at a glance,* available at http://www.oecd.org/dataoecd/21/15/41278761.pdf

OECD (2009) *Creating Effective Teaching and Learning Environments: First Results from TALIS.* Paris: OECD.

OECD (2010). *TALIS 2008 Technical Report.* Paris: OECD.

OECD (2011) Shanghai and Hong Kong: Two Distinct Examples of Education Reform in China, in *Lessons from PISA for the United States: Strong Performers and Successful Reformers in Education* (pp. 83–115). http://www.oecd.org/dataoecd/32/50/46623978.pdf.

Ofsted (2004) *Making a Difference: The Impact of Award Bearing In-service Training on School Improvement.* London: HMI 1765 survey of HEI based CPD.

Ofsted (2006) *The Logical Chain: CPD in Effective Schools.* London: Ofsted.

Ofsted (2009) *Twelve Outstanding Secondary Schools: Excelling Against the Odds.* London: Ofsted.

OHMCI (1996) *Success in Secondary Schools.* Cardiff: OHMCI.

OHMCI (1999) *A Survey of the Role of LEAs In School Improvement.* Cardiff: OHMCI.

O'Mara, A.J., Marsh, H.W. and Craven, R.G. (2005, December) *Self-Concept Intervention Research in School Settings: A Multivariate, Multilevel Model Meta-Analysis.* Paper presented at the AARE Conference, University of Western Sydney, Parramatta, Australia.

Opdenakker, M. C. and Van Damme, J. (2000) The Importance of Identifying Levels in Multilevel Analysis: An Illustration of the Effects of Ignoring the Top or Intermediate Levels in School Effectiveness Research, *School Effectiveness and School Improvement,* 11(1): 103–130.

Opdenakker, M.C. and Van Damme, J. (2006) Differences Between Secondary Schools: A Study About School Context, Group Composition, School Practice, and School Effects with Special Attention to Public and Catholic Schools and Types of Schools. *School Effectiveness and School Improvement,* 17(1), 87–117.

Opdenakker, M.C. and Van Damme, J. (2007) Do School Context, Student Composition, and School Leadership Affect School Practice and Outcomes in Secondary Education? *British Educational Research Journal,* 33(2): 179–206.

Opfer, V.D., Pedder, D. and Lavicza, Z. (2008) *Survey Report: Schools and Continuing Professional Development (CPD) in England – State of the Nation Research Project (t34718).* London: Report for Training and Development Agency (TDA) for Schools.

Opfer, D.V. and Pedder, D. (2010) Access to Continuous Professional Development by Teachers in England, *Curriculum Journal,* 21(4): 453–471.

Opfer, D.V. and Pedder, D. (2011) The Lost Promise of Teacher Professional Development in England, *European Journal of Teacher Education,* 34(1): 3–24.

Orr, D. (2004) *Earth in Mind* (10th anniversary edition). Washington, DC: First Island Press.

Orr, D. (2009) *Down to the Wire: Confronting Climate Collapse*. Oxford: Oxford University Press.

Osberg, L., Wien, F., and Grude, J. (1995) *Vanishing Jobs: Canada's Changing Workplace*. Toronto: James Lorimer.

Osborne, R. and Cormack, R. (1989) Gender and Religion as Issues in Education, Training and Entry to Work, in J. Harbison (ed.) *Growing up in Northern Ireland*. Belfast: The Universities Press, pp. 42–65.

Ozga, J. (2005) Modernizing the Education Workforce: A Perspective from Scotland, *Educational Review*, 57(2): 207–219.

Pease, T. (2009) *Going Out of Business by Design: Why Seventy Percent of Small Businesses Fail*. New York: Morgan James.

Peng, W.-J., Thomas, S. M., Yang, X. and Li, J. (2006) Developing School Evaluation Methods to Improve the Quality of Schooling in China: A Pilot 'Value Added' Study, *Assessment in Education: Principles, Policy and Practice*, 13(2): 135–154.

Peterson T.C. (2008) State of the Climate in 2008, *Special Supplement to the Bulletin of the American Meteorological Society*, 90(8): S17–S18.

Petty, G. (2009) *Evidence Based Teaching* (2nd edition). Cheltenham: Nelson Thornes.

PISA (2006) *Science Competencies for Tomorrow's World*. Paris: OECD.

Plewis, I. and Fielding, A. (2003) What is Multi-Level Modelling? A Critical Response to Gorard, *British Educational Research Journal*, 51(4): 408–419.

Prochnik, G. (2010) *In Pursuit of Silence*. New York: Doubleday.

Purdon, A. (2003) A National framework of CPD: Continuing Professional Development or Continuing Policy Dominance? *Journal of Education Policy*, 18(4): 423–437.

Purdon, A. (2004) Perceptions of the Educational Elite on the Purpose of a National Famework of Continuing Professional Development (CPD) for Teachers in Scotland, *Journal of Education for Teaching*, 30(2): 131–149.

Purkey S.C. and Smith M.S. (1983) Effective Schools: A Review, *The Elementary School Journal*, 83(4) Special Issue: Research on Teaching (Mar 1983): 426–452.

Quality Assurance Agency for Higher Education (QAAHE) (2000) *The Standard for Initial Teacher Education in Scotland: Benchmark Information*. Gloucester: QAAHE.

Raczynski, D. and Munoz-Stuardo, G. (2005) *Efectividad Escolar y cambio educativo en condiciones de pobreza en Chile*. Chile. Ministerio de Educacion. Division de Educacion General.

Raczynski, D. and Munoz-Stuardo, G. (2007) Chilean Educational Reform: the Intricate Balance Between a Macro and Micro Policy, in W.T. Pink and G.W. Noblit (eds) *International Handbook of Urban Education*. New York: Springer, pp. 641–664.

Ramaswamy V. (2006) Anthropogenic and Natural Influences in the Evolution of Lower Stratospheric Cooling, *Science*, 311: 138–114.

Rampey, B.D., Dion, G.S. and Donahue, P.L. (2009) *NAEP 2008 Trends in Academic Progress* (NCES 2009–479). Washington DC: National Center for Education Statistics, Institute of Education Sciences, U.S. Department of Education.

Rasbash, J. and Browne, W. (2001) Modelling Non-hierarchical Structures, in A.H. Leyland and H. Goldstein (eds) *Multilevel Modelling of Health Statistics*. Chichester: Wiley.

Rasbash, J. and Goldstein, H. (1994) Efficient Analysis of Mixed Hierarchical and Cross-classified Random Structures Using a Multilevel Model, *Journal of Educational and Behavioural Statistics*, 19(4): 337–350.

Ray, A. (2006) *School Value Added Measures in England: A Paper for the OECD Project on the Development of Value-added Models in Education Systems*. London: Department for Education and Skills.

Rea-Dickins, P., Yu, G., Khamis, Z. and Afitska, O. (2008) *Examination Underachievement: Is There a Language Factor?* A paper presented in BAAL (British Association for Applied Linguistics) Annual Conference, Swansea University, Wales, 11–13 September, 2008.

Reeves, J., Forde, C., O'Brien, J., Smith, P. and Tomlinson, H. (2002) *Performance Management in Education: Improving Practice.* London: Paul Chapman Educational Publishing in association with BELMAS.

Reeves, J. (2007) Inventing the Chartered Teacher, *British Journal of Educational Studies*, 55(1): 56–76.

Reezigt, G.L., Guldemond, H. and Creemers, B.P.M. (1999) Empirical Validity for a Comprehensive Model on Educational Effectiveness, *School Effectiveness and School Improvement*, 10(2): 193–216.

Register, R. (2006) *Ecocities: Rebuilding Cities in Balance with Nature.* Gabriola Island BC: New Society Publishers.

Reynolds, A.J. and Walberg, H.J. (1990) *A Structural Model of Educational Productivity.* DeKalb, IL: Northern Illinois University.

Reynolds, D. (1976) The Delinquent School, in P. Woods (ed.) *The Process of Schooling.* London: Routledge, Keegan and Paul.

Reynolds, D. (1982) The Search for Effective Schools, *School Organisation*, 2(3): 215–237.

Reynolds, D. (1987) The Consultant Sociologist: A Method for Linking Sociology of Education and Teachers, in P. Woods and A. Pollard (eds) *Sociology and Teaching.* London: Croom Helm.

Reynolds, D. (1994) *The Effective School.* A revised version of an Inaugural Lecture. University of Newcastle upon Tyne, October.

Reynolds, D. (2006) *Narrowing the Gap: Reducing Within School Variation in Pupil Outcomes.* Nottingham: NCSL.

Reynolds, D. (2006) World Class Schools: Some Methodological and Substantive Findings and Implications of the International School Effectiveness Research Project (ISERP), *Educational Research and Evaluation*, 12(6): 535–560.

Reynolds, D. (2008a) New Labour, Education and Wales: The Devolution Decade, *Oxford Review of Education*, 34(6): 753–765.

Reynolds, D. (2008) *Schools Learning from Their Best: The Within School Variation (WSV) Project.* Nottingham: NCSL.

Reynolds, D. (2010) *Failure Free Education? The Past, Present and Future of School Effectiveness and Improvement.* London: Routledge.

Reynolds, D. and Creemers, B. (1990) School Effectiveness and School Improvement: A Mission Statement, *School Effectiveness and School Improvement* 1(1): 1–3.

Reynolds, D., Creemers, B.P.M., Hopkins, D., Stoll, L. and Bollen, R. (1996) *Making Good Schools.* London: Routledge.

Reynolds, D., Creemers, B.P.M., Stringfield, S., Teddlie, C. and Schaffer, G. (2002) *World Class Schools: International Perspectives in School Effectiveness.* London: Routledge Falmer.

Reynolds, D. and Cuttance, P. (1992) *School Effectiveness: Research, Policy and Practice.* London: Cassell.

Reynolds, D., Harris, A., Clarke, P., Harris, B. and James, S. (2006) Challenging the Challenged: Developing an Improvement Programme for Schools Facing Exceptionally Challenging Circumstances, *School Effectiveness and School Improvement*, 17(4): 425–440.

Reynolds, D., Nicolson, R. and Hambly, H. (2003) Evaluation of an Exercise Based Treatment for Children with Reading difficulties, *Dyslexia*, 19: 48–71.

Reynolds, D. and Nicolson, R. (2006) Follow up of an Exercise Based Treatment for Children With Reading Difficulties, *Dyslexia*, 13: 78–96.

Reynolds, D. and Sullivan, M. (1979) Bringing Schools Back In, in L. Barton (ed.) *Schools, Pupils and Deviance*. Driffield: Nafferton.

Reynolds, D., Stringfield, S. and Schaffer, E. (2006) The High Reliability School Project: Some Preliminary Results and Analyses, in J. Chrispeels and A. Harris (eds) *School Improvement: International Perspectives*. London: Routledge.

Reynolds, D., Sullivan, M. and Murgatroyd, S. (1987) *The Comprehensive Experiment: A Comparison of the Selective and Non-selective Systems of School Organisation*. Lewes: Falmer Press.

Reynolds, D., Sammons, P., De Fraine, B., Townsend, T. and Van Damme, J. (2011) *Educational Effectiveness Research (EER): A State of the Art Review*, paper presented at the International Congress for School Effectiveness and Improvement, Cyprus, January 2011.

Reynolds, D. and Teddlie, C. (2000) *The International Handbook of School Effectiveness Research*. London: Falmer Press.

Reynolds, D. and Teddlie, C. (2001). Reflections on the Critics, and Beyond Them. *School Effectiveness and School Improvement*, 12: 99–113.

Reynolds, M. (1999) Standards and Professional Practice: The TTA and Initial Teaching Training, *British Journal of Educational Studies*, 47(3): 247–260.

RGZ (2006) *Zanzibar Strategy for Growth and Reduction of Poverty*. Author. Regional Government of Zanzibar.

Rickinson, M. (2005) *Practitioner's Use of Research*. National Education Research Forum Working Paper 7.5. London: NERF.

Riddell, S. and Brown, S. (1991) *School Effectiveness Research: Its Messages for School improvement*. Edinburgh: SOED.

Ridley, M. (2010) *The Rational Optimist*. London: Harper Collins.

Robinson, V., Hohepa, M. and Lloyd, C. (2009) *School Leadership and Student Outcomes: Identifying What Works and Why*. Wellington, NZ: Ministry of Education.

Robinson, M., Walker, M., Kinder, K. and Haines, B. (2008) *Research into the Role of CPD Leadership in Schools*. Slough: NFER.

Rosenshine, B. and Stevens, R. (1986) Teaching Functions, in M.C. Wittrock (ed.) *Handbook of Research on Teaching* (3rd edition. pp. 376–391). New York: Macmillan.

Rowe, K. (2006) Effective Teaching Practices for Students With and Without Learning Difficulties: Issues and Implications, *Australian Journal of Learning Disabilitie*, 11(3): 99–115.

Ruane, C. (Minister of Education) (2008) Education Minister's Statement for the Stormont Education Committee (31 January). Available online at: http://www.deni.gov.uk/index/85-schools/6-admission-and-choice/statement_for_the_education_committee_48_kb.pdf Accessed 14 August 2009.

Rutter, M., Maughan, B., Mortimore, P. and Ouston, J., with Smith, A. (1979) *15000 Hours: Secondary Schools and Their Effects on Children*. London: Open Books.

Sacco, J, and Schmidt, N. (2009) A Dynamic Multilevel Model of Demographic Diversity and Misfit Effects, *Journal of Applied Psychology*, 90(2): 203–231.

Sachs, J. (2003) Teacher Professional Standards: Controlling or Developing Teaching? *Teachers and Teaching: Theory and Practice*, 9(2): 175–186.

Salim, M. (2011) *Exploring Issues of School Effectiveness and Self-Evaluation at the System and School Levels in the Context of Zanzibar*. PhD thesis. University of Bristol.

Sammons, P. (1996) Complexities in the Judgment of School Effectiveness, *Educational Research and Evaluation*, 2(2): 113–149.

Sammons, P. (1999) *School Effectiveness: Coming of Age in the 21st Century*. Lisse: Swets and Zeitlinger.

Sammons, P. (2006a) School Effectiveness and Equity: Making Connections, Keynote lecture at the International Congress for School Effectiveness and Improvement, Florida, January 2006 http://www.leadership.fau.edu/icsei2006/Papers/Sammons%20keynote.doc

Sammons, P. (2006b) The Contribution of International Studies on Educational Effectiveness: Current and Future Directions, *Educational Research and Evaluation*, 12(6): 583–593.

Sammons, P. (2007) *School Effectiveness and Equity: Making Connections*. Reading: Centre for British Teachers.

Sammons, P. (2008) Zero Tolerance of Failure and New Labour Approaches to School Improvement in England, *Oxford Review of Education*, 34(6): 651–664.

Sammons, P. (2009) The Dynamics of Educational Effectiveness: A Contribution to Policy, Practice and Theory in Contemporary Schools *School Effectiveness and School Improvement*, 20(1) 123–129.

Sammons, P. (2010) Equity and Educational Effectiveness, in *International Encyclopedia of Education*. Oxford: Elsevier.

Sammons, P., Anders, Y., Sylva, K., Melhuish, E., Siraj-Blatchford, I., Taggart, B. and Barreau, S. (2008) Children's Cognitive Attainment and Progress in English Primary Schools During Key Stage 2: Investigating the Potential Continuing Influences of Pre-school Education, *Zeitschrift für Erziehungswissenschaften*, 10. Jahrg., Special Issue (Sonderheft) 11/2008 179–198.

Sammons, P., Day, C., Kington, A., Gu, Q., Stobart, G. and Smees, R. (2007) Exploring Variations in Teachers' Work, Lives and Their Effects on Pupils: Key Findings and Implications from a Longitudinal Mixed Methods Study. *British Educational Research Journal*, 33(5): 681–701.

Sammons, P., Hillman, J. and Mortimore, P. (1995) *Key Characteristics of Effective Schools: A Review of School Effectiveness Research*. A report by the Institute of Education for the Office for Standards in Education.

Sammons, P. and Luyten, H. (2009) Editorial Article for Special Issue on Alternative Methods for Assessing School Effects and Schooling Effects, *School Effectiveness and School Improvement*, 20(2): 133–143.

Sammons, P., Nuttall, D., Cuttance, P. and Thomas, S. (1995), Continuity of School Effects: A Longitudinal Analysis of Primary and Secondary School Effects on GCSE Performance, *School Effectiveness and School Improvement*, Vol. 6(4) 285–307.

Sammons, P., Nuttall, D. and Cuttance, P. (1993) Differential School Effectiveness: Results from a Reanalysis of the Inner London Education Authority's Junior School Project Data, *British Educational Research Journal*, 19(4): 381–405.

Sammons, P., Siraj-Blatchford, I., Sylva, K., Melhuish, E., Taggart, B. and Elliot, K. (2005) Investigating the Effects of Pre-school Provision: Using Mixed Methods in the EPPE Research, *International Journal of Social Research Methodology, Theory and Practice*, special issue on Mixed Methods in Educational Research (3): 207–224.

Sammons, P., Sylva, K., Melhuish, E., Siraj-Blatchford, I., Taggart, B., Grabbe, Y. and Barreau, S. (2007) *Summary Report: Influences on Children's Attainment and Progress in Key Stage 2: Cognitive Outcomes in Year 5: Effective Pre-school and Primary Education 3–11 Project (EPPE 3–11)*. Research Report RR828, London: DfES.

Sammons, P., Thomas, S. and Mortimore, P. (1997) *Forging Links: Effective Departments and Effective Schools*. London: Paul Chapman.

Santer, B.D. (1996) A Search for Human Influences on the Thermal Structure of the Atmosphere, *Nature*, 382: 39–46.

Santer B.D. (2003) Contributions of Anthropogenic and Natural Forcing to Recent Tropopause Height Changes, *Science*, 301: 479–483.

Scottish Executive Education Department (SEED) (2002a) *The Standard for Full Registration*. Edinburgh: SEED.

Scottish Executive Education Department (SEED) (2002b) *The Standard for Chartered Teacher*. Edinburgh: SEED.

Scottish Executive Education Department (SEED) (2003) *Continuing Professional Development for Educational Leaders*. Edinburgh: SEED.

Scottish Office Education Department (SOED) (1988) *Effective Secondary Schools*. Edinburgh: SOED.

Scottish Office Education Department (SOED) (1989) *Effective Primary Schools*. Edinburgh: SOED.

Scottish Office Education and Industry Department (SOEID) (1998) *The Standard for Headship in Scotland*. Stirling: SQH Development Unit.

Scheerens, J. (1990) School Effectiveness Research and the Development of Process Indicators of School Functioning, *School Effectiveness and School Improvement*, 1(1): 61–80.

Scheerens, J. (1992) *Effective Schooling: Research, Theory and Practice*. London: Cassell.

Scheerens, J. (2001) Monitoring School Effectiveness in Developing Countries, *School Effectiveness and School Improvement*, 12(4): 359–384.

Scheerens, J. and Bosker, R.J. (1997) *The Foundations of Educational Effectiveness*. Oxford: Pergamon.

Scheerens, J., Glas, C. and Thomas, S. (2003) *Educational Evaluation, Assessment and Monitoring: A Systemic Approach*. Lisse: Swets and Zweitlinger Publishers.

Scheffer, M. (2009) *Critical Transitions in Nature and Society*. Princeton, NJ: Princeton University Press.

Schildkamp, K. and Visscher, A. (2009) Factors Influencing the Utilisation of a School Self-Evaluation Instrument. *Studies in Educational Evaluation*, 35: 150–159.

Schleicher, A. (2009) International Benchmarking as a Lever for Policy Reform, in A. Hargreaves and M. Fullan M. *Change Wars*. Bloomington, IN: Solution Tree.

Schneider, B. and Keesler, V. A. (2007) Transforming Education into a Scientific Enterprise, *Annual Review of Sociology*, 33: 197–207.

Schoenfeld, A.H. (1998) Toward a Theory of Teaching in Context, *Issues in Education*, 4(1): 1–94.

Schug, M., Tarver, S. and Western, D. (2001) *Direct Instruction and the Teaching of Early Reading*. Hartland, WI: Wisconsin Policy Research Institute.

Schumacher, E.F. (1973) *Small is Beautiful: A Study of Economics as if People Mattered*. London: Blond and Briggs.

Scottish Executive Education Department (SEED) (2005) *The Standard for Headship*. Edinburgh: SEED.

SDLP (2011a) See http://www.sdlp.ie/index.php/the_issues/eleven_plus/ Accessed 15 February 2011.

SDLP (2011b) See http://www.sdlp.ie/index.php/the_issues/education/ Accessed 15 February 2011.

SELB (Southern Education and Library Board) (2011) Education Services: Post-primary Education (11–18 years). Available online at: http://www.selb.org/pupilparent/webpages/postprimary.htm Accessed 20 February 2011.

Sellstrom, E. and Bremberg, S. (2006) Is There a 'School Effect' on Pupil Outcomes? A Review of Multilevel Studies, *Journal of Epidemiology and Community Health*, 60 (2): 149–155.

Sen, A. (1999) *Development as Freedom*. Oxford: Oxford University Press.

Senge, P. (1990). *The Fifth Discipline: The Art and Practice of the Learning Organization*. New York: Doubleday.

Shavelson, R.J., Hubner, J.J., and Stanton, G.C. (1976) Validation of Construct Interpretations, *Review of Educational Research*, 46: 407–441.

Siraj-Blatchford, I., Sammons, P., Sylva, K., Melhuish, E. and Taggart, B. (2006) Educational Research and Evidence Based Policy: The Mixed Method Approach of the EPPE Project, *Evaluation and Research in Education*, Special Issue, Combining Numbers with Narratives, 19(2): 63–82.

Singer, E. and Kohnke-Aguirre, L. (1979) Interviewer Expectation Effects: A Replication and Extension, *Public Opinion Quarterly*, 43: 245–260.

Sinn Fein (2011) See http://www.sinnfein.ie/education Accessed 15 February 2011.

Slavin, R. (1996). *Education for All*. Lisse, The Netherlands: Swets and Zeitlinger.

Slavin, R. (2010) Experimental Studies in Education, in B.P.M. Creemers, L. Kyriakides, and P. Sammons, (eds) (2010) *Methodological Advances in Educational Effectiveness Research*. London: Taylor Francis.

Slee, R., Weiner, G. and Tomlinson, S. (1998) *School Effectiveness for Whom? Challenges to the School Effectiveness and School Improvement Movements*. London: Falmer.

Smith, F. and Hardman, F. (2000) Evaluating the Effectiveness of the National Literacy Strategy: Identifying Indicators of Success, *Educational Studies*, 26(3): 365–378.

Smith, A. and Robinson, A. (1996) *Education for Mutual Understanding: The Initial Statutory Years*. Coleraine: University of Ulster.

Smith, D.J. and Tomlinson, S. (1989) *The School Effect. A Study of Multi-racial Comprehensives*. London: Policy Studies Institute.

Smyth, E. (1999) *Do Schools Differ?* Dublin: Economic and Social Research Institute.

Smyth, W.J. and Shacklock, G. (1998) *Re-making Teaching: Ideology, Policy and Practice*. London: Routledge.

Snijders, T. and Bosker, R (1999). *Multilevel Analysis: An Introduction to Basic and Advanced Multilevel Modelling*. London: Sage.

Soros, G. (2008) *The New Paradigm for Financial Markets*. New York: Public Affairs.

Soulsby, D. and Swain, D. (2003) *Report on the Award-Bearing INSET Scheme*. London: TTA.

Spillane, J. (2006) *Standards Deviation: How Schools Misunderstand Education Policy*. Cambridge, MA: Harvard University Press.

Stallings, J. (1985) Effective Elementary Classroom Practices, in M.J. Kyle (ed.) *Reaching for Excellence: An Effective Sourcebook* (pp. 14–42). Washington, DC: U.S. Governing Printing Office.

Stinchcombe, A. (1965) Social Structure and Organizations, in J. March (ed.) *Handbook of Organizations*. Chicago, IL: Rand McNally.

Stoll, L. and Fink, D. (1994) School Effectiveness and School Improvement: Voices from the Field, *School Effectiveness and School Improvement*, 5(2): 149–177.

Stoll, L. MacBeath, J. and Mortimore, P. (2001) in J. MacBeath and P. Mortimore, *Improving School Effectiveness*. Buckingham: Open University Press.

Stoll, L. and Myers, M. (1998) *No Quick Fixes: Perspectives on Schools in Difficulty*. London: Falmer.

Strand, S. (2010) Do Some Schools Narrow the Gap? Differential School Effectiveness by Ethnicity, Gender, Poverty, and Prior Achievement. *School Effectiveness and School Improvement*, 21(3): 289–314.

Stringfield, S. (2010) Personal communication, email, 19/01/2010.

Stringfield, S., Millsap, M. A., Herman, R., Yoder, N., Brigham, N., Nesselrodt, P., Schaffer, E., Karweit, N., Levin, M. and Stevens, R. (with Gamse, B., Puma, M., Rosenblum, S., Beaumont, J., Randall, B. and Smith, L.) (1997) *Urban and Suburban/Rural Special Strategies for Educating Disadvantaged Children. Final Report*. Washington, DC: U.S. Department of Education.

Stringfield, S., Reynolds, D. and Schaffer, E. (2008a) Improving Secondary Schools' Academic Achievement Through a Focus on Reform Reliability: 4 and 9 Years Finding from the High Reliability Schools Project, *School Effectiveness and School Improvement*, 19(4): 409–428.

Stringfield, S., Reynolds, D., and Schaffer E. (2008b) *Improving secondary students' academic achievement through a focus on reform reliability*, Research Report for CfBT, Reading: CfBT http://www.cfbt.com/evidenceforeducation/PDF/High%20Reliability_v5%20FINAL2.pdf

Stringfield, S.C. and Slavin, R.E. (1992) A Hierarchical Longitudinal Model for Elementary School Effects, in B.P.M. Creemers and G.J. Reezigt (eds) *Evaluation of Educational Effectiveness*. Groningen: ICO, pp. 35–69.

Sun, H. C., Wang, X.D., Yuan, S.F., Hao, L.L., Liu, W.Z and Liu, Y. (2010) An Overview of the Status Quo, Weakness and Development of the Educational Effectiveness Research in China, paper presented at the 2nd International Conference on School Effectiveness and School Improvement and the 3rd Meeting of the Educational Effectiveness Academic Committee in China, 22–23 October 2010, Shenyang, China.

Sun, M.T. and Hung, Z. (1994) The Initiative Study of School Effectiveness, *Education and Economics*, 3: 1–5.

Sylva, K., Siraj-Blatchford, I., Taggart, B., Sammons, P., Melhuish, E., Elliot, K., Totsika, V. (2006) Capturing Quality in Early Childhood Through Environmental Rating Scales, *Early Childhood Research Quarterly*, 21: 76–92.

Sylva, K., Melhuish, E., Sammons, P., Siraj-Blatchford, I. and Taggart, B. (2010) *Early Childhood Matters: Evidence from the Effective Pre-school and Primary Education Project*. London: Routledge.

Tang, L. C. and Liang, L. L. (2005) An Exploratory Study on School Effectiveness Using Value Added Method, *Shanghai Research on Education*, 4: 24–26.

Tashakkori, A., and Teddlie, C. (1998) *Mixed Methodology: Combining the Qualitative and Quantitative Approaches*. Thousand Oaks, CA: Sage.

Tashakkori, A. and Teddlie, C. (eds) (2003) *Handbook of Mixed Methods in Social and Behavioral Research*. Thousand Oaks, CA: Sage.

Tashakkori, A. and Teddlie C. (eds) (2010) *Handbook of Mixed Methods Research*, 2nd edition, Thousand Oaks, CA: Sage.

Stephens, D. (2007) *Culture in Education and Development: Principles, Practice and Policy*. Bristol Papers in Education: Comparative and International Studies. Oxford: Symposium Books.

Teddlie, C. (2010). The Legacy of the School Effectiveness Research Tradition, in A. Hargreaves, A. Lieberman, M. Fullan and D. Hopkins (eds) *The Second International Handbook of Educational Change*. Dordrecht, The Netherlands: Springer.

Teddlie, C., Creemers, B., Kyriakides, L., Muijs, D. and Yu, F. (2006) The International System for Teacher Observation and Feedback: Evolution of an international study of teacher effectiveness constructs. *Educational Research and Evaluation*, 12: 561–582.

Teddlie, C. and Liu, S. (2008) Examining Teacher Effectiveness Within Differentially Effective Primary Schools in the People's Republic of China. *School Effectiveness and School Improvement*, 19(4): 387–407.

Teddlie, C. and Reynolds, D. (2000) *The International Handbook of School Effectiveness Research.* London: Falmer Press.

Teddlie, C., and Reynolds, D. (2001). Countering the Critics: Responses to Recent Criticisms of School Effectiveness Research, *School Effectiveness and School Improvement*, 12: 41–82.

Teddlie, C. and Sammons, P. (2010) Applications of Mixed Methods to the Field of Educational Effectiveness Research, in B.P.M Creemers, L. Kyriakides and P. Sammons, *Methodological Advances in Educational Effectiveness Research.* London: Taylor & Francis.

Teddlie, C. and Stringfield, S. (1993) *Schools Make a Difference: Lessons Learned from a Ten Year Study of School Effects.* New York: Teachers College Press.

Teddlie, C. and Tashakkori, A. (2009) *The Foundations of Mixed Methods Research: Integrating Quantitative and Qualitative Techniques in the Social and Behavioral Sciences.* Thousand Oaks, CA: Sage.

Thomas, H. and Martin, J. (1996) *Managing Resources for School Improvement.* London: Routledge.

Thomas, S. (2001) Dimensions of Secondary School Effectiveness: Comparative Analyses Across Regions, *School Effectiveness and School Improvement*, 12(3): 285–322.

Thomas, S. (2005) Using Indicators of Value Added to Evaluation School Performance in UK. *Educational Research Journal*, 26(9): 20–27.

Thomas, S.M. (2010) Assessment and Evaluation of Institutional Effectiveness, in McGaw, B., Peterson, P. and Baker, E. (eds) *International Encyclopedia of Education* (3rd edition). Oxford: Elsevier.

Thomas, S. and Peng, W.J. (2011) *Improving Educational Evaluation and Quality in China.* Final report to ESRC.

Thomas, S., Peng, W.J. and Gray, J. (2007) Modelling Patterns of Improvement Over Time: Value Added Trends in English Secondary School Performance Across Ten Cohorts, *Oxford Review of Education*, 33(3): 261–295.

Thomas, S.M. and Peng, W.-J. (2009) Enhancing Quality and Capacity for Educational Research, in D. Stephens (ed.) *Higher Education and International Capacity Building: Twenty Five Years of Higher Education Links*, Bristol Papers in Comparative Education. Oxford: Symposium Books, pp. 51–77.

Thomas, S. and Mortimore, P. (1996) Comparison of Value Added Models for Secondary School Effectiveness, *Research Papers in Education*, 11(1): 5–33.

Thrupp, M. (1999) *Schools Making a Difference: Let's Be Realistic!: School Mix, School Effectiveness, and the Social Limits of Reform.* London: Open University Press.

Tikly, L. and Barrett, A. (2007) *Educational Quality: Research Priorities and Approaches in the Global Era.* 9th UKFIET Conference, 11–13 September 2007: 248

Tikly, L, Haynes, J, Caballero, C, Hill, J and Gillborn, D (2006) *Evaluation of Aiming High: African Caribbean Achievement Project.* Research Report RR801. London: DfES

Tibbitt, J. (1994) Improving School Effectiveness: Policy and Research in Scotland, *Scottish Educational Review*, 26(2): 151–157.

Toffler, A. (1971) *Future Shock.* London: Pan.

Townsend, T. (1998) The Primary School of the Future: Third World or Third Millennium? in T. Townsend, *The Primary School in Changing Times: The Australian Experience.* London and New York: Routledge.

Townsend, T (ed.) (2001) The Background to This Set of Papers on Two Decades of

School Effectiveness Research, Special Issue Critique and Response to Twenty Years of SER, *School Effectiveness and School Improvement*, 12(1): 3–5.

Townsend, T. (ed.) (2007) *The International Handbook of School Effectiveness and Improvement.* Springer: Dordrecht, the Netherlands and New York.

Townsend, T. (2009) Third Millennium Leaders: Thinking and Acting Both Locally and Globally, *Leadership and Policy in Schools*, 8(4): 355–379.

Townsend, T. (2010) *Thinking and Acting Both Locally and Globally: From Sustainability to Regenerative Leadership.* A Keynote Presentation to the International Congress for School Effectiveness and Improvement Annual Conference, Kuala Lumpur, Malaysia, 4 January, 2010.

Townsend, T., Clarke, P. and Ainscow, M. (1999) *Third Millennium Schools: A World of Difference in Effectiveness and Improvement.* The Netherlands: Swets and Zeitlinger.

Training and Development Agency (TDA) (2009) *Strategy for the Professional Development of the Children's Workforce in Schools 2009–12.* London: TDA.

Tymms, P. B. (1992) The Relative Effectiveness of Post-16 Institutions in England (including assisted place scheme schools), *British Journal of Educational Research*, 18 (2): 175–192.

Tymms, P., Merrell, C., Heron, T., Jones, P., Albone, S. and Henderson, B. (2008) The Importance of Districts, *School Effectiveness and School Improvement*, 19: 261–274.

Ungerleider, C. and Burns, T. (2002) *Information and Communication Technologies in Elementary and Secondary Education: A State of the Art Review.* Paper presented to the Pan-Canadian Education Research Symposium, Montreal, April/May.

UNESCO (2000) World Education Forum: Dakar Framework for Action: Education for All: Meeting Our Collective Commitments, Senegal.

UNESCO (2004) *EFA Global Monitoring Report 2005: Education for All. The Quality Imperative.* Paris: UNESCO.

UNESCO (2009) *Learning for a Sustainable World: Review of Contexts and Structures for ESD.* Paris: UNESCO.

UNICEF (2007a). *Education Quality Framework.* Accessed 12 February 2009. http://www.unicef.org/infobycountry/china_statistics.html.

UNICEF (2007) *An Overview of Child Well-being in Rich Countries: A Comprehensive Assessment of the Lives and Well-being of Children and Adolescents in the Economically Advanced Nations.* Florence: Innocenti Research Centre.

United Nations (1987) *Report of the World Commission on Environment and Development: Our Common Future.* Annex to A/42/427 (Development and International Co-operation: Environment Bruntland Commission).

United Nations Population predictions http://www.un.org/esa/population/publications/longrange2/WorldPop2300final.pdf Accessed 15 December 2010

UUP (2010) Available online at: http://www.uup.org/index.php/news/education Accessed 15 February 2011.

Van Damme, J., Opdenakker, M., Van Landeghem, G., De Fraine, B., Pustjens, H., Van de gaer, E. (2006) *Educational Effectiveness: An Introduction to International and Flemish research on Schools, Teachers and Classes.* Leuven: Acco.

Van Damme, J. and Dhaenens, E. (2007) ISTOF Student, Leuven: Centre for Educational Effectiveness and Evaluation of the Catholic University of Leuven Belgium.

Van de Gaer, E., De Fraine, B., Pustjens, H., Van Damme, J., De munter, A. and Onghena, P. (2009) School Effects on the Development of Motivation Towards Learning Tasks and the Development of Academic Self-concept in Secondary Education: A Multivariate Latent Growth Curve Approach, *School Effectiveness and School Improvement*, 20(2): 235–253.

Van de Grift, W. (2007). Quality of Teaching in Four European Countries: A Review of the Literature and an Application of an Assessment Instrument *Educational Research, 49* (2) 127–152.

Van de Grift, W. (2009) Reliability and Validity in Measuring the Value Added of Schools, *School Effectiveness and School Improvement*, 20: 269–286.

Van der Wal, M. and Waslander, M. (2007) Traditional and Non-traditional Educational Outcomes: Trade-off or Complementarity? *School Effectiveness and School Improvement*, 18: 409–428.

Van der Werf, G., Opdenakker, M.-C., and Kuyper, H. (2008). Testing a Dynamic Model of Student and School Effectiveness with a Multivariate Multilevel Latent Growth Curve Approach, *School Effectiveness and School Improvement*, 19(4): 447–462.

Van Petegem, P. (2011) The Effect of Flemish Eco-Schools on Student Environmental Knowledge, Attitudes, and Affect, *International Journal of Science Education*, 33(11): 1513–1538.

Valenzuela, J., Bellei, C., Osses, A. and Sevilla, A. (2009) *Causas que explican el mejoramiento de los resultados obtenidos por los estudiantes chilenos en PISA 2006 respecto a PISA 2001. Aprendizajes y Políticas*. Available online at: www.fonide.cl Accessed 21 July 2010.

Verachtert, P., Van Damme, J., Onghena, P. and Ghesquiere, P. (2009) A Seasonal Perspective on School Effectiveness: Evidence from a Flemish Longitudinal Study in Kindergarten and First Grade, *School Effectiveness and School Improvement*, 20(2): 215–233.

Von Hippel, P. (2009) Achievement, Learning and Seasonal Impact as Measures of School Effectiveness: It's Better To Be Valid Than Reliable, *School Effectiveness and School Improvement*, 20(2): 187–213.

Van Velzen, W., Miles, M., Elholm, M., Hameyer, U. and Robin, D. (1985) *Making School Improvement Work*, Leuven: ACCO.

Wacquant, L. (2001) The Rise of Advanced Marginality: Notes on its Nature and Implications, *Acta Sociologica*, 39(2): 121–139.

Walberg, H.J. (1984) Improving the Productivity of America's Schools, *Educational Leadership*, 41(8): 19–27.

Wals, A.E.J. (2007) Learning in a Changing World and Changing in a Learning World: Reflexively Fumbling towards Sustainability, *Southern African Journal of Environmental Education*, 24(1): 35–45.

Wals, A.E.J. and Blewitt, J. (2010) Third Wave Sustainability in Higher Education: Some (Inter)national Trends and Developments, in P.Jones, D. Selby and S. Sterling (eds) *Green Infusions: Embedding Sustainability across the Higher Education Curriculum*. London: Earthscan, pp. 55–74.

Walsh, P. (2006) Narrowed Horizons and the Impoverishment of Educational Discourse: Teaching, Learning and Performing Under the New Educational Bureaucracies, *Journal of Education Policy*, 21(1): 95–117.

Wang, X.R. and Zheng, W. (1997) Introduction to Organisational Culture and Effectiveness of Schools, *Education Science*, 3: 53–57.

Waters, A. (2008) *Edible Schoolyard*. San Francisco, CA: Chronicle Books.

Watkins, C. and Mortimore, P. (1999) *Pedagogy: What do We Know? Understanding Pedagogy and its Impact on Learning*. London: Paul Chapman.

Watling, R. and Arlow, M. (2002) Wishful Thinking: Lessons from the Internal and External Evaluations of an Innovatory Education Project in Northern Ireland, *Evaluation and Research in Education*, 16(3): 166–181.

Weiss, L. and Fine, M. (2000) *Construction Sites: Excavating Race, Class and Gender among Urban Youth*. New York: Teachers College Press.

Wells, K. (1995) The Strategy of Grounded Theory: Possibilities and Problems, *Social Work Research*, 19(1): 33.

Welsh Assembly Government (2001) *The Learning Country: A Paving Document*. Cardiff: Welsh Assembly Government.

Welsh Assembly Government. (2002) *Narrowing the Gap in the Performance of Schools*. Cardiff: Welsh Assembly Government.

Welsh Assembly Government. (2005) *Narrowing the Gap in the Performance of Schools Project: Phase 2 Primary Schools*. Cardiff: Welsh Assembly Government.

Welsh Assembly Government (2006a) *The Learning Country: Vision Into Action*. Cardiff: Welsh Assembly Government.

Welsh Assembly Government. (2006b) *Beyond Boundaries: Citizen-centred Local Services for Wales*. Cardiff: Welsh Assembly Government.

Welsh Assembly Government (2008) *School Effectiveness Framework: Building Effective Learning Communities Together*. Cardiff: Welsh Assembly Government.

Welsh Assembly Government (2009) *National Standards for Educational Improvement Professionals in Wales*. Cardiff: Welsh Assembly Government.

Wenger, E., McDermott, R. and Snyder, W. (2002) *Cultivating Communities of Practice. A Guide to Managing Knowledge*. Boston, MA: Harvard Business School.

West, M. (2010) School-to-School Cooperation as a Strategy for Improving Student Outcomes in Challenging Contexts, *School Effectiveness and School Improvement*, 21(1): 93–112.

Whelan, F. (2009) *Lessons Learned: How Good Policies Produce Better Schools*. London: Author.

William, D. (2009) *Assessment for Learning: Why, What and How?* London: Institute of Education.

Wilkinson, R. and Pickett, K. (2009) *The Spirit Level: Why More Equal Societies Almost Always do Better*. London: Allen Lane.

Wilson, E.O. (1991) *The Diversity of Life*. Harvard, MA: Harvard University Press.

Wilson, E.O. (2002) *The Future of Life*. Harvard, MA: Harvard University Press.

Wimpleberg, R., Teddlie, C. and Stringfield, S. (1989). Sensitivity to Context: The Past and Future of Effective Schools Research. *Educational Administration Quarterly*, 25(1): 82–107.

World Bank (2005) *Expanding Opportunities and Building Competencies for Young People: A New Agenda for Secondary Education*. Washington DC: World Bank.

World Bank (2007) Tanzania–Zanzibar Basic Education Improvement Project. Zanzibar.

Wright, M. and McGrory, O. (2005) Motivation and the Adult Irish Language Learner, *Educational Research*, 47(2): 191–204.

Wright, M. and Scullion, P. (2007) Quality of School Life and Attitudes to Irish in the Irish-Medium and English-Medium Primary School, *Irish Educational Studies*, 26(1): 57–77.

Wylie, C. (1997) *Self-Managing Schools Seven Years On: What Have we Learned?* Wellington: New Zealand Council for Educational Research.

Wyse, D. (2003) The National Literacy Strategy: A Critical Review of Empirical Evidence, *British Educational Research Journal*, 29(6): 903–916.

Yang, H.-Q. and He, J.-H. (2008) The Application of Hierarchical Linear Model in Longitudinal Research on the Study of Education and Psychology, *Journal of Shijiazhuang University*, 10(3): 71–72 and 102.

Yin, R.K. (1994) *Case Study Research: Design and Methods* (2nd edition). Thousand Oaks, CA: Sage.

Young, M. (1971) (ed.) *Knowledge and Control.* London: Macmillan.

Yu, J.F. (2005) The Introspection and Future Development of School Effectiveness Research of Western Countries, *Studies in Foreign Education*, 6: 1–4.

Yu, G. and Thomas, S.M. (2008) Exploring School Effects Across Southern and Eastern African School Systems and in Tanzania, *Assessment in Education: Principle, Policy and Practice*, 15(3): 283–305.

Xie, X.Y. (2007) On the Rationality of Policy Restriction of 'migration' for the National College Entrance Examination, *Journal of Shaanxi Institute of Junior Managerial Personnel*, 20(1): 27–29 and 35.

Xue, H.-P. and Min, W.-F. (2008) A Study on Educational Production Function in Western Regions of China, *Education and Economy*, 2: 18–25.

Zhang, T., and Minxia, Z. (2006) Universalizing Nine-year Compulsory Education for Poverty Reduction in Rural China. *International Review of Education*, 52(3–4): 261–286.

Zhou, H. and Wu, X.W. (2008) School Performance of Migrant Children and its Determinants: a Hierarchical Linear Model Analysis, *Population Research*, 32(2): 22–32.

Index